Rapidex™ English Noting and Drafting Course

Prof. Shrikant Prasoon

Published by:
Rapidex PUBLICATIONS
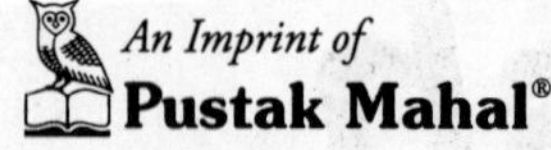
An Imprint of
Pustak Mahal®

Administrative Office and Sale Centre

J-3/16 , Daryaganj, New Delhi-110002
☎ 011-23276539, 23272783, 23272784, 23260518
E-mail: info@pustakmahal.com • *Website:* www.pustakmahal.com

Branch
Bengaluru: ☎ 080-22234025, 40912845
E-mail: pustakmahalblr@gmail.com

This book was earlier published under the title:
"Rapidex English Writing Course"

ISBN 978-81-223-1632-2

Edition: 2025

Printed at: Sharma Printers, Delhi

Contents

Publisher's Note

Thank you for choosing ***Rapidex* English Writing Course** for achieving perfection in your English Writing Skills. The course covers almost every segment of writing in detail. It has been designed and classified in 20 days so that each day is devoted to one particular segment of writing.

Every segment has its 'tips' and 'useful points' for effective writing. Numerous examples further enrich one's reasoning and learning.

This unique course covers entire gamut of writing ranging from personal, professional, business, legal, literary and many more. The course has been designed to suit the needs of professionals as well as students who aspire to take competitive exams or wish to apply for jobs, and those who wish to understand commercial/official correspondence.

To make the course readers-friendly, these icons have been used:

Exercises

The appendix given at the end of the book provides useful information on English Grammar, Glossary of confusing words and English Thesaurus of over 22,000 words.

The DVD accompanying the book would explain the use of **'MS-Word' software**, which is required for all sorts of writing. By using this DVD, you will be able to format, edit, print and save your files.

We hope the course will benefit to all those who want to improve their writing skills.

—Publishers

Salient Features of Writing

• Introduction and Instructions • Five Steps to Become an Expert • Why to Write?
• What to Write? • What Not to Write About? • How to Write?

Introduction and Instructions

This book is dedicated solely to writing: an essential need for preserving collected information, knowledge and human experiences for posterity, in different forms and styles.

Writing may have originated with symbolic picture-writing or it may have emerged in its advanced form from the most perfect and rich ancient language, Sanskrit. The history of writing is as old as human civilization and the need for writing is established since then. Civilizations have grown, because our forefathers wrote and preserved these writings, books, charts, illustrations, scriptures and treatises from decay.

Of all the means of expression – from sign to language, writing is the most difficult to master. Even the experts, masters and writers of dozens of creative, critical, analytical and philosophical books continuously strive to hone their writing skills.

As mentioned earlier, all sorts of writing skills have been taught in this book, but examples of each style have been kept to the minimum. Although it needs effort and practice to master the skills of reading and speaking, writing requires greater practice, knowledge and concentration. The age-old dictum that practice makes a man perfect is perfectly true.

It is easy to give topics for practice, but if examples are not given alongside in such a book, it will be of little practical value to readers. Accordingly, topics have been detailed first so that students or learners know what has to be incorporated, and what left out. Practice exercises have been given where required and only passages helpful for a learner have been included.

To master writing, the following things must be kept in mind:

- Accuracy is most important and mistakes must always be eliminated.
- Words contain ideas. The more words a person possesses, the more ideas one has at one's disposal. Enrich your vocabulary from others' writings.
- Consult a dictionary whenever in doubt. Always keep a big as well as a small dictionary handy. Small dictionaries can be used at most times, while the big ones could be consulted occasionally, when the smaller ones do not contain specific entries.

- The general rules of grammar are important too.
- If English isn't your first language, the best way to master it is by reading a lot of English writings, speaking and writing in English as much as possible.
- All writings contain errors. It is up to us to reread the text to correct errors. Spellcheck should be used by all writers working on computers.
- As far as possible, refrain from repeating errors.

Follow these tips diligently and your writing will improve by leaps and bounds.

Five Steps to Become an Expert

There are five tried-and-tested steps to become an expert. Such persons would include: a Reader, an Analyst, an Orator, and a Writer. If one could spare a few hours early in the morning between 5:00 and 8:00 am, when you are relatively free, it would be the best.

1. Reading: Reading is the most essential prerequisite to become an expert in writing or any other vocation. It helps to add to our bank of knowledge, day after day. The day one stops reading, one stops growing. Simply accumulating wealth will get one nowhere, unless this is backed by a robust knowledge. By reading and rereading, one begins to comprehend a topic better, as it boosts vocabulary and improves spellings.

People sometimes wonder what should we read? One could begin by reading the daily newspaper. Make sure to read this from begining to end: from each column; news items; ads; even obituary and tenders; sports pages; international page; financial page; share prices; star signs, etc. Leave out nothing. Moreover, read each item with undivided attention and concentration.

2. Comprehending: It is important to understand everything one reads. But remember that in the beginning, one will not understand everything one reads. Comprehension comes gradually as we read more and more about a particular topic. We then slowly begin analyzing what has been read, boosting the understanding further.

How understanding and analysis boost all-round comprehension is best illustrated by an example. Ask someone: How many sides does a coin possess? The prompt answer will be two – head and tail. This is not true. A coin has three sides: top, bottom and side, i.e., its thickness, which is the third dimension.

To understand a situation in its entirety, one needs to consider all three dimensions. In India, this is known as *manan* or *chintan* – deep and focused thought. That is why total comprehension is important while reading.

But never forget that this only comes through daily reading. While reading, if you come across something that is incomprehensible, pause and ponder over this particular point. By considering a point from all angles, one will understand it better, even registering the elements missed earlier.

3. Memorizing: Memory depends upon a functional mind. There are three layers to memory:

a. Whatever one does every day is always in the foreground of one's memory, ready for use. This is the functional memory or ready memory.

b. Sub-functional Memory is the second layer, which may not always come at one's bidding when required. It may sometimes come when needed; but at other times, despite desperate attempts to recall, it may elude a person. Yet, it may come back instantly and become a part of functional memory if someone else mentions something relevant.

c. Stored Memory forms a major part of both the previous types mentioned above. It can be the biggest, most useful memory. Stored memory comprises information that has been used repeatedly in the past. An alert mind can convert stored memory into functional memory as and when needed.

Repeated usage can sharpen one's memory. Infrequent usage may lead to gradual loss of that memory. A sharp memory can help orators and writers in their daily work.

4. Retention: All efforts will be wasted if one reads, comprehends but fails to retain what is read. Retention is most important for students, teachers and people from various walks of life. Those who retain information well are considered to possess a powerful memory. This is important to succeed in life.

Like other things, retention needs practice. Read poems and other text, then try to recall what has been read. Reading, rereading and revising lessons help students improve their power of retention.

5. Expression: Expression is of two kinds: oral and written.

(a) ***Oral Expression*:** Proper oral expression is imperative for speakers. It is important for all others in interviews, discussions, debates, general conversations, chanting or recitations, etc.

Speaking: Speakers need to have a strong voice and develop their own style of speaking. In the initial stages, speakers need to rehearse many times before speaking. Slowly, this becomes second nature. Speaking is an art that calls for correct accent and pronunciation. It is also important to avoid repetition and keep speeches as short as possible.

Chanting and Recitation: These practices can help speakers improve their skills. Chanting and recitation improves pronunciation as well as dialogue delivery and helps one develop into a skillful orator. By recalling mantras, poems or important quotes, a speaker can ensure s/he is perceived as being well-read and knowledgeable.

Dialogue Delivery: This is an important aspect of both reading and speaking. Persons who practise this and develop a natural command over their diction can become successful speakers, actors or stage personalities.

(b) ***Written Expression*:** Written words help one communicate with others and express oneself better. Such words help readers and examiners judge the writer and determine how knowledgeable the person happens to be. Writers, poets, authors and journalists are judged purely by their writings.

Why to Write?

'Why to write?', is difficult to answer. There are many reasons for writing, including expressing one's emotions and feelings. Oral and written communication help us express ourselves. But correct language is needed for both, otherwise the listener or reader may get wrong message.

A few of these reasons would include:

- Human beings write to maintain records for posterity.
- Writing is done for learning, exams, official work and self-satisfaction.
- Writings express personal ideas, experiences, spiritual revelations and other facets of life.
- Writing enhances personal communication skills.
- Writing helps carry out official duties via written communications.
- For many, writing can serve as a means of earning one's living.
- To discuss, debate and disseminate one's thoughts and ideas.

What to Write?

It is important to be clear about the topic and key messages that one wishes to write about. Without such clarity, the writing would be longwinded and meaningless.

Some writings could be meant to:

- Make an individual, a community, society, or country better, thereby making the world a better place to live in.
- Communicate better values and ethics to others, improving the overall well-being of society.
- Express certain experiences that could make life easier for others following the same path.
- Inculcate positive values so that negative emotions are curbed, thereby reducing suicide, crime, terror incidents and other negative happenings.
- Express noble and lofty thoughts for others and for posterity so that the forces of evil and negativity are overcome.

What Not to Write About

There are many things one should not write about.

These include:

- Negative values and ideas that breed negative sentiments.
- Ideas that divide humans and society.
- Ideas that spread evil thoughts among humans.
- Thoughts that fill others with negativity and hopelessness.
- Anything that goes against the law of Nature and disturbs natural peace and harmony.
- Ideas that alienate a person from family, friends and peers.
- Thoughts that hide reality or present an inaccurate picture.
- Ideas that cover up or condone crime and terror, including their magnitude.
- Thoughts that help envy, covetousness and lust grow amongst individuals.
- Defending indefensible actions of any kind.
- Writings that misguide others.
- Writing for some vested interest or the other.

How to Write?

Write the way you talk.

The key to simple and clear writing is "to talk" on paper to your reader. When you are writing, imagine that you're actually standing in front of your reader, and then write those words that you would use in your "talk." If you do so, the words will come out like the best of speaking.

To "talk" on paper, you may have to change your writing style. For example, you may have to give up writing in which you:

- use less familiar words like 'commence' instead of 'begin', or 'prior' instead of 'before'
- avoid using personal pronouns like 'I', 'we', and 'you.'

For simple and clear writing, you should:

- use simple, short, familiar words;
- use a variety of punctuation marks;
- use more personal pronouns;
- use contractions (sometimes).

TIPS

Remember that writing is largely an art, not a science. Even scientific writing is an art. Master the art of composing descriptive passages. Follow simple tips outlined below to write well. Keep practising as much as possible to improve writing skills. Always write short and correct sentences. Ensure the sentences are in the correct sequence that adheres to the proper flow of thought.

Other useful tips:

- Practise writing a thousand words daily.
- Begin a new paragraph to indicate new ideas. Write one point in a particular paragraph
- Use adjectives only where essential.
- Insert the correct prepositions.
- Use adverbs only where necessary.
- Use the correct punctuation marks.
- Don't repeat names unnecessarily. Instead, use pronouns.
- For brevity, minimize conjunctions.
- Verbs are action words that recreate motion. Make your verbs as strong as possible. The verb 'to be' (am, is, are, was, were) can be superfluous; eliminate it wherever possible. Use modern verbs where the past and past participle are formed by adding 'd' or 'ed'.
- Names of people, places and concrete as well as abstract things are to be handled with caution because English has multiple words for almost everything. From among them, choose the noun that works best and is most suitable for each expression.

- Use short words – those that are monosyllablic or have two or three syllables. These are usually more forceful than multiple-syllable words.
- Use the active voice as far as possible. In some cases, however, it is important to use the passive voice. Learn to ascertain when each is required.
- Avoid using different nouns, adjectives or adverb clauses in one principal clause. This makes the sentence unwieldy and difficult to comprehend. Begin each sentence afresh and keep sentences short.
- At appropriate points, use different forms of writings – anecdotes, quotes, statistics, events, incidents, contrary views, etc. – to make your writings interesting. But avoid any excess.
- Editing of documents is as important as pruning an overgrown garden to remove wild growth.
- Add a touch of humour if you know how to handle this. Humour makes writings entertaining and easier to read. But avoid forced humour. Humour should always be witty and refined.
- Once done with writing online, take a hard copy and read this closely to delete errors and refine as well as concise it further.
- In writing a book, ensure that the Preface, Foreword or Prologue as well as the Publisher's Note are brief, preferably just a page or two. Anything longer can put off readers.
- Never go overboard with exclamation marks. Use them sparingly and with discretion.
- Avoid swear words or those with abusive and derogatory connotations.
- Don't use words from other dialects or languages, unless imperative. Even so, always explain the meaning briefly.
- Mention details of places, persons or things if they are part of the theme, but avoid painstaking details.
- In describing something, mention details to augment authenticity. But don't include long, boring details, which will fail to sustain readers' interest.
- Omit unwanted repetitions.

While it is generally believed that adjectives and adverbs make the language more interesting, this is not always true. Use them only when necessary. For example, consider these two sentences:

The teacher marched to the blackboard.

The tall, heavily-built teacher slowly and steadily marched to the wall-mounted blackboard without looking back.

Both sentences communicate the same message but the latter is verbose while the former is easier to read.

Most people have learnt grammar in school but still write ungrammatical sentences. This is due to lack of Practice. Great writers never worry about grammar while writing because they use correct English as a matter of habit. That is why regular reading and writing are imperative to ensure mastery in writing.

TIPS

Even established writers sometimes forget the basics and would be none the worse from a refresher course of writing tips provided in this book.

Here are some useful tips for beginners as well as established writers:

- Practise writing at least 2,000 words every day. This will improve writing skills immensely.
- Don't be overly concerned about editing while writing the first draft. Writing and editing are two different things and the latter can come later.
- Although computer spellcheck is a handy tool, don't rely on it blindly. Always oversee spellcheck, and once done, closely scrutinize the hard copy of your manuscript.
- Later, submit your manuscript to a professional editor and proofreader for error-free text.
- An editor can completely transform a manuscript if it is lacking in something.
- Learn to be a good reader – this is the first step to becoming a good writer.
- Self-analyse your writings or get this done by others. Accept constructive criticism gracefully and make changes in your draft accordingly.
- If using a computer while writing, use the online Thesaurus, whenever required to improve your word power, and avoid repetition of words.
- Keep the writing simple, straightforward and to the point.
- Improve visual clarity while writing by using the 'Zoom' facility in the 'View' panel to increase the size of the text on your computer. This makes it easier to detect errors.
- Different points on a page should have some connecting thread to facilitate easy reading.
- Always use precise words that convey the right thought.
- Don't let 'writer's block' bog you down. Put down whatever thoughts first come to mind. As Chinese philosopher Lao Tzu said: "A journey of a thousand miles begins with the first step." If you still feel bogged down, take a break and set aside the writing for a few days. This will help you return to the task refreshed.
- Ensure accuracy and truth are maintained in the writings or else your credibility will suffer.
- Never worry about the length of your piece at the outset. First convey your thoughts effectively. Later, edit any unwanted text.
- If an article appears long, break it up with sub-headings.
- Short stories are best expressed between 500 to 1,200 words.

  When writing a short story, consider the following points:

  1. The reading time should not exceed 15 minutes.
  2. Etch out different characters elaborately so that readers can identify with one or the other.
  3. All words should perform either of two tasks: reveal a character and/or advance the narrative.

4. Pay particular attention to the beginning and the end, which are crucial, and connect the two closely as early as possible.
5. Introduce an element of surprise so that readers' interest is maintained till the end.

- Conversely, a novel could extend up to 60,000 or 70,000 words.
- The length of writings will depend upon the medium: a short story, novella, novel, poem, etc.
- The theme and readership or target audience determines the kind and range of vocabulary.
- An article should always begin with a short or medium-sized sentence (between 8 and 20 words). Never open with long sentences, which could instantly put off readers.
- Don't be a slave to a specific writing schedule. Words and ideas will surface at any time. Keep a notepad handy and jot down such thoughts instantly.
- Never copy others' phrases. Develop your own style.
- Write your draft spontaneously, without labouring unduly. Spontaneous writing flows and reads best.
- Whether fiction or essay-writing, never begin without a plot or theme in mind.
- Always pull out your old writings, reflect upon them, identify the shortcomings and learn how to become a better writer.

TIPS

How to improve the quality of writing is a perennial problem for all writers seeking to increase their readership and fan following. A high quality of writing sans errors is respected by readers and critics. Bad writing not only puts off readers, more often than not, it may fail to get published.

Here are handy tips to improve the aesthetic and grammatical quality of writing:

- Writings should never offend or irritate readers and create any negative feelings.
- All writings should be thought-provoking, entertaining, inspiring and enlightening.
- They should be compelling, clear and error-free so as to attract word-of-mouth endorsements.
- Written thoughts should reflect clear, ethical and spiritual values, which appeal to most people.
- Never write with the critics in mind; write with your readers in mind.
- Maintain an undercurrent of creativity in your writing and avoid carping criticism of anything.
- Even if you are writing something critical, do so creatively and humorously.
- Creative and critical writing are two different streams of thought; so keep them separate.
- There are three mental planes: conscious; subconscious and unconscious. Write consciously at all times to maintain clarity of thought.
- Although the subconscious mind can sometimes throw up enlightening thoughts, it needs the conscious mind to express this lucidly.
- Never underestimate the importance of correct spellings as well as proper usage of grammar and phrases. There are many good books lying largely unread in libraries, because the quality of writing wasn't top-notch.

- Always spend time in rewriting and editing your manuscript repeatedly to improve the quality.
- Don't base your writings on memory only. Always double-check your facts.
- Write with passion. This will propel your writings and thoughts to a higher orbit.
- Widen your mental and intellectual horizons by becoming a voracious reader and viewer of select writings and programmes. This will widen the depths of your knowledge and thoughts.
- Never write simply to impress readers and critics with your command over the language, thereby using words that are difficult to comprehend. Keep your writing simple.
- It is important to first have the big picture or topic in place, before moving on to the finer points.
- Make it a point to read business newspapers and magazines too.
- The moment you read a good phrase, unusual expression or new word, note it down instantly in a notepad. At the first available opportunity, use this in your writing.
- But remember, relevance is crucial while using new words or expressions. Do not use anything if it is not relevant to the context.
- Make it a point to play crossword puzzles. These help to boost vocabulary.
- Throughout your writing, remain focused on your theme and key messages.

Writing Introductions and Descriptions

• Self-introduction • Introducing Personalities — Authors, Awardees, Politicians, Sportspersons, etc. • Factual Description — Describing Occasions, People and Places

At various occasions, one needs to introduce oneself, family members, persons, places, products, meetings, topics, ceremonies, books, authors, poets, leaders, etc. While oral introductions are important, written introductions are also central to the book.Whether short or long, it is best to begin an introduction with a prominent point that encapsulates the theme of the topic. Concise language is important. Unwanted pronouns, verbs, adjectives and other words are to be avoided.

Self-introduction

People are asked to introduce themselves at various occasions in their life. While we may do it as a customary formality most of the time, we do not realize that what we say in our introduction is the first impression that people form about us. And it's this self-introduction that can go a long way in making or breaking a particular situation for you.

TIPS

- Induce humour in your speech. When you speak about your strengths and weaknesses, use some funny incidents that took place to highlight them better.
- Look at the audience while you speak. There's nothing that puts an audience off more than an orator who seems too absorbed in his notes or worse, has no idea where to look. Looking your audience in the eye gives them the reassurance that you are confident about what you're saying.
- You can also gesticulate with your hands. It will ease out any nervousness and give you a sense of confidence and self-assurance.
- Use anecdotes in your speech to explain things like achievements, etc. It not only makes the speech more interesting, it also gives it credibility.
- Never lie about your achievements, your strengths or your weaknesses in a self-introduction speech.
- Don't go on and on about yourself. You'll have a limited amount of time to talk, so make best use of it.
- Conclude your speech with a friendly note so that the people sitting in the audience feel that they had a direct interaction with you.

Introducing Personalities

Authors: Famous Indian English writer, Ruskin Bond is an essayist, story writer and a reputed writer of children's books. Bond has more than hundred short stories and essays to his credit. His fame rests mainly on three collections of short stories: *The Night Train at Deoli; Time Stops at Shamli and Our Trees Still Grow in Dehra.*

Ruskin Bond was born in 1934 at Kasauli, a suburban area in Himachal Pradesh. The early years of his childhood were spent in Jamnagar (Gujarat), Dehradun and Shimla, small cities where he grew up in the lap of Nature, but that were fast turning into modern cities. The changes offered insights into different kinds of life, feelings and emotions, which he captured and expressed so well in his writings.

In the course of a career spanning more than 35 years, Bond has proved to be a balanced thinker and prolific writer. He has written more than 30 books for children alone. He has also edited two anthologies: *The Penguin Book of Indian Ghost Stories* and *The Penguin Book of Indian Railway Stories.* Bond completed his first novel *The Room on the Roof* at the age of 17, for which he received the John Llewellyn Rhys Memorial Prize in 1957.

He received the Sahitya Academi Award for English Writing in India in 1992 for *Our Trees Still Grow in Dehra.* His non-fictional writings were collected in *Rain in the Mountains* and all his novels were published in one volume by Penguin India in 1993.

Awardees: On 17 December 2012, Author Prem P Bhalla received an award of ₹51,000 for his book, *Hindu Rites, Rituals, Customs and Traditions,* which answers scores of queries related to Hinduism.

Educated in Dehradun and New Delhi, Bhalla enjoys photography and travel. Besides running his own business, he is deeply involved with several social, welfare and educational institutions. He has been involved with the Rotary movement for more than 40 years.

Bhalla has written several self-improvement books and is particularly interested in the welfare of youngsters. He gives group lectures on personality and career development too. His books include: *It's time to live-up Smart, The Portrait of a Complete Man, Hello! Just Married or About to Marry, 7 Mantras to Excel in Exams* and *50 Moral Tales,* as well as the co-authored *The Book of Etiquette and Manners*, all published by Pustak Mahal.

Entrepreneurs: Jitendra Agarwalla is a successful entrepreneur and industrialist. Through all these years, he has made religion a core part of his personal and professional life. He has studied the Scriptures, practiced Yoga, confronted the toughest questions and yet come up with the most convincing answers. He is a multi-faceted personality.

The President's Scout Award Winner Jitendra Agarwalla represented his school and the District of Dhanbad, Jharkhand, in cricket and tennis. He was an SSI entrepreneur and the key figure behind the commissioning of three heavy engineering projects.

But his life changed completely with the arrival of his guru maharaj in 1996. Now his days are spent reading, reflecting and writing. As a result, he has authored *Who am I; Facets of Hindu Religion; Close Encounters with a Living God; Dolphin and the Flamingo;* and *The Religion Demystified.*

Politicians: Sheila Dikshit, Chief Minister of Delhi (1998-2013), first came to limelight when her administrative skills were acknowledged by none other than Indira Gandhi (Former Prime Minister of India) for doing a good supportive work for her father-in-law Sh. Uma Shankar Dikshit,who was a veteran freedom fighter and one of the close aides of Indira Gandhi. Sheila Dikshit was nominated by Indira Gandhi to the Indian delegation of the UN Commission on status of women. Thus began a journey for Sheila Dikshit in active politics and there has been no looking back ever since.

The popularity of Sheila Dikshit has largely been credited to all the developmental work that has gone into shaping the present Delhi. Some of the finest development works like the addition of Delhi Metro on to the Public Transport system have been widely acknowledged and the prime factors responsible for a vote of confidence to Sheila Dikshit by the people of Delhi.

Sportspersons: Anand's rise in the Indian chess world is meteoric. National level success came early for him when he won the National Sub-Junior Chess Championship with a score of 9/9 in 1983 at the age of fourteen. He became the youngest Indian to win the International Master's Title at the age of fifteen, in 1984. At the age of sixteen he became the National Champion and won that title two more times. He played games at blitz speed, earning him the nickname "Lightning Kid" ("Blitz chess" is known in India as "Lightning chess"). In 1987, he became the first Indian to win the World Junior Chess Championship. In 1988, at the age of eighteen, he became India's First Grandmaster.

Viswanathan Anand qualified for the Professional Chess Association World Chess Championship final by winning the candidates matches against Michael Adams and Gata Kamsky. In 1995, he played a title match against Kasparov in New York City's World Trade Centre. After an opening run of eight draws (a record for the opening of a world championship match), Anand won game nine using a splendid sacrifice on the queen side, but then lost four of the next five. He lost the match 10.5 - 7.5.

Anand has won the Chess Oscar in 1997, 1998, 2003, and 2004. His four Oscars ties him with Kasparov for the most ever, one better than Fischer's three. The Chess Oscar is awarded to the year's best player according to a world-wide poll of leading chess critics, writers, and journalists conducted by the Russian chess magazine 64.

Viswanathan Anand's game collection, My Best Games of Chess, was published in the year 1998 and was updated in 2001.

Factual Descriptions

TIPS

- To describe something as it exists is called a Factual Description.
- A factual description ensures that whatever is described vividly reaches readers. This needs correct observation and accurate expression. If the thing to be described is not present before one's eyes, one has to depend on one's memory and inherent knowledge. In this manner, factual description is an effective way to test the knowledge and language of a student.
- A student/writer has to be accurate in the description. The language must be simple and clear. The picture created should be sharp and easy to visualize.

- While writing a factual description, important details should not be left out and unimportant things need not be mentioned.
- Factual descriptions can be used to describe anything, animate or inanimate. But it is best to limit factual descriptions to as few words as possible. It is therefore important to be precise while writing all the three parts of a factual description: the beginning, middle and conclusion.
- Precision and orderliness is a boon, so keep the description orderly, precise, logical and simple.

Occassions

You are a student of Maharani Laxmibai Senior Secondary School, Gwalior. Your school celebrated the Diamond Jubilee Year of India's Independence. Write a 100–125 words report for your school magazine, describing the celebrations.

Diamond Jubilee of Independence Day: The entire campus of Maharani Laxmibai Senior Secondary School, Gwalior was decorated and lit as if a royal marriage ceremony were being solemnized there on the day it celebrated the Diamond Jubilee of India's Independence. The town's elite were in the campus sitting in the thousands or standing and talking in groups of hundreds. The function opened with the lighting of the lamp and a chorus of patriotic songs sung by the school's boys and girls.

All speakers, including members of the royal family of Gwalior, expressed the desire to save India's hard-won freedom and democracy at any cost through self-sacrifice. Patriotic fervour ran very high during the function. The vote of thanks was followed by a patriotic song praising martyrs, which marked the end of the function.

A Road Accident: The road accident I witnessed took place around two o'clock when traffic congestion was easing and vehicles were not bumping into the fender of other vehicles. What the drivers happened to be doing is a mystery but the car driver turned sharply and the bus driver failed to check the speed of his bus or apply the brakes in time.

Within the flicker of a second, the car and the bus had a direct collision. The driver of the car may have been killed instantly. When the vehicles were finally pulled apart, the car driver was dead. The other two people sitting in the rear had minor injuries.

No one from the bus was injured although they suffered a bad scare. The accident can safely be put down to rash driving by both drivers.

Investiture Ceremony: An investiture ceremony is a sacred consecration prevalent only among the followers of the Eternal Religion (Sanatana Dharma). It is popular as a sacred thread ceremony. It is akin to a rebirth into the realm of learning, knowledge and wisdom. Accordingly, those who have this ceremony performed are called *dwij* – the person who has a second life.

It is celebrated with much pomp and gaiety because of its social, psychological and spiritual impact on a growing child. A sacred thread is given, which the child wears throughout life. This is given when the head is tonsured after worshipping different gods and goddesses. Only then is the child allowed to recite the Gayatri Mantra, the most sacred mantra that imparts courage and confidence and indicates the way out of serious problems.

After this only is the person adjudged fit to learn the Vedas – the book of ultimate knowledge.

People

- In the Indian context, little importance has been given to dates and places of birth.This is because the names of places have changed many times and the sheer breadth of time is difficult to grasp. Moreover, Indian calculations of time in Kalpa and Yuga were done away with by the British.
- Indian philosophy is very clear that deeds are the most important.
- In the Indian context, the deeds and achievements of people must be described in detail.

Note: (See the section on Introducing Personalities)

Places

- In describing places, the broader description is as important as the minute details.
- One can begin with a brief history of the place and then describe other features, laying emphasis on important aspects and giving artistic details.
- The importance of places must be clearly highlighted.
- Historical, social and religious aspects can be dealt with briefly.
- Specialty such as fairs held or the time of big gatherings should be mentioned.
- In today's world when travelling is a regular feature of modern life, it is also important to describe the best time of the year to travel to specific places.
- Apart from domestic travellers, it is imperative to keep foreign tourists in mind while writing about places, particularly for travel magazines or travel columns.
- Therefore, also give details about the choice of foods available, both vegetarian as well as non-vegetarian.
- Also give a good description of the types of hotels and lodgings available.

EXAMPLE

The Red Fort, Delhi: With a circumference of more than 2.2 kilometres, the Red Fort was laid out by the banks of the River Yamuna in the 17th century. Mughal Emperor Shah Jahan built it with the intention of projecting Mughal power through one monument. But 'monument' is perhaps not the right word, particularly in the context of ancient times because it was more like a mini-city.

Unfortunately for the emperor, before he could move his capital from Agra to Shahjahanabad in Delhi, he was taken a political prisoner by his son Aurangzeb. The fort is a delight to explore – Imagine the Naqqar Khana (Drum Room) also called Naubat Khana (Welcome Room), where drums once loudly heralded the arrival of the emperor and the Diwan-e-Aam (Hall of Public Audience) resounded with the chants of the people.

Besides these, there is more to see such as Mumtaz Mahal, Rang Mahal (Palace of Colours), Khas Mahal (Emperor's Palace), Diwan-e Khas (Hall of Private Audience), the Hammam (bathing area) and Shah Burj. The fort has two main entrances – Delhi Gate and Lahori Gate. The latter received its name from the fact that it faces Lahore in Pakistan. Its entrance leads to Delhi's most crowded bazaar, Chandni Chowk, which is a must see.

The winter months (between October and February) are the best time to visit Delhi, as the summers can be very harsh, with the ever-present danger of sunstroke.

There is a Light and Sound Show every evening.

Summer timings: Hindi: 7 pm to 8 pm, English: 8 pm to 9 pm
Winter timings: Hindi: 6 pm to 7 pm, English: 7 pm to 8 pm

Qutub Minar, Delhi: The highest stone tower in India, the Qutub Minar was built in 1192 by Qutubuddin Aibak, the viceroy of Mohammed Ghori. Built to celebrate Ghori's victory over the Rajputs, the tower and the victory are significant because both heralded the birth of a new dynasty – the Slave Dynasty – which laid the foundations of the Delhi Sultanate.

The Minar is a 72.5 metres five-storey building. The first storey was completed in Qutubuddin's lifetime. Son-in-law and successor, Iltutmish, added the next three storeys.

The famous Iron Pillar lies within the complex, having stood for millennia without rusting, Quwwat-ul-Islam, the first mosque built in India, and the Alai Darwaza, the gateway to the complex, were erected by Alauddin Khilji. Entry to the Minar has been closed, since the tower became infamous for several suicides. Qutub Minar is a successful tribute to architecture and has many features that arrest one's attention, including some of the most delicate and ethereal carvings.

Address: Mehrauli, Delhi-Gurgaon Road.
Timings: 6 am to 6 pm

The Iron Pillar: The 7.2-metre-high iron pillar, standing within the Qutub Minar complex, is proof of India's advanced knowledge of metallurgy 2,000 years ago, as it continues to stand rust-free even today. It was built sometime between the 4th and 5th century AD as a Dhavaja-stambha (flagpole) of a Vishnu temple.

It was erected in the memory of King Chandragupta Vikramaditya (who ruled between 375 and 413 AD), according to Sanskrit inscriptions on the pillar. It was once believed that if the visitors somehow hugged the pillar, their wishes would come true. But now this practice has been prohibited by the authorities.

Address: Qutub Minar Complex, Mehrauli, Delhi-Gurgaon Road.
Timings: 6 am to 6 pm

Seemapuri— (A Slum Area): Seemapuri is a place on the periphery of Delhi but different in many ways, including living conditions. A slum settlement for Bangladeshi refugees, before their arrival it was wilderness, but is densely populated with migrants today. They live in mud structures, with roofs of tin and tarpaulin, devoid of sewage and running water. Some 10,000 rag pickers live here. Naturally, garbage is gold for them. It is their daily bread.

While children collect garbage, adults work as house servants and tea vendors. The old are left to the mercy of the elements and charitable people. Their daily struggles make it clear that poverty is a way of life for them.

Academic Writing

• Article Writing • Comprehension Passages • Paragraph Writing • Precis Writing • Essays

Article Writing

Such writing is an art and skill that can be developed by consistent practice, patience and diligence. In essence, an article is numerous paragraphs weaved together thematically, based upon a single topic.

In article writing, there is much scope for subjective thought and personal style, both in writing and presentation. An article must be written in one's own words and style as far as possible.

TIPS

The following points should be borne in mind while writing an article:

- Use simple, contemporary language. Avoid rarely-used or archaic words.
- Avoid lengthy sentences consisting of many clauses and connectives.
- Write about relevant issues, and avoid circumlocution, repetitions and digressions. But some important points should be elaborated.
- Articles should be split into several short paragraphs, each with a connecting thread of thought.
- They should be simple enough for readers to understand without referring to a dictionary.
- Ensure the article has a smooth, seamless flow.
- Articles that are written in an authoritative tone carry more credibility.
- Whereever possible, it is best to quote statistics and cite specific case studies to buttress a particular point.
- When such details are given, make sure you back it up with references or sources, since this adds to the credibility of the article and the author.
- A reference or source can be directly woven into the main text of the article or it can be given as a footnote.

- An article should, however, not contain an overdose of information on a specific topic.
- It is best to restrict an article to around 800 words, when writing for newspapers.
- When writing for magazines, an average of 1,000 to 1,200 words is fine.
- Some magazines, particularly foreign periodicals, prefer in-depth pieces of 1,800 words or more.
- It is best to procure previous issues of a periodical one is writing for and study their style and length of pieces used beforehand so that one can draft an article accordingly.
- There are times when one may have to write two or three articles on the same topic. In such cases, the writer may be faced with the problem of writer's block, not knowing how to begin or what to write in the second or third article. The trick is to use a different angle or perspective for each article.

  For example, suppose you have been commissioned by a healthcare magazine to write about the problem of 'Lack of Access to Healthcare in India'. In the first article, you could take a macro perspective and write about how this problem has persisted ever since Independence due to various factors.

  In the second article, you could focus on how healthcare delivery has failed because only the public sector has been heavily involved in healthcare and there have been many shortfalls due to this. The private sector has only been present in major urban areas, which does not address the problems of a large section of the populace.

  In the third article, you could focus on how public-private partnerships have boosted healthcare access in various nations worldwide and India could also benefit by promoting such a model, whereby quality and efficiency of healthcare delivery are assured, while also ensuring services are available at various price points so affordability is not an issue.
- The introductory and concluding paragraphs of an article should be written with due thought. While the introductory paragraph should create immediate interest, the concluding paragraph should end logically and never seem like an abrupt ending.
- Proverbs, quotations and poetic thoughts can be used in articles provided they are relevant and promote better understanding of the topic.

Fatty Liver and the Excessive Use of Alcohol: Fatty liver has long been a term associated with excessive alcohol consumption. Doctors now say that numerous non-alcohol-related cases are surfacing as well. Termed non-alcoholic fatty liver disease, its prevalence is being blamed on regular consumption of junk food. The situation is alarming with 25–30% of urban India's population suffering from the disease.

Doctors believe metabolic disorders such as diabetes, hypertension and obesity increase the risk of fatty liver. Weight gain, especially around the waist, is one of the main causes of fatty liver. More and more people are consuming junk food as they have little time for traditional Indian cooking simply because they live in big cities and eat junk food due to peer pressure and live a rushed existence. Although their mothers prepare traditional food, the young prefer to eat junk.

Today, we are facing the harmful consequences of leading such a lifestyle and ending up with a variety of problems caused by liver disease.

Douglas' Escape from a Death Trap: When Douglas was learning to swim in a pool, a strong boy one day threw him into deep water. Douglas was totally unprepared for something like this. Suddenly, fear gripped him. He had no idea what to do. Yet he tried hard to move his arms and legs so that he could save himself.

He swallowed some water and immediately sank to the bottom. He tried desperately to paddle to the edge of the pool. But the nine feet deep water seemed to be 90 feet deep. He felt like his lungs were about to burst.

Panic gripped him. He tried to call out but no sound came. Suddenly, he noticed railings at the edge of the swimming pool wall. He frantically moved towards them. Grabbing a railing, he then hauled himself out of the water. He had come out of the water just when it seemed that his lungs would burst. Douglas realized he had had a narrow escape.

Henceforth, he decided he would never go for a swim in the pool alone but would always make certain he had some friend or companion along with him.

Comprehension Passages

TIPS

- Before reading a chapter, one should quickly read the questions at the end.
- As one reads the chapter thereafter, it will be easier to identify the answers.
- After reading the chapter, reread the questions, comprehend them and only then answer each question.
- Underline names when they occur for the first time. Underline important statements and quotable passages. Reread them while turning the pages of the book again at a later date.
- If there are any other instructions, ensure you read them thoroughly before answering the questions.
- Use the tense of the question. Change the tense only if imperative.

'The Last Lesson'
by Alphonse Daudet

I started for school very late that morning and was in great dread of a scolding, especially because M. Hamel had said that he would question us on participles, and I did not know the first word about them. For a moment I thought of running away and spending the day out of doors. It was so warm, so bright! The birds were chirping at the edge of the woods; and in the open field back of the sawmill the Prussian soldiers were drilling. It was all much more tempting than the rule for participles, but I had the strength to resist, and hurried off to school. When I passed the town hall there was a crowd in front of the bulletin-board. For the last two years all our bad news had come from there—the lost battles, the draft, the orders of the commanding officer—and I thought to myself, without stopping: "What can be the matter now?" Then, as I hurried by as fast as I could go, the blacksmith, Wachter, who was there, with his apprentice, reading the bulletin, called after me: "Don't go so fast, bub; you'll get to your school in plenty of time!" I thought he was making fun of me, and reached M. Hamel's little garden all out of breath.

Usually, when school began, there was a great bustle, which could be heard out in the street, the opening and closing of desks, lessons repeated in unison, very loud, with our hands over our ears to understand better, and the teacher's great ruler rapping on the table. But now it was all so still! I had counted on the commotion to get to my desk without being seen; but, of course, that day everything had to be as quiet as Sunday morning. Through the window I saw my classmates, already in their places, and M. Hamel walking up and down with his terrible iron ruler under his arm. I had to open the door and go in before everybody. You can imagine how I blushed and how frightened I was. But nothing happened. M. Hamel saw me and said very kindly: "Go to your place quickly, little Franz. We were beginning without you." I jumped over the bench and sat down at my desk. Not till then, when I had got a little over my fright, did I see that our teacher had on his beautiful green coat, his frilled shirt, and the little black silk cap, all embroidered, that he never wore except on inspection and prize days.

Besides, the whole school seemed so strange and solemn. But the thing that surprised me most was to see, on the back benches that were always empty, the village people sitting quietly like ourselves; old Hauser, with his three-cornered hat, the former mayor, the former postmaster, and several others besides. Everybody looked sad; and Hauser had brought an old primer, thumbed at the edges, and he held it open on his knees with his great spectacles lying across the pages. While I was wondering about it all, M. Hamel mounted his chair, and, in the same grave and gentle tone which he had used to me, said: "My children, this is the last lesson I shall give you. The order has come from Berlin to teach only German in the schools of Alsace and Lorraine. The new master comes tomorrow. This is your last French lesson. I want you to be very attentive." What a thunderclap these words were to me! Oh, the wretches; that was what they had put up at the town-hall! My last French lesson! Why, I hardly knew how to write! I should never learn any more! I must stop there, then! Oh, how sorry I was for not learning my lessons, for seeking birds' eggs, or going sliding on the Saar! My books, that had seemed such a nuisance a while ago, so heavy to carry, my grammar, and my history of the saints, were old friends now that I couldn't give up. And M. Hamel, too; the idea that he was going away, that I should never see him again, made me forget all about his ruler and how cranky he was. Poor man! It was in honour of this last lesson that he had put on his fine Sunday clothes, and now I understood why the old men of the village were sitting there in the back of the room. It was because they were sorry, too, that they had not gone to school more.

It was their way of thanking our master for his forty years of faithful service and of showing their respect for the country that was theirs no more. While I was thinking of all this, I heard my name called. It was my turn to recite. What would I not have given to be able to say that dreadful rule for the participle all through, very loud and clear, and without one mistake? But I got mixed up on the first words and stood there, holding on to my desk, my heart beating, and not daring to look up. I heard M. Hamel say to me: "I won't scold you, little Franz; you must feel bad enough. See how it is! Every day we have said to ourselves: 'Bah! I've plenty of time. I'll learn it tomorrow.' And now you see where we've come out. Ah, that's the great trouble with Alsace; she puts off learning till tomorrow. Now those fellows out there will have the right to say to you: 'How is it; you pretend to be Frenchmen, and yet you can neither speak nor write your own language?' But you are not the worst, poor little Franz. We've all a great deal to reproach ourselves with. "Your parents were not anxious enough to have you learn. They preferred to put you to work on a farm or at the mills, so as to have a little more money. And I? I've been to blame also. Have I not often sent you to water my flowers instead of learning your lessons? And when I wanted to go fishing, did I not just give you a holiday?" Then, from one thing to another, M. Hamel went on to talk of the French language, saying that it was the most beautiful language in the world—the clearest, the most logical; that we must guard it among us and never forget it, because when a people are enslaved, as long as they hold fast to their language it is as if they had the key to their prison. Then he opened a grammar and read us our lesson. I was amazed to see how well I understood it. All he said seemed so easy, so easy! I think, too, that I had never listened so carefully, and that he had never explained everything with so much patience. It seemed almost as if the poor man wanted to give us all he knew before going away, and to put it all into our heads at one stroke. After the grammar, we had a lesson in writing. That day M. Hamel had new copies for us, written in a beautiful round hand: France, Alsace, France, Alsace. They looked like little flags floating everywhere in the school-room, hung from the rod at the top of our desks. You ought to have seen how every one set to work, and how quiet it was! The only sound was the scratching of the pens over the paper.

Once some beetles flew in; but nobody paid any attention to them, not even the littlest ones, who worked right on tracing their fish-hooks, as if that was French, too. On the roof the pigeons cooed very low, and I thought to myself: "Will they make them sing in German, even the pigeons?" Whenever I looked up from my writing I saw M. Hamel sitting motionless in his chair and gazing first at one thing, then at another, as if he wanted to fix in his mind just how everything looked in that little school-room. Fancy! For forty years, he had been there in the same place, with his garden outside the window and his class in front of him, just like that. Only the desks and benches had been worn smooth; the walnut-trees in the garden were taller, and the hopvine that he had planted himself twined about the windows to the roof. How it must have broken his heart to leave it all, poor man; to hear his sister moving about in the room above, packing their trunks! For they must leave the country next day.

But he had the courage to hear every lesson to the very last. After the writing, we had a lesson in history, and then the babies chanted their ba, be bi, bo, bu. Down there at the back of the room old Hauser had put on his spectacles and, holding his primer in both hands, spelled the letters with them. You could see that he, too, was crying; his voice trembled with emotion, and it was so funny to hear him that we all wanted to laugh and cry. Ah, how well I remember it, that last lesson! All at once the church-clock struck twelve. Then the Angelus. At the same moment, the trumpets of the Prussians, returning from drill, sounded under our windows. M. Hamel stood up, very pale, in his chair. I never saw him look so tall. "My friends," said he, "I—I—" But something choked him. He could not go on. Then he turned to the blackboard, took a piece of chalk, and, bearing on with all his might, he wrote as large as he could: "Vive La France!" Then he stopped and leaned his head against the wall, and, without a word, he made a gesture to us with his hand: "School is dismissed—you may go."

Write a Summary of 'The Last Lesson'

A boy named Franz is ready to go to school. He narrates the story. He is worried, as he has not learnt his lesson. He is afraid of the iron ruler of the teacher, Mr Hamel. From there till the end of the class, these events make up the story 'The Last Lesson', written by Alphonse Daudet. It is set in the background of the Prussian War (1870-71) when Bismarck attacked and captured France. It is the day when there was a bad order on the bulletin that from the next day German would be taught in place of French. It is the last class of the teacher Mr Hamel, who gives students the last lesson in French.

On the way, Mr Hamel sees a crowd around the bulletin board on the main street. In the classroom, he finds a changed atmosphere. The teacher was dressed in his best Sunday attire. Some elderly men were seated on the back benches. He painfully announces that he is not needed since German will replace French and this is his last class. The entire class is alert. The teacher delivers his best lecture. The students and others listen with rapt attention. The atmosphere is charged with emotion and there is sadness all around. Mr Hamel asks them to save French by learning it.

At the end, he declares, 'Victory for beautiful France'. Thereby, the story ends.

Introduce the story 'The Last Lesson'

The theme of the story 'The Last Lesson' reflects the pain, anxiety and suffering of the people enslaved by the conqueror and their loss of the freedom. The pain becomes almost unbearable when the right to learn and speak their language is snatched.

The story has a sub-theme; it is about the teacher-pupil relations and their attitude to learning and teaching. Through a local issue, a universal truth has been brought forth for understanding the importance of one's language and the impact due to loss of freedom.

Questions and Answers from the Text Book

(On the pattern of CBSE and NCERT)

Think as you read.

1. What was Franz expected to be prepared with for school that day?

   Franz was expected to be prepared about Participles from the book of Grammar. He had not learnt it. So he was afraid of being scolded.

2. What did Franz notice was unusual about the school that day?

   His teacher Mr Hamel was in his best Sunday suit. He was most polite. There was no scolding. The class was quiet and some elderly persons were sitting on the back benches. Everybody seemed sad.

3. What had been put up on the bulletin board?

   When Franz passed by the bulletin board he saw a crowd there. He could not ascertain the cause of anxiety. He learnt the reason in the classroom when his teacher Mr Hamel informed everyone that German would be taught in place of French from the next day.

4. What changes did the order from Berlin cause in school that day?

   The order from Berlin ejected French from the school. German was to be taught in its place. The French teacher, therefore, had to leave the school.

5. What were Franz's feelings about Mr Hamel and the change at school?

   Franz was sorry to know it was the last class of French lessons. He wouldn't learn it anymore. He felt his Grammar and History books were like Scriptures. He forgot all about the ruler and the fear of being scolded by his teacher.

Understanding the text.

1. The people in the story suddenly realize how precious their language is for them. What makes you think so? Why does this happen?

   The moment the people learnt that French is to be replaced by German, they felt a longing for their language. It is evident that old Hauser had brought an old primer. He kept the book open and tried to learn everything in a single day. He had his big spectacles with him. Franz considers his books to be friends that he can't part with, and the teacher tries to teach everything in the last lesson. This situation came about because Berlin had sent an order that French was to be replaced by German.

2. Franz thinks: "Will they make them sing in German, even the pigeons?" What could this mean?

   It means the fear of losing one's language. A mother tongue is more precious than anything else. The rulers suppress the language of the enslaved to rule over them for long. It shows the worries of the boy, Franz.

Talking about the text.

1. "When people are enslaved, as long as they hold fast to their language it is as if they had the key to their prison."

   Can you think of examples in history where conquered people had their language taken away from them or had a language imposed on them?

   This story is in itself a proof of this. German ruler, Bismarck, defeated the French army. An order comes from Berlin that French is to be immediately replaced with German. The language of the French people was forcibly taken away and German, the language of the new ruler, was imposed upon them.

   Indians had to learn different languages during 1,000 years of enslavement. But they held fast to their languages and eventually regained their freedom.

2. What happens to a linguistic minority in a state? How can they keep their language alive? For example: Punjabis in Bangalore; Tamilians in Mumbai; Kannadigas in Delhi; and Gujaratis in Kerala.

   All these examples are from India. India is a country with multiple traditions. Tolerance and peaceful living is its essence. Hence, there is no problem here. Since thousands of years before Christ, Indians have used, developed, lived with more than 1,600 languages and dialects.

   Usually there are serious differences between linguistic minorities and the majority, but not in India. Despite adverse statements by vested interest as many as 16 languages are recognized in the Indian Constitution, and great authors from each language receive National Awards for the growth and development of those languages. Every language should be respected and given its due space.

3. Is it possible to carry pride in one's language too far?

   Yes; one must be proud of one's language but not carry this too far to the extent of suppressing another language. Nothing is more precious than the language of one's country.

4. Do you know what 'linguistic chauvinism' means?

   Linguistic chauvinism means to fight for the promotion of one's language while looking down upon or suppressing other languages.

Questions and Answers for practice (Short)

1. Who is the writer of the story 'The Last Lesson'?

   The story, 'The Last Lesson' was written by Alphonse Daudet.

2. Who is the narrator of 'The Last Lesson'?

   'The Last Lesson' is narrated by a schoolboy named Franz.

3. Who are Mr Hamel and old Hauser?

   Mr Hamel is the teacher of Franz, the narrator of the story and old Hauser is a neighbour of the boy who sat on the backbench with an old primer.

4. What is the background of the story 'The Last Lesson'?

   The pain and suffering of the French people defeated in the Franco-Prussian war (1870-71) by German ruler Bismarck. It is set in the French districts of Alsace and Lorraine. The people were shocked and aggrieved to learn that by an order from Berlin they had to learn German in place of French.

5. What is the subject matter of the story 'The Last Lesson'?

   The subject is the last lesson given by the teacher Mr Hamel, when by an order from Berlin he is forced to leave the school he served for 40 years. The story brings out the reaction and sadness of the teacher, pupils and even the villagers at the news that French will no longer be taught in their schools.

6. Why did the schoolboy want to run away?

   The schoolboy Franz had to learn participles, which he had not. He was afraid of being scolded by his teacher Mr Hamel and scared of his iron ruler. So instead of going to school, he wanted to run away.

7. Where did Franz plan to spend the day?

   Franz wanted to run away and spend the day outdoors as the day was bright, warm and pleasant.

8. Why was there a large crowd at the bulletin board?

   There was a large crowd because the bulletin board revealed that French would be replaced by German.

9. How was the atmosphere at school?

   The school was quiet, still and peaceful.

10. How did the teacher react when Franz entered the classroom?

    Very politely, the teacher told Franz to go to his seat.

11. What did the teacher say when Franz failed to recite?

When Franz failed to recite, the teacher consoled and assured him that he wouldn't be scolded. He said that every day we promise ourselves to finish learning the next day but tomorrow never comes. So we all have a great deal to reproach ourselves on this count.

12. What did the teacher say about the French language?

Mr Hamel said French was the most beautiful language in the world and advised all to guard the language and declared: "When people are enslaved, as long as they hold fast to their language, it is as if they have the key to their prison."

13. What did the schoolboy feel when Hamel gave them new copies?

The boy liked the new copy that was given to them by their teacher. To him they looked like little flags floating everywhere in the classroom.

14. What did the teacher do at the end?

Mr Hamel tried to say something but could not say a word. So he turned to the blackboard, checked his emotions and wrote in big letters "Vive La France!" – which means 'Victory to France.'

Questions and Answers for Practice (Long)

1. Sketch the character of Mr Hamel as depicted in 'The Last Lesson'.

Mr Hamel is a teacher in the school of the narrator, Franz. Mr Hamel has created fear in the minds of pupils because he is strict and maintains discipline. He is a man of strong moral character. A patriot, he loves France and French from the depth of his heart.

He knows the meaning of freedom and the effects of slavery. He is not a traditional schoolmaster but an emotional intellectual. He maintains a balance between reasoning and emotions. He is well respected in the village. This is evident when the villagers sit in the classroom during his last lecture. They were there to pay their respect to the teacher.

2. Sketch the character of Franz as depicted in 'The Last Lesson'.

Franz is a normal schoolboy. When he has not done his homework, he fears being scolded or beaten with the iron ruler, so he thinks of running away and spending the day in absolute freedom in the lap of nature. But he has a conscience. The eager learner in him wins over and as a disciplined child he attends class, despite the fear of being scolded. He is a curious boy, watchful and intelligent. He shows due respect to his teacher.

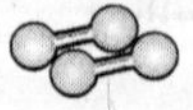

Exercise

Answer these short questions in about 40 words.

1. How did Franz reach his school?
2. How did the teacher treat him?
3. What were the changes in the school?
4. What were the changes in Franz?
5. What do you learn from the story 'The Last Lesson'?
6. Why did the teacher ask them to guard French?

7. Why were the pupils and people sad?
8. Why had the villagers come to the school?
9. What was the order from Berlin?
10. What happens to the language of a slave country?

Paragraph Writing

TIPS

- Paragraphs should be focused and to the point.
- Simple sentences are easier to read.
- All sentences should be related to the previous one and flow seamlessly.
- Each paragraph should be related to a specific point or train of thought. Multiple points should not be used in the same paragraph.
- Even if a long paragraph is based upon a specific point, it is proper to break it up into two paragraphs to facilitate easier reading.
- Short paragraphs are best for all kinds of writing.
- Longer paragraphs are usually used in books and novels.
- But it is best to limit each paragraph to a maximum of 150 words.

Cells and their types: A cell is a unit in which all life activities occur. The basic structure of every living being is composed of cells. Each cell lives its own life and simultaneously makes it possible for the living being as a whole to carry on its activities. The useful matter in the cell is the protoplasm, which carries on all the processes necessary for life. It takes in food and oxygen; changes some of the food into living matter; expels waste; repairs worn-out parts; and forms and reproduces itself.

There are plants and animals ranging from one-cell creatures to those with millions of cells. The most complicated cell structure is in humans. In humans and other higher animals, cells are organized in groups of a specific kind to perform a particular type of work. These are called tissues – such as bone tissues, muscle tissues, etc. When several tissues combine to perform a specific task, this becomes an organ.

In the human body, there are five important types of cells. Epithelial cells make up the skin and glands, and line the body vessels. Nerve cells make up the brain, spinal cord and nerves. Blood cells are found in the blood and lymph. Connective tissue cells make up the framework of body tissues.

Glands: A gland is an organ producing a chemical substance that regulates the body's metabolic activities. There are two kinds of glands: exocrine glands with ducts leading outside and ductless endocrine glands. Sweat glands secrete sweat via coiled ducts taken to the skin's surface. Digestive glands secrete digestive juices in the stomach and intestine. Salivary glands produce saliva. These are all exocrine glands. Endocrine glands secrete hormones; these are chemical messengers released directly into the bloodstream, and used to control metabolic activities such as growth and development.

The Brain: Located within the skull, the brain is well protected since it is a very tender part of the human body. The brain has three main parts: Forebrain, Midbrain and Hindbrain.

The anterior part is the forebrain. This includes the olfactory lobes (the centre of smells) and the cerebral hemisphere (the seat of intelligence). The midbrain includes optic lobes, the centre of vision. The hindbrain is the posterior part, which includes the cerebellum (co-ordination centre) and the medulla oblongata (centre of involuntary actions). The medulla oblongata continues behind the spinal cord.

All human functions are controlled by the brain. In other words, we only have to control the brain in order to have complete control over the Self. The brain is connected to each part of the body with nerves, which form a delicate nervous system. It receives messages and passes the orders that are immediately sent to various organs for necessary action.

The Process of Reproduction in Plants: Reproduction in plants is a unique and interesting process. A common flower has four parts. The green outer portion is made up of leaf-like Sepals. Within these sepals are the Petals. The reproducing organs of a flower lie within the petals. They produce seeds.

One or more Pistils are found at the very centre of the flower. Pistils are female organs. Around the pistils there is a ring of Stamens. The bottom of the pistil is an enlarged part called the Ovary. Inside the ovary are round Ovules which, at a later stage, become seeds. But they become seeds only when they are fertilized by the contents of Pollen Grains. Pollen grains are produced by the Stamen, which is the male organ of a flower. Most flowers have both organs but many flowers have only one organ.

Plants depend on wind, birds and insects for pollination. There is a sugary liquid on the surface of the ovary. The pollen grains absorb moisture and then they swell and grow. The grains are pushed down and become a tube. The tube keeps on growing down through the stalk of the pistil and through the wall of the ovary and then into an ovule. The contents of the tube then empty into the ovule and fertilize it.

Decoding DNA: DNA, or deoxyribonucleic acid, is a nucleic acid that is the chief constituent of the chromosomes carrying genetic information in the form of genes, necessary for the organization and functioning of living cells. The molecular structure of DNA was first proposed by JD Watson and FH Crick in 1953.

The DNA consists of a double helix of two strands coiled around each other. Each strand is made up of alternating pentose sugar (deoxyribose) and phosphate groups, with an organic base attached to each pentose group. There are four possible bases: adenise (A); guanine (G); cytocine (C); and thymine (T).

The bases on each strand are joined by hydrogen bonds, which are always poised in the same way. A always binds with T; and G with C. During replication, the strands of the helix separate and each provides a template for the synthesis of a new complementary strand, thereby producing two identical copies of the original helix.

This special property for accurate self-replication enables DNA to duplicate the genes of an organism during the cell divisions of growth and production of germ cells for the next generation.

Delhi Metro – the Green Mode of Transport: The advent of the Delhi Metro in the early part of the new millennium has led to a great change across Delhi in many ways. To begin with, had it not been for the Delhi Metro, the number of cars and buses on the streets would have been much more, causing higher and concentrated levels of pollution that would have affected all citizens.

Ironically, there was a major campaign to stop the Delhi Metro on the pretext that it was an exorbitant mode of transport as far as its development was concerned. Antagonists argued that for the money spent on building the Metro, thousands of buses could be made operational to carry passengers all across Delhi.

The critics totally missed the point that thousands of additional buses on Delhi's streets would have led to total traffic chaos, not to mention pollution levels being doubled. One shudders to think what the effect on public health would have been had the Metro not been introduced.

Moreover, buses as a mode of transport are not exactly safe for passengers since there have been many cases of pickpocketing where the victims have been stabbed when they resisted. Although pickpocketing incidents have also been taking place in recent years on the Metro as it has become overcrowded, the fortunate part is that no victims have been stabbed on board for the simple reason that the Metro has adequate security on the platforms and stations. In case pickpockets indulge in open violence, their chances of getting away would be slim because of heavy security at the gates, not to mention the CCTV cameras that are present all over.

This apart, in areas of Old Delhi such as Chandni Chowk, businesses that were on the verge of closure have now been attracting patrons once again. These businesses declined during the past years because clients found it almost impossible to reach there on time or find parking space when they did manage to reach. Consequently, clients moved to other parts of Delhi where it was easier to conduct business. The Delhi Metro changed all that as people can now reach Old Delhi easily, without having to worry about parking and other issues. This has revived many businesses in the past decade.

Whichever way one looks at it, the Delhi Metro has been a boon for everyone, besides being a green mode of transport. And it has only been a bane for Delhi's notorious auto drivers who love to fleece passengers every day. But now passengers have a reliable, secure and safe option – Delhi Metro.

Exercise

- Write a paragraph on Teacher's Day, which falls on 5th September.
- Write a paragraph on Children's Day, which falls on 14th November.
- Write a few paragraphs on the Book Fair organized at the Pragati Maidan.
- Write a paragraph on Global Warming.
- Write a few paragraphs on Water Pollution.
- Write a paragraph on 'Melting Antarctica'.

Précis Writing

TIPS

- Précis writing is the art of rewriting in brief, something written in detail.
- A good précis is only one-third or less of the original passage.
- It should be written in one's own words as far as possible.
- Précis retains all important ideas and leaves out unimportant details.
- A précis needs a suitable title.
- The best example of précis: The president of one country visited another. The counterpart of the host country kept speaking for 15 minutes. The translator simply told the guest: "Your honour! The president is praising you in the superlative." Thereby, 15 minutes of speech was reduced to one simple sentence.
- Grasp the central theme and read the passage twice at least.
- Note down only important ideas to form an outline.
- Now, rewrite the outline in your own words and give a title.
- Avoid personal comments.
- Don't break the précis into too many paragraphs though the original may contain many paragraphs.
- If possible, write the entire précis in one paragraph.
- In case of a really long story, there will be no choice but to have numerous paragraphs. But make sure the précis is as short as possible.
- Avoid the direct form of narration.
- Don't use the first person.
- Don't quote from the passage.
- Don't write: "In the opinion of the writer/the writer says" etc.
- Don't copy any sentence from the original passage.

- **Forgiveness: A Divine Quality**

Forgiveness is a rare word and divine quality that has retained its value since creation, although its characteristics were found and respected from time immemorial in all parts of the world, all languages and all religions. All preached it, and all the ancient writings are its living proofs. It is not limited to Hinduism or Christianity. It gets the same respect in all faiths, sects, groups and factions.

Whether they possess this quality or not, all people worldwide talk about its great benefits and recommend it as a panacea for all mental ills, common and uncommon anxieties and prevalent worries. The moment one forgives the other, the mind becomes relaxed. Growing tension is reduced to almost naught.

Forgiveness becomes easy when one believes in the law of *Karma*, deeds; *Satkarma*, meritorious deeds; and *Dushkarma*, immoral, illegal and unethical deeds. One is responsible for one's own deeds and gets rewarded or punished accordingly. These acts are *Sanchit*, accumulate; or *Prārabadha*, ongoing; or *Āgāmi*, to be performed in future.

Nature has numerous ways of punishing for wrong deeds and rewarding for good ones. It is in the law of Nature, imperceptible but guaranteed. There is no pick and choose in that law. It comes in the course of time or living. When one is not responsible for deeds or misdeeds of others, then one should not worry about the wrongs done by others towards him/her or others. Think in this light and you can forgive anyone for any crime: common, general or heinous.

A common saying goes: 'To err is human to forgive divine'. This concept can make you forgive others. But it empowers the ego. When you forgive someone be humble. It will enable you to forget the event. But when the ego grows then it is difficult to forget the incident. If one fails to forget the incident, it will come to mind off and on and aggrieve you. The unpleasant event will haunt you for long. So it is better to remember the 'forgive-and-forget' formula. One must keep in mind that forgiveness is not only divine but sublime too.

One forgives the other not for the sake of the other but for one's own sake, for getting rid of the tension and worries, and also for throwing revenge out of one's mind. If another misdeed is committed to punish or to take revenge or for personal satisfaction then there remains no difference between the one who committed the crime first and the other who committed the crime afterwards for the sake of revenge. It is far easier to punish someone or to take revenge and really difficult to forgive the misdeed.

If this is kept in mind then those that forgive are mentally and morally stronger than the wrongdoer. This was what Bāpu had in mind when he said: "The weak can never forgive. Forgiveness is the attribute of the strong."

Précis (Forgiveness): Forgiveness is a sublime quality in human character. By practice, it becomes part of one's nature. The moment one forgives someone for wrong acts, s/he becomes greater than the wrongdoer. Forgiveness ensures peace of mind to the wronged person. The person who forgives finds instant relief from tension and permanent freedom from the negative emotion of revenge. This peace is long-lasting and improves social relationships. This is the best benefit from forgiveness.

• **The Full Mind:** In a cup full of tea, if one pours more, it will overflow. The cup is already holding back whatever capacity it had. It is the gist of a tale of a Buddhist Monk. Our mind is like the cup already full to its brim and whatever is poured into it, overflows. The mind has no capacity to hold more. So, to enable the mind to understand and retain fresh, novel and meritorious ideas, it is essential to empty the mind, in the same way that the cup needs to be emptied first for refilling with freshly prepared hot tea. If the mind is also empty then it can hold more new ideas, essential for the growth of inner ability and skill. All our performance in any field depends entirely upon our ability and skill.

The mind incessantly creates numerous modifications every now and then. Naturally, one of the great occupations of the illumined minds has been to search out ways and means to check the mind from participating in races of different kinds. So in place of being swayed by the mind, man, in every age and every race, has tried hard to control mind. That is the reason that there are various ways and means of controlling the mind.

One of the best methods advocated almost everywhere and by every master and preceptor in this way or that is to 'empty the mind'. There are different ways and methods of emptying the mind. Despite differences in method the end everywhere has remained the same: "to go deeper and deeper and penetrate all the layers of mind and existence, to hit the centre and gain control over mind, our existence and thus over the self.

Spirituality always aims at the realization of the self, whether one believes in rebirth or not; in the law of *Karma* or not; or in the final enlightenment and *Nirvāna* or not. Those aims are different. The sole aim is one, the realization and enlightenment.

The most difficult thing is to begin emptying the mind. People don't believe that emptying the mind can be done; that the mind can be empty. No, the mind will never be empty but the important thing is to stop the negative energy from flowing faster, to make positive energy flow faster; and that way, initiate the formations of positive ideas by relegating negative ideas to the back seat, then displacing it and then ousting it completely. Negative connection is needed but the flux of negative ideas ruins one's life. Inner and higher growth begins the moment negative ideas are denied passage and positive ideas make headway.

Précis (Emptying the Mind): A mind that is always full can take in nothing more of value. The ideas already inside ensure there is no place for new ideas. One must keep emptying the mind periodically in order to throw out negative things and take in positive ideas. Such a person will keep making progress throughout life. Emptying the mind to allow new ideas is akin to the still water of a small pond that becomes dirty and polluted. The moment flowing fresh water enters, the polluted water is moved out. In this way, inner growth and positivity are assured.

• **Ideas and Learning Words:** All the ways of learning words are considered effective but imbibing them through ideas is a much better way of learning words because the association improves the power of recall. We have the mental power to learn everything intelligently and utilize them advantageously. It is our weakness that we fail to learn or retain what is learnt.

We must therefore learn words and other things in many ways, including associating them with specific ideas or thoughts. Knowledge is never ending and has no beginning or end. Every day we keep learning about new things and new words. Keep collecting words and using them in sentences in order to gain mastery over them.

The following way of learning words is interesting. One idea is taken and different words are given, which are deeply related to that idea. In the absence of those words you can't talk about the idea or the new words.

Also remember that everyone receives help from different persons in various forms. Therefore, keep helping others. If you share words and ideas with others you will grow mature and confident and your personal bank of ideas will also increase. Sharing and interacting with others is a novel way of learning words as well as grasping and expressing new ideas.

Précis (Learning Words through Ideas): There are different ways of learning words. The best way is via ideas. An idea is considered and all words related to that idea are collected and learnt. In this way, one learns by association, which can leave a permanent imprint on the mind. One will remember the association even if the actual meaning is forgotten. Another benefit of learning words via ideas is that words are spontaneously used in the correct context. For example, if one hears the word 'haute couture' for the first time, one can associate this with the idea of a fashion show. Immediately, all the related words will become associated with the idea of a fashion show, connecting it to haute couture or designing of fashionable clothes.

• **Shiva and Akshar Brahma:** Shiva is also known as *Akshar Brahma.* As *Akshar Brahma*, He neither does nor is attached, and yet is powerful and active. *Akshar* possesses *Sat, Chitta* and *Ānand.* Only *Akshar* is active and therefore *Akshar* is also popular as *Chetanā* or consciousness.

Creation depends on *pratishthā*, insertion, placement (*Brahma Tattva*), *jyoti*, light (Indra Tattva) and *yagya, anna*, feeding (*Vishnu, Agni* and *Soma Tattva*): *yagyo wai Vishnu*. The power that takes anna, digests it and converts it into energy is called Vishnu. When active inside the womb, Indra is known as Fire, and when active inside the womb, Vishnu is Soma. Creation is the combined effort of *nām-rupa* and *karma*.

One dynamic akshar tattva, in the form of *gati smuchchya* (*Brahman*), *Shuddha gati* (Indra), *Shuddh agati* (Vishnu), *sthiti garvitā gati* (Agni) and *sthiti garvitā agati* (Soma), becomes Fire. One *akshar* with dynamic connectivity becomes *Panchākshar*. As words are created with a, i, •, ri, and lri, five *akshars*, in the same way the meaning is also derived from the same five *akshars*. The sequence of the creation of akshar and derivation of meaning are the same. *Shabda* (word) and *Artha* (meaning) are deeply related. With the five *akshars*, five *Vikārs* originate, called *Viswashrishta*. From the *vikārs pancha jana* are created. When they are inter-mixed then *panchikrit prāna* originate. Then the *akshar Brahman* enters: *tat srishtvā tadevānu prāvishat*. They are collectively called *Shodashi Prajāpati*.

Précis (Akshar Brahma): Akshar – that which is neither lost, nor reduced but which remains intact – is the quality of the Absolute God, Brahma. It is a fact that he is both a static and dynamic force. He is pure force and purely static. All the opposite qualities arise and are possessed as well as given by Brahma. He is all the five gross elements, all the three genders, all the sound, alphabet and word. He is both Nada Brahma and Shabda Brahma. He is endless, infinite and indomitable. He is all and everything and in everything and everyone. So he is Akshar Brahma.

Essays

Short Essays

TIPS

- Short essays can be a brief version of longer essays.
- Your essay will require insight of your own, genuine essay writing brilliance.
- Based upon the topic, write down the key messages required. This will ensure a reasonable sequence to the flow of points.
- The introduction should grab the reader's attention – Remember this always.
- Always break up an essay into various points to facilitate drafting and smooth flow of reading.
- Elaborate the points in short paragraphs.
- Read the essay more than once to revise, correct and improve upon it.

Team Work: A team performs and sustains on the basis of personal and professional relationships. In both cases, coordination and cooperation are crucial to success. Instead of trying to be the centre of attraction, try to be one amongst all, an integral but vital part of a team, assisting others and accepting the occasional encouraging smiles that flash. Every action and reaction must be reciprocated. It makes no difference whether it's satisfactory or unsatisfactory, adequate or inadequate. It is reciprocated and that is enough to keep up the team spirit.

My own role in a team depends entirely on my skill, dexterity and performance. If I'm determined to perform a given task well and in time, only then can I hope to extend a helping hand to teammates. If I am lagging all the time, I will be expecting some help from this or that corner and will never be able to help others and learn how more work can be finished in a limited span of time.

I believe only they can prove and become good teammates who are active and efficient, know their work and responsibilities, and possess the ability to complete the work and fulfill responsibilities. They also prove to be good teammates who truthfully accept their weaknesses and decline to do something beyond their capacity. I prefer such teammates and cherish their contributions.

Worshipping the Sun: Ancient Indians were the first people to worship the Sun and they have been pioneers in many other things as well. They had a well-developed culture, civilization, language, literature, scientific knowledge and spiritual thought. Whether the world accepts it or not, the fact remains that ancient Indians with illuminated minds and high moral character gave human religion to the world and all other religions developed from it.

Read the history of ancient civilizations: India, Mesopotamia, Egypt, China, Greece, Rome and even that of the Mayans or Aztecs. There are many things in common with ancient Indian civilization. All of them believe in an all-powerful God. They may not accept Him as Brahman but their description fits into the picture. The other striking similarity is that almost all worshipped the Sun God: be it Ravi or Surya.

Study of Light: Light is the basis of the sense of sight and the perception of colour. It is made up of photons and produces rays. Light travels in a straight line and is faster than anything else in the known universe. Light travels at a speed of 300,000 kilometres per second. Distance is calculated by the time the rays take to reach another place. Light takes 8 minutes and 30 seconds from the Sun to reach the Earth. A light year equals 9.5 trillion kilometres.

Light can travel through air, transparent substances and even empty space. Modern scientists say sunlight is composed of three types of rays: Infrared; Ultraviolet; and Visible Light. The wavelength of each is different. Ultraviolet rays have the shortest wavelength while infrared rays, the longest. Ultraviolet and Infrared rays are invisible. Visible light consists of seven colours: violet; indigo; blue; green; yellow; orange; and red.

Converting Food into Glucose and Energy: The digestive system changes food into insulin and glucose. It is absorbed by the blood and the blood transmits it to the organs as pure energy. If such pure energy could be taken directly from the Cosmos, food would not be required. Ancient Indian rishis had developed a way, mostly through Yoga, of inhaling cosmic energy and thereby managed to live without food for months together. They had minimized their physical needs. They had control over their bodies and lived in a balanced way. Naturally, in all the literature available they have laid stress on two things: Control and Balance.

Sugar is our perpetual need, which has become a common problem in the modern age. People hardly realize that they will faint or may even die if their sugar levels plummet. It's the excessive sugar deposited by non-physical labour that causes problems and triggers all sorts of diseases. Sugar in itself is not a problem. The imbalance creates problems.

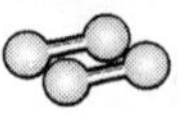

Exercise (Write short essays on the following)

- Five Gross Elements;
- Classification of Rocks;
- The Need for Forests;
- Negative Impact of Pesticides;
- Water Pollution.

Long and Detailed Essays

Hints on Essay Writing:

- An essay is something written on a specific topic.
- It is a series of paragraphs on one subject. Each paragraph deals with a different but relevant aspect of the same subject. The paragraphs are arranged to form a connected whole.
- An essay is an exercise in original composition, intended to test the expression of one's ideas in suitable words.
- In some jobs where content writing skills are essential, candidates may be given a written test and asked to write an essay on some topic or the other. It is, therefore, best to practice essay writing well in advance so that one is able to write well whenever required.

Selection of Subject

- Selection of a proper topic is essential. During exams, if there is a list of five or six topics, it is best to select a topic one is most familiar with.
- If such an option is not there, select a subject which is somewhat familiar.

Collecting Ideas and Framing Outlines

- Next, form a clear idea on the subject.
- The main ideas must be written as points or sub-headings.
- All related ideas should be noted to complete an outline of the subject.

Editing the Essay

- Read the outline from a reader or critic's viewpoint. Delete all irrelevant ideas.
- Once done, reread and edit any other irrelevant words or points missed out earlier.

Connecting Points

- All subsequent points must be connected to the central theme.

- If some points don't connect well, rewrite them so a connection is established.
- Points that still don't connect or flow well can be safely deleted.

Writing the Essay

- First write the introduction, preferably in one paragraph or a maximum of two.
- Next, each sub-heading should be considered based upon importance or sequence and written in two to three medium-sized paragraphs.
- While developing ideas, be as original as possible. Originality outshines borrowed ideas.
- Simple and original ideas are far better than lofty borrowed thoughts.
- All thoughts or points must flow logically and seamlessly one after the other.

Language

- The essay should be written in one's own words.
- Quotations should only be used occasionally.
- Nothing should be unnecessarily repeated.
- Specific thoughts should be given under related sub-headings.
- Grammatical mistakes or spelling errors should be avoided.
- Punctuation marks should be used appropriately.

Conclusion

- The conclusion is as important as the introduction and it should be equally striking.
- Specific points are given for excellent conclusions.
- The conclusion should be short and smooth.
- No essay should end abruptly or this will lead to deduction of marks.

Revision

Revision is the last and most important part of an essay. The points or mistakes missed earlier should be added or corrected during the revision. Having to write essays in haste could lead to errors, but this can be corrected by carefully rereading them later. That is why revision or rereading is so essential.

Air Pollution: The rise of industrialisation and globalization has led to higher levels of pollution throughout the world. Due to this, air pollution is one of the gravest threats to human health today. Air pollution increases day by day due to the rising number of vehicles that take to the roads every day. These include two-wheelers, three-wheelers and four-wheelers. With emissions norms not having been strict in earlier years, pollution has wrecked havoc with human health across much of the country.

Acid Rain is one of the most dangerous outcomes of air pollution. This consists of rain mixed with toxic elements such as nitrogen, sulphur and other harmful chemicals released by factories into the atmosphere. When these gases mix with moisture in the air, they form an acid compound and condense to form rain. When it rains, the chemicals mixed with rain also come down, damaging trees and other living beings.

Burning of garbage also adds tremendously to air pollution. Garbage contains plastic and other toxic elements, which release noxious fumes when burnt. For example, when computers and refrigerators are dismantled, they emit harmful gases and other dangerous pollutants that are hazardous to life. Some microscopic particles emitted via fuel combustion from automobiles, power plants, industrial processes, etc. are able to penetrate the deepest parts of the lungs. These toxic particles are associated with higher morbidity and mortality rates, respiratory and cardiovascular diseases, asthma, cough, throat dryness, chest discomfort, thoracic pain and headache. Children, the elderly and the sick are most susceptible.

We must consciously do our best to check air pollution and make this Earth a better place to live in. For this, multiple measures will need to be taken, including phasing out polluting vehicles, using stringent air pollution control norms, ensuring strict checks and fines for polluters as well as other relevant steps.

The Evil Effects of Corruption: In the past decade, corruption has become one of the biggest banes of India. Scam after scam is being uncovered, which is hurting India's image and impacting the India brand story among overseas investors and the global community. The 2G scam, Coalgate, the Commonwealth Games scam and a host of other scandals have sullied the India growth story. With scams being uncovered at regular intervals, it has given thc Opposition parties an excuse to keep disrupting Parliament regularly. Due to this, for the past two years the UPA Government was virtually paralyzed and unable to pass any worthwhile legislation. This led to almost everyone accusing the Manmohan Singh Government of being afflicted with 'policy paralysis'.

But it is the country that has had to pay a terrible price for this. Lack of governance and the non-passage of important Bills meant that many problems were being swept under the carpet. Two years down the line, this has ended with terrible consequences, which has affected the common person especially hard. Inflation has persisted stubbornly, the price of food grains and other consumables have kept rising each month, the rupee has depreciated sharply against the dollar, going from ₹ 52 to ₹ 68 within the span of 15 months or thereabouts. This has meant that the salaries of most people are no longer sufficient to meet monthly expenses.

The effects of corruption across the country have been truly devastating. While almost all people have been blaming the present government for the mess the country now is in, the fact remains that all of us are to blame in some way or the other.

We are to blame when we elect the wrong persons to power, despite knowing they do not have a clean record. We are to blame when we have the chance to vote but fail to do so. We are to blame when we witness wrong things being done but choose to keep silent so that our situation is not disturbed and we are not forced out of our comfort zones. We are to blame when we patronize some so-called godmen who are nothing but frauds. We are to blame when we do not support committed bureaucrats and honest politicians.

The only way corruption can be curbed in the country, if not banished altogether, is if each of us decides to act, decides to exercise our vote during the next elections, decides to do something concrete about corruption by ourselves not indulging in corrupt practices and not supporting others who do so.

Let us not lose hope in the battle against corruption. Let us never forget that there is always another alternative, a third alternative or a fourth alternative. This can only happen if we stop supporting just one or two parties believing in the TINA (There is No Alternative) myth. There is always an alternative – if only we allow it to rise and support it.

Remember, about a hundred years ago, the United States of America was exactly where we are today. Yet, by introducing a series of legislations and measures to curb corruption, they have managed to bring down its level drastically in the US.

There is no reason on Earth why India cannot do the same. In the 2014 General Elections, we simply need to believe that we can bring about change and vote wisely for this to then happen sooner or later.

Real Estate Regulation Bill— a Boon for People: The introduction of The Real Estate (Regulation and Development) Bill 2013 will be a real boon for common people who have struggled for decades to have a roof over their heads in India, given the exorbitant rates of flats and other housing projects. The Bill will undoubtedly protect the interests of end-users who, for years, have been fleeced, harassed and hoodwinked by builders of all hues. The Bill seeks the regulation and promotion of India's real estate sector and will ensure that sales of plots, flats and other properties are done in an efficient and transparent manner.

Naturally, while prospective flat seekers and other stakeholders have largely welcomed the Real Estate Bill, the builders' lobby has voiced their dissent and disapproval, stating that the Bill will only increase hurdles for the real estate development industry, leading to delays in project approvals and launches and thereby inflating the final costs to buyers.

But flat owners and other end-users are refusing to buy these arguments and assert that these are just scare tactics and attempts to derail implementation of the Bill. They insist that for years they were left at the mercy of builders who used many tricks of the trade to harass and intimidate them into agreeing to their one-sided terms and conditions when buying any property across India.

For instance, builders sell flats as per built-up and super built-up area, yet they continue to charge buyers for car parking and other facilities. This is a fraud, since such additional charges could only be justified if flats were being sold based upon their carpet area, not super built-up area. Built-up and super built-up areas are supposed to take into account all the extra areas that encircle the building or complex. So if flats are sold as per such criteria it simply makes no sense to then charge extra for parking and other facilities. In other words, buyers end up paying twice for the same facilities.

Moreover, builders launch projects, sell flats and collect funds even before all their permissions have been acquired, which is against the law. The new Bill will ban these transgressions and make builders accountable for such violations. It now remains to be seen whether the laws will ultimately be implemented in toto or simply end up being on paper like a host of other laws.

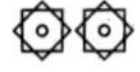

Preparing Job Applications, Resume/Bio Data, SOP's, Recommendations

• Job Applications • Resume/Bio Data • Statement of Purpose (SOP) • Recommendations

Job Applications

TIPS

1. Remember that the immediate objective of your application is not to secure the job but to get a chance for an interview.
2. Highlight your qualities briefly.
3. Give complete particulars, as desired by the prospective employer, in a simple and straight forward manner.
4. Avoid using stereotyped sentences like 'hoping for the favour of an early, assuring of my best services'....etc.
5. Type the application neatly and correctly.
6. The format should be like that of a business letter.
7. Do not send cyclostyled applications, or pre-printed application forms with details filled in.
8. Always send the original typed copy and not the duplicate copy.

 **Application which includes the details of Resume.**

Dear Sir,

In response to your advertisement in 'The Hindustan Times' dated 8th April 2017, I wish to apply for the post of Private Secretary to the Managing Director.

I graduated from University of Delhi in 1996 securing 76% marks in B.A. (Hons) English.

This was followed by a one year Secretarial Course at the well-known Reliance Secretarial Institute, New Delhi, from where I acquired proficiency in Business Correspondence, Shorthand, Typing, Operating Computer and Secretarial Practice.

At present I am employed with Bright Light Company, New Delhi, as an Office Assistant. The present job calls for handling of routine correspondence besides other Secretarial Work. My shorthand and typing speeds are 120 and 60 w.p.m. respectively.

Having lived in various parts of the country I can speak Hindi, Punjabi and Marathi fluently and have working knowledge of Gujarati and Bengali.

I am 25 years old, excellent in health, and had been a good player of hockey during my college days. My work with the present employer has been highly appreciated (testimonials are attached) but I feel that your job offers greater scope for career growth and use of my potentiality.

I take the job with a great sense of responsibility, enjoy the challenge of new situations, and expect to make a positive contribution to your organization.

Hope to get an interview call from you.

Thanking you,
Yours faithfully,
(signature)

Encl: Testimonials

EXAMPLE **Application with Separate Resume.**

Dear Sir,

In response to your advertisement in 'The Hindustan Times' dated 8th August 2017, I wish to apply for the post of Private Secretary to the Managing Director.

At present I am employed with Bright Light Company, New Delhi, as an Office Assistant but feel that your job offers greater scope for career growth and use of my abilities.

I take the job with a great sense of responsibility, enjoy the challenge of new situations and expect to make a positive contribution to your organization.

Hope to get an early interview call.

Thanking you,
Yours faithfully,
(signature)

Encl: Copies of testimonials

Bio-data

Name	:
Date of Birth	: April 15, 1976.
Present Address	:
Permanent Address	:
Academic and Professional Qualifications	: B.A. (Hons) English from University of Delhi in 1996, securing 76 % marks. One year course of Secretarial Practice at Reliance Secretarial Institute, New Delhi. Proficiency in Business Correspondence, Shorthand, Typing, Operating Computers, & Secretarial Practice. Shorthand/Typing speed. 120 / 60 w.p.m. respectively.
Working Experience	: Presently working with Bright Light Company, New Delhi, as Office Assistant The job involves handling of routine correspondence, filing taking dictation and answering visitors' queries.
General Qualifications	: Can speak Hindi, Punjabi and Marathi fluently and have working knowledge of Gujarati and Bengali.
Personal Details	: Excellent health. Have been a good player of hockey during college days.
Present Emoluments	:
Salary Expected	:

The present trend is slightly different. Mostly the applicants send a resume to the prospective employer alongwith a Covering Letter. This Covering Letter may be as small as that of two-three sentences, but in the style of a formal letter. A few examples of such letters are given below:

1) Dear Sir,

With reference to your advertisement in the Times of India dated 22nd November, 2017, for the post of an Executive Secretary, I wish to offer my candidature.

I am enclosing a copy of my bio-data for your perusal and kind consideration.

I hope to hear from you about the date of interview.

Yours Sincerely,

2) Dear Sir,

In response to your advertisement in the Employment News dated..., for the position of Accountant, I would like to apply for the same.

I am sending herewith a copy of my resume/ curriculum vitae for your consideration.

Could you let me have an interview with you at an early date ...?

Yours Sincerely,

3) Dear Sir,

I have come to know through reliable sources that there exists a vacant post of Sales Engineer in your esteemed organization.

Please find enclosed a copy of my resume for your perusal and kind consideration.

Should you require any further information, the same will be provided to you at the time of interview.

Hope to hear from you,

Yours Sincerely,

Resume/ Bio-Data

Let us study how to frame a good resume, in the latest style, which is the first interface of a candidate with the potential employer:

- The employer should get an idea by the first glance itself. Thus make it briefer and stick to the points only. Ideally a resume should be of one page or maximum two.
- Sell yourself using friendly language, addressing only the employer's need, without using large paragraphs and repetitions.
- Make the 'experience portion' clearer, mentioning how long, in what capacity, and what you have done for the previous organizations. It has to be specific, measurable, action-oriented and realistic.
- Be candid and unambiguous so that the employers feel comfortable in hiring your services.
- Don't write much about your hobbies and interests, age, height, weight, etc. unless it is relevant to the position.
- Make it neat and clean, in good stationery as well as absolutely error-free.
- Avoid using the pronoun 'I' like "I have conducted…etc." Use only "conducted ..."

Resume of a senior level Executive Secretary in the latest style.

K. RAMACHANDRAN PILLAI
17F, Pocket A-I,
Mayur Vihar-III,
Delhi-110096.
Ph. Resi: 91-11-2615270
Email: kr.pillai@gmail.com

Experience: 15 years of service as Executive Secretary and Personal Secretary providing support to Senior Management functionaries in large Indian Corporate Houses and Multi-Nationals. (Starting from the latest is as below):

- Currently attached to the Managing Director, PSINct Consulting Solutions, a $2 billion multi-national with HQs in US, as Executive Secretary. Besides routine Secretarial Tasks, work includes coordination, communication with sister companies and counterparts spread across the globe, team-oriented assignments, drafting and editing of key materials, handling MD's personal work, etc.
- 3 ½ years in Xerox as Secretary to GM-HRD and then CEO-Staff Affairs. Besides Secretarial work, updated and edited the company's personnel policy manual; designed and implemented events and programmes; arranged residential and non-residential training programmes and other management development programmes; Handled preparation of minutes and training related materials, maintained interaction and communication with company's JV partners; excelled in drafting and editing key and critical business related correspondence.
- Six years in Godrej (an Indian Giant group) as a Steno Secretary, where besides Secretarial Work, had to handle customers all over the world.

- Three years in camphor and Allied Products Ltd. as a Steno-Typist. Work included inter-company/ departmental coordination and general office work, liaison with import, export and insurance people.

Qualifications: B.Com from the University of Kerala. Pre-Degree Course in the first division and first rank in the district.

Tech. Qualifications: Kerala Govt. Technical Examination Diploma in Typewriting & Shorthand. Speed 60 w.p.m. and 100 w.p.m. respectively.

Software knowledge: MS-Word, Excel, Power Point, eMail and Internet and a little exposure to Adobe Page-Maker.

Training Exposure: Have undergone:

- Five-day Course on TQM; familiar with Quality Tools and Processes;
- A course on Train the Trainer;
- Kaizen Principle in work-life;
- Six months Banking Training in Canara Bank;
- Well exposed to ISO tools and processes.

Merits & Recognition: Won prizes/ Certificates in English Elocution, Essay Writing, Debates, Many times winner of Long Term Productivity Awards, etc.

Personal: Highly interactive, team-oriented & empathic, good communication skills, principled, religious, honest, candid and hard-working.

General Job Application

Starting the letter:

1. In response to your advertisement in 'The Times of India' dated 8 August 2017, I wish to apply for the post of Office Superintendent in your institution.
2. I have learnt from reliable sources that the post of Labour Welfare Officer in your office has fallen vacant.
3. I am interested in the vacancy you have advertised in 'The Hindustan Times' dated 8 July 2017, for the position of Sub-editor and wish to offer my services for the same.
4. This is to enquire whether you have a vacancy of an Office Assistant in your office.
5. I understand from Mr. Sunil Kumar, one of your suppliers, that you wish to appoint a Sales Engineer.
6. As Mr. Arun Kishore will be leaving your office on 31st July, I wish to offer my service for the same post.
7. I wish to offer my services for the post of Sales Officer which, as I understand, falls vacant by the end of this month.
8. This is to apply for the post of Sales Manager in your office which you have advertised in 'The Times of India' dated 8th September, 2017.

9. With reference to your advertisement in 'The Statesman' dated 21st May, 2017, I wish to offer my services for the post of Steno-typist in your organization.
10. I have learnt from a reliable source that the post of Accountant is lying vacant in your office. I wish to offer myself as a suitable candidate for the same.
11. In response to an announcement made in the Employment News on 10th August, 2017, I wish to apply for the post of a Translator (Hindi to English).
12. Going through Employment News, I found that a situation of a lecturer in English is lying vacant in your college. I offer myself as a candidate for the same.
13. Please refer to your advertisement in 'The Times of India' dated 14th July, 2017, for the post of a Law Officer, I wish to offer my services for the same.
14. Having come to know through a monthly bulletin of your Deptt., that you need a travelling Salesman, I offer my services for the same post.
15. Through a circular issued from your office, I have come to know that the post of a Draftsman is lying vacant in your office. I offer my candidature through this application.

Middle portion of the letter is given separately in the forthcoming pages:

Closing the letter:

16. I look forward to hearing from you.
17. I trust you will consider my application favourably and give me a chance to meet you personally.
18. I would appreciate an interview with you when I could give you more details about myself.
19. I can come for an interview, at any time convenient to you. I enclose a self-addressed and stamped envelope so that you could respond to me.
20. I look forward to the opportunity of a personal interview.
21. I shall be grateful to you for an interview call at your convenience.

Various Job Applications

(Middle portion of the application for all types of jobs)

There are two different types of applications — one containing the particulars in the application itself and the other with a bio-data attached separately. Their samples have already been given. You can select anyone of those, according to your requirement.

Here we give particular samples of various types of approaches for different job applications.

Private Secretary

1. I completed my education in June this year and have been employed as an Office Assistant with Bhatia Electric Company. Although I do not have long experience, I am hard-working and take the work with great sense of responsibility. I am confident that your Managing Director will find me a competent Private Secretary.
2. For more than two years, I have been working as P.A. to the Sales Manager, India Trading Corporation. I am confident that I would prove to be a competent Personal Secretary to your Managing Director.

3. Although I am working in the same capacity in India Marketing Agency, I am applying for this job as your company is well-established and can offer greater scope for career advancements.
4. I have good knowledge of word processing and can work on MS Office, besides handling emails and Internet browsing.

Accountant/Accounts Assistant

1. I am a Commerce Graduate from University of Mumbai and have good knowledge of Accountancy, Auditing, Income Tax procedure and Company Law.
2. I can also draw up Balance Sheets and Profit and Loss Accounts.
3. Apart from my work as Accountant you may find my knowledge of Secretarial work also useful.
4. Now I have enough experience to take independent charge of maintenance of Accounts, preparation of bills and writing of account books.
5. I am computer literate and friendly with the software Tally.

Cashier

1. I passed B.Com from University of Delhi in 1995, securing 52% marks and specialised in Book-keeping and Accounting.
2. I am, therefore, quite well versed in book keeping and billing, etc.
3. Having worked for three years as a Cashier in the Delhi Textile Emporium, I have the requisite experience for the job.
4. I am computer literate and have fair knowledge of the software Tally.
5. If your rules require a security deposit I am willing to do so to a reasonable extent.

Typist-cum-Clerk

1. I can type accurately at a speed of 60 w.p.m.
2. I am excellent in word processing on Computer and familiar with MS Word, Excel and MS-Outlook.
3. I am fairly acquainted with office work such as filing, indexing, etc. and also possess elementary knowledge of book-keeping.
4. I have also been attending short-hand classes for the last six months.
5. I have the ability to work for long hours and can cope with work pressure easily.
6. I take the work with a great sense of responsibility.

Labour Welfare Officer

1. I have studied Labour Welfare at the Delhi School of Social Studies, and am a registered member of the Labour Welfare Officers' Association.
2. I speak Hindi, Punjabi, Bhojpuri and Bengali fluently, and this enables me to deal easily with labour hailing from different parts of the country.
3. I am well-versed in labour and factory legislation and possess the requisite qualifications as provided under the Factories Act.

4. On account of my present job in the textile mill, I have adequate experience in handling industrial labour.
5. I have done a short-term course in computer and know its basics.

Librarian

1. I completed my MLISC (Master of Library & Information Science) from IGNOU in 1999 securing 60% marks.
2. I am fully conversant with the DEWEY decimal classification systems.
3. I can competently manage all aspects of Library routine, including classifying and cataloguing of books and periodicals.
4. I have worked in computerized environment and am familiar with the relevant software.
5. I am good at various search methods which include CD search and Internate surfing.

Driver

1. During my five years of driving career I have not had any accident.
2. I have never been challaned even for minor violations of the Traffic Rules.
3. I have fairly good knowledge of automobiles and can do minor repairs.
4. I am ready for a trial any time, at your convenience.

Nurse

1. I completed B.Sc. in Nursing from the University of Delhi in 1996 and am a registered member of the Trained Nurses' Association of India.
2. I also hold the St. John's Ambulance Certificates of Proficiency in First Aid, Nursing and Hygiene.
3. My work has generally been appreciated by my superiors.
4. I can undertake both medical and surgical nursing and have long experience in handling children and the aged.

Personnel Officer

1. I hold an M.A. degree in Social Science from University of Mumbai and have also completed a correspondence course in Personnel Management from the London School of Correspondence Courses.
2. I have sound knowledge of modern principles and practices of personnel management, aptitude tests, work incentives, etc.
3. I am also acquainted with the methods of merit rating and performance audit.
4. I have five years' experience as Assistant Personnel Officer in a public sector undertaking.
5. A short-term course on computer that I have undergone with NIIT, Delhi, has enabled me to improve my productivity during my career.

Stenographer

1. My Short-hand and Typing speeds are 140 and 70 w.p.m. respectively.
2. I have also completed a course on book-keeping and secretarial Practice.
3. I am good at English and thus can handle correspondence independently.

4. If required, I can also work in the capacity of a Secretary.
5. I am good at MS Office Software like Word, Excel, Power Point and Access, besides handling email and Internet.

Store-keeper

1. I am fully conversant with the theory and practice of store-keeping.
2. Having worked as an Assistant Store-keeper with Mehta Surgical Company for two years, I have fairly good knowledge of handling and recording stocks.
3. I am fully conversant with all aspects of store-keeping.
4. Since I have also worked on a computerised Store Management System, I could increase my productivity by 200%.
5. On account of my training and experience, I am in a position to discharge efficiently all duties that are assigned to me as an storekeeper.

Telephone Operator—Receptionist

1. I have good command over spoken English and can also converse fluently in Hindi.
2. I have a pleasing personality and a well-modulated voice, and can handle all enquiries on the telephone.
3. I can handle the most modern EPABX and other voice storage systems.
4. I have completed a three months course of Telephone Operators and Receptionists from Reliance Commercial Training Institute, New Delhi.
5. I do maintain all my official contacts on computer and am well-versed on how to appropriately manipulate these data.

Private Tutor

1. I am a IInd class Commerce Graduate from the University of Delhi and have been giving private tuitions for the last ten years.
2. As I have been an English teacher in Delhi Public School for five years, I am familiar with all school requirements.
3. I can coach your child in all subjects and guarantee his/her progress in the subjects he is weak in, at present.
4. We can, of course, discuss the terms and conditions when we meet.

Typist

1. After completing my SSLC in 1999 with 2nd division I attended the Delhi Typewriting Institute and have now acquired good speed and accuracy in typing.
2. Besides office routine I can do simple invoicing and tabulation work, etc.
3. I can also cut stencils well and can operate any standard duplicating machine.
4. I am very good at computers and can work on Windows 8, especially all software on MS-Office.

Salesman

1. Besides being a Commerce Graduate, I have taken a diploma in Business Management and Control and other subjects related to retail sales.
2. For the last three years, I have been working as a part-time Salesman for a well-known cosmetic company and my sales, on an average, have exceeded ₹ 50,000/- a month.
3. I am in perfect health and prepared to travel anywhere in India.
4. I have a way with people and know the art of persuading prospective customers into placing orders.

Sub-Editor

1. I also have a diploma in Journalism from University of Delhi.
2. Since June this year, I have been working as an apprentice with 'The Hindustan Times' and as a result have become conversant with the process of producing a paper.
3. I am proficient in English and can process data in a computerised environment.
4. I have also freelanced with most of the publishing giants in Delhi.

Hotel Cook

1. I hold a diploma in catering from the College of Catering, University of Mumbai.
2. For two years, I have worked as an Assistant to my father who was the Chief Cook at the famous Leela Vilas Hotel in Shimla for more than 15 years.
3. I can prepare Indian, Continental as well as Chinese dishes.
4. At times, I have prepared meals for more than 100 people at very short notices.

Manager

1. I completed M.B.A. from the College of Business Administration, Hyderabad in 2016, securing 87% marks and have done a one year course on Computers.
2. I have three years experience as Assistant Manager in Bharat Auto Industries, Yamuna Nagar.
3. I can handle matters regarding Accounts, Finance, General Administration and Board Meetings competently.
4. My work with the present employer has been highly appreciated, as I have managed to establish harmonious relation with the staff and the management.

Mechanic

1. I have specialised in the working of Internal Combustion Engines, Electric Motors and allied subjects from the Polytechnic Institute Delhi.
2. As a trainee at the Polytechnic, I have had the opportunity to dismantle car engines and reassemble them.
3. As an apprentice with Yantra Industries since last year, I have efficiently handled engines of various types and makes.
4. Having worked for some time in a tool manufacturing industry, I have acquired the knowledge of various types of tools required for the repair and servicing of engines and machines.

Technician

1. I have completed a two year diploma in Mechanical Engineering from the Industrial Training Institute, Malviya Nagar, New Delhi.
2. As an apprentice with Pratima TV company, Ghaziabad, I have also acquired fairly good knowledge of electronics.
3. My present job has given me adequate experience in various technical jobs like welding, soldering, wiring, etc.
4. I can also deal with customers, if my job demands.

Teacher

1. I completed M.A. History in 1995, from the University of Mumbai securing 76% marks. In 1996, I got B.Ed (Bachelor of Education) from the same University securing 78% marks.
2. I have been teaching English and Geography to IX and X standard for the last two years, in a Municipal School in Pune.
3. For more than five years, I have been giving private tuitions to high school students.
4. I have an impressive personality and have the knack of handling students well.

Space Seller

1. After completing B.Com. in 1978 I have been working as Space Seller on behalf of "Blend", a monthly magazine published from Nagpur, with a circulation of 25,000 copies.
2. The monthly average of advertisement business which I procured for the magazine has always been at least six times of my remuneration.
3. I have been an active campaigner of advertisements for "Perception" a Kolkata monthly, with a circulation of more than 18000 copies and have established good contacts in the advertising circle in Mumbai.

Air Hostess

1. I am fluent in English as well as Hindi and interested in hospitality industry.
2. As desired by you in the advertisement, I have a pleasing personality and am modest in approach.
3. I am unmarried and prepared to undergo any vocational, aptitude and physical tests that may be necessary to prove my suitability for the job.

Apprentice

1. I have been taking keen interest in everything mechanical ever since my childhood.
2. Of late, I have also got exposed to computer applications and am good at CAD.
3. Basically, being interested in mechanical work I have a small workshop at home in which I tinker about. I have also forged certain hand-tools.
4. The stipend you offer during my apprenticeship is acceptable to me.
5. I am of good health and take pride in working with my hands.

Canteen Manager

1. I have taken a Diploma in Hotel Management and Catering from the Catering College, Mumbai.
2. I can efficiently supervise a large kitchen equipped with all modern cooking appliances.
3. I have also studied dietetics and nutrition thoroughly and can prepare meals for a big group.
4. For two years, I have worked as an Assistant to the Canteen Manager of M/S. Globe Industries, Faridabad.

Draftsman

1. My work with the present employer has been highly appreciated and I was also sent to West Germany for an advanced course in this line.
2. During my three years of service with Delhi Engineering Company, I have gained valuable experience in structural and mechanical drawings.
3. I am extremely good at all the related software and have worked in a computerised environment.
4. I have also done some architectural sketching and tracing.
5. My plans and blue-prints in the present job have been frequently praised for their accuracy as well as in the overall perspective.

Headmistress of School

1. I am M.A. M.Ed. from University of Mumbai and have specialised in modern methods of education.
2. I have 15 years of experience as a senior teacher and two years experience as an Assistant Headmistress in reputed High Schools in Delhi including St. Francis Public School.
3. I am fully conversant with the administrative functions of a large educational institution.
4. I have a knack for handling children, and along with maintaining discipline, I can win their confidence and love.

Hotel Manger

1. I have five years experience as Assistant Manager in the well-known Badshah Hotel of Mumbai.
2. I am conversant with all aspects of hotel management, from daily menus to security and from public relations to arranging conventions.
3. I can fluently speak English, Hindi, Punjabi and Gujarati and also have working knowledge of French.
4. I have the experience of working in a computer-friendly environment.
5. I have sufficient experience in handling foreign guests.

Lawyer for Industrial Concern

1. I have five years experience as Legal Adviser to M/S Delhi Steel Industries.
2. I have passed the L.L.M. examination and have sound knowledge and experience of Industrial Legislation, Factory Act, Labour Law, etc.

3. On a number of occasions I have represented my Company in legal disputes in the High Court and the Supreme Court.
4. For more than three years, I have worked as an Assistant to the reputed legal expert of Mumbai on Industrial Legislation, Mr. F.M. Kanoonwala.
5. I generate most of my documents and affidavits on a computer without depending on a typist.

Publicity Officer

1. I have a diploma in Journalism from Nagpur University and have also done a correspondence course in Publicity, Public Relations and Advertising from the London School of Journalism.
2. I have a good knowledge of computer and all related software and I am an expert in design and lay-out.
3. As an Assistant Publicity Officer for Rose Cosmetics Ltd., Nagpur. I have conducted several successful advertising campaigns, trade fair, road-shows, etc.
4. I am well versed in printing and production techniques and also conversant with all publicity media like Press, Radio and T.V. etc.

Press Reporter

1. I have a Diploma in Journalism from the Punjab University.
2. I am excellent in handling English language besides being good in Hindi and Punjabi.
3. I am computer literate and can generate reports on computer.
4. I was closely involved in the publishing of the students' newspaper brought out by the University Department of Journalism.

Sales Manager

1. As an Assistant Sales Manager, I have been able to achieve creditable sales results and exceed the targets.
2. I have a sound knowledge of maintaining accounts and modern business methods specially in sales management.
3. I am known in my field for effectively handling tough sales related problems.
4. I have a good knowledge of modern methods of publicity, public relations and advertising which are prerequisites to sales.
5. I know how to generate spread-sheets and sales statistics on a computer.

Travelling Salesman

1. I have five years'experience in door-to-door sales canvassing of various consumer products.
2. I am prepared to travel to any part of the country and find pleasure in meeting people.
3. I am in excellent health which, I believe, is essential for a travelling salesman.
4. I know the art of dealing with people and can speak English, Hindi, Punjabi, Bengali and Gujarati fluently.

Agent

1. As the sole representative of Gala Cosmetics Ltd., for entire Maharashtra, I have built up personal contacts with all major cosmetic dealers in the state.
2. Although I am new to this line, I am confident of performing well in the business on account of my old contacts in the city.
3. I am confident that my connections in the trade circle will result in a large turnover for your firm in this region.
4. We could negotiate the agency terms at an early date and I would accept any reasonable offer.

Accounts Assistant

1. I have passed B.Com degree examination from the Punjab University with 90% marks in Advanced Accounts.
2. I have been an apprentice with Dena Bank, Karol Bagh, New Delhi, for more than 6 months.
3. I can easily maintain the books of accounts of any type of business.
4. I have a good handwriting and can speedily enter data into a computer. I am also familiar with the software 'Tally'.

Lecturer

1. Apart from having a good academic record, I have also published papers in literary journals like Humanities Review, etc.
2. I am a writer and one of my books was chosen for an award by the Maharashtra Literary Conference.
3. I am a good orator and have often compered many cultural programmes during college days.
4. I am fond of teaching and I make it interesting for the students.
5. Despite the fact that I have done M.A. in Hindi, I have also good command over the English language.

Copy-writer in Advertising Agency

1. I have done a correspondence course in Advertising from the London School of Correspondence Courses.
2. I have made a special study of the 'copies' of leading Indian advertisers, and my paper on this subject has been appreciated by the London School of Advertising.
3. I have a flair for writing and can produce forceful and punch packed 'copy' on any product.
4. I can also visualise advertisements and have working knowledge of lay-outs.
5. My basic knowledge of computers has made my work more productive and speedy.

Engineer

1. I completed my B.E.(Electrical) from I.I.T. Kanpur, in 2016 securing grade A (90% marks).
2. I have worked as an apprentice engineer for 4 years with Hindustan Electric company, Kolkata, and am very familiar with computerised environment.
3. I have more than 2 years of experience in working at power generation plants.
4. I have also been designing and making small electrical gadgets for everyday domestic use.

Advertisement Manager

1. Over the years I have managed to establish close personal contacts with all major advertising agencies in Delhi.
2. I also have personal contacts with many major advertisers in Kolkata.
3. I have more than 5 years of experience in coordinating the activities of Creative Departments and the Studio. I am very good at softwares like Adobe, Coreldraw, Photoshop, etc.
4. I also have sound knowledge of block-making, offset printing and various other production techniques.

Shop Assistant

1. I have passed the Higher Secondary Examination.
2. I can speak Hindi and English fluently.
3. I have a pleasing personality.
4. I like any job involving public dealing and can be successful at the counter of any commercial establishment.

Proof-reader

1. I have a sound knowledge of English and am very good at spellings.
2. I know all the signs of proof-reading and can read proofs without omissions.
3. I have freelanced for the New Book Publishing Company, on assignment basis.
4. I am used to working on a computer and very familiar with most of the types/fonts, designing magazine lay-outs and book pages, etc.

Statement of Purpose (SoP)

TIPS

1. Explain your proposed course of study. List your reasons for wanting to pursue that line of study.
2. Detail any experience you have had in your chosen field of study.
3. Read the school's brochure and talk to current students to get an idea of the type of student the school wants.
4. Check your SOP for grammar and typing errors.

EXAMPLE

The need of the hour are MR professionals who are true managers - managers who have to facilitate a radical change in the way market research is looked upon today; very often as an activity done by a separate cell and an end in itself. I see myself, as an MR professional, using research as an actionable tool, incorporating cutting edge methodologies, getting the needed results while saving time and money. I want to turn it into a dynamic instrument, use it to feel the pulse of the market, make probabilistic predictions about the market through sophisticated tools and ultimately get involved in product innovation and strategic planning.

To achieve this, I would like to gain exposure to the latest practices adopted by the trend makers in the field of market research and information systems. To this end, I would probably want to work with a leading international market research firm that would enable me to help corporations leverage their focus. I would like to bring this acquired expertise back to India, and use it to help companies to grow in the stiffly competitive market. I see market research as a sensitive and flexible instrument to be applied with insight, imagination and creativity.

The ability to work in a fast-paced setting with time sensitive jobs made my summer internship at Pepsi a further step to learning. I was a part of a number of marketing promotions of the company on a local scale. My project on customer research on a key stock keeping unit required consumer profiling and a high degree of qualitative analysis through a study of buyer behaviour using research tools like focus group interviews and perceptual mapping. Based on this study, I have planned and implemented marketing promotions to capture the home segment, within given budget constraints. I had carried out a pre-launch survey based study for an antioxidant brand that helped the company identify its target segments.

Apart from these, working on various school projects has given me varied experience on the basis of which I have decided that MR is where I would like to base my future. A career in MR would give me an opportunity to work across boundaries of industry definitions with a number of industries ranging from consumer goods to innovative communication and high tech markets.

I possess a broad-based management education. But, in order to attain what I am aiming for, I believe that I require a sharply defined and focused course in marketing research. The expertise to analyze the marketing as well as the strategic problems faced by companies and implement corresponding solutions is what I want. An international exposure coupled with the immense opportunity in the Indian marketplace will help in breaking new ground in Indian marketing research.

I want to attend the University of Maryland's Master of Marketing Research Programme for several reasons. The focussed structure of the course will help me concentrate and work towards the attainment of my career goals. The internship provided within the MMR course work would help me gain exposure, insight, knowledge and hands-on experience with real time work environment. I am impressed with the quality of education provided by the university in terms of the well-structured curriculum and the recognized faculty. I look forward to shaping my career in the halls of University of Maryland.

Recommendations

TIPS

- In a recommendation, someone's name is recommended for admission, appointment, award, promotion, etc.
- A recommendation highlights the positive qualities of the person and justifies his/her eligibility for admission, job, promotion or award.

- Recommendations are usually written by teachers; officers; heads of institutions; politicians, in-charge or noted social workers.
- A recommendation refrains from mentioning weaknesses of the person.
- The tone is balanced: neither mild nor too enthusiastic.
- A practical approach adds meaning and value.
- The language in a recommendation is correct and learned.
- It shows the writer understands what's expected from a candidate and the qualities required.

To Whomsoever it May Concern

To the best of my knowledge and opinion, Shalini Gupta possesses a strong hold on the faculties that she has mastered, which are different and many. She believes in growing equally from the inside as from the outside. She has been doing this consistently and apparently improving both in her desk work and in dealing with clients of value, giving much-needed service well in time. She has accomplished many things within a year – sincerely and diligently via self-study, sharp and deep thinking as well as straight and clear dealings. There are certain spheres where she has shown greater interest. She has improved and covered them well to show balanced growth. I'm sure she can do justice to any job with her technical skill and other facets and thereby serve any institution ably and skillfully.

To Whomsoever it May Concern

I have known T K Parmeswaran for the past 15 years, ever since he worked directly under me as a Trainee Executive in 1998-99. I have always found him to be extremely hardworking and diligent. Howsoever difficult and time-consuming the task, he has never shied away from responsibility. In fact, on many occasions he has even volunteered to take on an assignment, despite knowing he would have to stay late to complete it or even come in on a Saturday. It is this extra sense of responsibility that is inherent in him from a young age that endeared him to me and all the other management personnel. In all difficult assignments that others would think twice about before taking up, he was my Man Friday whom I could always turn to without fear of being let down. I have absolutely no hesitation in recommending him for any job, howsoever difficult, since I believe he has the wherewithal and the attitude to get things down. I wish him all the very best in his future endeavours and would recommend him for any post without hesitation – secure in the knowledge that I am recommending one of the best persons ever to work under my watch.

Business Letters & E-mails

• Business documents • Business Letters • Business Report Writing

Business Documents

Every form of writing has a distinct style, depending on its purpose. Business documents also have a distinct style. Business documents are meant to convey information clearly and in a manner whereby the reader understands the message immediately. Although there is no specific formula for writing a business letter or a report, these documents do follow certain guidelines.

All kinds of business documents, be it a half-page memo or a 300-page report, are prepared in a sequence of steps, which are described below.

Pre-writing Stage: Here, the writer plans the document and collates the information required to write it. If one is writing a report, some background research may be carried out. In an office, even if the boss dictates a short letter, the personal assistant may still need to check letters or memos mentioned in the letter just dictated.

There are three points to bear in mind:

- What is the purpose of the message?
- Whom is the message addressed to?
- What exactly should the message say?

While these questions may be self-evident in the letter dictated to the PA, a report on the month's sales performance, for instance, may require close consideration of these questions.

Once these are answered, the writer could move to the next step – the actual writing of the letter.

Writing: With the preliminary stage undertaken, one can proceed to the next step.

Organising: The document will be organised as per its purpose. One could arrange the contents step by step in a numbered list if the document is an instructions manual, or a letter outlining how to repair a defect. On the other hand, if it is a letter to a customer announcing a special sale, the large discount may be the first thing to be highlighted. The format chosen will depend on the purpose of the document.

Outlining: An outline separates the contents of a large document into smaller manageable parts. It summarises the message and the sequence in which this will be conveyed, so that the thoughts flow logically from one step to the next. The outline is akin to the blueprint of a building. The more detailed the outline, the easier it will be to write the actual letter or report.

A report is likely to contain tables of figures and, if required, even bar charts or pie charts. The tables and charts can be planned while preparing the outline.

First Draft: With the outline ready, one can begin on the first written draft. Do remember that the first draft is only a working draft and not the final document. It is best to complete the entire first draft before editing any section. As one writes the subsequent sections, one may need to revisit earlier paragraphs and make changes. Therefore, editing the draft is best done after the document is completed. Often, the main part of the document is drafted first. The introduction and conclusion are best drafted after the main points have been written.

While preparing the first draft, always remember the objective of the document and to whom the document is addressed. This will ensure inconsistencies are avoided.

Editing or Revising: Once the first draft is completed, it is time to edit or revise the document. It is good to keep a checklist handy for revision. Ensure that:

- All facts and figures are accurate.
- The ideas flow logically and there are no internal inconsistencies or contradictions.
- The language is clear and grammatically correct.
- There are no spelling and punctuation errors.

Some general rules that apply to all types of business documents have been covered here. Some of the steps can be skipped if the document is short and simple. But no matter how short or straightforward the document may be, ensure that revisions and corrections are done carefully.

The following pages will now closely consider specific examples of business documents.

Business Letters

(Main Characteristics)

"Good correspondence is the soul of successful business. Without correspondence there can be no trade. Modern business is the greatest romance of the age. It spins out money which can buy law and life."

A business letter needs a careful drafting because a well-written letter can go a long way in producing desirable results. It may clinch a sale, sort out a complaint or fetch a customer. It is a very straight forward document, but, at the same time, friendly and conversational in tone. It is also a substitute for a personal talk or conversation on a telephone.

Let your letter be a credit to yourself and your firm. Such a letter cannot be written by just anybody. It is an expert's job. If the letter has mistakes and faulty constructions it can do serious damage to business dealings.

However, there is nothing very complicated about these letters. In every company, large amount of business and considerable sales are done through mail. Thus, every letter has its bearing on the balance sheet. Every outgoing letter is a spokesman of the company's policy. It is silent but not dumb. It helps to increase the reputation of the firm. It opens markets and outlets for goods and services. It is a way to make profit.

Since the business has become extremely complicated nowadays, the ability to write good business letters is an asset. The correspondence between the head office, branches, production units and sale depots makes the functioning of a company smooth. Thus, a letter has both internal and external uses and importance.

Considering the fact that a letter gets only a few minutes of the reader's attention, the message must be clear, correct and concise. The letter should be well-organised as to perform multiple functions of conveying a message, building goodwill and creating a favourable response. It is difficult to avoid negative ideas but what matters most is how they are put. A skilful correspondent handles the negative attitude with a tactful positive approach. Almost all negative ideas can be put in a positive way, e.g.,

	Negative	**Positive**
1.	We cannot despatch the consignment until you inform where it is to be delivered.	We shall despatch the consignment as soon as you let us know where it is to be delivered.
2.	We shall be careful to avoid delay in future.	We shall take care to ensure prompt delivery in future.
3.	Unless the old dues are cleared,further goods cannot be despatched.	You are risking your own goodwill by delaying our payment.

Everyone has a style of his own. But, however good it might be, there can be scope for further improvement. A good style is an asset to a writer. And it can be perfected with practice and training. For an effective letter, the correspondent must have a clear knowledge of the product, the services or the subject he is dealing with. And he must put all this with a flow of good and impressive language.

For an organisation or a commercial set-up, correspondence has a vital bearing on its relations with customers. Invaraibly, the prime need for giving a clear-cut and simple message is that there is no difficulty in understanding the message conveyed.

Simple and natural language is the key to good business correspondence. The letter should be friendly in tone and content. In your telephonic conversation you would not say, "It is regretted that the goods cannot be delivered today." Rather say, "I am sorry, we cannot deliver the goods today." Thus, the letter should be framed keeping in view what the situation demands, and with as much simplicity as one spends with the other.

TIPS

For writing effective business letters, we are giving some useful tips below:-

1. While writing a business letter keep in mind whom you are writing to. Give all the information he needs clearly so that there is no guessing on his part.
2. Catch the attitude of the incoming letter and reply accordingly.
3. Use conversational language in the letter, wherever required.

4. Be clear, courteous and precise. Avoid ambiguity.
5. Be as polite and polished as possible.
6. Avoid using high sounding words. If the letter demands, the reply should be elaborate and detailed one.
7. Discard stereotyped language.
8. Use effective phraseology.
9. Avoiding monotony and dryness, introduce variety in the letter.
10. A long letter should be divided into paragraphs.
11. The opening should be particularly catchy, as it has lasting impact on the reader.
12. Revise the letter before closing it.
13. Avoid repetitions.

The tips explained in detail:

Keep your letter's reader in mind: This can be best done by keeping the reader's point of view in mind. Anticipate his feelings, requirements and give sure and subtle replies. Visualise the letter's impact on yourself. If it is impressive and effective, the job is done.

Catch the attitude: The reply should be in tune with the letter received. Think out the objective clearly and then reply accordingly. Skill, tact and practice are necessary for tackling different queries and approaches.

Use natural and conversational language: The letter's tone should be friendly and natural. It should be simply written to convey a message for impressing the reader:

Avoid	Write
I have pleasure in informing you	I am pleased to tell you (or to say)
Please be good enough to advise us	Please let us know

Write clear and definite language, avoiding ambiguity: Think before you write. Express yourself in clear and simple language. Avoid using stereotyped language. It should not cause reader's guessing, but being definite. It should also be unambiguous.

Be courteous and considerate: 'Courteous' does not mean that unnecessary adjectives are used. E.g., 'Your esteemed order', etc. Your approach should be on the positive side without meaning any discourtesy.

Avoid business jargon: Avoid the use of words and phrases which the reader fails to understand easily. Jargons are the words that are specific to a subject and should not be used in general letters. The letter should be short, simple and to the point. Lengthy letters bore the reader.

Avoid	Write
We express our regret at being unable to fulfil your order on this occasion with customary promptness.	We are sorry we cannot meet your present order immediately.
Under active consideration	Being considered
With reference to	About

In connection with	For
It should be noted that	Please note

Discard stereotyped language:

Modern business letters do not use old terminology that make the letters stereotyped.

Avoid	Write
Adverting to your letter	Referring to your letter
We beg to acknowledge	We have received
Your esteemed favour to hand	Received your letter
The favour of your early reply will oblige.	An early reply is expected
Under separate cover	Separately
Your goodself	You
Kindly take into consideration	Please consider
Assuring you of our best attention at all times.	We will pay full attention We assure you of the best of our attention.

Use effective phraseology:

The letter should be simple and easily understandable. Use of familiar and easy words is desired.

Avoid	Write
Communication	Letter
Will you be good enough	Will you please
In the near future	Soon, shortly
It gives much pleasure	I am pleased; I am happy
We will execute your order expeditiously	We will process your order promptly
We beg to acknowledge receipt of your favour	Thanks for your enquiry/order

Introduce variety:

Avoid monotony and repetition. Use active voice on the whole but for variety use passive voice at places.

Avoid	Write
Please let me know at once if you are unable to deliver the goods or not.	If you are unable to deliver the goods, please inform me/us immediately.
We have noted with surprise the contents of your letter.	It was with surprise that we noted the contents of your letter.
We despatched the goods on 15th.	The goods were despatched on the 15th.
You did not sign the order form.	The order form was not signed.

Opening and closing of effective letter:

A. Opening:

Although 'Thank you for your letter', This refers to your letter' etc., are normally used one can introduce variety with expressions like 'I was glad to receive your letter', 'When I received your letter of.........' etc.

B. Closing:

Avoid	Write
We shall deal promptly with any orders you place with us.	Your orders will be dealt with promptly.
Thanking you in anticipation.	Thanking you/Thank you.
Hoping to hear from you soon.	I hope to hear soon from you
Trusting this meets with your approval.	I trust you will approve of this.

Revising the letter:

Peruse your letter before signing and revise if necessary before mailing it. Also put the following questions to yourself:

(i) Is the letter impressive?

(ii) Is the letter well drafted?

(iii) Are spellings and punctuation correct?

(iv) Is the message clear and simple?

(v) Does the letter fulfil the reader's needs?

(vi) How would you, yourself, react to such a letter?

If all the above questions have a positive reply, your letter is ready to be mailed.

Business letters comprise a major part of a secretary's or PA's written communication. This is especially true if you work in sales, trading or general business. In case your organisation undertakes research and analysis (such as a market research bureau or a consultancy firm), one will also generate large volumes of reports, which will be covered in the next section.

Since they form such an important part of a secretary's job, business letters will be covered in detail in the following sections.

Parts of a Business Letter:

Regardless of their purpose, most business letters contain the following basic parts:

1. Heading or Letterhead
2. Dateline
3. Inside Address
4. Reference Lines (Attention, Personal and Confidential, Subject)
5. Salutation
6. Body

7. Complimentary Close
8. Signature
9. Stenographic Reference
10. Enclosures or Copies

Heading or Letterhead: In most cases, the heading of a letter is simply the printed letterhead on the company stationery giving the company name, address, phone number(s), and perhaps the name of an officer or correspondent.

If the stationery one is using does not have a printed letterhead, type the company name, address, and phone number in the upper right-hand corner of the paper about one and a half inch from the top and flush with the right margin.

Dateline: All business letters should contain the correct date typed under the letterhead. The date is a record when the letter was written and may serve as an important reference. For example, if there are doubts about an order or shipment, a contract, or a reply to customer complaints, the dated copy of a letter in the office file will verify when this was written and what was officially stated. Try to mail the letter on or close to the date typed under the letterhead. The postmark on the envelope and the date in your letter should correspond as nearly as possible.

Inside Address: The inside address is typed below the dateline. It is single-spaced and placed flush against the left margin. The inside address contains the name, title, company division or department (if any), mailing address, and pin code of the receiver. For instance:

Ramesh Trivedi,
Treasurer,
Finance and Accounts Department,
Ramdev and Co.
45 Dalal Street,
Mumbai 400 001

Reference Lines: In some cases, one will want to draw special attention to the subject of the letter or single out a particular person to whom the letter is addressed in a company. Use a reference line for this purpose.

The reference 'Personal and Confidential' is typed in initial capitals and underlined before the inside address as follows:

Personal and Confidential
Ms Shailaja Nanda,
Vice President,
Business Development Department,
Investment Credit Bank of Mumbai,
20 North Avenue,
Delhi.

Salutation: After the inside address or reference line, the salutation is typed two lines down, flush with the left margin, and followed by a colon. The salutations for the above inside addresses are as follows:

Dear Ms (or Miss or Mrs) Anand,
Dear Mr Jain,
Dear Ms (or Miss or Mrs) Shah,
Dear Mr Singh.

If the recipient's name is not known, but one does know that a man or woman is being addressed, the salutation would be:
Dear Sir,
Dear Madam,

If one is unsure who the receiver will be, use a title or some general greeting for the salutation:
To Our Friends at The Gymkhana Club:
Dear Manager:
Dear Executive:
Dear Members:
To the Sales Staff:

Block Format is the most commonly used layout for business letters, as it is easy to compose on a computer. In block format, the entire text is left-aligned. (See page no. 72)

Body of the Letter: The body of the business letter begins two lines below the salutation. The body can be typed in block style with no paragraph indentations or semi-block style in which the paragraphs are indented. Do remember, there is no 'correct' style. The one used could be a matter of personal choice or company preference. Paragraphs are generally typed single-space with double spaces between different paragraphs.

Even for a short letter, it is proper to divide the body into at least two or three paragraphs. This makes the text easier to read and presents the message more clearly. A typical plan for a three-paragraph letter would look like the following:

- Paragraph one: Begin with information that catches the reader's attention and refers to some need or interest of the reader. One way to do so is to imbed the 'you' into a letter.
- Paragraph two: Bring in your involvement, what role you are playing, what service or information you have to offer. At this stage, put 'you and I' into the letter.
- Paragraph three: End the body of the letter with the action or idea that you want the reader to consider or with the results you would like to have. In this paragraph, keep the 'you and I' in the reader's mind, but emphasise 'you'.

The example below follows the basic plan of the business letter just described:

In your letter dated 10 October, you mentioned your company was purchasing an IBM office system with a main computer and several terminals and printers. You requested a quote of our acoustical covers for micro-printers.

I am happy to report that we can offer you a substantial discount on a bulk order of 20-25 acoustical covers. These covers will fit any micro-printer and can be adapted to fit printer options such as single-sheet feeders and track feeders. They will reduce printer noise levels by 80%. Studies have shown that lower levels of noise in the office boost worker productivity and efficiency.

The discount offer expires on 30 November. You can take advantage of our discount by phoning in your order, using our toll-free number 1-800-444-2222. I would be happy to arrange for shipment directly to your home office or warehouse.

Notice that the writer mentions the reader's needs in the first sentence. The following paragraph describes how the writer can help satisfy that need. The closing paragraph outlines the desired actions for the recipient and the writer. The plan of the letter helps the writer be concise, specific, and direct.

Complimentary Close: The complimentary close is typed one double space after the body of the letter. It can be centred on the page or set flush with the left or right margin. The preferred complimentary close for most business letters is 'Sincerely', although some companies also use 'Yours truly' or 'Sincerely yours'.

The closing is followed by four lines and the typed name and title of the person sending the letter. In rare instances, when the letter is not typed on letterhead stationery, the company name and address follow the name and title of the sender. A phone number or extension may also be included if the writer wishes to receive a quick reply to the letter. An example is given below:

Sincerely,

Rama Reddy,
23, Village Road,
Post Office Tillenkota,
Guntur.

Signature: The writer signs his or her name in ink in the space between the complimentary closing and the typed name. If you are signing for someone else using a stamped signature, put your initials after the signature and on the same line.

Stenographic Reference: These reference initials refer to the person who is sending the letter and the typist. The sender's initials are typed in all capitals, followed by a colon or a slash, then the initials of the typist in lowercase letters like: FWW:tg or FWW/tg.

Stenographic reference initials appear one double space below the last line of the typed signature and are set flush with the left margin. In some companies, only the typist's initials, in lowercase letters, are used. If you type your own letters, omit the reference initials.

Enclosures or Copies: This designation is typed one single space below the stenographic initials. It alerts the reader to the fact that material has been enclosed with the letter or that copies of the letter have been sent to others. One may want to list the enclosures or simply indicate how many have been included. The reader can then check to make sure all the material is enclosed. In general, list the names of those receiving copies of the letter.

Encl: Brochure of Hotel
Tariff Plan
Road Map

Cc: Mr Asit Banerjee, Sales Manager
Ms Supriya Sule, Inventory Supervisor

Format of a Business letter

Format styles used most often in business letters include Block, Modified Block and Semi-block Indented and Simplified. The main differences among them are the placement of the date, complimentary close, and signature block, and the use of paragraph indentations.

Full Block is the easiest format to use, since all lines are flush with the left margin. Some prefer a more balanced appearance, however, in which the date, complimentary close, and signature all begin near the centre of the page, as in Block and Semi-block. Simplified, a newer format, is gaining popularity. It eliminates the problem of gender-specific salutations by doing away with the salutation line altogether.

Whichever format you adopt, be consistent. Do not mix styles. Be consistent and use the same style throughout the entire letter. The appearance of your letter on the page will influence the reader's perception of your message.

Language and Style: Business letters follow the same basic rules as all business writing. Pay particular attention to the following when drafting a business letter. Even if the letter has been dictated, keep the same guidelines in mind when finalising the draft:

- Ensure Accuracy. Double check all figures, dates and specifications. Check name spellings and ensure that the final letter is neatly typed and free of errors.
- Check that the tone of the letter is appropriate for the recipient and the subject matter. A formal tone is usually appropriate for most business letters.
- Check to see that sentences and paragraphs are clear in content and not excessively wordy. One paragraph should express only one central thought.

Structure of the Letter: The letter should have a structure consisting of the opening paragraph, the main body and the closing paragraph. The details are below:

Openings: The opening paragraph indicates the purpose and subject of the letter. For example:

We received your report that the FX-100 printer manual was missing from your shipment. Our customer service department is looking into the matter.

The reader needs to know immediately what the letter covers and your reason for writing.

Body: Paragraphs in the body of the letter spell out the main points and indicate the goal one would like to achieve via the letter. In the given example, the body of the letter would detail the steps the customer service department is taking to locate the missing manual and what the company intends to do. These paragraphs can vary in length, depending on how much detail and information the reader requires.

Closing: The closing paragraph should be only one or two sentences long. It indicates the action you wish the reader to take or expresses appreciation for the reader's understanding or patience. Make sure you restate any pertinent information or mention items by name that you refer to again. If you open with a statement of need or a problem, then close with a statement of action to address the need or a solution to the problem.

For example, in the opening paragraph above, where the missing printer manual was noted as the problem, the closing paragraph providing a solution may read as follows:

We appreciate your patronage and wish to provide satisfactory service to all our customers. A new copy of the manual is being couriered to you immediately.

It will be clear that the style of business writing focuses on the presentation and appearance of documents, which remain as important as what is written.

Block Format: Block Format is the most commonly used layout for business letters, as it is easy to compose on a computer.

In block format, the whole text is left-aligned.

A template of a letter in block format is given below:

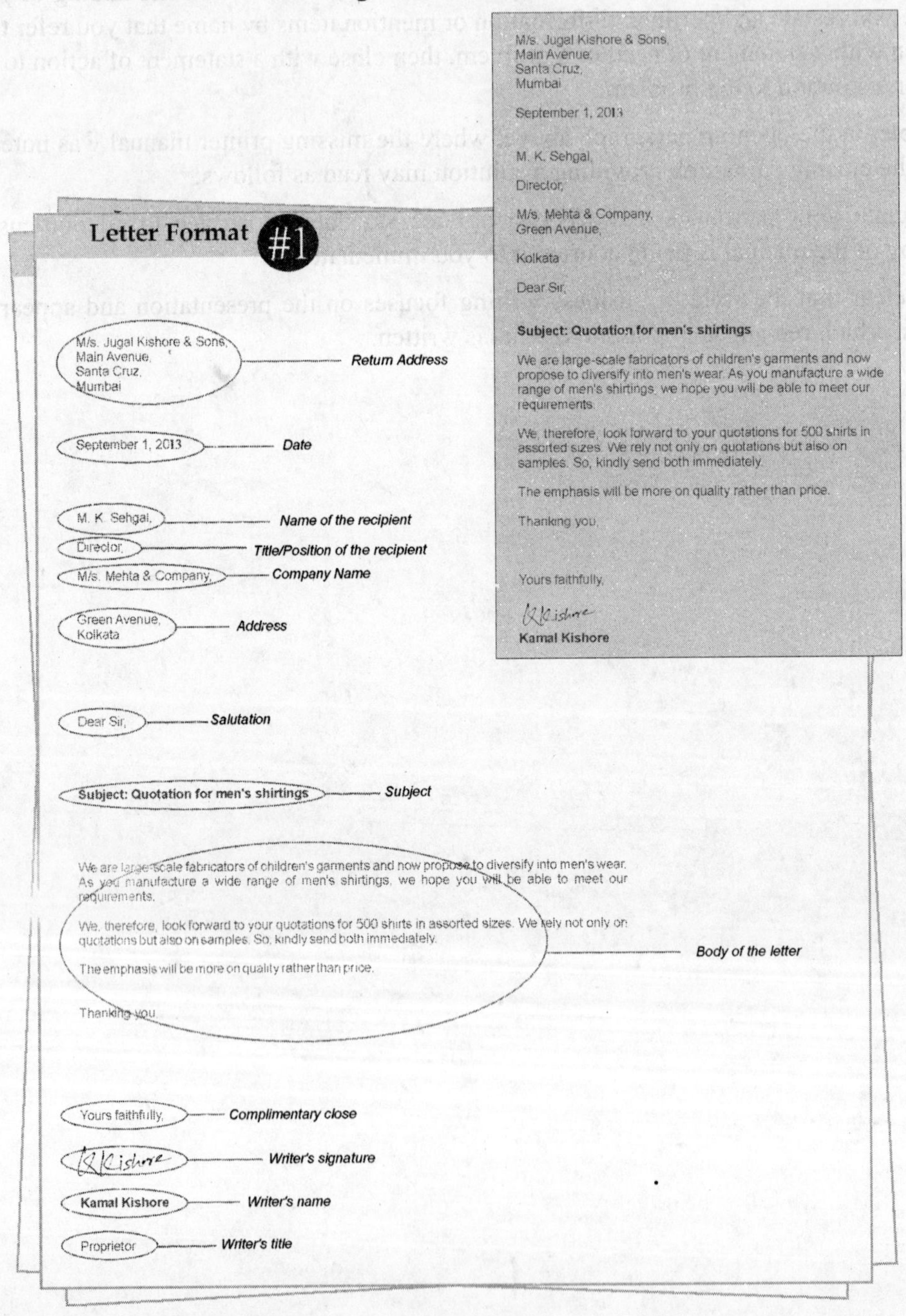

Modified Block Format: In Modified Block Format, certain elements of the letter are aligned to the right.

A template of a letter in modified block format is given below:

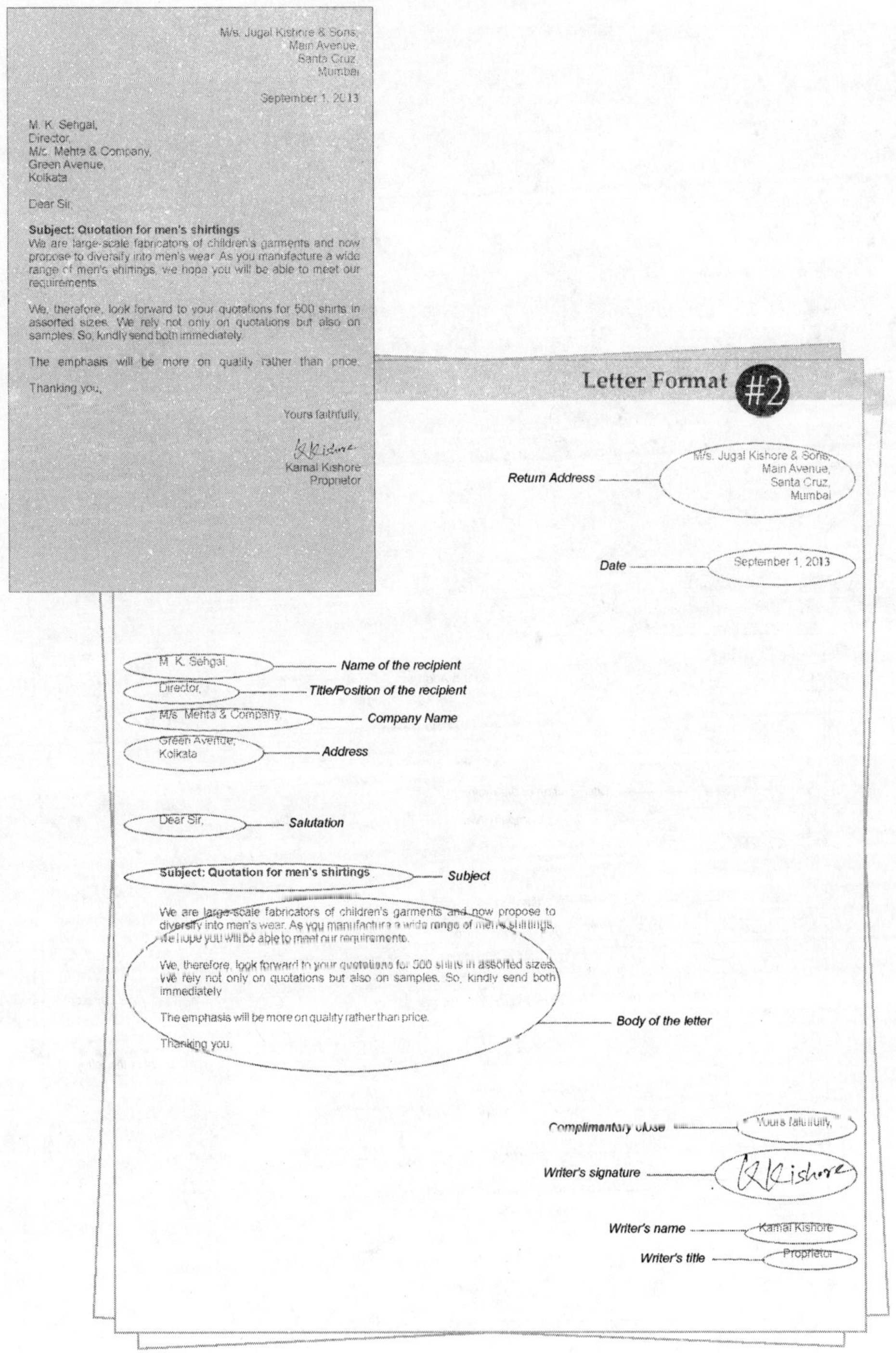

M/s. Jugal Kishore & Sons,
Main Avenue,
Santa Cruz,
Mumbai

September 1, 2013

M. K. Sehgal,
Director,
M/s. Mehta & Company,
Green Avenue,
Kolkata

Dear Sir,

Subject: Quotation for men's shirtings

We are large-scale fabricators of children's garments and now propose to diversify into men's wear. As you manufacture a wide range of men's shirtings, we hope you will be able to meet our requirements.

We, therefore, look forward to your quotations for 500 shirts in assorted sizes. We rely not only on quotations but also on samples. So, kindly send both immediately.

The emphasis will be more on quality rather than price.

Thanking you,

Yours faithfully,

KKishore
Kamal Kishore
Proprietor

Semi-Block Indented Format: In Semi-Block Indented Format, the return address is aligned to the right, and the first line of every paragraph in body is indented.

A template of a letter in semi-block indented format is given below:

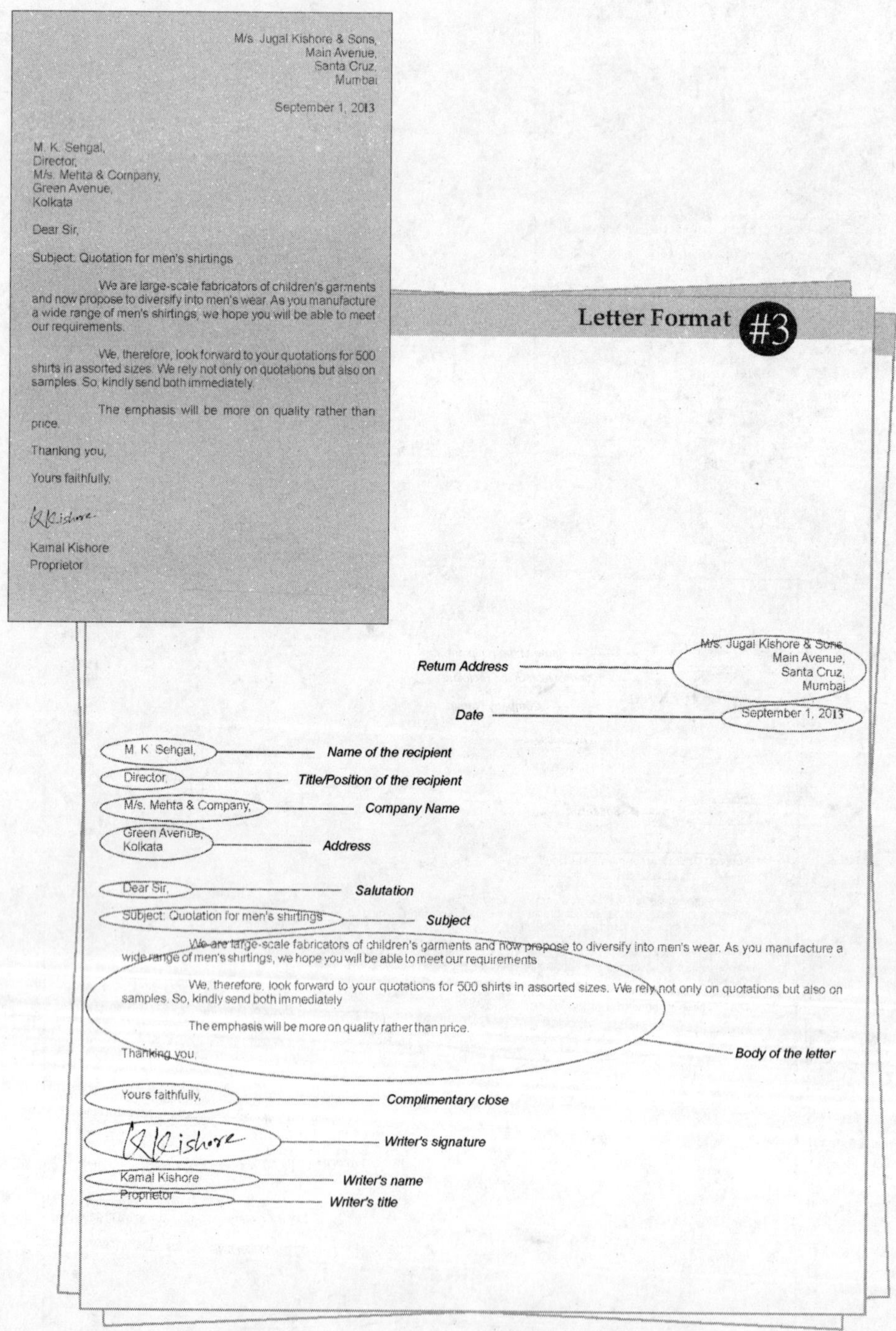

M/s. Jugal Kishore & Sons,
Main Avenue,
Santa Cruz,
Mumbai

September 1, 2013

M. K. Sehgal,
Director,
M/s. Mehta & Company,
Green Avenue,
Kolkata

Dear Sir,

Subject: Quotation for men's shirtings

We are large-scale fabricators of children's garments and now propose to diversify into men's wear. As you manufacture a wide range of men's shirtings, we hope you will be able to meet our requirements.

We, therefore, look forward to your quotations for 500 shirts in assorted sizes. We rely not only on quotations but also on samples. So, kindly send both immediately.

The emphasis will be more on quality rather than price.

Thanking you,

Yours faithfully,

K Kishore

Kamal Kishore
Proprietor

1. Letter of Enquiry

From
Sebastian & Co.,
Sabina Park,
Gorakhpur, UP.

Dated: 18th July, 2017

To
Godrej India Ltd,
23, Cross Road,
Mumbai.

Sub: Enquiry about Agency in the Area

Dear Sir,

We are two-year-old wholesalers of consumer items. We feel your famous products have a good market here but there is no wholesaler in this region, as a result of which your products are not reaching consumers.

We have the experience, distribution network and sufficient capital to distribute your products to small shopkeepers in the area. Moreover, we have a good reputation in the area and good backing from nationalized banks. You could make enquiries through your Marketing Officer to confirm these facts.

Please let us know your terms and conditions for an agency in a particular area and how much goods we need to sell per quarter. Please send your wholesale price list too.

Awaiting a prompt reply...

Thanking you,
Yours Faithfully,

Sudhansu Shekhar
Managing Director
Sebastian & Co.

2. Letter of Quotation

From
The Manager,
Celia Garments,
Sonepat, Haryana,
Dated: 15th July, 2017

To
The General Manager,
New Jersey India Ltd,
Mumbai.

Sub: Request for Quotation of Rates of Automatic Garment Sewing Machines

Dear Sir,

We have been manufacturing readymade garments for the past five years. Lately, we have revamped our entire setup and enlarged our supply field. We need more machines to cater to rising demand.

Please send us the quotation of rates of Automatic Garment Sewing Machines of different sizes and for different purposes. Also state the mode of payment and delivery, along with terms and conditions and details of the warranty.

Also send the latest catalogue to enable us to choose machines of our liking and requirement.

Thanking you,
Yours truly,

~ ~

Manager

Celia Garment

3. Letter placing orders

SEEMA ELECTRONICS
C/67, Kali Ghat Market,
Sheikhpura,
Muzaffarpur, UP.
Ref. No: 8/293,

Date: 12.09.2017

To
The Manager,
Vishal Electronics Pvt. Ltd.

E-6, Outer Ring Road,
Prashant Vihar,
New Delhi.

Sub: Order for Electronic Goods

Dear Sir,

We have gone through your catalogue and the terms of supply. These are okay with us. Please send the following items through Transport Receipt through SBI, ADB, Sheikhpura:

- 6 pieces Multimedia Speaker;
- 6 pieces Single Door Fridge;
- 6 pieces Double Door Fridge;
- 6 pieces Window AC;
- 6 pieces Z-Line Microwave Oven;
- 6 pieces 64-cm TV.

Thanking you and assuring you of our cooperation.

Yours truly,

~ ~

Shashank Tripathi

Manager

4. Letter of complaint (wrong billing or short supply)

SEEMA ELECTRONICS,
C/67, Kali Ghat Market,
Sheikhpura,
Muzaffarpur, UP.
Ref. No: 8/332

Date: 02.10.2017

To
The Manager,
Vishal Electronics Pvt Ltd,
E-6, Outer Ring Road,
Prashant Vihar, New Delhi.

Sub: Request to Refund Extra Money Charged through Wrong Billing

Dear Sir,

With reference to our order no. 293 dt 12.09.2013 and your bill no. 616723 dated 26.09.2017, we have to draw your attention to a discrepancy in billing. The rate of 64-cm TV was quoted as ₹ 17,500/- each but in the bill the rate is ₹ 19,500/-. Two thousand rupees excess money has been wrongly charged for each TV.

Please check the details and refund us ₹ 12,000/- via DD and oblige. Please do ensure such mistakes do not occur in future.

Looking forward to your cooperation...

Yours truly,

~ ~

Shashank Tripathi

Manager

5. Letter of Request

From
Arya Priyamber,
Elite Distributors,
Motihari, Bihar.

To
The Executive-in Charge,
Tata Indicom,
Bihar Zone,
Patna. (Bihar)

Date: 09.12.2017

Sub: Request for Provision of STD/ISD on Telephone No. 64522704

Dear Sir,

I purchased a Tata Indicom connection for Internet only and I received Telephone No. 64522704 in the year 2017. Now I feel the need for STD and ISD connections.

Therefore, please provide me STD and ISD facilities with a dynamic lock for this telephone. I have already filled up requisite application form and deposited two copies of my recent photographs.

I shall be grateful if the facility is provided at the earliest.

Thanking you,

Yours faithfully,

~ ~

Arya Priyamber

Business Report Writing

Business reports are written for numerous reasons. At the beginning of your career, you may be asked to type either a dictated report or a report based on notes that have been dictated to you over a period of time. Later, it is quite likely that you may be entrusted with report writing based upon the data collected by you. For example, you may be told to collect monthly sales information from salesmen working in your department and prepare a consolidated monthly report for the approval of your boss.

If you work for a consulting company or a legal firm, you may prepare preliminary reports as a matter of routine. Regardless of whether you write reports from dictations, or prepare virtually independent reports, as a secretary, it is important for you to know the basics of business report writing. The finer points of writing reports are therefore explored in this section.

Some reports are requested by higher management to explore an area of interest for the company. For instance, the company may ask your boss to prepare a report on the opportunities for your company's products in the overseas markets. Other reports may be routinely prepared, such as annual reports, monthly sales reports, or quarterly production reports. Additionally, the government requires many written reports from businesses each year to ensure their compliance with government regulations and other regulatory orders.

In many cases, a written proposal may be made to a client, followed by a full report after the proposal is approved. For example, a market survey proposal is followed by a complete market survey report after approval of the proposal. A report may also precede a proposal and serve as part of the background information on which the proposal is based. For example, your firm may publish a study on the energy problems of small businesses. Your company would then write a proposal to small firms detailing how an energy survey could help them save money. If a firm accepts the proposal and hires your company to carry out the survey, then the results of your survey would be used for a final report for the client.

Some written reports may be only a page or two, much like a detailed memo or a long letter. The content and form of these documents usually follow a set format, as in the case of monthly sales reports, inventory reviews, etc.

In this section, however, we will focus on reports written on an assigned topic at the request of management. The topics might include evaluating the communication skills of employees or determining the best marketing strategy for the next year. For such reports, you will have to determine the content and format yourself, with inputs from your boss.

When you are asked to write a report on an assigned topic, you can safely assume that there are similar reports in the company's files, written by earlier employees. Study some of these reports so that you understand the company format and style for reports.

As in the case of most of business documents, writing reports is also a two-step process. Each step is examined below.

Planning and Prewriting

Purpose: As in the case of letters, memos, and other business communication, begin by establishing the purpose of the report. Assume that you have been asked to prepare a report on involvement of employees in the management decision-making process.

Scope: Your first task is to determine the exact scope and objective of the report. Is it to evaluate the pros and cons of involving employees in your own firm? Are you also to study the results of this technique that other firms may already have tried? If you are not sure about the purpose of your assigned topics, ask questions from your boss and other colleagues until you can state the scope and objective in a sentence or two.

Audience: You should be able to answer who is the intended audience. Determine whether the report will be written for top management, the government or for other firms in the same industry. Also determine whether the report will be made available to middle and line management or also to workers and the support staff at the shop-floor level.

Contents: Once you have determined the audience, ask yourself what they need to know. For instance, they may need background information on employee involvement. Interview those who are awaiting the report to find out what they would like included and use those answers to guide your research. Put yourself as much as possible in the readers' place.

Finally, you will arrive at a list of topics that the report will cover. For this discussion, assume that the report will be read by top management. Also, assume they would like to know if introducing employee involvement in management decision-making will improve quality of decisions, increase productivity, and boost employee morale.

Research: All the above indicates that you will need to research how employee involvement has worked in companies similar to yours. The data you gather will have to be analysed in terms of productivity, decision-making methods, efficiency, revenues, accident rates, turnover, morale, and labour-management relations. Your report will require drawing conclusions and making recommendations about whether employee involvement is appropriate for your firm.

Outlining and Final Draft: The detailed outline serves as the basis for writing the final report. The outline gives you the chance to go through your data and organise it. You can carefully evaluate what should be included and what discarded. The analysis will help you evaluate what the information means, and what conclusions and recommendations one should make.

The outline should be detailed enough to help you develop each section of the report, yet flexible enough so that you can change it if necessary. The outline is your way of thinking through the structure and content of the report in detail. Final adjustments and corrections can be made when you write the first draft.

An outline for your report on employee involvement might look like the following:

1. Summary or synopsis: Here you will summarise the major points of the report and the conclusions.
   a) Employee involvement can be used in medium-sized companies to improve labour-management relations, develop human resources within a firm, improve

productivity and efficiency, develop better decision-making processes, and increase overall company performance;

b) Employee involvement needs to be introduced carefully or it will not be successful. Top management and labour leaders must be committed to the process and seek to involve workers and middle and line managers. Adequate training in employee involvement procedures must be provided. The success of the method depends on commitment and education of all participants.

2. Introduction. Here you will explain the reason for writing the report.

   a) Purpose of the report: To determine if employee involvement is suitable for our company;

   b) Scope of the topic: Definition of employee involvement and its application, and description of what will be covered in the report;

   c) Methodology: How data were gathered and analysed;

   d) Structure of the report: The organisational approach you have chosen.

3. Historical review of employee involvement in India.

   a) Introduction of employee involvement in the Indian private and public sectors;

   b) Overall success and failure rate of the method;

   c) Comparison of Indian and foreign programmes, focusing on the USA, Japan and Europe.

4. Evaluation of employee involvement in medium-sized firms.

   a) Interviews, questionnaires, and data from published literature revealing characteristics of successful and unsuccessful programmes;

   b) Description of firms chosen and explanation of their programmes;

   c) Summary of findings.

5. Evaluation of your firm and employee involvement.

   a) Current structure and organisation of firm;

   b) Ways in which employee involvement would impact the firm, the pros and cons.

6. Conclusions and recommendations.

   a) When instituted and administered properly, employee involvement improves a company's productivity, decision-making process, profits, morale, labour-management relations, and development of human resources;

   b) Recommend that employee involvement be instituted in your company;

   c) List of conditions for instituting and administering programme successfully; they include commitment from management and labour leadership, selection of training and education programmes, means of administering and gradually phasing in new system, follow-up and monitoring;

   d) Estimate of time and cost to institute programme and get it running effectively.

7. Bibliography.

8. Appendices.

   a) Charts of four companies showing increase in productivity, morale, revenue, decrease in absenteeism, turnover and labour-management conflicts;

   b) Questionnaires used and transcripts of selected interviews with workers and management in four companies;

   c) Summary of historical data from government reports.

After developing and refining the outline, one is ready to write the final report. As one can see from the above, all the data has been collected, analysis has been completed and conclusions have been drawn by the time the outline is ready. Writing the actual report is now a matter of penmanship. The subsequent sections will provide readers with all the guidelines required to write reports.

Effective E-mails: Of all forms of Internet activities, email is probably the most popular one for business communication. In the USA, almost 90% of all business users use the Internet for sending and receiving email. While the present percentage is much lower in India, it has been growing rapidly for the past few years.

Thanks to globalisation, trade has spread all over the world. Therefore, a means of rapid communication, almost as fast as a phone call, but much cheaper, has become essential for business. Not surprisingly, with email communication becoming central to daily office activities, you will need special skills to deal with this swift means of communication.

Accordingly, one needs to learn the right way to deal with incoming emails, compose effective outgoing emails and maintain correct email etiquette, just as one would for any other form of business communication.

Controlling Your Inbox: Since you may expect a large number of emails from business contacts, Internal emails from colleagues as well as many promotional emails trying to sell products and services, you should institute some simple rules to deal with what comes into your inbox (the folder in which email software downloads email).

As soon as you open the email software's inbox, determine as quickly as possible the action you wish to take with each email. For instance, you may decide to:

- Delete it;
- Archive it;
- Defer it for later response;
- Generate an action from it;
- Respond to it immediately.

It is a good idea to first delete unimportant emails that require no reply and no action. Next, defer emails that can wait by transferring them to a separate folder (perhaps marked 'Pending') that you can create in your inbox. You will now be left with the important emails that require a reply or some specific action. These can be either forwarded to your boss, or printed out by you and submitted to the boss along with other mail.

Outgoing E-mails: Getting inbound email under control will ensure a big productivity boost. To get the best out of email communication, however, you will have to think about the emails you have to send. If you want your emails to produce results that you actively seek, you will need to craft messages that are concise and easy to deal with. The following guidelines should help.

Purpose: Before you type a new email, be sure you have clear answers for two questions:

1. Why am I writing this email?
2. What do I expect the email to accomplish?

Think about your email from the recipient's point of view; carefully thought out emails are concise and easy to understand for the recipient. They will get you an equally careful response.

Types of E-mails: There are three basic types of business emails:

1. Providing information: "Simran Mann will be in the office on Monday at 10:00 a.m."
2. Requesting information: "What action has been taken on the customer's complaint?"
3. Requesting action: "The sales personnel are required to attend a meeting in the Sales Manager's office on Tuesday at 2:00 p.m.."

It should be immediately clear to your recipient which type of email has been received. Insert a descriptive subject line and get the details and context fitted into a sentence or two. You may write an actual 'topic sentence' that clarifies what the email is about and what response or action the recipient should take.

Since the board meeting on Monday has been moved from the Executive Meeting Room to the Conference Room, could you please make sure that the Conference Room has been reserved and that the caterer has been notified about the location change? Please email me today by 5:00 p.m. and confirm.

It is a good idea to assume that no one will read more than the first sentence of your email. Therefore, making the first sentence strong and clear is the best way to attract attention and convey the most important information in that sentence.

Strong Subject Line: You can help your recipient understand why you have sent the email and to quickly determine the response or action it requires. To do so, compose a 'Subject:' line that summarises the most important points in the message. For example:

- Lunch rescheduled to Friday @ 1:00 p.m.;
- Please resend the Monthly Budget zip file;
- HELP. How do I defrag my C drive?
- Thanks for the new printer – works well!

In the body of the message, it is important to keep the total length to just one screen page. By doing so, you convey the message to the recipient without the need to scroll the page on the monitor screen. If it is absolutely necessary to extend your email beyond one page, then summarise the salient points in the first page and send this as the main email. Enclose a longer document containing the details as an attachment to your email.

Define the Action Required: If your message requires action, you may consider a standardised text header just under the subject line that specifies the action required and the priority of the email.

Here is a possible header design you may incorporate in your email:

This email is:	[ ] actionable	[ ] for info	[ ] social
Response needed:	[ ] yes	[ ] no	
Urgency:	[ ] immediate	[ ] soon	[ ] none

Email Etiquette: *Importance of Email Etiquette:* As the use of the Internet spreads in India, there is a good chance you will increase the use of email to communicate with others, including your boss, colleagues, clients, or prospective employers.

Like the business letter or a business report, emails also reflect upon the organisation and the individual sending the email. While there is need to be pithy and concise on the one hand, it is also necessary to prevent the appearance of carelessness or lack of good manners on the other hand.

Some messages get right to the point, perhaps too quickly. The writer wastes no time asking for what s/he needs without bothering to be polite. Sometimes, a form of shorthand is used. For example:

"Can u plz send info on careers?"

While this style may be appropriate for instant messaging to your close friends, it is not suited for writing to a business correspondent.

Sometimes there are glaring errors, such as misspellings and poor grammar. Because your correspondence says a lot about you and your company, you should be aware of some basic email etiquette, sometimes known as Netiquette.

Netiquette Basics: Follow these guidelines to make sure your emails create a good, professional impression about you and your company:

- Do not drop 'please' and 'thank you' for the sake of brevity.
- Do not use first names in business emails, unless you know the recipient personally.
- Remember to spell the names correctly and add the appropriate salutation such as Mr, Mrs, or Dr.
- Use a friendly, helpful but not over-familiar tone in your messages.
- Do not use 'emoticons' in a business message. Emoticons are symbols such as smiley faces that look like:).
- Do not use all uppercase letters in your message. It would seem like you are shouting at the recipient.
- Do not use abbreviations such as 'plz' when you mean to say please, or 'thnx' in place of thanks.

Spelling, Grammar, and Attachments: Most email software such as Microsoft Outlook or Windows Outlook Express has a built-in spelling checker. Use it to correct spelling mistakes before sending the email.

Good grammar is important. You may use a less formal tone in emails than what is used in business letters. But it is best to limit the level of informality.

Limit attachments to the minimum. If you have lengthy reports to send as email attachments, it is important for you to know what computer software is available with the recipient. Otherwise, the attachment cannot be read by the receiver.

Plain text can be opened by any computer user. It is, therefore, preferred as the first choice. Depending on the subject, however, you may have to send reports and attachments as Microsoft Word documents, Excel spreadsheet or as Adobe Acrobat documents. Make sure the recipient has the required software. Otherwise, the attachment cannot be read.

Personal & Social Letters

• Personal Letters • Social Letters • Greetings and Congratulations • Letters of Sympathy

Although personal letter writing or for that matter even business letter writing has become a forgotten art in the present day of e-mails and internet but it is always a joy to receive a personalised card or letter from your loved ones – friends, family, colleagues, etc. Letters are tangible evidence that someone took the extra time to write and send you something because you are special to them. Let's retrive the vanishing art!

Personal Letters

Personal letters are those which are written to relatives and friends. At one time or the other, all of us are called upon to write such letters. These letters can be carriers of information, messenger of love and sympathy, promoters of harmony and harbingers of peace and tranquility. A good personal letter must appear natural.

Social Letters

These are usually written in the context of a social obligation. The occasion can be happy or unfortunate. These can also be written to make enquiries, lodge complaints and convey congratulations.

Some typical occasions are:

1. Greetings and Congratulations;
2. Thanks;
3. Invitations;
4. Condolences;
5. Sympathy;
6. Educational matters;
7. Office matters;
8. Landlord and Tenant;
9. Complaints;
10. Between Couples;
11. Apologies;
12. Matrimonial Replies;
13. Family Letters.

• **Form and Arrangement:** The (From) Address: We begin a letter with a heading which is the address. In Britain, it is customary to write your full postal address at the top right-hand corner of the notepaper or letter-pad. The name or number of the house or building is followed by the name of the road or street, and then the name of the village, town or country. The date is written after that. Here are some typical styles of writing addresses:

4/45, SBP Buildings,
Roop Nagar,
Delhi-110007.
April 2, 2017.

The address given at the top-right hand side of a letter is usually the one to which you wish replies to be sent. Thus, if you write from home but are going to stay at another place in the near future, you can mention this new address preceded by the word 'from'.

From: Hotel Cortina,
Napean Sea Road,
Mumbai-400 001.
July 14, 2017.

If a person is staying at another person's house, the name of the owner is written above the address and is preceded by the letters 'C/o.' which denotes 'care of':

C/o. Dr. P.C. Gupta,
4/40, Roop Nagar,
Delhi-110007.
March 20, 2017.

• **The Date:** There are five principal ways of writing the date on a letter:

1. Sunday, 10th September, 2017
2. 10th September, 2017
3. September 10th, 2017
4. 10-09-2017
5. 10/9/2017

• **Address and Inside Address:** As for personal letters, the lay-out or style differs from person to person. However, there are some formal personal letters, almost like commercial correspondence, in which case the addressee's address is written in the letter itself on the left-hand side of the page below the Date and above the salutation.

10th September, 2017

M/s*. Pustak Mahal Pvt Ltd.,
J-3/16, Ansari Road, Daryaganj,
New Delhi-110 002

Dear Sirs,

---

* M/s. is the short form of Messrs which is the plural form of Mr., and the last line of Inside Address is normally under-lined.

Dr./ Mr./ Mrs./ Miss R N Gupta,
350, Civil Lines,
Srinagar,
Kashmir

This address should be same as the one written on the envelope. In fact, sometimes in business letters, when 'window envelopes' are used, the letter is folded in such a way that the Inside address actually becomes the "To Address" on the Envelope, being visible through its window.

Yes, the letter becomes ready for despatch after signature and you have to put it in an envelope and write the "To Address" on the envelope. In case of Personal Letters, normally one can omit writing the "To Address" inside the letter. The letter can simply start with the salutation. Always write the address correctly and clearly.

- **Salutation:** Mostly letters begin with 'Dear…' written from the left-hand margin. This is called "salutation."

While addressing someone elder, one begins the letter using salutations such as 'Dear Father', 'Dear Aunt', etc. But while writing to a friend or so, 'Dear' is followed by the person's first name or even the nickname.

Dear Sharada, or Dear Charu,

(Sharada is the name and Charu is the nickname)

There must be a comma after the salutation. The text of the letter and the first word of salutation begin with capital letters:

Dear Ram, Dear Rita, Dear Tony, Dear Johny,

As a rule, the text of the letter should begin leaving space for 5 alphabetical letters from the margin as in the case of starting a paragraph. (It may vary from place to place).

Dear Mala,

What a long time…

As one's relationship develops, the salutation can reflect various degrees of increasing cordiality, intimacy, friendship or love.

Dear Sonia, My dear Naresh, Dearest Sonia, My dearest Sonia,
My dearest, Darling, etc.

And thus such a letter becomes a very personal message; an instrument for exchange of love and affection between two persons.

While writing a personal letter to someone who is not a close friend or to someone who is treated with respect, the salutation begins as:

Dear Mr…, Dear Mrs…, Dear Miss…

followed by the person's surname. People are addressed in a letter as they are addressed in a conversation, especially in social letters.

But if the name is not known, it can start saying "Dear Sir" or "Dear Madam", etc.

When writing to a firm we use "Sirs" in place of "Sir." For example " Dear Sirs,"

• **Body of the Letter:** After salutation the body of the letter starts. This can be divided into three parts – (i) Introduction, (ii) Main message/ information or the descriptive middle portion (iii) Conclusion. There are no strict rules regarding the body of letter of Personal Letters, which can be flexible and changeable according to the relation of the sender and receiver.

(i) Introduction: Following are some examples that could be used to introduce the body of Business Letters. A few of them hold good in case of Personal Letters too.

1. Thank you for replying/ responding to my letter so promptly.
2. I have just received your letter.
3. Thank you for your prompt reply.
4. It was nice to hear from you after such a long time.
5. You will be glad/sorry to learn…
6. Thank you for your letter dated…
7. Trust this finds you in good health and cheers.
8. Thank you for your letter No… dated… regarding…
9. We thank you for your letter No… dt…
10. Received your letter No… dated… on… (subject)…
11. We have received…
12. We are in receipt of your letter No… dated… regarding…
13. This refers to your letter…
14. This has reference to your letter…
15. With reference to your letter…
16. According to your letter…
17. Referring to your letter No… dated… regarding… we would like to say that…
18. This is with reference to your letter…
19. This is in response to your letter No… dated…
20. This is in connection with your post-card dated…
21. Please refer to your letter No… dated… on the subject of…

22. We would like to inform you that…
23. This is to state that…
24. This is to inform you that…
25. This is to request you that…
26. We are pleased to…
27. We have pleasure in informing you that…

(ii) Message or Descriptive Middle Portion: This is the main part of the letter. Here we answer the questions or supply the information asked for. In case of personal letters, we also try to include interesting and important things. No stereotyped text can be exemplified here as this differs from case to case and from time to time. Its size may be as big as two-three pages or as brief as a line or one paragraph. It is dependent on the message to be communicated but in case of business letters, it has to be brief and descriptive.

(iii) Conclusion: The personal letter, usually, ends with a wish. Here are a few examples:

1. Please give my Best Wishes/ love/ regards to…
2. I hope to see you soon (or hear from you soon)
3. Everyone here joins me in sending you love/ wishes.
4. Wishing you a quick and complete recovery and…
5. Thanks a lot and be in touch.
6. Please convey our regards and respects to all there.
7. Have a nice time.
8. Have an enjoyable vacation.
9. Cheers.
10. Take care.

• **The Complimentary Close:** Most of these close with the subscription "Yours…" and the 'Y' in 'Yours' must invariably be in Capital Letter.

When writing to friends, one can close a letter just as one likes – with expressions of deep affection or familiarity. The most common endings of personal letters are:

Yours,
Yours sincerely,
Yours very sincerely,
Yours affectionately,
Sincerely yours,
Affectionately yours,
Sincerely,
Love,
With love,

Complimentary Close is always followed by a 'comma' as in case of "Salutation".

• **The Signature:** Underneath the Complimentary Close, you put your signature. Always put your signature clearly. If the letter goes to known personal circle, initials will be enough instead of a full signature, whereas, if it is formally addressed to someone, your full signature and name will be necessary.

If the letter is typewritten, the writer's name will be typed leaving space for signature above. A woman could indicate whether she is married or not by writing 'Mrs' or 'Miss' with the name after her signature. If she does not want to indicate whether she is married or unmarried Ms is used before the name, pronounced/ miz.

• **Post Scripts (P.S.):** These are permissible when something important has been left. These are put after the signatures, starting on the left-hand side of the paper. Generally, this should not exceed 2 or 3 lines.

Letters of Greetings and Congratulations

At one time or another all of us are required to write Letters of Greetings or congratulations to our friends, colleagues, acquaintances or relatives. The main purpose of these letters is to share the happiness of others making the social ties more cordial and everlasting. Thus, the less formal these letters are the better it is. One should express one's happiness in a simple and natural way. The important occasions which call for greetings/congratulations are classified below:

• **Birthday Greetings:** It is customary all over the world to send birthday greetings. Of course, children's birthdays are celebrated with more gaiety and fun than that of adults. But even for adults and old people, it is ideal that we send Greetings on such occasions. Everyone wishes to be greeted on his/her birthday, and people do it to cement the mutual relations with the warmth of love, affection and cordiality.

Start the Sentence with an expression of happiness:

1. Thank you for your invitation to attend your birthday party/ function.
2. It was very nice of you to invite me/ us to your birthday party…
3. What a pleasant surprise to know that the coming Monday is your birthday!
4. How delightful/ interesting it is to learn that you are celebrating your birthday next week!
5. I am desperately/ eagerly waiting to join you in your birthday party, next week.
6. Thanks a lot for inviting me to your birthday party next week. I like to share your joy of the occasion.
7. It will be a matter of great pleasure for me to attend your birthday party.
8. I express my joy and happiness on the eve of your birthday celebrations.
9. Accept my heartiest greetings on the eve of your birthday celebrations.
10. Thank you for your birthday invitation. It has given me immense pleasure.
11. Thank you for inviting me to your birthday party. I am looking forward to attending it.
12. I convey my heartiest congratulations and wish you many happy returns of the day.
13. Please accept my best wishes on this happy occasion.
14. I join all your friends and family members in wishing you a very happy birthday.

After congratulations, convey Good Wishes for future happiness:

15. I take this opportunity to wish you all success for the long life ahead.
16. May all happiness and prosperity be with you in the days to come.
17. May you live long life to enjoy the fruits of all your labour.
18. I wish this birthday to be followed by many more such happy occasions in your life.
19. May every day in future be like your birthday/ be as rosy as this happy day.

Expressing inability to join the birthday function:

20. It's really very kind of you to have invited me to your birthday party, but I'm sorry I won't be able to make it as I will be out of town that day.
21. It was very nice of you to invite me/ us to your Birthday party.
22. It was very kind of you to invite me/ us to your birthday celebrations.
23. It's a pleasure being invited to your birthday party, but, I am sorry I can't make it as I'm ill.
24. I, of course, wanted to join your birthday party, but, I am badly tied up with business affairs.
25. As my sister is leaving for the US on that day, I regret, I won't be able to attend it/ make it.
26. Had I not to go out on tour, I would certainly have been amongst your guests/ with you on this happy occasion.
27. I wish I could participate in/ attend the function and meet you all but due to unavoidable official commitments, I regret, I will not be able to make it.

Inform about sending some gift:

28. Very shortly, you will receive/ Through my brother I am sending a small gift from my side as a token of my love and affection for you.
29. I hope you would like the small gift I have sent to you today by post.
30. I've bought a nice gift for you which I will give you when I come down to Delhi next month.

Closing by summarizing the message:

31. Wishing you all success,
32. With all my felicitations,
33. Congratulations and best wishes,
34. Wishing you the best of luck,
35. Hope to hearing from you soon,
36. Thank you very much for remembering me.

My dear...,

What a pleasant surprise to know that the coming Monday is your birthday![3] It will be a matter of great pleasure for me to attend your birthday party.[7]

Please accept my best wishes on this happy occasion.[13] I wish this birthday to be followed by many more such happy occasions in your life.[18] It is really very kind of you to invite me to your birthday party, but, I am sorry I won't be able to join as I will be out of town on that day.

Very shortly you will receive a small gift from my side as a token of my love and affection.[28]

Wishing you the best of luck,[34]

With regards,

Yours sincerely,

• **Congratulations on Engagement / Marriage:** While writing letter on someone's engagement/ marriage, express your feelings and sentiments as warmly as the occasion obviously warrants. If one is writing to someone close, its length cannot be prescribed.

At the very outset express your happiness:

1. How happy/excited I am to learn about your engagement/ marriage!
2. How excited I was when I received your wedding invitation card!
3. The other day, when Mohan brought the news of your marriage/ engagement, I was quite thrilled.
4. My happiness and joy knew no bounds when I came to know about your marriage.
5. I am truly overjoyed to learn about your daughter's wedding/ engagement.
6. The happy news of your engagement/ wedding has given tremendous pleasure to all of us here.
7. You don't know how eagerly I am looking forward to attend your wedding
8. Thank you for your invitation to attend your marriage with Gita on (date).
9. Thank you for your kind invitation to the wedding of your son/ daughter with... on (date).
10. It has been a pleasure to hear about the long awaited event/ most important event in your life, taking place on (date).

After expressing happiness, convey congratulations:

11. Please convey my best wishes to your daughter/ son.
12. God bless you on this happy occasion.
13. With many thanks for the invitation, please accept my congratulations/ best wishes on this memorable occasion in your life.

In order to convey your special interest on the occasion, add one or two sentences in praise of the person/s fiancé/ fiancée:

14. I am happy to know that you are getting married to a girl of your own choice.

15. My sister, who once happened to be a college-mate of your fiancée, tells me that she is a remarkable girl.
16. Your fiancé, who is our family friend, is a very fine chap.
17. It is of great delight to know that your fiancée is a lecturer in a local college.
18. I must say that you really are very lucky to have him/ her as your life-partner.
19. I am certain that you two will make a happy married couple/ an ideal match/ couple.
20. Now with your daughter married off to such a good family, your worries are over.
21. I am pleased to learn that your daughter-in-law is not only sweet but highly educated too.
22. It is really great that your would-be son-in-law is such a senior executive at such a young age.
23. I know your fiancée well and I am convinced that she will make an ideal/ a good wife.

Marriage bestows a social privilege, but, it also means new responsibilities. It will not be out of place to mention about it. Preferably these sentences are written by elderly people to the youngsters:

24. With all my heart, I wish you a blissful conjugal life.
25. One thing you should not overlook is the fact that marriage means many compromises and adjustments.
26. You are committing yourself to a great responsibility and I wish you all success in sailing through it.
27. But, see to it that you act as a cementing factor in the new family.
28. I take this opportunity to wish both you and (the 'wouldbe's name) a long and happy married life.

Enquiries about the date of marriage can be made, if the letter is being written on the occasion of engagement:

29. Please let me know when the marriage is going to be solemnized.
30. I hope it takes place as early as possible.
31. If I can be of any service during the wedding, please let me know.
32. It has been very thoughtful of you to have chosen October for wedding when the weather is going to be pleasant.

Close by summarizing the message:

33. Congratulations, and Best Wishes to the newly weds.
34. Please convey our best wishes to your son/ daughter for a long and happy married life.
35. Wish you/your ….(son/daughter/nephew/niece) a very happy married life.
36. I am eagerly looking forward to joining you on this occasion.
37. Best of luck in life.
38. Hope you won't mind my absence in the functions, but don't forget to see us with your sweetheart when you are in Delhi.

39. I wish I could participate in/ attend the functions and see you all there, but, owing to prior engagements/ pre-occupation/ unavoidable official commitments/ being out of town, I regret I will not be able to make it.
40. I was holding back this reply on the hope that I would be able to make it, but, due to the last minute change in plans, I regret I will not be able to attend the functions.
41. As things stand now, I hope to be able to participate in the function unless some problem crops up at the last moment/ unless I happen to be out of town.
42. I am just waiting to arrange a gala party in honour of your marriage after the great event.
43. Congratulations and wish you a happy married life.

Dear ...,

How excited I am to learn about your engagement![1] Congratulations and Best Wishes for a happy married life. I am happy to know that you are getting married to a girl of your own choice.[14] I am certain that you two will make an ideal couple.[19] You are now committing yourself to a great responsibility and I wish you all success in sailing through it.[26] Please let me know when the marriage is going to be solemnized.[29] I am eagerly looking forward to joining you on this occasion.[36]
Best of luck in life.[37]

With love and regards,

Sincerely Yours,

• **Congratulations on the Birth of a Child:** A child's birth, has a unique importance in one's life. On this momentous occasion, you can share the parents' happiness by sending them a note of felicitations. The parents of the new born would be delighted to receive it. Normally, the greetings should be addressed to the parents but sometimes it can be sent to the grand parents when the parental couple happens to be quite young. Greetings on such occasions make the social ties lasting too.

Start the letter by expressing your happiness on getting the good news:

1. I was very happy to know that you are now the mother of a lovely baby girl.
2. I am delighted to learn that you have now become the proud father of a pretty little boy/girl.
3. How excited I am to learn that somebody has arrived to fill the gap of loneliness in your life!
4. The news fills me with joy. I know how long you have waited for a child.
5. Everybody at my place/ at our end is quite thrilled to know that you have been blessed with a baby boy/ girl.

Convey your heart-felt congratulations after greeting the birth of the baby:

6. Hearty congratulations.

7. Congratulations to you both on becoming the proud parents.
8. Please accept my heartiest congratulations on this occasion.
9. My best wishes are with all three of you.
10. Best of Luck/ Wishing you all the Best.
11. Congratulations and I am very eager to see your cute baby.
12. Congratulations on becoming the proud parents / grand parents of a cute baby girl/ baby boy.
13. My wife joins me in sending you the best wishes.
14. Congratulations on being the proud parents.

A few sweet words about the child can add to the pleasure of the parents:

15. I join you to welcome the new member of your family.
16. I can well imagine how thrilled you are as you have always wished for a baby girl.
17. I am happy for Manisha also as she always wanted a little brother.
18. The baby, I am sure, will be a source of joy to both of you.
19. I can well imagine how thrilled you are by the birth of twins – (a boy and a girl).
20. The baby, I hope, is as pretty as the parents.
21. Hope he/she brings to you all luck and prosperity.
22. With a daughter and a son, now your family is happily/ ideally complete!
23. I know that the silence/ loneliness in your life has, now, been broken by a naughty little boy/ girl.

Wish for parents' well-being after writing about the newly born:

24. Your son must be quite excited at the feeling of becoming/ having become a proud father.
25. Wishing the baby good health and long life.
26. You must be quite excited at the feeling of having become a father.
27. It is nice to learn that your daughter-in-law and grand-child are keeping good health.
28. I hope, both the mother and the child are keeping good health.
29. Hope the mother and the child are keeping well. Take care.
30. I am truly concerned about your wife's health. I hope everything will turn out well.

You can further show a personal concern by writing a few more things about the child:

31. Please inform me when the christening ceremony is going to take place.
32. Please inform us of the christening ceremony as it takes place.
33. Let me know when the name-giving ceremony is being held.
34. I hope you have consulted a good astrologer to cast the baby's horoscope.
35. I have a few good books on child care which I think you must read.

At the end, extend your good wishes and blessings to the baby:

36. We wish your new baby/ new born grand-child a long and healthier life.

37. I hope your child turns out to be a brilliant young man in the years to come.
38. The child is really lucky to have got such loving parents.
39. I am sure your child will be the shining star of your family.

Give an affectionate ending to your letter if you have shown your willingness to see the child:

40. I will be visiting you when you return from the maternity home.
41. I am dying to see you and your baby.
42. I will make it a point to see you and the baby when we come to Delhi next.
43. I shall pay a visit to you next time I am in Delhi.
44. There are occasions when I really curse myself for being in a foreign country, unable to see the dear ones.
45. Cheers.

Dear ...,

I am delighted to learn that you have now become the proud father of a pretty little girl.[2] Please accept my heartiest congratulations on this occasion.[8] I can well imagine how thrilled you are as you always wished for a baby girl.[16] I hope, both the mother and the child are keeping good health.[28] Please inform me when the christening ceremony is going to take place.[31] I am dying to see you and your baby.[41]

With regards,

Sincerely yours,

Congratulations on Success in Examination: It is quite natural for anyone to feel proud of his success in an examination. On such occasions a word of praise goes a long way to inspire him/her and boosts the morale. This would also help him improve his performance.

Convey your happiness:

1. How excited I was to find your roll number in the newspaper and know that you have passed your M.A. in first division!
2. It is thrilling to learn from Ramesh that you have passed the Higher Secondary Examination with flying colours.
3. I am very happy to know that you have passed your B.A. in first division.
4. We are thrilled to hear that your son has passed the Higher Secondary Examination with very good marks.
5. You can't imagine my excitement at the news of your becoming a doctor.
6. My heart is filled with joy to learn that you are now a full-fledged engineer.
7. This news came as a pleasant surprise that you/ your son/ your daughter have/ has passed B.Com degree exam with first rank.

8. It was great to know that you/ your son (daughter) have/has passed the BA Hons. Examination with distinction.

Congratulate in sweet words:

9. Accept my heartiest congratulations on your creditable success.
10. Congratulations. You have kept up the tradition of being always higher in the rank/ merit list.
11. You have held the dignity of our institution high and memorable.
12. Our congratulations to your son on his remarkable success.
13. Please convey our congratulations and love to your son/ daughter on his/ her remarkable/ brilliant success.
14. My wife joins me in congratulating you on your brilliant success.
15. Your success is an achievement which you can be proud of.
16. You must be thrilled at realizing your lifelong ambition of becoming an I.A.S. officer.
17. It's really a splendid achievement and we are all proud of your success.

Express good wishes for a bright future:

18. Now there is scarcely any doubt about your becoming a lecturer.
19. We hope that you get a cadre of your choice and are nearer to your home.
20. With your excellent academic record it will not be difficult for you to get a good job soon and share your father's responsibilities.
21. Have you made up your mind for the future plans?
22. What are the further plans of your son/ daughter?
23. I am quite sure you will be an asset to your profession.
24. Now you are well qualified to shoulder the responsibility of your father's business and make it more flourishing.

Making enquiries about his future plans shows your personal concern for the person:

25. What do you intend to do now?
26. Are you planning to go abroad for higher studies?
27. Do you plan to expand your father's business or go in for higher studies?
28. You must have started looking for a suitable job by now.
29. Why don't you drop in one of these days, so that we can discuss about your future plans?
30. As Sujata is a promising student, I hope you will encourage her to study further.

Due appreciation of a few other things can also be made:

31. Such good result is the outcome of your hard work.
32. There is, of course, no doubt that your success is the outcome of your hard work.
33. You have maintained and followed the splendid tradition of your family.
34. Why don't you try for the I.A.S./ Management / Engineering?

35. It's all the more creditable that you have achieved such a brilliant success despite your recent illness.
36. It's really creditable for you to have done so well with a full time job.

In the end, you can wish again for the person's future glory:

37. I am sure you have a bright future.
38. (I) hope your future will be as bright as your present.
39. Please convey our blessings and good wishes to your son for a bright future.
40. I wish that you surpass all previous records in the years to come.
41. I wish that the field you have chosen offers you more satisfaction and success in the coming years.
42. Best Wishes.

Dear ...,

How excited I was to find your roll number in the newspaper yesterday and know that you have passed your M.A. in first division![2] Accept my heartiest congratulations on your creditable success.[9] Now there is scarcely any doubt about your becoming a lecturer.[18] Such good result is the outcome of your hard work.[31] Hope your future is as bright as your present.[38]

With love,

Yours sincerely,

• **Congratulations on Promotion:** The promotion of a person in his job speaks of his talents and competence. Such an occasion calls for congratulations. It conveys the message that you find your happiness in his happiness.

First of all, convey the pleasure:

1. How delighted I am to know that you have become the Marketing Manager of your firm!
2. It was great to know that you...
3. I am extremely happy to learn about your promotion to the post of Zonal Manager.
4. It was great to know about your promotion to the next rank.
5. It is good to know that you have finally accepted the promotion which you were evading because of the fear of a transfer.
6. It is very reassuring to know that the long awaited promotion has finally come through.
7. I was overjoyed to learn that you have been taken out of the typists' pool and promoted as the Private Secretary.
8. The news of your promotion has come as a great delight to all of us here.
9. We were highly delighted to know that you have become the...

Thereafter extend greetings:

10. Please accept my heartiest congratulations on your elevation to a higher post.
11. Hearty congratulations on your recognition.
12. Hearty congratulations on your deserving promotion.
13. Congratulations on your promotion which was already due.
14. Please accept my congratulations on this befitting recognition of your merits.
15. Please accept my felicitations on getting such a high rank/ post.
16. Our felicitations on your deserving recognition.
17. My wife joins me in congratulating you on this occasion/ your promotion.
18. Though a little late, your turn has come at last.

Give expression to your confidence in the person's capabilities to rise up to the expectations:

19. There is no doubt that you were the most deserving of all the candidates considered for promotion.
20. Greater responsibilities, of course, mean more work but I know you never shirk hard work.
21. Promotion means more accountabilities and I am sure you will be able to accomplish your tasks efficiently.
22. This promotion will, of course, mean additional responsibilities and I am sure you will discharge them efficiently.
23. You have, now, got what you deserve and I am sure you will still rise in your career.
24. It means that your organization has good faith in your capabilities and it expects more from you.
25. As you have been given a position where you have to take decisions, your responsibilities have increased, but I am confident of your abilities to shoulder them.
26. As this is a responsible post, you may have to work harder than before, but I have no doubt that you will meet the challenge and earn the admiration of your employers.

Wishing for a continued rise in the career:

27. I am sure you will continue to climb the ladder of success.
28. I wish you to add many more feathers to your cap.
29. However, take care that success does not go to your head.
30. It is just a beginning and many more are in the offing.

Talk of some bright aspects of the promotion:

31. Now, you will have to be more discreet in deciding things since so much depend upon them.
32. Your promotion has again proved that only the fittest can come up.
33. Your company has, of course, taken a very wise decision in promoting you to such a key position.
34. The Government has given due recognition to your performance by promoting you out of turn.

35. It is only a beginning and we are sure that you will keep on ascending in your career.
36. We are sure you will add more and more feathers to your cap.

Close the letter with your good wishes for the person's success in the new position:

37. Your promotion speaks itself about your capabilities.
38. This promotion was not only due, but you deserved it also.
39. I am sure you are able to meet the new challenges efficiently.
40. Wishing you the best of luck in your challenging task.
41. Hope, tolerance and foresightedness guide you while discharging new duties.
42. (I) hope you make a popular officer.
43. Our good wishes are always with you for further promotions in your career.
44. Good Luck for your future successes and keep in touch.

Dear...,

The news of your promotion has delighted all of us here.[8] My wife joins me in congratulating you on this occasion.[17] There is no doubt that you were the most deserving of all the candidates considered for promotion.[19] However, take care that success does not go to your head.[29] I hope you are able to meet the new challenges efficiently.[39] Our good wishes are always with you for further promotions.[43]

With regards,

Yours sincerely,

When you conclude a personal letter you could add usages like:

Good Luck,

Keep in touch,

Take care,

Bye,

Cheers,

See you,

- **Congratulations on Winning a Prize/ Successes/ Awards etc.:** Winning a prize is a very satisfying experience. On such happy occasions one wants one's happiness to be shared. Thus, by sharing his/her happiness you can inspire the individual to win more laurels.

First of all, express your pleasure:

1. It's very exciting/delightful to learn that you've come in the merit list of the Higher Secondary Examination.

2. The exciting news that you've won the first prize in the competition organised by the Indian Literary Academy, has filled us with joy.
3. It's very thrilling to hear that your university has named you the 'Sportsman of the Year' and awarded you a gold medal.
4. How delighted I am to know that you've been awarded the scholarship for higher studies abroad !
5. It's difficult to express in words my joy at your getting first prize in the All India University Elocution Competition.
6. I'm as happy as you, if not more, at your coming first in the International Children's Painting Competition.
7. It was really great/amazing to know that…
8. We were proud to know/ hear that you won the first prize …
9. Felicitations on your having won the first prize in the … competition.
10. We were sure that you could make it happen.

Now give your heart-felt congratulations:

11. Please accept my heartiest congratulations on this glorious achievement.
12. Please convey to your son my hearty congratulations and blessings on his great achievement.
13. Please accept my hearty congratulations on securing a higher position in the merit list.
14. My wife/ mother joins me in congratulating you on this happy occasion.

Praise his merit for winning the prize:

15. In fact, your splendid performance and the subsequent reward haven't come as surprise, because I know that you are an ace debater/painter/athlete.
16. I was sure that a brilliant boy like your son could definitely top the list.
17. This recognition of your talents was, in fact, long overdue.
18. This is another well-deserved addition to the prizes you have already won.
19. Your hard work and passion for perfection alone could bring such reward in hand.
20. It was heartening to see you rise unbeatably in the competitions.
21. You have made your parents and friends proud of your achievements.

Discuss the expected good results of winning the prize:

22. With a gold medal in hand it won't be difficult for you to manage a scholarship for higher studies abroad.
23. This award has, of course, confirmed your reputation as a writer.
24. These are the landmarks that will get counted in your long span of career.
25. Having won this high recognition, you can now make a name in the national as well as international competitions.
26. It's really fortunate of you/ You are really lucky to have won this scholarship as you will, now, be able to continue your studies without any financial difficulty.
27. With the help of the prize money/ award money, you will be able to go ahead with your creative writing without any financial problems.

28. With this excellence in debating, you might well turn out to be an important public speaker in future.

Make this occasion a source of happiness for everyone in the family:

29. Your parents must be feeling very proud of you./ You have made your parents really proud.
30. All your friends here are extremely proud of your distinguished achievement.
31. You must be feeling really proud of your son.
32. How we wish we were as talented as you!
33. My family is overjoyed at your impressive performance.

Once again, extend your good wishes at the end of the letter:

34. This is just the beginning and many such awards will follow you.
35. I wish you to add many more feathers to your cap.
36. I hope your very talented daughter achieves many such distinctions in life.
37. (I) hope you continuously strive to better your record.
38. Best Wishes for a distinguished and bright future.
39. Keep it up and you will reach the peak of fame.

Dear ...,

It is very exciting to hear that your university has named you the 'Sportsman of the Year' and awarded you a gold medal.[3] Please accept my heartiest congratulations on this glorious achievement.[11] In fact your splendid performance and the subsequent reward have not come as a surprise because I know that you are an ace athlete.[15] Having won this high recognition you can, now, make a name in the national as well as international competitions.[25] Hope this is just the beginning and many such awards will follow you.[34]

My best wishes for a distinguished and bright future.[38]

With regards,

Yours sincerely,

When you write too personalised a letter, you could use a usage like one of the following according to the context:

Congratulations...
Fabulous...!
Great...!
Wonderful...!
Amazing...!
Fantastic...!
Terrific...!
Marvellous...!
Miraculous...!

Letters of Sympathy

The tragic events/ sad occasions on which letters of sympathy are written may be classified as under:
(i) Financial loss;

(ii) Failure in examinations;

(iii) Accident;

(iv) Illness;

The emotional stress in a letter of sympathy is toned down as against the letter of condolence because the loss of property has less significance than the loss of life. Still, the reader must be able to get genuine sympathy from the letter.

The outlines of a letter of sympathy are as under:

(i) Regrets on getting the tragic/ sad news;

(ii) Happiness over saving the precious life and sustaining lesser loss;

(iii) Innocence of the reader over the event;

(iv) Enquiries about recovery/ revival;

(v) Offer of help;

(vi) Repetition of sympathies and good wishes.

Sympathy on Loss/ Damage

Start your letter with regrets on getting the news:

1. I am extremely sorry to learn that a part of your house was destroyed when the fire broke out yesterday.
2. It was very distressing to learn about the theft in your house last Monday and the loss of valuables.
3. It was very upsetting to learn about the loss you have suffered in the business deal last month.
4. How sad it was to know from your letter that recently some miscreants damaged your car while attempting to steal it.
5. I am extremely sorry to learn about the theft of your suitcase in the train.
6. I am quite upset to learn about the damage occurred to your house because of the recent earthquake/ floods/ blast in your city.
7. I was quite disturbed to learn about your loss of BHEL contract over a small technical point.
8. It is quite sad to learn about the loss of your prized lottery ticket.
9. I am sorry to know about the loss of your lovely dog, Rover.

Express your relief on lesser loss:

10. At the same time, I am relieved to learn that all of you are physically safe.
11. However, it is a matter of relief that the damage was of a minor nature.
12. It was, however, quite fortunate that nobody was in the house.

13. It was, however, fortunate that your jewellery was in a locker at the bank.
14. I am relieved, however, to see that the loss is not such that your flourishig firm cannot bear.
15. It is quite a relief to learn that police has got some clues about the theft.

Convey your belief in the reader's innocence:

16. Don't get tensed over this matter. After all it was not your fault.
17. I think with a little care you could have avoided the loss.
18. I suggest that you get your household goods insured now.
19. One could not, possibly, have foreseen such a recession in business.
20. I am sure it was none of your fault.
21. Please don't take it to heart. One should learn to take these things in the stride.
22. You must, of course, have done your best to minimise the loss.

Mention anything else of importance:

23. I am confident that your business skills will help you make up for this loss very soon.
24. I hope you have contacted the insurance people immediately.
25. I hope the health authorities in your city have taken precautions against the possible epidemic, which the floods are likely to bring.
26. The Government will certainly do something to help you and others affected by this natural calamity.
27. As your son is an engineer, the repairs of the house can be done speedily at a moderate cost.
28. Have you reported the loss to the police?

Extend your offer of help:

29. Don't worry. You have many good friends and I will be happy to be of any help to you.
30. I am sure your loss will be shared by others too.
31. May I offer you financial assistance to help you tide over the difficulties?
32. I would be happy to help you in any way on this occasion.
33. We have two dogs of excellent breed. You can take one of them.
34. You are most welcome to come and stay with us while your house is under repairs.
35. I have contacted my brother who is the IG of your city, and he has promised full cooperation.

Repeat your sympathies:

36. You have all my sympathies on this unfortunate event.
37. I feel extremely concerned about your loss.
38. Please convey my deepest sympathies on the sad event to everybody at your home.
39. My wife joins me in sending her sympathies on this sad occasion.
40. Best wishes for a quick recovery.

My dear...,

It was very distressing to learn about the theft in your house last Monday and the loss of valuables.[2] At the same time I am relieved to learn that all of you are physically safe.[10] I suggest that you get your household goods insured now.[18] Have you reported the loss to the police?[28] You have all my sympathies on this unfortunate event.[36]

With good wishes,

Sincerely,

Sympathy on Accident: Basically the contents of this letter are the same as those written on the occasion of loss or damage.

Express your grief on getting the news:

1. I am extremely sorry to learn from your father that you met with an accident yesterday.
2. It is quite distressing to learn from your brother that you had a fall and have broken a leg.
3. It is quite upsetting to learn that you had a scooter accident yesterday.
4. It was quite sad to learn that yesterday your wife suffered burns while cooking.

Sympathy on Illness: The contents of this letter are similar to those written in the event of a loss or an accident.

Start the letter with a show of your concern:

1. I am quite disturbed to learn from your brother that you have been hospitalised for quite a few days.
2. It's quite upsetting to learn that you are suffering from jaundice.
3. I am quite distressed to learn that your wife has developed post operation complications.
4. It is quite disturbing to learn that your new born baby has developed some problem.
5. It was quite disturbing to learn today that you have been down with typhoid for the last many days.
6. I was quite worried to know that you had to be hospitalised because of your liver problem.
7. It's quite shocking to learn that your brother has got tuberculosis.
8. Your chronic diabetes is indeed a source of worry to me.

Make enquiries about the treatment:

9. I am sure you are getting the right treatment from an experienced doctor.
10. Don't feel allergic towards Allopathic treatment, if you feel better than before.
11. Why don't you get yourself examined in the All India Institute of Medical Sciences.

12. I wish, the specialist you are consulting now, makes the right diagnosis.
13. Has your surgeon advised an operation?
14. Don't worry; it is a minor problem and perfectly curable.
15. You need not worry. T.B. is perfectly curable now.

Ask if you can be a source of help:

16. My wife can take care of your children while you are away in the hospital.
17. Can I be of any help as long as you are in the hospital?
18. I am enclosing a recommendation letter of Dr. Gokhale. I am sure it will help you a great deal to get good treatment.
19. I have asked my daughter to take food for your children regularly till you are in the hospital.

Repeat your good wishes:

20. We all are waiting eagerly for you to get well.
21. Get well quickly/ fast.
22. I am sure you will be back from the hospital soon.
23. We all miss you badly and are eagerly waiting for you to return from the hospital.
24. Vikas is planning to host a party when you return from the hospital.
25. Everybody in our family is praying for the speedy recovery of the child.
26. I don't think it will take more than a week to get discharged from the hospital.

My dear...,

I am quite disturbed to learn from your brother that you have been hospitalised for quite a few days.[1] Has your surgeon advised an operation?[13] My wife can take care of your children while you are away in the hospital.[16] I am sure, you will be back from the hospital soon.[22]

With good wishes,

Sincerely,

• Diary Writing • Dream Writing • Notes • Writing Experiences • Instructions • Travelogues • Memoirs

Personal Writing

Learning is a modification of views, ideas and skills. It is a continuous expansion of the mental horizon. Yes, indeed, it is a ceaseless growth. Such a collection of views and ideas come under personal writing. The most wonderful and important part of our learning is that we learn from everything – from persons of all ages and hues; places small or big; animals pet or wild; in short, everything means something. Some believe we learn from mothers, teachers, books, libraries and the electronic media. The fact is that we learn equally from friends as well as enemies. Friends encourage us and guide us, while enemies challenge us, forcing us to grow stronger and wiser. Even visiting new places teaches us something. The experiences and sights of such places must be recollected, written and stored safely. A few decades later, these will be invaluable assets. One may meet a varied mix of people wherever one goes. Such interactions enrich us and need to be noted. It is easier to write an autobiography if a person collects all diverse materials throughout life. But one should avoid writing anything negative, immoral or vulgar, even under the guise of being truthful or a realist. Never write anything you may be ashamed of in future. Writing is always for future, never for the past. Even past events and history are written for the future. Write only something worthy of being written about and useful for the future. This would include your immediate future and the distant future of children, grandchildren and great grandchildren.

Diary Writing

Some people are fond of noting down the important things that they do during the day in their personal diaries. While this may seem unimportant or trivial to others, to the diary writer it is an important activity that keeps him connected with the day-to-day happenings in his life.

Most diary writers tend to note down the events of that particular day before they retire for the night. Some are in the habit of making entries in their diary at all times during the day when opportunity permits.

The art and habit of diary writing gradually seems to be passing away with the advent of such 'online diaries' such as Facebook and Twitter, where people constantly update their timelines with whatever they have done during the day. It is possible that within a generation diary writers may fade into extinction; thanks to the popularity of online annotators.

But that will be a sad day indeed because the joy of recollecting past events through a 40- or 50-year-old diary is something that Facebook or Twitter simply cannot match. Imagine the immense delight of a son/daughter or grandson/granddaughter on discovering the diary of the father or grandfather that throws light on many untold happenings and events.

Such diaries would be like a magic gateway into the past – into a world that no longer exists and which the grandchild would never know of, except through the diary of his grandparent.

Success and Hobby: Today, I will write what I feel about my success and hobby.

I don't know whether my nature and pastime has helped me move ahead or forced me to lag behind. But one thing is for sure – despite the fact that I've not been getting the desired grades and expected percentages and my test scores are not up to the mark, I'm not worried because I feel I possess a lot of internal energy and strength and complete all tasks quite easily and mostly in time.

I have an innovative streak and can't confine myself within boundaries. I don't feel satisfied with the way words are used, ideas expressed and phrases formulated. Unusual adjectives are my specialty. I'm a thinker. It's a part of my inner being. Irrespective of the work at hand I keep on thinking about new ways and means to be adopted to accomplish something different or at least in a different way. I try to convey everything effectively.

Gardening is my favourite pastime. I love to be among colourful, fragrant flowers. I nurture them and in return I receive a lot of energy, freshness and happiness. The garden is my favourite place and flowers my friends.

I am also extremely fond of reading, a habit that I cultivated in my early childhood. There is a peculiarity about my reading habit and even the selection of books. I rarely opt for bestsellers. A few that I had read in the past appeared completely superficial. They had adventure and romance but lacked natural flow. Reading diverse material – particularly poetry, novels, stories and the daily newspaper – has given me a lot but in return has taken much of my time and kept me engrossed for long hours. Poetry purifies the soul and novels allow insights into the minds of people from all strata of society.

Some say these things have adversely affected my performance and grades, but I feel enriched. Personal satisfaction is more important than what others think of me.

Ethical Problem: It happened just last year and the memory is still vivid. When I write this, the events are playing like a new CD running live happenings. Although there is a committee to manage the Polo Games, since my Uncle has much faith in me, he deputed me to supervise the tournament and guide the participants off and on the ground. The summer vacation had just begun. I happily accepted my Uncle's offer because it gave me the chance to be at the Polo Ground and play some rounds daily. My Uncle and I are ardent Polo practitioners. It's our hobby as well as passion.

I have been passionate about horse riding and been pursuing it actively since childhood. Recently, I began playing polo too. My interest in polo developed on account of my Uncle, who owns many polo ponies and is a keen polo player.

During the League stage, though we played well, our Juvenile Team could not qualify for the Semis. But my Uncle's Team entered the Final. The Final began and within seven minutes of play my Uncle converted a nice pass into a goal. About ten minutes later, my Uncle's team was leading 1–0 when it began raining – the first shower of the season. We could not allow the match to continue as the field had turned slippery. No further play was possible.

It was easy to call off play but it was not clear who should be the winner. The team leading 1–0 had a clear edge over the other. I had to take the decision. The Umpires referred the matter to me as I was the Tournament Coordinator. This put me in a dilemma.

I went up to the mike to announce my Uncle's Team as the winner. But when I touched the cold iron of the mike, a feeling ran through my veins and I unhesitatingly declared both teams as the joint winners. The pleasure on the face of the players and spectators and the instant prolonged clapping told me I had passed the moral test when my sense of ethics was challenged. I had not missed the finer points of an unprejudiced decision.

Of course, my Uncle's Team was not pleased with the decision. But sometimes in life we have to take some decisions that are in the better interests of everyone but may not please some people. The important thing, I feel, is to make sure that we have not taken the decision with any personal bias or vested interest.

Dream Writing

There are three types of dreams: Daydreaming; Dreaming in Sleep; the Dream of Life. Daydreaming is useless imagination and pure wastage of time and energy. Don't waste time on daydreaming. Dreaming in sleep can be of two types: meaningless and meaningful. Most dreams are easily forgotten. They seldom reach the conscious memory. But certain dreams recur and can be recalled. Such dreams should be recalled and their meaning deciphered. Everything is symbolic in such dreams and is directly related to urgent steps or precautions to be taken. The dream of life is conscious dreaming; it is goal-oriented. Inner planning and hard work make such dreams come true. Most successful persons state it was their dream to accomplish something or the other. One must note down such dreams in a diary and keep adding pointers on how to realize this dream.

Daydreaming: I have enough paternal land. In four acres of land, I will get a deep and wide pond dug up. This will be a big water reservoir with drinking water as well as water for irrigation. In this pond, I will begin both pisci-culture and pearl culture. Around the pond, I will have fruit trees planted, mangoes, litchis and some herbal plants and blackberries to keep the water fresh and medicated. The villagers will receive fresh drinking water free of cost.

After two years, I will earn at least ₹ 100,000 per annum by selling the fish alone. In six years, I will earn about ₹ 400,000 annually from fruits. After 25 years, I will earn a minimum of ₹ 500,000 from big and bright pearls harvested from cultivating oysters. This will augment my earnings immensely and my family expenses will be drastically reduced due to the other produce from the agricultural land.

I'll become the richest, most-sought-after man in the area. What a bright, happy and prosperous life I will then lead!

Dreaming in Sleep: He had to reach that place. He was moving fast but it was a hot day and it was not easy to travel on the dusty road. He wished he could drink a glass of water. He decided to do so at the next temple. He heard someone asking a young man: "When will you go to the akhāra for jhandā?"

He looked behind and saw a rickshaw coming. It had no passenger. He called out but the rickshaw driver turned onto the side road. He moved ahead. Two trains were coming fast from different directions. He could be run over! He quickly jumped out of harm's way and just then, he snapped awake and realized it was only a dream.

Dream of Life: There are seasons when something appears attractive and enchanting. In the same way in history, there are phases when one or another sector has surpassed others. Today, it's the age of the IT boom and Management needs. These two sectors are amongst the most alluring careers.

I entered this arena and I'm here to stay. It's personal ambition that forces one to make better and forceful attempts, to use more energy and ingenuity for achieving a self-designated goal, to rise up and cover distances for greener avenues and new pastures. I'm sure that an MBA degree will empower me to clear obstacles and help me rise and grow. That is the reason that I'm making an all-out effort to acquire the degree.

With right earnestness, I have been making proper efforts and moving in the right direction. While studying for my Bachelor's degree, apart from general subjects, I covered Econometrics to Marketing and Sales Operations. The Course of Master of Arts in Business Management opened new and attractive vistas before me. I was deeply interested in what I had opted for and determined to prove my mettle.

Consciously, I learnt the new vocabulary, its nuances and subtleties. Each word and phrase brought novel ideas and widened my views and horizons, amply enriching me. Now, the business world is not a mysterious entity or unknown phenomenon to me. As I have done intensive and extensive research in capital market analysis applying qualitative research methods, I have a clear concept about HR management; organizational needs and strategies; finance; market manipulations and corporate governance. I know the micro and macro facts of organizational culture that will shape my success in the future.

I have already worked with one of the largest KPOs and know the roles and responsibilities, making customized sales collaterals, pricing a project and coaching and mentoring new members. It has boosted my confidence and courage, which will assist me in my task because I have both knowledge and insights.

Now that I know the business world reasonably well, I feel all the more captivated by its ups and downs, highs and lows. I want to join the MBA course in ____________ University because it is a very prestigious institution and has maintained its reputation of producing the most successful CEOs in good numbers.

It will prepare me and make me well equipped to face future challenges, solve all problems, grow to my heart's content and remain at the top level till the end as a renowned CEO.

Writing Notes

TIPS

There are three types of notes:

a) Personal notes are important personal memorandum; reminders; instructions or notes that are to be expanded later on. Such notes are for self use, written on the spur of the moment.

b) Study notes are utilized by students and scholars to remember important points while studying in the classroom. These notes are taken down instantly as the lesson is underway.

c) Official notes are put down in files by clerks for the officers to peruse and take action as required. These notes are written after reading specific papers in relevant files; after considering the applicable law and then forwarding this to the officer or senior for specific action.

Clerks undertake the job of writing notes, which is their official duty. Similarly, for students notes are important to understand lessons and to prepare for exams. The same holds true for scholars, who need notes for discussion, teaching, thinking and writing.

a) EXAMPLE **(i) Personal Notes**

- After 37 years Indane and HP Gas papers are required.
- They have asked for it, when I'm sure 70% people must have lost their papers.
- They run an office and have no paper. Why?
- Father bought the connection in 1965, much before my birth.
- Where did he keep the papers?
- It is difficult to prove that the gas connection is mine.
- I must meet Pathakji the Advocate.
- Many affidavits will be needed.
- I better get this job done right away, otherwise it will be much more troublesome later on.
- Hereafter, I will make it a point to file all my important papers in a separate folder.

EXAMPLE **(ii) Yearly Budget**

Category	Budget Amount	Actual Amount	Difference
INCOME:			
Wages and Bonuses			
Interest Income			
Investment Income			
Miscellaneous Income			
Income Subtotal			

INCOME TAXES WITHHELD:			
Federal Income Tax			
State and Local Income Tax			
Social Security/Medicare Tax			
Income Taxes Subtotal			
Spendable Income			
EXPENSES:			
Home:			
Mortgage or Rent			
Homeowners/Renters Insurance			
Property Taxes			
Home Repairs/Maintenance/HOA Dues			
Home Improvements			
Utilities:			
Electricity			
Water and Sewer			
Natural Gas or Oil			
Telephone (Land Line, Cell)			
Food:			
Groceries			
Eating Out, Lunches, Snacks			
FAMILY OBLIGATIONS:			
Child Support/Alimony			
Day Care, Babysitting			
Health and Medical:			
Insurance (medical,dental,vision)			
Out-of-Pocket Medical Expenses			
Fitness (Yoga,Massage,Gym)			
Transportation:			
Car Payments			
Gasoline/Oil			
Auto Repairs/Maintenance/Fees			
Auto Insurance			
Other (tolls, bus, subway, taxi)			

Debt Payments:			
Credit Cards			
Student Loans			
Other Loans			
Entertainment/recreation:			
Cable TV/Videos/Movies			
Computer Expense			
Hobbies			
Subscriptions and Dues			
Vacations			
Pets:			
Food			
Grooming, Boarding, Vet			
Clothing:			
Investments and Savings:			
401(K)or IRA			
Stocks/Bonds/Mutual Funds			
College Fund			
Savings			
Emergency Fund			
Miscellaneous:			
Toiletries, Household Products			
Gifts/Donations			
Grooming (Hair, Make-up, Other)			
Miscellaneous Expense			
Total Investments and Expenses			
Surplus/Shortage (Spendable income minus expenses & investments)			

b) EXAMPLE **Study Notes**

Shakespeare's RII – Act I, Sc I	
Who?	RII (1367-1400) King (1377-1399), cousin of HB, (son of Black Prince) HB (1367-1413) Henry Bofingbroke Hereford, son of JG, became Henry IV. TM (1366-1399) Thomas Mowbray, Dk of Norfolk, enemy of HS, Died exiled. JG (1340-1399) Advisor to RII, Dk of Lancaster. (4th son of Edward III).

When?	After Dk of Gloucester's death + HB became Dk of Hereford. Shortly before the death of John of Gaunt. (Late 1398 - early 1399).
Where?	Main – Treachery, enmity, image. Minor – Flattery, Trust, Forgiveness.
Action?	RII worries about treachery. HB + TM enemies, wan'na fight - claim e/o traitors to RII. HB claims TM killed Glouc. – TM denies. RII wants to settle dispute w/o bloodshed. HB + TM won't forgive e/o – must keep honour . . . concern w/ reputation RII reluctantly allows HB + TM to duel on St. Lambert's day.
Char?	RII – Appears neutral, wise monarch (so far). No vice evident yet . . . HB + TM – stubborn, Mutually hateful. Both flatter RII + worry bout image
Q:	How did Dk of Gloucester die? (RII ordered his death – cf. history) St. Lambert's day – When? (Sep 17) What symbolism? (Royal martyr, slain in c. 699 for speaking out against King Pepin's adultery.)

c) EXAMPLE **Official Notes**

The T.A. Bill presented by ____________ is in order. The required photocopies of the tickets and bills are attached, checked and found proper. The amount for the night halt has been deducted as it is not allowed in this case. There was no advance given to him.

The bill can be passed and payment made accordingly.

Sd. ________________

Date: ________________

Writing Experiences

TIPS

- When personal experiences are written in detail, it can become an autobiography or serve as one's written experiences that could eventually become an autobiography.
- Important experiences that show a major impact on one's life must be written for future reference and also for future generations.
- This is because the experiences of senior or elder persons can guide others decades later. All human experiences become a valuable guide for others to avoid similar obstacles and overcome hurdles. That is why experiences need to be written.
- Note down experiences honestly and while they are still fresh in one's mind. Half-forgotten or concocted experiences are meaningless and should always be avoided.
- Such personal experiences could later form the material for books of fiction too.

Experiences

Bad Apples in College: It is an accepted fact that college is the seat of learning, a place for character building and personality development, an institution to mould minds and shape the future generation of the country.

But this does not mean that colleges are only filled with wise and sensible people. All kinds of negative, unsavoury characters can be found among students and sometimes even among the faculty. So while some students can be extremely hard working, there are others who are downright lazy and malicious.

In the first year itself, students split up into many groups, each inimical to one another. The louts and the indisciplined can be found hanging out together outside the classrooms in bigger groups. The studious and industrious will be found studying together in class and tend to stay together even outside class. The latter are, however, few in number and usually end up topping the class during exams.

In the beginning, I used to feel sick and scared of the unruly elements – it is very risky to obey or disobey such elements. If you follow their diktats, you may end up in trouble with the administration. If you disobey, they may harass and hound you mercilessly. In short, whether you do or don't, it's Hobson's choice.

I was usually in two minds in such situations on whether to report such ruffians to the principal or not. I spoke to a few friends who were not interested in complaining and reluctant to appear as witnesses before the principal. Then I remembered the famous line of Sri Aurobindo: "The mighty perish in their might." As I recalled this, calmness descended upon me.

Soon, I realized that the rowdies don't possess the guts to learn or acquire the power of knowledge. They are rotten fruit who can't stand simple wisdom. They don't want anything to do with studies and learning. They are fearful that a simple test will have them totally exposed as ignoramuses and morons.

Years later, as I look back upon those days in college and catch up with old friends, I find that most of the studious ones have got somewhere or the other in their professional lives, making a name for themselves. As for most of the louts, they have fallen on bad times, are without worthwhile jobs or simply twiddling their thumbs at home, doing nothing. A few of them who are doing something are into unenterprising jobs or professions.

Sri Aurobindo was right – the so-called mighty goons have finally perished into mighty nothingness, while the studious are still shining brightly.

A Situation that Challenged Personal Values: Though there was no complaint against me, I was tense. It was all about a purchase I'd made. I was the one to invite quotations, inspect the wares and then approve them. I had placed the orders and made the payment. But someone else had signed the cheque.

There were rumours of unfair dealings. I knew the rumours were deliberately brought to my notice by a jealous employee of the organization. Originally, he was the candidate for the post. But the management decided to appoint a fresher. An ad was published and I was lucky to get the post. But he felt sidelined. Jealousy was the immediate result and the consequences were now apparent.

I was worried. I had no idea whether the management knew about the rumour or what they thought about it. I was worried because I felt my reputation could be tarnished and this would jeopardize a bright career if others believed the rumour. The total purchase amount was only ₹ 44,000, but it could damage my reputation irrevocably.

I thought over the matter and concluded that one factor led to this rumour. Spurious software and hardware was available at cheaper rates in the market. The original, branded software is much costlier. That may have helped him spread this unscrupulous story.

To counter the rumour, I wrote two separate letters, one to the Microsoft distributor and another to the HP distributor requesting them to send their experts to test whether the wares were genuine or fake. Their executives visited the office, inspected the wares and tested them. They declared them to be genuine. Then I asked them to quote the recent price. The total price matched that given in the bill.

The rumour was killed immediately and all suspicions about my credibility neutralized.

Writing Instructions

TIPS

- Written instructions can be given by any person for personal, professional or official purposes.
- Writing proper instructions is therefore important, particularly because today instructions are passed on instantly via emails.
- The subject, person addressed to and organization must be written at the top.
- Then instructions are written point wise or in different paragraphs and signed at the end.
- The date should be put down to keep track of when the instructions were imparted.
- Family or personal instruction can be passed on directly to the concerned person.
- Official or other instructions must be sent to the recipient through easily available means such as email, SMS, direct chat, etc.

To the DTP Operator

Dear Shweta,

Please note these points and carry out the changes accordingly:

- Two pictures of Buddha won't look good. The first picture should be replaced with something else, may be a stupa or a symbol related to Buddha.
- There should be no dash before Mahakavya. Delete it.
- Change the black background to yellow.

- ISBN number is mentioned in the Royalty Page. Please check. The book and its cover should be complete in all respects.
- What is the Font used? If you can find a more suitable font, replace this one.

Sd/-
Chief Editor

Instructions to a gardener

- Prepare the three beds in the east for plantation.
- Enrich with manure kept in the far south-western corner.
- Buy 20 plants each of chrysanthemum, dahlia and marigold.
- Plant each of them as discussed earlier in person.
- Water each sapling after planting.

Mālika

Travelogue

A travelogue is a person's account of a journey to another country or place. It can either be a written report with many factual details or a narrative story about personal impressions and experiences that is supported by images.

TIPS

1. Decide on the purpose of your travelogue. Whether it is for a magazine, for friends or just for yourself, determine your writing style.
2. While traveling, take notes about what you see, places that you visit, and people you get acquainted with. Keep a diary of your impressions. If you don't have enough time to write, perhaps a recorder would be a smart option for keeping a diary. Also, collect various brochures, tourism maps, and guides. They may come in handy when you start writing a travelogue.
3. Take as many pictures as possible. A photographer doesn't necessarily need to capture an historic or famous place. Sometimes, a photo of a crowded street, neon signboard, or an old man, conveys a stronger impression of a place you've visited than the images of monuments that anyone can see on the Internet.
4. When you return home, take time to review your recordings. Sort them out by date, personal importance, or based on any other criteria. Choose photographs which best illustrate the brightest moments of your journey.
5. Create an outline of your travelogue. This must not be a detailed report yet. The outline is necessary for you to structure your thoughts and to see if the story flows logically and is easy to understand.

6. After you've completed the outline, write the full travelogue. Try to make it as interesting as you can. Add vivid descriptions, historic and factual information, and educate your readers on the customs and traditions of the country that you've visited.

Memoirs

Writing your personal memoir can be a great way to share your story. You may have life lessons to pass on or a fascinating history to share. Even if you are not a writer, you can still create a memoir to provide a family heirloom for future generations.

TIPS

1. Start by making a list of all the important dates and events in your life. Check old records to ensure the information that you are providing is accurate. Do not dwell on too many details at first; you can always go back to things later.
2. Jog your memory by looking at old photos or reading your journals. If you find yourself forgetting significant details, these items will help you remember things more clearly.
3. Begin writing after you gather your information. When you write, you should try to focus on the big stories rather than technical details. Provide important dates, but you do not need to go into great detail about the less important stuff.
4. Be sure to include the goals that you still wish to accomplish. A memoir can be just a glimpse of your life; it does not have to be considered your entire life story.
5. Approach a publisher or place the document in a safe place. Let your family members know about it and inform them on where you plan to keep it.

List of Memoirs for Reference:

- *Dream of Our Fathers – Barack Obama*
- *Don't Call Me Mother – Linda Joy Myers*
- *Look Me in the Eye – John Robison*
- *Marley and Me – John Grogan*

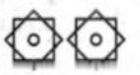

Literary Writing

• Tales, Narratives and Stories • Child Fiction • Rhymes • Verse • Poem • Fiction

TIPS

- **In literary writing, it is the writer who speaks from beginning to end, be it a story, novel, poem, epic or play. In novels, the writer may identify himself/herself with one character, which is taken as his or her mouthpiece throughout the book.**
- **The writer's beliefs are paramount for a literary creation, which holds across ages.**
- **Literary writings survive for centuries and have permanent value.**
- **The responsibility of a literary writer is therefore manifold.**
- **The writer should be well educated, experienced, with mastery over a chosen language, a robust philosophy and positive message for future generations. Only if these facts hold true should one opt for literary writing.**
- **Do not be fooled by such ads: "You too can be a writer. Take your pen; some paper and start writing. We guarantee its publication." This is simply meant to part with your money.**
- **Publication, sale and earnings are different things and the standards of literary creation are different. Many great books were published posthumously and are popular till date. Many writers acquired fame only after their demise.**
- **Literary writing should be creative and laden with eternal values. It must make and never mar.**
- **Literary writing is different from general writing in many ways. The most important difference is the depth and breadth of meaning. The other point is the use of adjectives and prepositions.**
- **One example will highlight the difference:**

Chānakya is known for:
Destroying and Creating;
Demolishing and Establishing;
Uprooting and Planting;
Over-ruling and Framing Rules;
Disturbing and Managing;
Displacing and Governing;

- In literary writing, the essence is written and the explanation is left to the discretion of readers and their capacity to analyze and extract the meaning. The deeper the meaning extracted, the greater the pleasure.
- In general writing, repetition is abhorred, but in literary writing it is exalted. Judicious repetitions enhance the meaning.

I was left alone but I was not alone. I was with trees, with leaves and fruits and grass and the living beings around. I was one with Nature, one with the Cosmos, one with the Earth and one with the sky. Then I started getting light; light from all around. It was all light. I was light. I became light. I'm light. There was light. There is light in me as much as there is light outside me. I'm still a part of the cosmic light. I was not alone, I was with light and in light; a lighted being; an enlightened one.

There was light and light and only light: light of knowledge; light of life; light of the cosmos; the light connecting the inner light with the cosmic light. It was the beginning of revelation and it lasted till the completion of awakening and even after that. The light is still in me, around me.

Then it dawned on me. It came as light. Then everything dawned on me. Then I perceived all. Then everything was revealed to me. Then I received everything. I received all knowledge. Then I received all wisdom. It was immense and infinite. It is immense and infinite. It is Truth: Universal and Absolute.

The realization of the ultimate truth of reality unfolded in stages like a lighted lotus unfurling its petals. It was the lotus of light. I had already crossed over many stages of detached and calm thinking, and was somewhere in a supra-conscious state. The chatter of mind was over a long time ago. I was somewhere in the transcended thought ready to enter the state of exalted rapture; of the purest joy and of purest and complete knowledge. It was hiding. But it opened as myriads of the lighted petals of myriads of the lotus of light.

There was peaceful upheaval; tempestuous tranquility; soundless speed of the lighted and the lighted silence of the Cosmos. All and each opened up with supernatural fastness and superb finish from the tiniest to the biggest; from me to all; from the tree to infinity. All and each came to me. I'm all and each.

Infinity was now in me. I was infinity. I'm infinity. I'm infinity with the wisdom. Wisdom will stay with me. Wisdom will live in me with infinity.

- Actually, words are not difficult or easy; they are either known or unknown. Unknown words are treated as difficult while the known words are already a part of one's thinking. It is generally believed that in literary writing unknown words are deliberately used but it is not correct. The best writing is always simple and straightforward.
- One thing is very clear: almost all the literary writers first practise hard and evolve a language and style of their own. Their way of expression; syntax; epithets are different. With that

idiosyncratic idea and style they describe a situation; a scene or a character. A conscious reader will know them, before finishing the first book of a renowned writer that he happens to read.

- Although most literary writers give conclusive endings, some writers prefer to leave the conclusion open-ended. In other words, it is left to the imagination of the readers to decide what could have happened in the end.
- But leaving endings open-ended is an art that not every author masters.
- It is best to read the works of various authors to have a better idea of how they conclude their stories.
- Keeping the above hints in mind, start writing and evolve a style of your own.

Tales, Narratives and Stories

TIPS

- At a cursory glance, stories, narratives and tales are the same or say similar things. They contain a story. Yet, there is a difference.
- Stories generally refer to modern short stories.
- Narratives basically deal with the narrative technique, which is akin to story telling.
- All narratives may not be stories.
- Tales are associated with moral tales or ancient stories.
- Generally, all three are stories that can be finished in one sitting.
- Basically in the Indian context, they originate from oral traditions when a kathā vāchak would narrate a story in a religious congregation or social gathering. During the Mughal period, the same tradition was almost overtaken by court appointed nagamā nigārs, but story telling survives.
- In oral traditions, story tellers and the listeners were face to face. According to the mood and need, the story teller lengthened or shortened the story.
- Like poems, enchantment in stories depends upon the receptivity of readers.
- Every story contains characters, dialogues and events.
- Every story shows a definite movement towards the climax. Howsoever feeble or strong, every story has a climax.
- In anti-climax stories, the climax occurs in the beginning; thereafter the events and incidents are described leading readers to the ending that has already been described in the beginning.
- Stories impart pleasure, wisdom and moral lessons. Moral teaching is the blissful characteristic of Indian stories.
- By birth and nature, Indians are natural story tellers.

Tales

Happy Work Force: One day, a person was passing through a street. A worker was breaking large pieces of stones into concrete. All the time he was saying something in a peculiar tone that combined anger and pain. Out of curiosity, the man stopped to listen to the worker. He was venting his grievances against God, society and virtually everyone. The tone was definitely abusive and there was no repentance in it.

The man went up to the worker and asked a simple question, "What are you doing?"

"Don't you see, I'm cursing my fate," was the instant reply. The tone was harsh.

The man stepped back. In the meantime, another worker passed by with an iron-basket on his head. He was whistling happily. With a jerk he threw the basket down, hurriedly filled it up with concrete chips and turned back with it, whistling the same happy tune.

The man noted the difference. The nature of work was similar. In all probability, the wages were the same. Yet one worker was cursing his fate and the other one was whistling happily.

The man waited for the other worker to return and then repeated his question, "What are you doing?"

The reply was prompt, "Oh! I'm constructing a temple." There was both pleasure and pride in the tone.

The man looked at the half-constructed temple and realized that the difference in their approach was the difference in philosophy that they followed. Their approach to the same work made them different.

Success or failure lies therein. It's not the nature of work that makes the difference. It's the approach and philosophy of a particular person that makes all the difference. Here, literacy, knowledge, wealth or poverty makes no difference.

Narrative

Lāwanyawati, the wife of Hariswāmi: Slowly and surely, King Vikram Sen reached the rosewood tree and picked up the human corpse with the laughing Vetāla in it, and put it up on his shoulder; and confidently and fearlessly, free from the feelings of carrying a dead body, walked faster but silently towards the Buddha Monk.

The Vetāla in the dead body on the shoulders of King Vikram said, "O Emperor! Now, listen to a very short story.

"There is a very ancient city famous as Varanasi. There lived a Brāhmin named Devaswāmi. He was well respected by the king. He was very rich and had a son called Hariswāmi. Hariswāmi had an extremely beautiful wife named Lāwanyawati. When the creator became wise and skilled after creating Tillottamā and other apsarās, then had He created Lāwanyawati at leisure.

One night, Hariswāmi slept with his beloved wife on the roof under the cool and soothing rays of the moon, tired after copulation. At that very night a young Vidyādhar (Genie) named Madanvega (the force of the sex god), who used to travel in the sky as he wished, passed through that roof. He saw the incarnation of beauty sleeping by her husband. He could not control his love and passion for her. He lifted her up while in sleep and eloped with her through the aerial way.

After some time, Hariswāmi awoke and did not find his beloved wife.

He was worried, "Where has she gone? Is she angry with me? Or is she hiding somewhere to watch my reaction and make a mockery of me?"

Many ideas flashed through his mind. He was thinking and searching for her at each possible place: thoroughly on the roof, in the rooms on the terrace, in the balcony, in the rooms below, in the kitchen and at other places. But he did not find her.

He came out and looked in the garden but his beloved wife was nowhere. He was desperate now. His worries had changed into fear of some terrible incident.

Out of passionate agony, he began crying loudly: "Ah! Moon-faced beloved! Where are you? Oh! With a body like the rays of the Moon! Where are you? Ah my beloved Lāwanyawati! Where have you gone? You were equal to this moonlit night in beauty so out of jealousy the night has hidden you somewhere! Where are you? The moon that used to give me pleasure with its soothing rays is now burning me like hot embers. It is imparting pain like poisoned arrows."

Hariswāmi spent that night weeping in anguish for his wife but the pain of separation failed to subside. In the morning, the Sun wiped out the darkness from the world but not from the heart, mind and life of Hariswāmi. His pitiable weeping and painful cry increased hundred-fold. His relatives tried their best to console him but he had lost his only and best possession. He was not satisfied and could not get contentment. Logic is a weak substitute for the love lost.

He was in a half-mad state. He would go to different places and remember incidents and pleasant moments that they had spent together: "I had sat with her here! We had taken bath here! Here she finished her makeup! It is here that we enjoyed and spent our leisure!" He kept repeating and crying bitterly for his lost beloved wife.

His friends, brothers and relatives gave him solace by saying, "Why are you killing yourself? She is not dead as yet so, she must be somewhere. Instead of weeping for her at this place, search for her in other places. There is no wealth greater than patience. You can get her back if you search for her patiently."

This gave him the right kind of solace. After some days, he came to his senses and decided to give away everything that he had to Brāhmins and to go on a pilgrimage to wipe away his sins. If his sins were wiped out then was a chance he can get his beloved back. Thinking along these lines, he took a bath and then decided to act as planned.

The next day he arranged a feast that was open to all. Many different delicious dishes were cooked; Brāhmins and the poor were fed well and he gave all his wealth in charity to them. He retained only a small amount of his wealth and went on the pilgrimage.

The summer came. The Sun grew hot. It's hot lion-like rays began burning and wiping out greenery from the fields. The wind too grew hotter after being touched by the hot breath of the lovers in separation. It blew hot and burnt travellers on their way. The ponds dried up. They became muddy first and then cracks appeared as the burning rays evaporated the water.

The birds cried when they found the trees and their leaves drying and withering. They expected the spring but it seemed like it had separated from the seasons. Nature was teaching them about patience and endurance.

During such a hot summer, one day Hariswāmi reached a village, burnt by the hot sun, aggrieved at the separation from the beloved wife, thirsty and hungry, tired out of traveling. He was in search of food and shelter.

He saw some Brāhmins having a meal at the house of a Brāhmin named Padmanābha. He went there silently and stood at the gate motionless, holding the frame of the door with one hand and his back touching its panel. The Brāhmin had performed some yagya and had arranged a feast for the Brāhmins.

The kind and compassionate wife of that Brāhmin thought, "O hunger is painful! It belittles all! He is someone who needs food. He is standing with his head down. He seems to have come from some distant place and seems weak. He deserves food."

Thinking so, that sincere housewife took a pot full of milk mixed with butter and sugar and gave it to Hariswāmi and said, "There is a pond nearby. Please sit there and eat this."

Hariswāmi took the pot and said, "As you wish."

He went to the pond and placed the pot under a banyan tree before entering the pond to wash his hands and legs.

In the meantime, an eagle came with a black snake caught in its talons and sat on the tree just above the pot of milk. It began eating the snake. At this time, saliva mixed with poison came out of the mouth of the snake and dropped down into the pot.

Hariswāmi washed his hands and feet, cleansed his mouth and returned back to the pot. He had no knowledge of what had happened during his absence. He was hungry and ready to eat his meal. He finished it in no time.

But immediately afterwards, he felt the burning sensation of poison. "Oh God – the sweet dish has turned to be poison for me!"

So saying, he staggered and somehow walked up to the house of the Brāhmin who had performed the yagya.

He said, "O Brāhmini! Your food has changed into poison for me! Be quick! Call someone who can neutralize the effect of the poison. Otherwise, you will be guilty of killing a Brāhmin."

The sincere housewife exclaimed, "How did this happen?"

She was restless. She called a person for his treatment. But before he was taken care of and administered medicine, the eyes of Hariswāmi turned pale and he collapsed.

The Brāhmin who had performed the yagya was very angry with his wife. Though she was innocent and had done nothing wrong, yet she was exiled.

So she decided to undertake penance at some pilgrimage site and travelled to a holy place.

After finishing the story, Vetāla asked, "O Emperor! From amongst the snake, the eagle and the Brāhmini who gave food in charity, who was responsible for the death of the Brāhmin? This was debated in the court of Dharmarāja, the god of religion, but it remained undecided. Now, O Ruler of Kings, you should state who is to be blamed for the killing of the Brāhmin! Remember, the curse is hanging there if you tell a lie despite knowing the truth."

Vikram again had to break his silence. He had heard every bit of the narrative intently. He answered honestly, "Who is to be blamed for the killing of the Brāhmin? The snake was enslaved. It was not free and an enemy was eating the snake. It can't be blamed for Brahmahatyā. The hungry eagle also did not see anything. It was trying to satisfy its hunger. It too can't be blamed. The couple or one of the two who fed a guest who came suddenly also can't be blamed because they were performing yagya and doing something religious. So they are not to be blamed. I think he would be blamed for Brahmahatyā who would blame any of these three for the death of the Brāhmin without thinking about it."

After saying this, the king was silent again.

Vetāla heard it and vanished from the king's shoulder, and went to the tree where he resided.

Short Story

Zoo Employment: An M.A. in English, a brilliant student well equipped in the art of teaching and writing, was unemployed and hungry. Before his meagre savings were finished, he had tried to get some articles published in newspapers but to no avail. He tried to give tuitions but failed to get any students.

Unemployed and hungry, he walked around in desperation and reached a zoo. Without a second thought, he entered the zoo and went inside the zoo office. He went straight to an official and said: "I'm hungry, have no money and am ready to do anything to earn enough to feed my hungry body."

The official replied: "Oh yes! There is a vacancy for a deer. You can fill it."

And the M.A. in English became a live deer in the zoo. The dress was not cozy and smooth but he did not dare complain. He was out in the wide green field among trees. Suddenly, he saw a huge lion walking towards him. He was scared like never before. He was expecting food for becoming a deer. But here it seemed he would be food for a hungry lion.

He prayed to God: "O God! Have mercy on me! I'm not a real deer. I'm an M.A. in English."

The lion walked up, hit him on the head and said: "Oh, Shut up! I'm an M.A. in Hindi!"

Child Fiction

All authors in general – and writers of children's books in particular – need advice both about writing and being published. These are different categories because there's a difference between advice to a new writer and advice to someone who wishes to get his work published.

Due to the emphasis on publishing, we sometimes forget that writing and publishing are different activities. Publication doesn't have to be the goal of all writing.

TIPS

Advice to the Writer: An aspirant should ask himself/herself a question and answer it silently. Are you ready and equipped to write books for children?

If yes, proceed; if not, read the following tips and get set for the test.

- As much as possible, read all available children's books and magazines.
- Visit libraries, school and shops to go through books.
- Build a good collection of books in your personal library.
- Read books analytically.
- Compare your writing to others' writings. Note down the similarities, dissimilarities, important points and then train your mind to catch the peculiarities as well as general patterns.
- Ponder whether you wish to follow them or create your own style. Remember: novelty is better than repetition.
- Once the first draft of your manuscript is ready, show this to children in your family or the neighbourhood. After they read it, solicit their feedback. This will give you valuable insights on how to improve it before finally submitting it for publication.

Mental adjustments are needed because books for children have to be written with a limited vocabulary. Analyse the vocabulary of kids between six and ten years of age. Then express yourself in a child's simple language.

Even simple language can be truly evocative if you master your way with words.

Children's Books: Writing children's books can be really exciting. Begin with simple stories on school events, ceremonies, festivals and functions wherein children participate. Then move on to their travels; moral tales; anecdotes; and jokes. Then move to things that improve their taste and language; things that facilitate their proper growth and make them better human beings.

You have found a whole new world and entered it. All activities are for your pleasure. Enjoy it and write for children. Don't leave anything in the middle. If you have begun then finish it. Take care of everything for improvement but never be worried about something ill-written. You have the option to throw it into the dustbin any time you want. Don't be in a hurry to throw it. Keep it. Years later, it may give you an idea for a far better piece.

Picture Books: Writing picture books can be irresistible. Most picture books are for kids between three and eight years of age. To write well for children:

1. Remember your child-self, your feelings, childhood memories, worries and pleasures.
2. Prepare your own sketches or hire the services of an amateur artist. This will cost less.
3. Create your writing time and mull about what to write, how to write and be adventurous.

4. Welcome your ideas as you would welcome a guest. Don't think negatively about anything regarding children. Avoid accidents; deaths; defeats; crimes; cheating; immoral acts. These are not proper for sensitive, eager, tender minds.
5. Read old and new picture books. Then try to change them; improve them; rewrite them, adding a few things of your own. It will hone your skill.
6. Visit bookstores and libraries. Become acquainted with the person in charge of children's books who may know about workshops, writing groups, and school visit opportunities.
7. Read books on creativity.
8. Collect fairy tales; village tales; tales of adventures; and childhood tales of various kinds.
9. Cultivate the worthy habit of revision. Repeated revisions of a story, article or book will improve the writing immensely.

Advice to Writers Seeking Publication

1. If publication is important for you, learn about the field. Find out what's being published. Read reviews of picture books and browse bookstores.
2. Picture book publishing is a collaborative process between the author, illustrator, editor, art director and, sometimes, the editor-in-chief and marketing staff. If you need total control of the process, it's best to publish your own manuscript.
3. Publishing is a business. Wonderful books get published; wonderful manuscripts don't. A publisher needs to be convinced a manuscript will sell well when it competes with 5,000 other books.
4. Be prepared for rejection and don't let it push you into dejection. Editors receive thousands of unsolicited manuscripts and good manuscripts sometimes end up being rejected too due to work pressures.
5. Collect information about catalogues of different publishers of children's books. There are specialist publishers for different types of books.
6. Know the advantages and disadvantages of small and large presses.
7. Submit your best work intelligently. Find out about the submission process.
8. Be persistent. It is not easy to ensure a manuscript is accepted.
9. Be passionate about your work. Value the process of writing and the honour of writing for children. Having a book published probably won't change your life, but being committed to writing and children could change your life and the life of your readers.

Equality and Strength: Once a rat went to a highway and as he moved along, he suddenly heard music and noise. He looked ahead. The king was sitting on an elephant and a crowd was moving towards him. The rat saw the elephant, which was moving in royal fashion. The rat imitated the elephant's movement and felt he was better than the fat elephant. He was proud of being a rat.

People were singing and dancing. The elephant was well decorated. The royal dog and cat were sitting by the king's side. The rat felt jealous of the elephant. Both had four legs and a tail, the rat thought. But the elephant's nose was too long. The rat was smart and fast, yet people were not looking at him. They were all looking at the elephant that was wearing ornaments on its forehead. It was only their size that differed. To the rat the elephant was simply a giant.

Suddenly, the rat looked at the cat and the cat also noticed the rat. The rat smelt danger and scurried away quickly into the tall grass where his hole was located. He forgot everything about being better than the elephant.

Moral: Basic similarities in organs do not mean two creatures possess equal strength.

The Travellers and the Purse: Once, two persons were travelling along a road. Suddenly, one of them saw a red silk cloth lying by the roadside. He picked it up. It was a heavy silk purse. He opened it. There was money in the purse and some precious gemstones. The finder said, "I am very lucky. I have found a purse full of money and costly stones."

The other man said, "Don't use the singular. Don't say, 'I have found a purse'; say "We have found a purse." When we are moving together, we must share the riches and face the dangers together."

"Oh no!" said the first man. "I found it and it is mine. I will not divide the riches. You have no share in it."

Just then, they saw some people come rushing towards them with thick sticks in their hands. They were looking for something. The first traveller whispered, "We are in deep trouble if they find the purse with us."

The second man said, "Don't say 'we'; say 'I'm in deep trouble."

The crowd stopped and searched both men. They found the purse on the first man and began beating him mercilessly. The other man said nothing and remained silent.

Moral: Share your good fortune and others will share your misfortune.

The Wolf and the Crane: Once, a wolf was gulping down his prey very fast when a bone got stuck in his throat. He tried hard to spit it out or swallow it in but the bone remained stuck in his throat. As a result, his throat swelled up immensely.

The wolf was in great pain. He could neither eat nor drink. He requested many animals to help him and take the bone out but none of them agreed to help the greedy and wicked wolf.

The wolf was dying. He was in a fix. He was lying on the ground. Just then he saw a crane. The crane had a long beak. The wolf thought that the crane could easily remove the bone out of his throat in a jiffy.

He walked slowly to the crane and requested it politely to remove the bone from his throat because he would otherwise be dead if the crane did not help him.

"I'll give you ample reward for your great help," he said.

At first the crane declined to do so, but the wolf seemed in great pain and in real danger of losing his life. So the crane agreed and pulled the bone out with his long beak. The wolf was relieved of the pain.

He then moved away without a word. The crane reminded the wolf that he had promised a reward if the bone was removed from his throat.

The wolf said, "It is the greatest reward that I did not bite off your head when it was in my mouth, you fool!"

So saying the wolf walked away without looking back. The crane realized he was a fool to have listened to the wicked wolf.

Moral: Never believe the wicked.

Rhymes

TIPS

- Rhymes are poems or songs for tiny tots.
- Meaningless words strung together are not Rhymes.
- Real Rhymes are meaningful.
- Nursery Rhymes are the most popular form of this art.
- While tiny tots may not understand rhymes, these are explained to them by teachers or parents.

God

Life is God and God is life;

Light is God and God is light;

Praise God and pray to God;

For all are Godly and all is God.

Incy Wincy spider

Incy Wincy spider climbed up the water spout,

Down came the rain and washed poor Incy out,

Out came the sunshine, and dried up all the rain, so

Incy Wincy spider climbed up the spout again!

Incy Wincy spider climbed up on my chair

He climbed up my arm, and then hid in my hair,

He tickled my leg, and tickled my toes,

Then Incy Wincy spider sat on my nose!

Verses

- Verses are a part of poems and songs.
- Verses are simple rhyming compositions.
- Verses are used when writing for children or writing stories.
- Verses are generally metrical and rhyming compositions.

EXAMPLE

Suggestion

"Look at the food."
The dish said to spoon:
"Green vegetables are a boon.
They digest very soon.
But cucumbers harm at noon.
Eat less to enjoy health good."

Work for Cakes

"In churches the priests and nuns
Leave the work half done;
To grant forgiveness
To free others from their sins;
With ethical means.
O father! Pray to the Sun."
Said the son:
"Work in the field and garden;
Be grain laden and fruit laden;
For eating cake and bun,
In the presence of Sun."

Thus Spoke the Thorn

A light breeze arose
And pushed a fully grown rose
Towards a mature thorn
Which felt lone and forlorn.
It pierced the petals unaware
Made the rose in dismay stare.

Then the thorn thus spoke sadly:
"Bad enough
I don't wish but I'm rough.
Meditative, relaxed, aggressive and envious;
I didn't know, it's certainly obvious
That you were so close and tender.
By nature I'm a born offender."

Poems

TIPS

- Poems are never reasoned out; they flow from the inner being.
- If the poetic sensibility is missing, a person can't become a poet despite the best tips.
- Even if a writer has poetic sensibility, practice is still mandatory to improve skills as a poet.
- Poems should be poetic, if not, it is verse.
- Even if a poem is not metrical, it should be rhythmical.
- Poetic metre depends upon the use of accented and unaccented syllables; and their alternate placement.
- Rhythm depends on its sonorous and mellifluous qualities.
- When ready to compose, arrange the essence of your thoughts in layers and compose it well in rich meaningful words and pleasant ways. Then recast it.
- Keep it hidden for sometime then read it as a reader. Mark the points you would like to change. Then read it as an unprejudiced critic and mark the weaknesses. Leave it for some time. Then, recast it as a poet.
- Read the final version once again. Only then, make it public.
- Poetry contains both words and pleasant order; it also contains ideas, emotions and wisdom.
- Poetry is high in perception, wide in attitude and deep in meaning.

- Many poets were enlightened beings, who were thereby able to write about their experiences and perceptions on a much higher plane.
- In modern times, Walt Whitman is regarded as one of the most enlightened poets in the world.
- The beauty of a poem lies in the fact that each time a person with heart and mind reads a poem s/he discovers enhanced pleasure as well as deeper and different meanings.
- Most poets look upon the art as a passion indulged in for self-expression and pleasure, not as a profession or a means of livelihood.
- Really popular poets are, however, still able to have their poems published in the form of books.
- While translations of popular poems are done, the translated poems tend to lose some of their idiomatic flavour.

Daffodils

- William Wordsworth

I wandered lonely as a cloud
That floats on high o'er vales and hills,
When all at once I saw a crowd,
A host, of golden daffodils;
Beside the lake, beneath the trees,
Fluttering and dancing in the breeze.

Continuous as the stars that shine
And twinkle on the milky way,
They stretched in never-ending line
Along the margin of a bay:
Ten thousand saw I at a glance,
Tossing their heads in sprightly dance.

The waves beside them danced; but they
Out-did the sparkling waves in glee:
A poet could not but be gay,
In such a jocund company:
I gazed–and gazed–but little thought
What wealth the show to me had brought:

For oft, when on my couch I lie
In vacant or in pensive mood,
They flash upon that inward eye
Which is the bliss of solitude;
And then my heart with pleasure fills,
And dances with the daffodils.

Poets in the Indian Context

- Treated as jewels, poets were prized possessions and regular members in the court of almost all Indian kings right up to the Mughal period. They also advised kings.
- On many occasions, Kalidas was sent as ambassador and returned successful. Such poets succeeded in securing favourable treaties and much bloodshed was easily averted.
- During the Middle Ages, the poet Rahim was made a commander in Akbar's army and successfully negotiated many tough situations.
- Mrs Mahadevi Verma was a Principal in Allahabad and a successful administrator.
- Poetess Sarojini Naidu led many regional movements against the British and eventually became the first lady Governor in free India.
- Dharmavir Bharati edited Dharmayug for decades.

Autumn Song

- Sarojini Naidu

Like a joy on the heart of a sorrow,
The sunset hangs on a cloud;
A golden storm of glittering sheaves,
Of fair and frail and fluttering leaves,
The wild wind blows in a cloud.

Hark to a voice that is calling
To my heart in the voice of the wind:
My heart is weary and sad and alone,
For its dreams like the fluttering leaves have gone,
And why should I stay behind?

Stories/Fiction

1. In writing stories or fiction, one must consider many important things such as the following:
   a) ***Plot:*** A plot is essential. Both in the shorter and longer version of stories, plots are imperative to ensure the interest of readers is held at all times.
   b) ***Theme:*** A central theme is another basic need. A plot is the larger area wherein the characters move, while the theme is the central point around which the characters revolve. The theme determines the philosophy and actions of the characters and gives readers something to think about and remain engrossed.
   c) ***Planning:*** Everything is planned in advance. A good writer leaves nothing to chance. He plans everything in detail and then begins framing the story.
   d) ***Dialogues:*** These can make or mar characters and thereby the story. If descriptive passages lay importance on some aspect of the character but the dialogues are in direct antithesis, then the story is doomed. Dialogues are written keeping in mind their relevance to the theme.
   e) ***Characters/people:*** E M Forster prefers to say "people" because all the persons in a story or novel are not characters. When they are actively part of the events, they become characters: minor or major, according to the role played. In *A Passage to India* the pankha puller is a character, although he never speaks.
   f) ***Milieu:*** The totality of the literary work creates a milieu and makes readers a part of that milieu, becoming fully absorbed in it. They identify themselves with different characters, incidents and the milieu. The more the readers are absorbed, the greater is the creation.
   g) ***Philosophy:*** Nothing can compete with the inherent philosophy of life that flows throughout a classic work. Knowingly or unknowingly, the attitude of the writer gets enough expression to be recognized easily even by those readers who have no knowledge of different schools of philosophy. Great philosophies help in inner growth, shape life as a whole and remain active even when the body perishes. Such creations are immortal.
2. Write positive things that benefit the larger societal good and ensure the work is remembered for years to come.
3. It makes little difference whether a story is short or long as long as it enriches readers.
4. A story without substance has no subsistence.
5. Positive writings improve social thinking and promote human as well as moral values.
6. Remember, during his entire writing career, Chandradhar Sharma Guleri wrote only one story titled *Usne Kahā Thā* and became immortal in the history of India's 20th century fiction.

The Cobra Couple: "Man has words and ideas. Man has spoken, written, painted and sculptured love in myriads of ways but his love is usually superfluous. It is only skin deep. He will have to learn sincerity and depth in love from the animals, particularly from snakes."

He was turning out to be a philosopher. I had said nothing to make him serious but perhaps he felt the superfluity in the house of and in the behaviour of our hosts whom he summarily rejected. After coming out of their drawing room, he said impatiently: "I'll send my sister to a poor man's house but won't allow her to come to these fellows. They will need a few centuries to become civilized." He may have been carrying that bitterness.

"How can animals, particularly deadly snakes, teach us love?" I laughed sarcastically.

He didn't say anything for quite some time. Then he asked me to stop the car at a cigarette shop. Fortunately, there was a tea stall and juice stall where I had stopped the car.

He asked me: "What would you like: tea or juice?"

"Tea…"

He went out, ordered tea, bought a packet of cigarettes, returned back, opened the windows, settled inside, took out a cigarette, lit it, took a few puffs and said: "I'll tell you a story; not exactly a story but an incident. It happened when I had just entered college and had no faith in any supernatural elements. Modern science has divided our faith. We are neither faithful nor faithless. What I saw and heard shook me hard.

"My sister is married to a teacher who has a flour mill in Aranyarāja. It has an ancient and famous temple. It is said that Lord Krishna asked the Pāndavas to pray to Lord Shiva in this temple when they were spending the last days of their exile. They had taken shelter in Champakāranya, which was under the rule of Maharaja Virāt at that time. As a woman Arjuna fought a battle.

"It was Sunday. I was on the way to my sister's place. It was the month of Shrāvana. There was a light drizzle. I was enjoying the chlorophyll-filled paddy crops that seemed to be savouring the rain more than me. They were literally 'tossing their heads and dancing in the breeze'. A huge gathering on the road ahead disturbed the dreamy sight. They were looking towards a paddy field. I followed their gaze. I saw a cobra with its hood half raised. It was restless. It moved its head from side to side. It was looking towards the crowd but not in a particular direction. Suddenly, I spoke without thinking.

"It just came out of my mouth, 'The cobra is dancing.' Many men looked sharply at me. A senior person said, 'No, she is weeping.'

"'Why?' My question was natural.

"'Don't you see? Her husband is lying by her,' he retorted.

"Then I surveyed the place. Up till now I had seen only the snake with raised hood. For the first time, I saw a large dead snake lying beside the other living snake. I looked at the man questioningly.

"In reply, he said angrily: 'Man has invented guns. He carries it for his protection but every time he is hunting innocent animals. In this case, a man took his gun out and killed one of the pair while they were copulating. He killed the male and when the female chased him, the coward fled in his jeep. She then returned back to her dying husband. But she has seen his face in the eyes of the male. She will definitely find and kill him.'

"Both the anger and pain were clear in his emotional voice. I looked towards the coiled cobra that was protecting the dead body of her husband.

"How do you know that it's a female cobra? It could be the male," I asked.

"'She is smaller and her hood is not so wide. She has not that bright colour of her husband on her head. Though dead yet his head is glowing,' he explained.

"I remained there for about an hour. People praised her love for her mate and were angry with the man who killed her companion. It is said that cobras wait for 12 years to take revenge. We forget our dead after 12 days. It is said that snakes have photographic lens in their eyes. The face of the killer is printed on the retina and that picture file is transferred to the mate's eyes. She would now know the killer. Will she succeed in taking revenge?

"She remained in my mind. I was still thinking about her strange behaviour when I reached my sister's place. As I began narrating the tale to her she looked up sharply. She had heard about the incident and gone to see the snake. My sister mentioned that the killer was Ramāyana Singh.

"I knew Ramāyana Singh well. A rich farmer and wrestler, he was extremely rude. He had shown his rough tongue and uncivilized behaviour when we had met for the first time. But later, he became friendly towards me. As I was talking to my sister, he landed up.

"Without replying to his rough greeting, I asked him a straight question, 'Why did you kill the cobra?'

"He sheepishly confessed: 'I don't know. I had not seen the female snake. I only saw the cobra. He saw me, raised his hood and hissed. For a moment, I was afraid. But the next moment I took my loaded gun, aimed and fired. Then I saw her. She first went to the cobra, touched him, and found that he was dead. She then turned towards me, hissed hard and rushed towards me. I ran to my jeep and returned home. Since then I'm living like a fugitive. I feel I'm a murderer. I have heard a lot about her. I have thought about killing her to end her suffering but failed to muster enough courage. Someday I'll gather enough courage and kill her.'

"He wiped away sweat from his brows. My sister brought a glass of water. He took it, drank the contents and left the place.

"The next day, I was ready to return. Just then there was some uproar. People were rushing in one direction. Someone cried aloud: 'The Nāgina has bit Ramāyana Singh.'

"We were stunned. We too joined the rush. Just then a person came from the site. He was almost breathless. He stopped and said hurriedly: 'Ramāyana Singh was going to the temple for poojā. When he reached there, he saw the Nāgina and decided to kill her. He stopped the jeep and came out with his gun. The paddy had grown higher. He was able to see her but unable to take good aim. People tried to stop him. But he was determined to kill her. He took his shoes off, crossed the ditch onto the embankment, took aim and shot her head off. Her headless body danced for some time. Slowly, it stopped moving. Even the movement of the tail stopped.'

"Ramāyana Singh had returned, worn his shoes and was looking at the dead cobra. People began returning but no one liked his heinous crime. He boarded his jeep. But suddenly he complained that something was pricking his toe. He stepped down from the jeep. He removed his right shoe and turned it upside down. The head of the Nāgina tumbled out. By God's grace her head had landed into his shoe. She had then stayed alive till she bit him. He could not stand up. He sat down and fainted. Foam began coming out of his mouth. The snake-bite experts arrived. They began treatment but his condition deteriorated fast."

He stopped and then began speaking again, "Fear and wonderment were written on all the faces around Ramāyana Singh. It was not only extraordinary but supernatural too. It was not easy for the shot head to fall directly into the shoe of the killer. The paddy crop would not have been a great hindrance. He could have still shot her from there. What compelled him to take his shoes off? What gave him the idea of crossing over to the embankment? Revenge and death must have been secretly conspiring against him; otherwise, there was no need to go there to kill her. Strange are the ways of Nature! Stranger are the means of divine justice!

"Another man came and announced his death. The sound of loud crying confirmed the death. We went to see him for the last time. On my way to the bus stop, I stopped near the field where the cobra couple was first spotted."

He took a long and deep breath and then fell silent. He took out another cigarette.

I opened the other door of the car, brought a bottle of water for him and ordered two more cups of hot tea. Both of us needed it badly.

Novels/ Fiction

TIPS

1. Novels are fictional prose narratives of considerable length and complexity, dealing imaginatively with human experiences via a connected sequence of events involving a group of persons in specific settings.
2. The genre encompasses a wide range of types and styles: comic; romantic; social; political; biographical; realistic; historical, etc.
3. The typical elements of a conventional novel are the plot, character, setting, narrative method, point of view, scope, myth and symbolism.
4. A novel differs from short stories in that short stories focus upon a single significant episode, event or scene, involving a limited number of characters, while novels have no such limitation.
5. Novels are not bound by economy of setting and concise narration.
6. Characters in novels are fully developed via many different actions and dramatic encounters.
7. A novel concentrates on creating, developing and explaining the mood as well as the story and its events, describing them in longer, painstaking detail.
8. Novella or novelettes are shorter forms with a compact, pointed plot, often realistic and satiric in tone. These are often based on local events, individual tales or tales gathered into collections.

9. A novella or novelette is used to describe a work of fiction of intermediate length and complex in nature. It falls between a short story and a novel.
10. Anti-novels are a type of avant-garde novels that depart from traditional novelistic conventions, ignoring elements such as the plot, dialogue and human interest.
11. Anti-novelists deliberately avoid intrusion of authoritative personalities, preferences or values trying to overcome readers' habits. They do it to challenge the expectations of readers.
12. The term 'anti-novel' was coined by Jean-Paul Satre in 1948.
13. Hindi novels too have their own charm, particularly novels by Ajneya; Jainendra; Premchand; Phanishwar Nath Renu; Yashpal; Bhagawati Charan Verma; Bhagawati Prasad Bajpei; K M Munshi; Rangeya Raghava; Chatursena Shastri; Bimal Mitra; Chanakya Sen; Shankar; Mahashweta Devi; Shivani; and Hazari Prasad Dwivedi.
14. It is best to read these novels in Hindi. Translations of novels and stories usually tend to lose their flavour because some words and phrases simply cannot be translated accurately or convey the full meaning of the original version.
15. Begin writing a novel only if you have much to offer to the posterity. If not, confine yourself to story writing.

Famous novels for reference:

Wuthering Heights by Emily Brontë
Vanity Fair by William Makepeace Thackeray
Oliver Twist by Charles Dickens
Pride and Prejudice by Jane Austen
Picture of Dorian Gray by Oscar Wilde
Frankenstein by Mary Shelley
Man in the Brown Suit by Agatha Christie
The Godfather by Mario Puzo
The Good Earth by Pearl S. Buck
The Time Machine by H.G. Wells
The Room on the Roof by Ruskin Bond
The God of Small Things by Arundhati Roy
A Suitable Boy by Vikram Seth
The Namesake by Jhumpa Lahiri

• Scriptures Writing and the Scriptures • Hymns & Psalms

Spiritual Writing and the Scriptures

TIPS

- Spiritual writings are often considered scriptures, but they are different. Spirituality is personal growth and scriptures are general instructions believed to be dictated by God or messengers of God or by godly figures. All scriptures are sacred books, but all spiritual writings are not sacred.
- The youngest scripture is the Guru Granth Sahib in Gurumukhi, the scripture of Sikhism.
- One can create and foster spirituality internally. Know the Self and the Cosmos to be spiritual.
- The entire cosmos is a configuration of triple energy or triple form or tri qualities. It is another tri, tri-guna or tri-qualities – Tamas, Rājas and Sattva – that deals with lower, middle and higher character; mundane, royal and pure; physical, mental and spiritual. It shapes the mind, character, growth and progress of a person. It determines one's yearning and the changes that occur.
- We always grow from within. But only the outer growth is noticed and the inner growth missed. Spirituality is the belief that all our strength lies inside because of the divinity within us.
- The growth seems to be in fractions or parts but this is not so. We are divided into infinite fractions. Modern scientists call them cells, which exist in all organs in different systems. All the systems are one system; though divided, the body is one system like the cosmos. The rishis knew this and taught us: *yat brahmānde tat pinde* – whatever is there in the cosmos is there in the body. But ordinary people don't realize this truth.
- Our body is not all that we possess. The body is only the outer garb for inner life – Prāna Tatva, the living spirit and soul. Besides the physical body, we possess an immensely powerful 'Spiritual Self'; that is the life and 'I' of each person.
- In the words of Swami Vivekanand: "Always think of the body as your house. The people and the world are all absolutely unreal like a dream. Always think that the body is only an inert instrument. And the Ātman within is your real nature."
- Each one has a body but no one is the body. The body is not the person though it belongs to the person. The person is neither his/her hands nor legs; neither head nor toe; neither intestine nor

heart. S/he pervades all: the whole body. As the pervading entity in the body s/he is a soul. Each one has a soul but s/he is not the soul. A person is both the body and the soul in it. So each one possesses and belongs to both his/her physical self and spiritual self: Body and Soul.

- The dilemma of modern humans is that we cater only to physical needs and ignore the spiritual need. As a result the body, wealth and luxury grow, but the soul weakens and becomes empty.
- The body is not life, but there is life in the body.
- We are not the body in which we are. The body is needed to foster the life-force, i.e., Prāna Tatva or Spirit, the ātmā or the soul to be more precise; for its growth, development, refinement and possible salvation, Moksha, freedom from the endless cycle of birth-death and birth or rebirth. In that sense, all our births are rebirth.
- Whenever we are miraculously saved, it is said to be a rebirth. For that very purpose of growth, refinement and salvation, one must keep the body healthy and fit to perform greater and wholesome deeds to take care of all sorts of life on the Earth: both human and non-human. That is the purpose of life.
- Ancient rishis said the body is a vehicle and important only as a vehicle on the way to spiritual realization and salvation.
- Human beings' primary identity is with the spirit and not the body. Maintaining a fit and healthy body is a requirement for the eternal spirit, so that it can achieve mystical union with the Ultimate Reality – the Absolute God or the Brahman.
- Self or Soul is the spirit that transcends the body. Self is a part of the Absolute God. The Self never dies. It takes rebirth, rather many rebirths. In this sense, it is eternal as death can't touch it. Eventually, it merges with the Brahman and is freed.
- Meditate and feel all these things by yourself to be spiritual.

Born, Ruled, Died: There was a king who wished to know how other kings ruled and what great things they did that they were loved and respected by their subjects and were immortal. In a few years, his learned historians and litterateurs collected and brought a cartload of books before the king.

"Oh no! I can't read all these books. Write it in short so that I may finish it," he said.

A few years later, the learned men brought 15 volumes for him to read.

"Oh no! I can't read all these books. I don't have many years before me. Write it in short so that I may finish it," he looked longingly at the lovely leather-bound books.

Some years later, the learned men brought three volumes for him to read.

"Oh no! I've grown quite old. I can't read all these books. Write it in short so that I may finish it."

After some years, the learned men brought the summary in one volume for the king to read. But he was on his death bed. His minister came to him with the book. He touched the book remorsefully and said: "Oh no! I can't read the book. It is my time for departure. Yet I want to know what they did. Please tell me in short."

"All the kings were born, they ruled and died," the minister said. But the king was not alive to hear this.

Perform as many righteous deeds as possible without waiting for an auspicious time to begin. Time is fixed and once lost can never be regained.

Ungovernable Temper: A Zen Master was delivering a lecture on self-control. When the lecture was over, a new Zen student came and told the teacher: "Master, I have an ungovernable temper. Help me get rid of it."

"You have something strange," said the teacher. "It is not healthy to possess an ungovernable temper or be possessed by one. Are you sure you have an ungovernable temper?"

"Yes Master," the student accepted candidly.

"Then show it to me," the Master told him.

"Right now I cannot show it to you."

"Why can't you?" the Master asked.

"It arises suddenly."

"When it arises suddenly at some instigation, incident or unknown entity, then it cannot be your own true nature," said the teacher. "If it were, you would be able to show it to me any time. Why are you allowing something that is not yours to trouble your life?"

Thereafter, whenever the student felt his temper rising, he recalled his teacher's words and controlled his anger. In time, he developed a calm and placid temperament.

Tranquility can be maintained as insights are developed and attained with the right approach and positive attitude.

Spiritual Thinking: 'There is God' and 'Does God Exist?' are two different aspects of the same truth. One will have to show the existence of God in order to deny His existence but the first expresses faith while the latter expresses doubt and faithlessness.

There is nothing new in this question. Since primeval time, the existence of God has been simultaneously accepted and denied. Indian Demons or western Satans have always denied God and fought against godly figures, while the general masses and the wise have accepted and worshipped God. After Darwin's theory of evolution, a dangerous gulf was created between scientific doubt and religious faith. Western mind is torn between the two and at present there is demand to teach both the Scriptural Truth and scientific truth in classrooms.

It's easy to deny God in the age of complete faithlessness. It's really a challenge to impart faith to such people. There must be an effort to empty the mind and hearts of modern humans first and then fill it with God and Faith. Modern man needs faith, and a lot of it. Tied fast to the useless pillar of materialism; humans are accelerating development but destroying nature.

The view "Is there God?" would have been most welcome had this been raised with open-mindedness. Without open hearts and open minds, humans will never discover the Ultimate Truth.

The Principle of Dharma: Sharman, the King of Vidarbha, was facing various problems. Many border provinces were revolting and declaring themselves free from the Vidarbha kingdom. King Vidarbha did not wish to crush rebellions through war by killing thousands of men and turning many citizens into widows and orphans. But this was considered to be his weakness.

The king was against severe punishment, particularly death sentence. Due to this, many subjects lost their fear of the king and stopped paying taxes. So, although expenses remained the same, income was drastically reduced. Consequently, even royal officials gained in strength and were doing as they pleased. Activities of physical pleasure grew in and outside the palace and spirituality was sacrificed for petty gains.

In such a scenario, the king once saw immense light before him and felt the presence of some divine being. With folded hands, he bowed before the deity and asked: "Who are you and what do you want?"

"Rājan, I'm your Rāja Laxmi! I'm not feeling comfortable here. So I'm deserting you," the deity replied.

In the same soft voice, the king replied: "As you wish Māte!"

And the Goddess of Wealth and Prosperity left him.

Another day, a different deity appeared. After a similar exchange between the two, this deity also deserted the king. One by one, all the deities deserted the king.

One night, another deity appeared. Now, the king knew that this deity would also desert him. But for his satisfaction he asked: "Who are you and what do you want?"

"Rājan, I'm Dharma! All else have left you. I too want to go away!" the deity replied.

The king protested: "How can you desert me? I have been righteous! I have done nothing wrong! I've always followed your dictates! No, you can't leave me! When the others left, I said nothing, but I can't be separated from my Dharma! You can't go! Please stay back."

The king was right. He had done nothing immoral, unethical or unrighteous. Dharma accepted this contention and replied: "*Yathā Astu*! As you wish!"

He returned and did not desert the king. Since Dharma was with the king, Laxmi returned. One by one, other deities also returned.

Dharmah Rakshite Rakshatih! Protect Dharma and you will be protected by Dharma!

Hymns and Psalms

TIPS

- When poetry exhibits balance, control, faith and hope, and exudes sweetness, fragrance and absolute pleasure, it becomes a Hymn or Psalm.
- Hymns are composed mostly on God or religious and spiritual topics but Psalms can be composed on anything with the above conditions and qualities.
- Hymns and Psalms contain religiosity, righteousness, morality and spirituality.

A Hymn to the Absolute God

Bless this Earth, O Lord! We pray,
Keep it rich and free from decay. Bless…

Bless the creatures unwilling and weak,
Keep the greenery so feeble and freak.
Peace everywhere pleasure must stay. Bless…

Give us wisdom and a heart that feels,
Body strong and a mind that heals,
Able to live together and play. Bless…

Save us all from ego and arms,
Less high roofs, many rich farms,
Rays only soothing and pleasant bay. Bless…

A Psalm to Present-Day Life

Life of a man was lighted vane.
Life of a man is the darkest lane.
Don't be a writer or pleader very great,
Live with love but not with hate.

Be a man loving and humane,
Not a beast cunning and profane.
Life of a man was lighted vane.
Life of a man is the darkest lane.

Don't be a trader or business tycoon,
Don't finish riches of the Earth so soon.
Be her child stout and sane,
Grow not enmity, grow only grain.
Life of a man was lighted vane.
Life of a man is the darkest lane.
We cut ourselves with each green tree,
We are imprisoned with each bird free.
Deeds of men are really bane.
Humanity is in a state of wane.
Life of a man was lighted vane.
Life of a man is the darkest lane.

Whether the winter or the spring,
Music eternal flows from within.
Be the tune of showering rain,
Pure from beginning and without stain.
Life of a man was lighted vane.
Life of a man is the darkest lane.

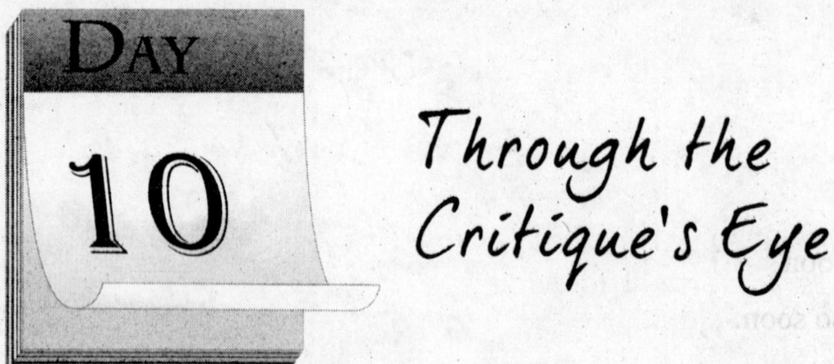

Through the Critique's Eye

• Preface/Foreword • Preview • Review • Analysis

Preface/ Foreword

TIPS

- A Preface is also referred to as a Foreword, Prelude, Introduction, Prologue or Preamble.
- Before writing a Preface, the entire manuscript should be read closely and important points, salient features, highlights or inconsistencies marked.
- Idiosyncratic ideas and other points should also be flagged off as these are to be highlighted in the Preface.
- Peculiarities of the work, individual style and other novelties should be included in the Preface.
- The Preface should be short, precise and well written.
- The Preface writer should not talk about himself or herself. That is digression. Concentrate on the manuscript and its writer.

Preface

After much deliberation, consultation and analysis, this series of Short and Complete Dictionaries was carefully planned and meticulously prepared with the sole aim of helping users by giving them something really handy. It can be placed on reading tables or carried anywhere easily. Each of them will become a companion, a true friend and guide.

All the expert editors of the team are masters in their respective field and experienced writers. They have given time and completed the cherished project with the full attention, alertness and diligence at their command. The entries have been wisely selected and liberally explained. As a result, each Dictionary in this Series contains all the words related to and used in the course of learning and teaching that subject and using them in talks, articles or writing books.

These will be the prized possessions of students, teachers and scholars alike; and, accordingly, are essential for every library.

This series contains separate dictionaries on the following very important subjects:

Computer	**Difficult words**	**Education**
Geography	**History**	**Library**
Management		

We proudly hand over the series to the readers for their use.

—Chief Editor

Foreword: Prof. Shrikant Prasoon was my classmate and colleague. I know him since 1962. We collected our B.A. Hons. Degrees together from M.S. College, Motihari and worked together for more than a decade in S.N.S. College. In 1985, he was transferred to L.N.D. College but we have attended numerous meetings and functions together and organized many, both separately and in collaboration. He is a very diligent and intelligent person.

Apparently, Prof. Prasoon has read a lot; numerous books in Hindi, English, Sanskrit and Bhojpuri. He has a rich library of his own. Undoubtedly, he has understood and digested them well. He is an able thinker and can easily and meaningfully co-relate different ideas. He says he has a weak memory and does not rely on it so much, so he hurriedly writes the ideas that crop up in a diary or on a pad. But I feel he has a lively, sharp memory and collects material painstakingly.

Happily, Prof. Prasoon has an idiosyncratic style of expression: both oral and written. He is a great orator and prolific writer. With such inner power and knowledge, he has been able to write great books that are really very useful to all. Moreover, he has a definite and humane purpose behind the creation of each work. He tries to bring all closer to Nature and to save the natural wealth and ambience for better growth, healthy living and a happier future.

Prof. Prasoon's Netaji Subhash Chandra Bose is a small but complete book. The presence of the towering personality of Netaji is the specialty of the book. Netaji may not be in the world but he is in the hearts and minds of people, which is more important than the physical presence. Netaji was a great patriot and visionary. He tirelessly tried to transform his vision into reality. His greatest contribution is that he created a strong pedestal for us and gave us the will to stand erect and hold our heads high. The patriotism that suddenly enters our blood the moment his name is mentioned is an apt tribute to his personality that is well presented in Netaji Subhash Chandra Bose.

I congratulate both the writer and the publisher for bringing out such a book.

—Prof. Ram Niranjan Pandey
Retired Reader
The Department of Political Science
Motihari

Preview

TIPS

1. Check if you have read the same author earlier to highlight his other works.
2. Assess the author's writing style and mention that in your preview.
3. Mention the plus points of the book in terms of how it can appeal the readers and the visibility in the market.

After reading the manuscript of *Iron Lady: Mrs Indira Gandhi* by Prof. Shrikant Prasoon and completing the Preview of the book, I began reading another manuscript of his ready for publication. This was *Netaji Subhash Chandra Bose*. I liked his spirit and attitude. I have seen and felt the nationalist feelings in his songs and the cultural programmes he arranged every year on 25th of December.

After finishing this manuscript, I came to the conclusion that Prof. Prasoon is bent upon reminding modern Indians that the rich cultural heritage, great civilization, unfathomable knowledge, learned men and political heroes of this country are something to be proud of.

Prof. Prasoon has worked with me for more than 20 years. I've heard him on many occasions and read several books of his. It's difficult to say whether he speaks better or writes better. He has command both over his tongue and fingers. His expressions are very apt and appropriate.

In *Netaji Subhash Chandra Bose* it is very clear that Prof. Prasoon adores Netaji. Prof. Prasoon has intelligently, diligently and truthfully presented his views and painted different facets of Netaji's personaliy. He has clear conception about his great deeds and achievements. So, he has written the book with ease and dexterity. He is a disciplined writer and maintains the rhythm he starts with. He has an uncanny ability to finish a book in his own way and before expiry of the deadline that he himself fixes.

I'm confident that like his other books, Netaji Subhash Chandra Bose will be welcomed, enjoyed and appreciated by national and international readers.

—Prof (Dr) SNP Sinha
Retd Head of the Dept. of Political Science
L N D College
Motihari
Bihar

Reviews

TIPS

- Reviews are written in much the same way as Previews.
- The major difference is that the Preview is written before the publication of the work and Reviews are written after its publication.
- The other difference is that a Preview is always appreciative of the book and rarely critical, while a Review can be appreciative as well as critical, highlighting the minor and major shortcomings of the book.
- In both writings, one must concentrate only on the author and the contents of the book.
- In both, extraneous or irrelevant matters are not included.
- Both must contain some citations from the book.

Gulliver's Travels: There are few great satirists who manage to judge their work so finely that it can be considered both a rip-roaring, fantastical adventure story suitable for children and adults alike, as well as a searing attack on the nature of society. In *Gulliver's Travels*, Jonathon Swift has done precisely that, and has bestowed upon us one of the great works of English literature in the process. A tale recognised far more widely than it is read, the story of Gulliver–a traveller who is, in turns, a giant, a tiny figure, a king and an idiot–is both excellent fun, as well as thoughtful, witty and wise.

Swift has a deft eye for an excellent image, and an uproarious, often bawdy sense of humour. In writing Gulliver's Travels, he has created a legend which endures up to our times and beyond.

The Jungle Book: *The Jungle Book* is one of the works for which Rudyard Kipling is best remembered. The Jungle Book falls in line with works like Flatland and Alice in Wonderland (which offer satire and political commentary, underneath the genre title of children's literature). Likewise, the stories in *The Jungle Book* are written to be enjoyed by adults as well as children–with that depth of meaning and symbolism that delves far beyond the surface.

Relationships and events related in *The Jungle Book* are important to any human being, including adult men and women, with or without families. While the tales can be read, or children may listen to them from an older reader, these stories need to be re-read later, in high school, and again in later adult life. They are enjoyable in every subsequent reading and the longer one lives, the broader is the frame of reference one has against which to draw the stories into perspective.

The Kipling stories offer a marked perspective of a reminder of human origins and history as well as animal. As the Native American and other Indigenous Peoples often state: All are related under one sky. A reading of The Jungle Book at age 90 will reach several more levels of meaning than a childhood reading and both are just as brilliant an experience. The stories can be shared inter-generationally, with interpretations shared by all. The book is a group of stories that are actually quite good for "Grandparents in the School" types of family literacy programmes of the current day.

Analysis

TIPS

- An analysis must be three-dimensional. All three dimensions of the topic should be considered, analyzed and posited in a balanced way without prejudice to any side even when outlining one's views.
- Social, political, religious, scientific, environmental or economic – all sorts of problems should be analyzed in the same manner.
- If one cultivates the habit of balanced analysis, one could easily analyze and deal successfully with one's own general and specific problems: personal, familial and social.
- While considering different dimensions, the points should be noted and compared before the final write-up.
- Analytical language should be brisk and showcase in-depth knowledge. Without this, an analysis is superficial.
- Never write an analysis on anything where one's knowledge is lacking.

Cell Phone Use Risks Impotence . . . Avoid Mobiles to Remain Potent: Excessive use of mobile phones over the long term could make people infertile and unable to bear children. This fear was not unfounded and confirmation has come from the WHO (World Health Organization), which said cell phone radio frequencies and electro-magnetic fields (EMF) could cause brain tumours and in some cases turn men infertile.

The radiation from electronic equipments – particularly mobiles, computers and TV – are dangerous and said to affect many organs. Apart from the above ailments, loss of hearing is another danger.

After a recent global survey, the WHO classified radio frequency and EMF as being "carcinogenic to humans." In other words, cancer causing. Even prolonged low exposure to such electronic gadgets can cause headache; difficulty in concentration; behavioural problems as well as emotional disturbance in children, adolescents and adults too.

A committee has recommended revision of the levels of non-ionizing radiation emitted by cell towers 24x7. Small birds and bees are said to have been badly affected by such radiation, with some species hurtling to extinction. For example, once present across India in the thousands, sparrows are no longer as visible as they once were, with EMF radiation being cited as one of the major reasons for their precipitous decline over the past two decades.

Accordingly, doctors and healthcare experts recommend that people should not use mobile phones continuously for long hours. Instead, all calls should be kept as short as possible. If long conversations are unavoidable, these should be made from landlines as far as possible. Moreover, when speaking on mobiles, people should keep varying usage between the right ear and the left, rather than speaking from one side only.

The harmful health effects of radiation could be prolonged and chronic, warn the experts, with children being more susceptible.

The Effects of Caste-based Reservations: Reservations are a complex, longstanding problem in India. It is difficult to present all these issues in one article. Sections of society have been equally divided into protagonists and antagonists when it comes to the issue of reservations. More than six decades after Independence, it makes little sense to continue with this practice in a major way, but due to various pulls and pressures, no political dispensation dares to restrict only to the deserving the benefits of this practice that has been having a major impact on society.

While there is no doubt that reservations for the truly downtrodden and below-the-poverty line sections should continue for some more time, it is counterproductive to have reservations for various groups who possess the wherewithal to compete with others on a more or less equal footing but still seek to capitalize on reservations to gain an unfair advantage over others. While equality and rights for all are cherished human values, the better-off sections should not be allowed to exploit a system that is actually meant for those who are indeed deprived.

By bringing sundry sections under the ambit of reservations, a disservice is being done to a principle meant for the really deserving. In this way, merit takes a backseat and undeserving candidates end up filling many seats and denying the truly meritorious their rightful place under the sun.

All five fingers will never be equal and this should not be the goal of any dispensation. We must remember that heterogeneity bears fruits while homogeneity remains infertile. It is important to let all sections bloom in their own way and have an opportunity based upon merit to rise in society. But this is not possible when a majority of seats are reserved *en masse* for various sections in society simply because they fall under some category or the other that may have historically been deprived but today are no longer so.

In such situations, it is important to take into consideration the true status of people at this point in time, rather than going by yardsticks and definitions that may long since have become outdated.

This will serve the interests of the large majority and the larger good, rather than pandering to the interests of select groups. Curbing undue reservations is one of the many steps we need to take to make certain India becomes a truly egalitarian and fair-opportunities society that does not deny or debar the truly meritorious simply because they do not come under one category or the other.

Imaginative Writing

• Features • Speech Writing • Drama/Plays • Monologue • Songs • Satire/Humour/Lampoon

Features

TIPS

- **In feature writing, characteristics as well as special and distinctive parts are included to present a full perspective about an important news or topic.**
- **Feature articles are used in newspapers and feature films are based upon such stories.**
- **Features are presented to emphasize something special about the subject.**
- **In features, important aspects must be focused on, emphasized, highlighted and promoted.**
- **Never write a feature story without collating all the facts or without proper planning and sequencing.**
- **A feature must include all aspects; attributes; characteristics; circumstances; details; facets; traits and other qualities, if any.**

Yoga: The science of Yoga is one of several unique contributions of India to the world. It seeks to discover and realize the Ultimate Reality through yogic practices. Yoga is one of the six systems of Indian philosophy, *Bhārtiya Darshan*. Today, Yoga is practiced worldwide and numerous changes have been brought about and new names given to some select *asanas* of this ancient, most dependable practice.

Known for its physical and intellectual aspects, Yoga is essential both for physical and mental wellbeing; for peace and prosperity in life and personal growth in religion and spirituality. Holding the view that the world was created in stages, Yoga attempts to reverse this order so that a person re-enters his or her state of purity and consciousness. It may require several lifetimes to pass through this.

Ācharya Patanjali – the founder of Ashtānga Yoga – hailed from the district of Gonda, which was called Ganara during ancient times and is in present-day Uttar Pradesh. With his immaculate achievement of creating a system for the betterment of human life, he became a Maharishi, and is revered for the invaluable gift of Ashtānga Yoga. He prescribed control of Prāna (life-breath) as the means to control the body, mind and soul. This helps a person gain skills as well as think and work in a balanced way. Good health and inner happiness then follow.

Ācharya Patanjali's 84 yogic postures effectively enhance the efficiency of the respiratory, circulatory, nervous, digestive and endocrine systems, as also that of many other organs. Yoga has eight limbs where Ācharya Patanjali shows the attainment of the ultimate bliss of God in Samādhi via the disciplines of yam, niyam, āsan, prānāyām, pratyāhār, dhyān and dhārna. These seven limbs lead one to successful Samādhi, whereby one is united with the Absolute Cosmic Power.

In its eight limbs, the first two stages are ethical preparations emphasizing morality, cleanliness and devotion to God. The next two stages are physical preparations that condition the body to make it supple, flexible and healthy. The fifth stage involves control of the mind and senses to withdraw from outward objects. The remaining three stages entail the cultivation of increasingly concentrated states of awareness, which ultimately lead to release from the cycle of birth-death and rebirth.

The practice of Yoga has gained global popularity because of its scientific approach and direct benefits. Yoga holds an eminent place as one of six philosophies in the Indian philosophical system. Ācharya Patanjali will forever be remembered and revered as a pioneer in the science of self-discipline, happiness and self-realization.

Satellite Collisions in Space: On 10 February 2009, two communication satellites collided in orbit. It was the first clash of its kind that occurred in space and was caused by the fault of scientists who could neither control one of the satellites nor pass on the information to the other country. The news came long after the disaster and the date and time of collision was not mentioned in the newspaper. The scale of this crash was unprecedented.

But it is not the first collision and definitely not the last one. In 1996, French Spy Satellite Cerise was hit at a speed of 50,000 kmph by a wheeling fragment left from an exploded Ariane Rocket. In June 1983, the windscreen of US space shuttle Challenger was chipped by a fleck of paint measuring only 0.3 mm that hit it at a speed of 4 km per second or 240 km per minute.

The present collision occurred nearly 800 km over Siberia. This collision involved a US Iridium Commercial Satellite, which was launched in 1997, and a Russian Satellite Cosmos 2251, which was launched in 1993. The Iridium satellite weighed 560 kg and the Russian satellite nearly a tonne. It is claimed that the Russian satellite spun out of control. The claim was made by an orbital debris scientist, Mark Matney of the Johnson Space Center in Houston. They had no idea about the number of pieces created by the collision. It could have been hundreds or even thousands.

Scientists accepted the fact that they knew what was going to happen. Yet neither Russia was informed nor any efforts made to avoid the collision. They perhaps wanted to witness the effects of the collision. If so, it can be deduced that the collision was planned.

When the satellites collided, instantaneously a cloud of debris shot forth, posing risks even to the International Space Station. The United States refused to give details on the pretext that the damage was yet to be assessed. NASA (US National Aeronautics and Space Administration) stated, "It will take weeks to determine the full magnitude of the crash."

A computer image of the debris floating in the sky was issued and shown on select channels and published in chosen newspapers. People neither got a good view nor came to know fully about the incident.

According to the European Space Agency, there are 12,000 man-made objects in orbit around the Earth. Another report says that the number of man-made debris in space is around 17,000. Watchdog group Space Security Index says that there are more than 300,000 orbital objects and billions of smaller pieces.

The particles of debris travel at immense speeds and carry enough energy to wreck a satellite or depressurize a spacecraft. Debris in orbit keeps increasing day by day. It includes micro-particles, massive fuel tanks, drifting derelict satellites, parts of spent rockets, pieces from satellites or pieces of final stage launchers that either disintegrated or exploded as some fuel may have been left in it. A report claims that orbital debris is now the biggest threat to satellites, surpassing the dangers of liftoff and return to earth.

In this scientific world, humans may never sleep in peace and security.

Pune: Real Estate and Education

Real Estate in Pune: In the year 2006, six government properties in Mumbai were sold for more than ₹600 crores each. Soon there was a boom in the real estate markets in Mumbai and Pune. The latter is growing faster and prices of residential and commercial plots, apartments, and shops in and around Pune are soaring.

Yet more people are trying to purchase property in Pune and its suburban areas. The reasons for the growing interest are the serene, clean atmosphere, proximity to Nature, the opportunity for work and business, expected high returns from property and, above all, the fact that Pune is fast becoming India's Educational Capital.

Educational Pune: As a result, students from all over the country and across the globe are streaming into Pune in droves. The more the students, the greater the number of faculty and resources in education management, and the more the infrastructure needed to accommodate the influx of people and the need to arrange classes as well as hold extracurricular activities, including sports and athletics.

Many constructions have been completed in record time and more are progressing in full swing. The need for libraries and auditoriums is also being felt and construction work has begun.

Combined together, all these have transformed Pune and the suburban areas into colourful, delightful and active hubs. Pune shows its firm faith in *Vasundhavai kutumbakam* or universal brotherhood, and is proving to be one place that can represent humans all across the globe.

Restructured Pune

The areas where construction is at its peak, where the population has multiplied in the last few years and where all sorts of property are in great demand include: Law College Road; Talegaon; Baner; Kalyani Nagar; Kondhwa; Kothrud; Aundh; Kharadi; Pimple Nagar; Vishrant Wadi; Wagholi; Bavdhan; Hadapsar; Mukund Nagar; Chichwad; Unri; Wakad; Bhandarkar Road; etc.

Amongst these places, Kothrud stands out for its advantageous position. A suburb in the southwest of Pune, it is close to the city centre. This explains its explosive growth and why it is termed the fastest developing suburb in India. Many housing finance companies and banks are offering home loans on easy terms.

Last year, many Non-Resident Indians (NRIs) visited Pune. Most were seeking information about buying property. That gave birth to a new concept called the NRI Lounge, floated by a property dealer.

Speech Writing

All forms of written communication have their specific do's and don'ts. Speech writing is no exception. While writing a speech for oneself or on behalf of another, it is important to bear three points in mind: the theme or topic, the target audience and event for which it is being prepared, and the time allocated for the speech.

Besides the above, a writer should also bear in mind whether the speaker is a male or female, because the gender could change the tone of a speech. It is also important to be aware about the background of the speaker. If the speech is being written for a celebrity, business person or a politician, it would be in the fitness of things to study all the past speeches of the speaker in order to ascertain his or her bent of mind.

Apart from the theme, you will also need to ask the speaker whether s/he has any specific talking points or key messages, which you should focus upon while drafting the speech. If the key messages have not been ascertained in advance, despite writing an excellent speech, you may find that the speaker tells you to rewrite the entire speech because it does not flow as per the key messages s/he has in mind.

The purpose or event for which the speech is being written as well as the target audience it will be delivered to happen to be equally important. For instance, although the topic and speaker may be the same, the speech may take on totally different overtones depending on whether the target audience is male or female, students or business persons, etc. Every speech has to be written taking into account the target audience and the event in question.

With all the above points taken care of, the speech needs to be drafted with a passion and a purpose that may not ordinarily be present in other forms of writing. For example, if you are writing for a politician who is preparing to fight the upcoming elections, the speech will need to be extremely assertive, with phrases that would seem hyperbolic in other forms of writing but are not at all out of place during an election campaign. Anything short of that will make the masses think the leader in question won't be able to deliver, since s/he lacks the charisma and assertiveness to tackle tough issues.

Naturally, such a speaker needs to come across as lively, assertive and self-assured, which can only happen if the speech is imbued with passion and purpose.

A speech that is written without taking all the above points into consideration is likely to be rejected or may end up being revised repeatedly. Once you have followed the above pointers and prepared the first draft of the speech, note down the specific lingo or phrases that the speaker favours by reading and rereading his/her past speeches.

Thereafter, edit and revise the speech by incorporating the speaker's favourite words or phrases in the speech. More often than not, the speaker will be pleasantly surprised to read your first draft and may very likely approve the first effort with minimal or no changes.

Be sure you do not exceed the time limit by a wide margin. Depending on the style and speed at which the person speaks, you will have to accordingly limit your word count. A 10-minute speech, for instance, should not exceed a one-and-a-half page. Bear in mind that the person will not read the speech at breakneck speed, but interject it with normal pauses while establishing eye contact with the audience or emphasizing specific points.

Also ensure you do not include jargon, uncouth words, sexist terms or other politically incorrect phrases that could embarrass the speaker or antagonise the audience. Any facts or figures quoted in a speech would need to be substantiated to the speaker separately via footnotes or comments that do not comprise the main text of the speech. This ensures that in case there are questions after the speech, the speaker will be able to field queries even from combative members of the audience who may seek to belittle or disprove any assertions in the speech. If you are unsure about a particular fact, howsoever outstanding it may seem, do not use this under any circumstances as it could backfire later.

The Greatest Speeches of All Time: Some of the best speeches ever delivered have been those that came from the heart and made an instant connect with the audience. While writing speeches, the writer should therefore make it a point to place himself/herself in the shoes of the speaker and imagine oneself making the impassioned speech that is now being written.

Amongst some of the greatest speeches of all time are • Abraham Lincoln's Gettysburg Address delivered on 19th November 1863 (which inspired • Dr Martin Luther King Jr's speech more than a century later); • Winston Churchill's Inauguration Speech, delivered on 13th May 1940 (when it seemed Great Britain was in danger of being overrun by German forces during World War II); • Swami Vivekananda's Chicago Address made before the World Parliament of Religions, Chicago on 11th September 1893 (introducing the salient features of Hinduism to the world); • Mahatma Gandhi's Mumbai Address made before the AICC on the eve of the Quit India Movement on 8th August 1942; and • Jawaharlal Nehru's Midnight Speech addressed to the Indian Constituent Assembly just before India's Independence on 14-15th August 1947.

In the new millennium, two speeches that have acquired iconic status are • Barack Obama's Audacity of Hope speech made on 27th July 2004 at the Democratic National Convention in Boston (which he delivered as a candidate for the Illinois US Senate) and Apple founder • Steve Jobs' Stay Hungry, Stay Foolish speech made on 12th June 2005 as a commencement address at Stanford.

To inspire aspiring speech writers, two iconic speeches have been reproduced below, one by Swami Vivekananda (unedited version) and the other (edited version) by Dr Martin Luther King Jr., both of whom inspired the entire world by the sheer power of their oratory.

Swami Vivekananda's Welcome Address – Chicago, 11th September 1893

Sisters and Brothers of America,

It fills my heart with joy unspeakable to rise in response to the warm and cordial welcome which you have given us. I thank you in the name of the most ancient order of monks in the world; I thank you in the name of the mother of religions, and I thank you in the name of millions and millions of Hindu people of all classes and sects.

My thanks, also, to some of the speakers on this platform who, referring to the delegates from the Orient, have told you that these men from far-off nations may well claim the honour of bearing to different lands the idea of toleration. I am proud to belong to a religion which has taught the world both tolerance and universal acceptance. We believe not only in universal toleration, but we accept all religions as true. I am proud to belong to a nation which has sheltered the persecuted and the refugees of all religions and all nations of the earth. I am proud to tell you that we have gathered in our bosom the purest remnant of the Israelites, who came to Southern India and took refuge with us in the very year in which their holy temple was shattered to pieces by Roman tyranny. I am proud to belong to the religion which has sheltered and is still fostering the remnant of the grand Zoroastrian nation.

I will quote to you, brethren, a few lines from a hymn which I remember to have repeated from my earliest boyhood, which is every day repeated by millions of human beings: "As the different streams having their sources in different paths which men take through different tendencies, various though they appear, crooked or straight, all lead to Thee."

The present convention, which is one of the most august assemblies ever held, is in itself a vindication, a declaration to the world of the wonderful doctrine preached in the Gita: "Whosoever comes to Me, through whatsoever form, I reach him; all men are struggling through paths which in the end lead to me." Sectarianism, bigotry, and its horrible descendant, fanaticism, have long possessed this beautiful Earth. They have filled the Earth with violence, drenched it often and often with human blood, destroyed civilization and sent whole nations to despair. Had it not been for these horrible demons, human society would be far more advanced than it is now.

But their time is come; and I fervently hope that the bell that tolled this morning in honour of this convention may be the death-knell of all fanaticism, of all persecutions with the sword or with the pen, and of all uncharitable feelings between persons wending their way to the same goal.

Excerpts from Dr Martin Luther King Junior's speech at the March on Washington, 28th August 1963; the spellings in the speech are as per American English.

I am happy to join with you today in what will go down in history as the greatest demonstration for freedom in the history of our nation.

Five score years ago, a great American, in whose symbolic shadow we stand today, signed the Emancipation Proclamation. This momentous decree came as a great beacon light of hope to millions of Negro slaves who had been seared in the flames of withering injustice. It came as a joyous daybreak to end the long night of their captivity.

But one hundred years later, the Negro till is not free. One hundred years later, the life of the Negro is still sadly crippled by the manacles of segregation and the chains of discrimination.

One hundred years later, the Negro lives on a lonely island of poverty in the midst of a vast ocean of material prosperity.

One hundred years later, the Negro is still languishing in the corners of American society and finds himself an exile in his own land. So we have come here today to dramatize the shameful condition.

In a sense, we have come to our nation's capital to cash a check. When the architects of our republic wrote the magnificent words of the Constitution and the Declaration of Independence, they were signing a promissory note to which every American was to fall heir.

This note was a promise that all men, yes black men as well as white men, would be guaranteed the inalienable rights of life, liberty, and the pursuit of happiness.

It is obvious today that America has defaulted on this promissory note insofar as her citizens of color are concerned. Instead of honoring this sacred obligation, America has given the Negro people a bad check, a check which has come back marked "insufficient funds." But we refuse to believe that the bank of justice is bankrupt. We refuse to believe that there are insufficient funds in the great vaults of opportunity of this nation. So we have come to cash this check — a check that will give us upon demand the riches of freedom and the security of justice. We have also come to this hallowed spot to remind America of the fierce urgency of now. This is no time to engage in the luxury of cooling off or to take the tranquilizing drug of gradualism. Now is the time to make real the promises of democracy. Now is the time to rise from the dark and desolate valley of segregation to the sunlit path of racial justice. Now is the time to lift our nation from the quick-sands of racial injustice to the solid rock of brotherhood. Now is the time to make justice a reality for all of God's children...

...I say to you today, my friends, even though we face the difficulties of today and tomorrow, I still have a dream. It is a dream deeply rooted in the American dream.

I have a dream that one day this nation will rise up and live out the true meaning of its creed: "We hold these truths to be self-evident: that all men are created equal."

I have a dream that one day on the red hills of Georgia the sons of former slaves and the sons of former slave owners will be able to sit down together at a table of brotherhood.

I have a dream that one day even the state of Mississippi, a state sweltering with the heat of injustice and sweltering with the heat of oppression, will be transformed into an oasis of freedom and justice.

I have a dream that my four little children will one day live in a nation where they will not be judged by the color of their skin but by the content of their character.

I have a dream today.

I have a dream that one day, down in Alabama, with its vicious racists, with its Governor having his lips dripping with the words of interposition and nullification, one day right there in Alabama little black boys and black girls will be able to join hands with little white boys and white girls as sisters and brothers.

I have a dream today.

I have a dream that one day every valley shall be exalted, every hill and mountain shall be made low, the rough places will be made plain, and the crooked places will be made straight, and the glory of the Lord shall be revealed, and all flesh shall see it together.

This is our hope. This is the faith that I go back to the South with. With this faith we will be able to hew out of the mountain of despair a stone of hope. With this faith we will be able to transform the jangling discords of our nation into a beautiful symphony of brotherhood. With this faith we will be able to work together, to pray together, to struggle together, to go to jail together, to stand up for freedom together, knowing that we will be free one day...

Drama/Play

TIPS

- Plays have much in common with fiction writing.
- Like them they are divided into symbolic plays, comedies, tragedies, historical, imaginative, psychological and political genres, etc.
- The big difference is that dramas are written in dialogues, brief descriptions, a line or two of a scene being given before the beginning and the characters being mentioned.
- The story moves and the characters, situations and events are described only via dialogues. If the dramatist wishes to convey something only to the audience and does not wish to inform other characters on stage, he writes this in brackets (or aside) before the character reveals it on stage. The other characters then ignore the statement as though they never heard it.
- In plays or dramas, everything is conveyed and expressed via dialogues or monologues or what the character says to himself and aside for the audience.
- Dramas are written in Acts; preferably three or five Acts. The Acts can have many scenes. Acts can be compared to sections in a book, while scenes can be compared to chapters.
- The number of scenes in an Act can vary.
- There are many One-Act Plays. Such plays can be easily staged.
- A One-Act Play can have many scenes but remains confined to the central topic.
- A drama can be compared to a novel while a one-act play is like a short story.
- Suitability for stage presentation is the acid test of a drama.
- Since plays are usually presented within three hours, the story begins and ends within the shortest span of time. They cannot linger for days, weeks or months. This is known as the **Unity of Time.**
- With plays being presented on one stage at a specific place, the scenes or Acts can't occur at different places and are so written as to be confined to one place. This is known as the **Unity of Place.** Houses and streets can change but the Unity of Place is always maintained.
- Unmanageable stage scenes such as those of a battlefield or big congregation or riots, etc. can't be presented on stage. Information regarding such scenes is, therefore, conveyed to the audience via characters and dialogues. This is known as **Unity of Action.**

- The three Unities of Dramas must be maintained.
- Dramas are based on dialogues. Dialogue writers are crucial for dramas. Practice writing dialogues as outlined earlier and then begin writing plays.
- Read a few dramas in Hindi and English to understand them well and get fully acquainted with the art of writing them.
- Hindi dramas have a classical form and most of them maintain the Unity of Time, Place and Action while there are variations in European dramas and most of their plays have failed to maintain the three unities. Even tempests, suicides and murders have been shown on stage.
- Before venturing to write dramas, one must read as many dramas as possible to become acquainted with the art of writing them.

List of famous playwrights and their plays:

1. *A Doll's House – Ibsen*
2. *Wating for Godot – Samuel Beckett*
3. *Halfway House – Mohan Rakesh*
4. *Ghashiram Kotwal – Vijay Tendulkar*
5. *Famous plays of Shakespeare*

Monologue

TIPS

- Monologues are long dialogues delivered to oneself.
- Monologues can be informative and instructive.
- Monologues may be confined to a specific topic or situation.
- If a single actor speaks in different voices, it is mimicry, not a monologue.
- A monologue may reveal the inner character of the speaker.

The famous Monologue from Shakespeare's play Hamlet:

To be, or not to be: that is the question:

Whether 'tis nobler in the mind to suffer

The slings and arrows of outrageous fortune,

Or to take arms against a sea of troubles,

And by opposing end them? To die: to sleep;

No more; and by a sleep to say we end

The heart-ache and the thousand natural shocks
That flesh is heir to, 'tis a consummation
Devoutly to be wish'd. To die, to sleep;
To sleep: perchance to dream: ay, there's the rub;
For in that sleep of death what dreams may come
When we have shuffled off this mortal coil,
Must give us pause: there's the respect
That makes calamity of so long life;
For who would bear the whips and scorns of time,
The oppressor's wrong, the proud man's contumely,
The pangs of despised love, the law's delay,
The insolence of office and the spurns
That patient merit of the unworthy takes,
When he himself might his quietus make
With a bare bodkin? who would fardels bear,
To grunt and sweat under a weary life,
But that the dread of something after death,
The undiscover'd country from whose bourn
No traveller returns, puzzles the will
And makes us rather bear those ills we have
Than fly to others that we know not of?
Thus conscience does make cowards of us all;
And thus the native hue of resolution
Is sicklied o'er with the pale cast of thought,
And enterprises of great pith and moment
With this regard their currents turn awry,
And lose the name of action.--Soft you now!
The fair Ophelia! Nymph, in thy orisons
Be all my sins remember'd.

Songs

TIPS

- Like other literary writing, composing songs needs some special qualities and language skills. Knowledge of music; singing; and the ability to play different musical instruments are added qualities.
- Songs can be sung with or without musical accompaniment. It is, however, easier to sing songs when music plays in the background.
- Songs may be traditional, folk or love songs or even simple lyrics.
- Songs were earlier passed on through oral traditions, which are still popular.
- Today, songs are mechanically recorded on cassettes, CDs and DVDs.
- Good songs mostly express emotions.
- In India, Hindi Bollywood songs have ruled public imagination for decades.
- Up to the 1970s, Hindi songs were mostly composed by shayars (poets), which is why melody ruled supreme.
- Thereafter, the shayars faded or retired and the era of geetkars (song composers) began.
- Poets wrote refined songs with in-depth meaning, working days and weeks on one song.
- Lyricists or song composers of today are known to compose songs while travelling and even waiting in airport lounges for their flight. Such songs naturally lack true meaning and depth.
- That is why modern song can't hold a candle to pastoral or folk songs, some of which were sung by village ladies to celebrate different occasions, particularly marriages and harvests.
- Classical songs were patronized by the elite who knew and appreciated the art.
- Song writing has today largely been reduced to a commercial proposition, which is why melody has taken a back seat in most cases.
- Aspiring song writers should aim to become shayars rather than geetkars; this is the only way true melody can be reintroduced into songs.
- The quality of songs has deteriorated so much because the focus is on quantity not quality, since the late 1970s.
- The senseless focus on quality can be gauged from the fact that former Bollywood singer Kumar Sanu entered the Guinness Book of World Records in 1993 for having sung and recorded 28 songs in a single day!
- This feat was achieved because Kumar Sanu was going on a month-long singing tour, so all his music directors and producers wanted to complete their pending songs before he left.

Satire/ Humour/ Lampoon

Satire is one of the most difficult type of humour to write because unless you are witty and full of humour, it could even get you into serious trouble.

1. A satire is a literary work holding up human vices and follies to ridicule or scorn.
2. An effective satire points out how stupid, ridiculous or silly someone or something is in the garb of humour. The readers have to read between the lines to understand the connection.
3. A satire can be in the form of an essay, poem or even a short novella.
4. Pick your subject carefully. The more visible and serious the target is, the easier it is to satirize them.

EXAMPLE

Dryden's "Mac Flecknoe," a masterpiece of satire: John Dryden wrote "Mac Flecknoe" to satirize another English writer, Thomas Shadwell (1642-1692), author of eighteen plays and a small body of poetry. Dryden and Shadwell had once treated each other amicably but became enemies because of their differing views over many things particularly because Dryden was a Tory; Shadwell was a Whig.

Mac Flecknoe

All human things are subject to decay,
And, when Fate summons, monarchs must obey:
This Flecknoe found, who, like Augustus, young
Was call'd to empire, and had govern'd long:
In prose and verse, was own'd, without dispute
Through all the realms of Non-sense, absolute.
This aged prince now flourishing in peace,
And blest with issue of a large increase,
Worn out with business, did at length debate
To settle the succession of the State.
And pond'ring which of all his sons was fit
To reign, and wage immortal war with wit;
Cry'd, 'tis resolv'd; for nature pleads that he
Should only rule, who most resembles me:
Shadwell alone my perfect image bears,
Mature in dullness from his tender years.

Shadwell alone, of all my sons, is he
Who stands confirm'd in full stupidity.
The rest to some faint meaning make pretence,
But Shadwell never deviates into sense.
Some beams of wit on other souls may fall,
Strike through and make a lucid interval;
But Shadwell's genuine night admits no ray,
His rising fogs prevail upon the day:
Besides his goodly fabric fills the eye,
And seems design'd for thoughtless majesty:
Thoughtless as monarch oaks, that shade the plain,
And, spread in solemn state, supinely reign.

• News • Reports • Articles • Editorials • News Releases or Press Releases • Obituary/ Condolence • Columns

Useful Information on Media and Newspapers

- A person who writes for newspapers is called a journalist and one who reports for the electronic media is called a reporter.
- Journalism is an extremely popular and respected profession.
- Journalists are the torchbearers of the fourth estate or fourth pillar in the modern age of information.
- During the last two decades, journalism has grown fast because of computerized printing as well as the rise of the electronic media.
- Today, the online or digital media is also making its presence felt across the world which includes web portals, Facebook and Twitter.
- Writing for the media can be extremely gratifying because publication, broadcast, telecast or upload happens within hours or days.
- Depending on their forte or specialization, journalists work on specific beats.
- Every form of writing is in demand across various avenues of the media.
- With the rise of mobile phone cameras, citizen journalism has become popular, whereby people shoot pictures the moment something unfolds before their eyes and send this to the media.
- But fabricating news is not correct. Researching and collecting information and news is the proper way to rise in journalism. Those who take shortcuts lose creditability.
- Besides this, shortcuts in journalism can also land a person in jail. A news reporter of a West Bengal news channel was jailed after it was discovered that he had instigated some rioters and hoodlums to assault a girl while he supposedly shot this 'live' for his channel. One of the assailants included a person known to him and that is how the entire conspiracy was uncovered.
- As journalists, it is important to develop written and verbal communication skills.
- There are courses, diplomas and degrees that enhance one's skills as a journalist. A higher salary is assured with such qualifications, since it reduces the practical learning curve.
- Freshers out of college and without specialization in journalism and mass communication are also hired by the media, albeit at lower salaries.

- Such persons join as trainees and are then trained on the job.
- Some freshers are hired as interns and may or may not receive a stipend during the internship.
- Do remember that there is a great difference between a career in print journalism and one in the electronic media.
- While careers in the electronic media can pay twice as much or more than the print media, the job is more hectic, with six-day weeks being the norm and in some cases even a full week.
- Careers in print journalism can be less strenuous but would again depend on whether one is working for the mainstream media (daily newspapers and business or political magazines, which could be weekly, fortnightly or monthly) or the non-mainstream media (niche magazines and trade publications that are usually monthly or fortnightly).
- The mainstream print media adheres to a six-day week, while the non-mainstream media usually follows a five-day week.
- The mainstream print media naturally pays higher salaries since the deadlines and work pressure are much higher here.

News

TIPS

- Whatever the topic, a news item is brief and to the point. Longer news is usually published as an article or feature story.
- There are limited pages for articles and feature stories in newspapers.
- Most of the pages are devoted to general, local, official, social, political, religious, state, national and international news.
- Entertainment news is usually carried in separate colour supplements.
- While reporters and journalists contribute the news, it is the Sub-editor, Copy Editor or Desk Editor who edits and rewrites the reports to make them suitable for printing.
- All news should be true and verified before being published.
- Printing the wrong or incorrect news and then issuing denials in subsequent issues tarnishes the creditability of a periodical.
- The size and placement of the news item depends on its importance.
- News items that are too long are edited by the desk editors as per the space available on a specific page.
- As a freelance journalist, it is best to study the paper, its writing style and preferences so that the news item could be written accordingly and assured of publication.
- Sometimes news reports are commissioned and accepted by periodicals but still not published due to space constraints or other issues. In such cases, the freelance reporter or journalist is still paid remuneration, which is termed a 'kill fee'. But this is usually less than the actual remuneration paid for published reports.

Rig-Veda: The First Scripture: Recently, the UNESCO declared Rig-Veda as a World Heritage. It is good news for humanity that the first Scripture that deals with the eternal religion has been recognized by a world body. The reason for this is because the Rig-Veda (and the Vedas) are not meant for a specific sect, caste or community – they are addressed to all human beings as they reveal the Universal Truth.

The Rig-Veda revealed the Universal and Eternal Truth about the Brahman, the Creator; the Absolute Almighty God; who is Formless and Foremost. The Almighty pervades the entire Cosmos and reveals Himself in the Ātmanah, which means He is at the core of everything in this realm. He is nāpti and niyantah, the Subtlest and the Largest Infinite Entity of the Cosmos; the Satyam, Gyānam, Ānanadam Brahman: the sat chitta ānand Brahman; eko devo sarvabhuteshu. He is One God of the Cosmos; eko aham bahushyam; He is One who became many.

The concept of such an Absolute, Almighty God is common to all religions of the world.

Death Penalty for 16 December Perpetrators: After a long wait of nine months, the perpetrators of the 16 December assault and rape of a paramedical student have finally been sentenced. As expected, the judge has sentenced four of the accused to death, while one committed suicide in his cell a few months ago while the trial was underway.

The sixth accused was not tried along with the rest simply because he happens to be a minor and accordingly cannot be tried and sentenced as per adult laws. He was separately tried and handed over a three-year sentence, which he has to serve in a Juvenile Justice home. Having already served almost a year, the youth should be out after a couple of years.

The 16 December rape-cum-murder of the paramedic student, who has been christened Nirbhaya (fearless) by the print media, has become a turning point of sorts for such heinous crimes. The general outcry across India has meant that the laws have been repealed so that the perpetrators of rape will no longer get away lightly. Depending on the severity and depravity of their crime, they can end up spending their life behind bars, even if they do not end up being hanged to death.

There has also been a clamour amongst many sections of society seeking to change the laws that govern juvenile criminals. This is because many cases have occurred in the recent past, whereby young under-aged criminals have taken advantage of their minor age to commit heinous crimes, secure in the knowledge that they were protected by law and would not have to undergo stringent punishment in jail but instead spend three years or less in a remand home.

Recently, quite a few murders and rapes have been committed by minors who were smug about the fact that they could not be arrested and tried as per regular laws. But such minors have been turning out to be a menace for society. In many cases, the crimes these juveniles have perpetrated are against minor girls and boys.

It is imperative that misguided activists speaking up for juvenile criminals realize that the lives of innocent law-abiding minors and other citizens cannot be endangered by criminal juveniles who have no compunction in killing, raping and maiming.

The other specious argument extended is that many of these juveniles happen to be from impoverished backgrounds and may themselves have been brutalized as children. Again, it should be clear to all citizens that past poverty or suffering cannot give a licence to some minors to take the law into their own hands and wreak vengeance on others.

There is no justification whatsoever for the oppressed to themselves turn into oppressors. And in situations where they do, they should have to face the full music and let not so-called mitigating circumstances be allowed as fig-leaf excuses.

In fact, in many countries, juveniles face stricter punishment when they commit heinous crimes. Moreover, unlike India, not everywhere is the age of a juvenile defined as those below 18 years. The age limit for juveniles in India needs to be lowered and the definition altered in case of diabolic crimes.

Only if such changes are brought about in the Indian Penal Code will women, children and others become truly safe from criminally-inclined juveniles who will stop at nothing to get what they want. Again, it should be reiterated that poverty and past suffering cannot be a blanket excuse or mitigating circumstance in such situations.

Reports

TIPS

- A report is a factual description of an issue, problem or an incident; or an objective evaluation or analysis of an event, celebration, survey or an accident.
- It contains details of what happened as well as where, when and how it happened.
- It contains details of rescue and relief in the case of an accident, flood, fire or other natural or manmade calamity.
- A Report on events/functions/celebrations contains details of the following:

Name and Nature	Occasion	Date, Time, Place, etc.
Chief Guest	Inauguration	Activities
Message	Prizes, if any	Vote of Thanks

Format of a Formal Report:

- Sender's name and designation
- Receiver's name and designation
- Date, Place, Heading
- Body of the Report: Introduction; Content; Major Events; Other happenings; End of Events; Conclusion (with recommendations for action required).
- Sender's Signature, Name, Designation.

Types of Reports:

1. Cultural Function/Book Release/Sports Meet
    - Occasion, Organiser, Sponsor

- Date, Venue
- Chief Guest, Crowd, Participants, Speakers
- Highlight of the Programme
- Annual Report/Prize Distribution
- Specialty
- Message by the Chief Guest, Dignitaries
- Vote of Thanks

2. Accident/Calamity/Robbery/Disturbances
   - Headline as the title
   - Occasion, Reason, Motive
   - Brief details
   - Casualties, damages, etc., if any
   - Witness accounts
   - Relief needed and provided, if any
   - Steps taken
   - Conclusion
3. Exhibitions/Visits/Camps
   - Place, Person, Occasion
   - Organiser, Sponsor, if any
   - Duration, Date
   - Presence, participation, visitors
   - Description in brief, as applicable
   - People's response
   - Conclusion. Success or Failure
4. Competitions
   - Occasion, Organiser, Sponsor, if any
   - Date, Venue
   - Nature, Objective
   - Chief Guest, Crowd, Participants, Speakers
   - Highlight of the Competition
   - Prize Distribution
   - Specialty
   - Message by the Chief Guest
   - Special Remarks
   - Vote of Thanks

5. Workshops/Seminars/Debates/Recitations by Poets

- Why? What for? For whom? By whom?
- Date, Venue
- Nature, Objective
- Chief Guest, Crowd, Participants, Speakers
- Happenings/activities in brief
- Aids used
- Interactive session
- Valedictory session
- Expert's comments
- Vote of Thanks
- Conclusion

6. Campaign/Rallies/Drive

- By whom, for whom?
- Date, Venue
- Nature, Objective
- Chief Guest, Crowd, Participants, Speakers
- Activities
- Display material: placard, banners, pamphlets, etc.
- Comments, Remarks
- Success or Failure?

To
The Editor
School Magazine

Annual Sports Day Celebrated

The Annual Sports Day of Solomon Public School was celebrated in the School Campus on 21th December 2013. The ground wore a festive look with colourful canopies and flags all around. The track gave it a hue of a great event. The event began when the Mayor N K Govil lit the torch and declared the meet open. All students and staff were present on the field but it was the presence of numerous guardians that made it a memorable event. 200 selected boys and 100 selected girls participated in 30 events, which included races, jumps, throws and boxing.

Prizes were distributed by different senior guardians after each event. Class 12 received the Champions trophy. The Principal Mr M Manu offered the Vote of Thanks. The meet concluded over lunch.

News Reports

Q. You are a staff reporter of The Hindu, New Delhi. You have witnessed a road accident involving a lorry and a Maruti car at Mathura Road. Write a report in 100–125 words.

Speeding Lorry rams into Maruti 800; car driver critical

– Reporter

At 7:30 this morning, an overspeeding lorry on Mathura Road hit a Maruti 800 car and smashed it from the rear. The car driver apparently wanted to stop the car and had slowed down, but the lorry driver either did not notice it or lost control of his vehicle and rammed the Maruti from behind. Although the car was badly mangled, luckily there was no one on the back seat. Nevertheless, the driver was seriously injured. He was immediately rushed to Indraprastha Apollo Hospital, which was barely a kilometre away the accident site. The driver is in critical condition and his survival is uncertain. The lorry driver fled the scene but the cleaner was taken into custody and he then divulged details about the driver and the lorry owner. The police are on the lookout for the absconding driver.

Ratan Tata Bids Adieu

Cyrus Mistry Takes Over

On Friday 28 December 2012, corporate icon Ratan Tata retired as the Chairman of the Tata Group after a 50-year run, predicting that India's growth would re-establish itself after the 'passing phase' of a difficult environment, which will most likely continue well into the next year.

Turning 75 on this day, Ratan Tata kept away from the Mumbai House Headquarters of the $100 billion group and spent time with employees at the manufacturing facilities of Tata Motors in Pune.

Cyrus Mistry, the 44-year-old Chairman-designate, who is likely to take over as Tata Group Chairman tomorrow, visited the office today. He was groomed for the assignment by Ratan Tata over the past year.

MCD to Auction Unused Vehicles

Various vehicles of the Municipal Corporation of Delhi, which have been lying unused for several years, would now be auctioned. These include cars, trucks, tractors, excavators, etc. The civic agency is hoping to earn as much as ₹ 5 crore from this auction. Many parts of such vehicles have been stolen. The junk vehicles are sites for mosquito breeding, which is indeed a big hazard in Delhi considering that dengue has already claimed a few lives this year.

Most of these vehicles had become unserviceable as long as 10 years ago but they were not auctioned by the civic agency. The MCD has kept the reserve price at 5 crore. "The condition of the vehicles has worsened over the years resulting in depreciation of value," revealed an MCD employee.

Nearly 25 Ambassadors, 212 Tata Tipper Trucks, 19 refuse removal trucks, three sewer jetting machines, and five motorcycles among others would be put up for auction.

Exercise

1. As a reporter of The Times of India, New Delhi, write a report on the fire in a marketplace that you witnessed.
2. You are working as a reporter for the Hindustan Times. Write a report on your meeting with the Union Home Minister.
3. Write a report on a Healthcare Conference in not more than 150 words.
4. Write a report on a sports event in not more than 150 words.
5. You are working as a reporter for the India Today. You attended a seminar on 'The Joys of Eye Donation'. Write a report on the conference in not more than 150 words.

Articles

TIPS

- Articles provide information either in brief or in detail.
- Somewhat like essays, they are yet different in form, content and technique.
- While articles are direct, essays are more circumspect.
- Articles are written on different topics under the sun.
- The standard word count for articles in newspapers is around 800 words.
- It is important to cover all aspects of a subject in concise and correct language.
- When articles are written on behalf of other persons, the key messages or talking points are noted and the flow of the article is based upon these points.
- Articles are best written with an unprejudiced mind.

As a social worker, you have observed that youngsters keep increasing their academic qualifications without proper direction. Many fail to find employment, creating the problem of the educated unemployed. Some then drift into unsocial activities. Write an article in 150–200 words on how the problem of the 'educated unemployed' can be solved.

Youth Lack Direction: Worldwide, today's youth seem to lack focus, especially in India. Simply interested in short-term gains, they think that a slew of diplomas and degrees will get them a fancy annual package with some esoteric designation. Once through with their education, they want a job quickly and feel that senior posts suit them best. A junior designation has them baffled, as they haven't heard about the learning curve and seem to believe they can hit the ground running, despite lacking practical job experience. Once in the job market, they are hit hard by reality when they fail to find a job despite myriad applications and multiple interviews.

After remaining unemployed for a year, it gradually dawns on them that they lack specific job skills. In such a situation, it is best for them to take up a job as an intern, if nothing else comes their way. Once they have a few months' experience, if they prove their worth, they could most likely be absorbed by the company where they did their internship. Failing this, they still stand a better chance of getting a job elsewhere, backed by the certificate of internship.

The Need for Forests: The world's forests are the life element of the Earth. She lives through them, breathes through them and looks after her infinite number of children through plants and forests. The latter contain immense resources and unimaginable natural wealth.

Modern science says that climatic and relief features greatly influence the growth of forests, while the fact may be just the opposite for we all know that forests are a great relief in themselves and capable of changing the climate. It's hard to tell whether they were created by the climate or they created the climate. As interdependence is the principle of Nature, one can safely assume both influenced each other.

Under all circumstances, forests influence our life, whether we live in the forests or far away from them. One thing is clear: no life on Earth can survive for long without the trees and forests.

Water Cycles: There are three states of matter: solid, liquid and gaseous. Water is found in all the three forms. At the poles or on the high peaks of mountains, it is in solid form; in the air it is in the form of gas or as moisture. Air carries it and the sun rays create them. All water bodies have water in liquid state.

During summers, the sun's rays change water into vapour, which rises and is carried away by air currents. This moisture-laden air cools at a height, forms droplets and comes down in the form of rain to quench the thirst of plants and animals, which wait endlessly for rains.

At specific high level, which is known as the freezing point, water freezes into solid ice. Under heat, it melts and becomes water again. The change of water from one state to another and again to water is called water cycles.

This is the Creator's greatest way to purify dirty and salty water by heating it and changing it into vapour and re-changing it into fresh drinking water. Rainwater is the purest water if collected from a clean place in a clean container. It's also a part of the greater cycle of life and the eternal system.

Green Buildings in India: As climate change and global warming keep wrecking havoc in various countries year after year, it is time that everyone realizes the importance of reducing the carbon footprint of all commercial activities. One way to do so and to reduce the impact on the environment is through the promotion of green buildings in the construction sector.

Unlike conventional structures, green buildings use minimal amounts of energy, consume less water, conserve natural resources, generate less waste and create spaces for healthy, comfortable living. Green buildings minimise environmental impact and happen to be healthier, since they utilize less energy, thereby saving occupants more money in the long term.

While green buildings found favour in developed countries in the last century, these structures only appeared in India in the new millennium. Officially, India's green building movement began in 2001 when the Indian Green Building Council (IGBC) was launched. Represented by all construction industry stakeholders – corporate, government, nodal agencies, architects, product manufacturers, institutions, and son on – IGBC seeks to serve as a single-point solution provider and key facilitator for all green building activities in India.

Commercial or residential, a green building should adhere to specific parameters during three crucial phases: before construction, during construction and after construction. Broadly, the steps before construction comprise site selection, soil and landscape conservation, health and wellbeing of the inhabitants, conservation and efficient utilisation of energy as well as management of other resources and wastes. Barring site selection, all the other parameters apply during construction too. In the after-construction phase, measures are taken to maintain and operate the building in an energy-efficiency manner.

All green structures adopt a practical, climate-conscious approach to design. Geographic location, the prevalent climatic conditions and the use of local, low-energy materials are typical factors driving the construction. This practical approach is crucial in ensuring there is minimal environmental impact during the construction of the building as well as in its future life cycle.

But green buildings across the country could vary because India hosts five climatic zones: hot and dry; hot and humid; moderate; cold; and composite. Incidentally, although unaware about the concept of green buildings, ancient Indians built such structures by using materials like wood, mud and stone, which controlled vagaries of the weather without expending immense amounts of external energy to keep the internal temperatures under control.

As the concept of green buildings spreads, it would be possible to create a green zone in which all structures adopt an environment-friendly approach, creating a healthier environment that curbs the heat-island effect. The creation of many such green zones in cities and towns across India would enable the country to slash annual energy consumption and reduce its overall carbon footprint.

With green buildings gaining popularity, India has three primary rating systems for such structures: IGBC, GRIHA and BEE. While IGBC has been mentioned earlier, GRIHA denotes 'Green Rating for Integrated Habitat Assessment' and BEE refers to the Bureau of Energy Efficiency. Whereas GRIHA considers various conditions and requirements specific to the design and construction of green structures in India, BEE set up a Star Rating Programme for office buildings in 2009 to accelerate energy-efficient activities in commercial buildings. Where BEE considers the actual performance of a building vis-à-vis specific energy usage in kWh/sq m/year, IGBC provides the LEED (Leadership in Energy and Environmental Design) ratings for green buildings in India as per stringent US norms.

Given that green buildings have a lower impact on the environment, the government should take all measures for their promotion by permitting lower taxes or tax holidays for such structures.

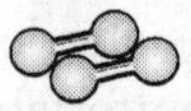

Exercise

Write articles on the following within 150 words:

- The Meaning of Modernity;
- Scientific Study of Light;
- The Process of Reproduction in Plants;
- Types of Joints;

- The Food Chain;
- The Body as a Factory.

Editorials

TIPS

- Editorials usually appear in the middle section of a newspaper on the left page, extreme left panel. This is referred to as the Editorial or Op-Ed page.
- Newspapers usually publish anywhere between one and three editorials every day.
- Editorials are usually written by senior journalists specially assigned for this task and need not necessarily be written by the editor.
- Without exception, editorials reflect the official stance of the newspaper.
- Editorials are written on the burning topic of the day or the past few days.
- Editorials are written in a balanced manner keeping the larger interests of society in mind.
- Such writings take a stance on government or regulatory policies, endorsing or criticizing them, as required.
- Some editorials take a nuanced, neutral stance, simply placing the facts before readers and inviting them to draw their own conclusions.
- In trying to lead from the front, an editorial should ensure it does not mislead readers.
- Such pieces are written after careful thought and not on the spur of the moment, since the primary purpose is to guide readers.

Implications of the Food Security Bill: On the face of it, India's Food Security Bill is a landmark legislation that could ostensibly ensure that no one in India goes hungry to bed. Promulgated as an ordinance a few weeks earlier, it was subsequently passed as a Bill before the ordinance lapsed. The entire world has been watching as the drama to pass the historic Bill played out in Parliament over the past few months. While people on opposite sides of the political divide have applauded or criticized the Bill for various reasons, almost all political parties have broadly supported it.

Some business analysts have, however, voiced serious disquiet over the long-term ramifications of the Bill. Make no bones about it – the Congress and the UPA have only pushed for the Bill with political dividends in mind. As Congress stalwarts have repeatedly stressed, this is a "game-changer." In other words, they expect it to win the UPA a third term in office. No one in the Congress has, however, paused and pondered over the consequences to the Exchequer and India's fiscal deficit.

Not surprisingly, the rupee fell yet again and the stockmarkets tanked after the Bill was passed. Analysts are clear that fiscal consolidation will be under severe strain, despite the Finance Minister's assurance that there would be no problem in funding the foodgrain outlays as per the Bill.

It is, however, important to note that some social scientists have voiced support for the Bill and stressed that this will not add unduly to the fiscal deficit, since the country was anyway making provisions to save almost 90% of foodgrains before the historic Bill came to be passed. Hopefully, the latter will be proved right and the consequences for fiscal consolidation will not be too difficult to bear.

Call the MNCs' Bluff on Pharma Patents: The issue of pharmaceutical patents and safeguards for innovation and research in the pharma industry has long bedevilled India. While the multinational pharma companies have kept crying themselves hoarse that India has not been recognizing and rewarding research in pharma, Indian companies and the regulatory authorities believe the MNCs are taking the argument too far and overpricing their drugs under the pretext of humongous research spends.

There can be little doubt that pharma research costs millions of dollars. At the same time, it must be stated that in many cases these huge amounts are not spent solely by the foreign pharma companies. Such research costs are underwritten by their governments and the government's research entities, which themselves conduct pharmaceutical research. But these facts are conveniently glossed over by the MNC's.

The other bone of contention between foreign pharma companies and the Indian government is the stand on patent extensions or what India prefers to term evergreening – the nefarious practice of making minor process changes during the manufacture of existing drugs in order to claim an extension on the patent. The Indian authorities strictly debar evergreening, which is a contention that the Indian courts also upheld in the case of Novartis' cancer drug, Glivec.

Novartis and other foreign firms have cried foul and claimed this means MNCs will no longer be interested in introducing new drugs in India or investing in new plants or research-oriented units within the country.

While this may be true to some extent, it needs to be borne in mind that the Indian drug market is vast – something which foreign entities can hardly afford to ignore. More so when profits in the West are beginning to plummet, especially since Big Pharma stares at a patent cliff – a period that has already begun whereby blockbuster drugs are reaching the end of their patent cycle. Thereafter, these patented drugs are open to be manufactured by generic companies, who then sell these drugs at a much lower rate than their branded versions.

Given these harsh realities, the MNCs can hardly afford to bypass the Indian market and not feel the pinch themselves. It is about time the Indian authorities call the bluff of these MNCs and stand firm by their laws on patents. When it comes to the question of patient lives, patents cannot be the overriding concern – patient wellbeing must.

News Releases or Press Releases

News releases – popularly referred to as Press Releases – are the most journalistic of all business communications. They are written to inform the public about events sponsored by, or occurring within a company. Therefore, they are public relations messages, promotional pieces, or announcements to the public. News releases may announce promotions within a company, changes in product line, creation of new departments or divisions, expansion, diversification, new products, mergers, and acquisitions. Such releases may be used to publicise grand openings, research findings, unusual events, humanitarian projects, and any other 'newsworthy' item.

The content or data from news releases is published in newspapers and periodicals, without it becoming apparent that the news item in question has actually emanated from a news release. They may also be splashed on radio and television. For example, a company may achieve a breakthrough in some life-saving drug. Since public interest in such a drug will be high, parts of the news release announcing the new drug may appear on television news channels.

Before proceeding any further, it is important to clarify why this section has been titled, News Releases or Press Releases. Although universally referred to as a Press Release even by public relations agencies (the main disseminators of news releases worldwide) and the media (the major recipients), this term is inappropriate in the Internet era.

To begin with, the term 'Press' is derived from Gutenberg's printing press, and primarily denotes the print media. In this day and age, however, it is not only the print media that is invited for a News Conference – again, inappropriately referred to as a Press Conference – but the Electronic Media too. The latter includes all the news channels, who are nowadays more vociferous than the traditional print media.

Besides the print and electronic media, the news is also disseminated to the online media, social networks and wire services, all of which flash the news almost immediately, unlike the traditional Press or print media, which may take a few hours or a day to come out with the news.

Furthermore, the emphasis of the releases put out by PR agencies is on the News element. Given all these factors, the word Press Release is clearly inappropriate and needs to be replaced by the more relevant News Release.

Understanding the News Release: News releases are usually sent to the media by public relations agencies and the Corporate Communications department of public and private companies. In general, though, a news release can be sent to the media by almost any entity, public or private. But each news release only stands any chance of being carried if it contains a newsworthy element, which will be discussed shortly.

If you are working in the Corporate Communications department of a company, it is likely you may be assigned the task of drafting and disseminating the company's news releases. Remember that news releases can be among the most creative and enjoyable writing assignments if you possess the passion for it. They stress not only basic information but also elements of human interest.

Because new releases may receive widespread attention, one must ensure that every sentence is accurate, clear and truthful. A misquote, an ambiguous statement, or wrong data will damage a company's reputation and hurt your own interests too. Since a news release is an extremely important document, make sure your draft is approved by your boss or a senior before it is released.

Preparatory Steps

Step One: Identify the Story: The first step in preparing the news release is to identify the newsworthy 'angle' in each topic assigned to you and research the story thoroughly. For example, say your company has discovered a way to triple the charge of cell-phone batteries, with a single charge now lasting for two days. In itself, this discovery is newsworthy.

But suppose the person who made the breakthrough happens to be a 17-year-old high school student hired by the company as a summer trainee. The story now has a strong human interest element and will attract the national media. Your company will receive credit not only as a technology leader but also as a supporter of school student research.

Once you have identified the story, follow these steps:

- Establish the details – Remember the five Ws of journalism: who, what, where, when, and why. If you cannot answer all of them, do more background research and procure additional information.
- Verify the facts – Remember the three rules of journalism: accuracy, accuracy, and accuracy. Check your facts by consulting at least two sources until you are confident the information is correct.
- Obtain permissions – Secure permission from a responsible source in the company to make the information in your news release public. Never assume that the data you have may be freely shared with the public. If you have secured permission from a superior, or if your superior has requested the release, give the person a preview of what you intend to write. Ensure you have explicit approval for the use of specific information.
- Choose the media you will use – Generally, the news release will be meant for general distribution and can be sent to all media and appropriate associations and individuals. In some cases, however, you may want to select a specific publication or media outlet for specialised news releases. If the material is urgent and needs immediate release, electronic and social media as well as the wire services are best. If the release has considerable detail, such as a list of names or scheduled events, the print media are better. Choose the media before you begin writing, as your choice can influence the presentation.

Step Two: Writing: Most companies have a standard format for news releases. The general rules for such a format are as follows:

1. If the company does not have a standard news release format, type 'News Release' centred at the top of the first page. Do bear in mind, though, that it is not mandatory to type 'News Release', since the email subject line and the format make it clear it is a news release.
2. At the top right-hand side of the first page, type 'For Immediate Release'; this informs the media that the release can be carried immediately.
3. The headline of the news release comes next, followed by the sub-heading.
4. Then follows the body copy of the news release, which begins with the dateline, followed by the lead paragraph that contains the five W's.
5. If the five W's cannot be answered in the first paragraph, answer most of them and the remainder should then follow in the second paragraph.
6. The quote from the chief spokesperson or the CEO or other management person should preferably appear in the second or the third paragraph.
7. Ideally, a news release should be restricted to one page only, which would ensure it is most likely carried.
8. After the body copy, the news release could end with 'For further information, please contact'.
9. If the news release runs to more than one page, type 'More' at the bottom of all pages, except the last one.
10. Type (–End–) or # # # at the bottom of the last page to indicate the end of the release.

News releases are almost always written in the 'inverted pyramid' style. In this form, the most important facts appear first. Answer the five Ws in the first paragraph itself as far as possible. Succeeding paragraphs provide supporting details and further explanations. It is best not to use stylistic tricks such as surprise endings or posing questions that are not answered until the final paragraph. Your readers should be able to scan your story quickly for the main points. Remember, other stories and events are competing with yours.

The inverted pyramid style is used to ensure that in case the media only uses the first paragraph or two due to space constraints, the most important elements of the news still get carried.

Where the headline of a news release is concerned, it is important to avoid complex, flowery titles. It is best to keep the headlines short, informative and preferably 'search engine' friendly. To ensure the latter, use more popular synonyms. For instance, if 'pharmaceutical' and 'healthcare' (or 'style' and 'fashion') could both be appropriate in a headline, it is better to use the latter, since this is more 'search-engine' friendly.

Headlines should be eye-catching. One trick to achieve this is to use alliterative headlines. Consider the headline: Apollo ties up with Ericsson across India. The same headline would be more memorable and eye-catching if it were alliterative (repetition of the first alphabet): Apollo announces all-India alliance with Ericsson.

The headline is followed by the subhead, which should be in one line if possible, with a strong hook like the headline. The subhead should contain important details not present in the headline. In some cases, the subhead would be akin to a summary of highlights.

Before drafting the news release, ensure it is newsworthy, else the media will not carry it. If a newsworthy element is missing, it is important to conduct a thorough background research on the topic and discover some news peg that would interest the media.

The body copy of the news release then begins with the dateline, which may read: New Delhi, 02 October 2013. Remember that the dateline should never read October 2, 2013. In this format, not only does one need to use a comma between the day and the year, it is also incorrect, although this style is used universally. Remember that the second is born first, followed by the minute, the hour, the day, the week, the month and the year. The dateline should therefore reflect the proper chronological sequence.

The dateline is followed by the lead, which is the first sentence in the body text. Make the lead as eye-catching, informative and newsworthy as possible. A weak lead may prompt the journalist to stop reading and immediately discard the news release.

Avoid the passive voice in news releases. The active voice makes news releases more catchy and crispy. Instead of saying: 'They entered into a partnership with the Mittals' say: 'They partnered the Mittals'. Instead of: 'The judge exhibited an extremely critical stance due to the frivolous RTI petition' simply state, 'The frivolous RTI petition angered the judge'.

Avoid all clichés and jargon, since this can turn off readers as well as journalists. Use jargon and technical terms only if you are writing a technical or medical news release. The same mindset is important while writing quotes. In case of an event, never pen a head honcho quote that goes:

"We are happy to announce that..." Be assured the media will most likely ignore such a quote. A quote from the top management should always contain insights that the rest of the release may not convey. Such quotes add credibility to a news release.

Keep all paragraphs short. Short paragraphs move the story along and cover the main points quickly while holding the reader's interest. As mentioned earlier, restrict the news release to one page or at the most two pages. Do remember that anything beyond that is usually not carried in India, although in the West news releases can run up to five and six pages.

A concise release is more likely to be read and distributed. Aim for a conversational, journalistic style. Make your language lively and fresh. Avoid superlatives like 'brilliant company executive' or 'outstanding corporate achievement'. Most editors will simply delete them, even if they do not end up junking the release.

A news release usually ends with the company's boilerplate, which generally goes as: About ________ (name of the company). The boilerplate contains one or two concise paragraphs about the company and its activities. Please make certain that you do not lift matter from the boilerplate to pad up quotes or other parts of the news release. The boilerplate should contain standalone or exclusive information.

Step Three: Revising: Revise the news release keeping the following points in mind:

1. Have I answered the five Ws?
2. Is the language lively and crisp?
3. Have I placed the most important statements first and supported them with facts in subsequent paragraphs?
4. Are the paragraphs concise?
5. Have I checked all the facts and obtained permission?
6. Is the human interest aspect properly highlighted?
7. Have I checked for grammar and spelling errors?

It is important to proofread the news release carefully before releasing it to the media. Well-written news releases enhance the reputation of your company and help your own career quite significantly, while unwanted errors will dent the image of a company and hurt your professional career.

Below is the template of a news release to help you adhere to the guidelines.

FOR IMMEDIATE RELEASE

Headline Headline Headline Headline.

Sub-head/Summary Sub-head/Summary Sub-head/Summary.

New Delhi, 03 October 2013: (First paragraph should contain the lead and answer: Who, What, When, Where, Why?).

(Second paragraph: Quote from CEO/senior management).

(Third paragraph: Relevant information about product or service, including benefits).

(Fourth paragraph: Additional details).

(Fifth and, preferably, the last paragraph: must conclude with final details and quote, if required).

Restrict quotes to two/three spokespersons.

About the Company (Boilerplate):

(This matter must NOT be repeated in text above).

For further details, contact:

Contact person:

Company name:

Telephone/Mobile number:

Fax number: (optional)

Email:

Website/URL:

# # #

If there is more than one page, at the end of the page write...

—more—

If there are more than two pages, replace —more— with

—2—

—3—

At the page bottom on the right, say:

Page 1 of 3, Page 2 of 3, Page 3 of 3

Obituary/ Condolences

TIPS

- Obituary is a way to remember departed souls and to pay them tribute.
- Nowadays, obituaries are confined to newspaper ads and serve two purposes simultaneously: the departed soul is remembered and the entity established by him/her receives publicity.
- Gone are the days of tomb writing, particularly Epitaphs or poetic lines written on stone in graveyards.
- A famous Epitaph:

  "Here he lies where he longed to be;

  Home is the sailor, home from sea."

- Since an obituary is printed in newspapers, a photograph usually accompanies it.
- The tone and wording of obituaries is exaggerated, yet reserved.
- The names of close and prominent relatives may be mentioned in obituaries.
- Condolences are part of obituaries. Condolence meetings may be announced in obituaries.

EXAMPLE

In the loving memory of
(Photograph)
Late ___________
17.08.1937 to 29.12.2005
Seven years have passed since you left us.
But not a single day has passed without your fond memories.
You continue to live in our hearts and minds.
We miss you every moment.
Deeply remembered by
The ___________Family;
____
____

EXAMPLE

(A photograph is usually given in the centre or left side)

Sad Demise of Dr D N Sinha

21.12.2017

With profound grief we inform about the sad demise of our beloved father Dr D N Sinha on 21.02.2017. All are requested to attend the rituals performed to pay homage to the departed soul on the following dates:

1.1.2013

Dashkarma

2.1.2013

Dwādashā/Brahma Bhoja

Sons and family members

202, P P Colony, Buxar; Mob: 09343436284

Condolence: Traditional

Condolence Message

A condolence meeting was held on ________at 3 pm in the college hall to mourn the sudden and premature demise of Prof. R D Sharma who succumbed to a heart ailment. The students, staff, teachers and elite of the town praised him and his contributions and expressed their sad feelings. They prayed for peace for the departed soul and wished that God may give strength and courage to the bereaved family members to bear the pain and loss. They silently prayed for two minutes.

— Principal

Condolence: Non-traditional

Real Tragedy

The painful news of Ritu's death in an auto accident in Delhi shocked everyone. She was a promising, ambitious girl who was sincerely pursuing her career in Media Management when the Maker stopped her breath. It is a real tragedy. If her call had not come so unduly and unfortunately, nothing could have stopped her inevitable path to name, fame and glory.

May she rest in peace and return soon to resume her journey on Earth and her passionate pursuit.

— Her grieving but proud family

Columns

TIPS

- Newspapers and magazines, even web portals, have dedicated columns written by senior journalists, authors, politicians and celebrities or renowned persons from various domains.
- These columns appear periodically (daily, weekly, fortnightly, monthly, etc.), depending upon the arrangement between the columnist and the periodical.
- Celebrity columns can be extremely popular, with some regular readers first turning to the regular column of their favourite columnist before turning to the other pages.
- Although most columnists are experts in their domains, nowadays even authors who are not really authoritative writers still end up with regular columns. This is done by using the services

of Public Relations consultancies, which have direct relations with the media and manage to "place" their client's writings in various periodicals regularly.

- Becoming a columnist on one's own merit takes years of hard work and recognition in one's industry before being invited to write columns.
- Once one achieves this position, it is simply a question of choosing a suitable topic to write about periodically or writing on the topic or theme provided by the periodical.
- As a columnist, it is important to write authoritatively and be sure of all the facts and statistics used in one's column.
- Extremely popular columnists even have their columns syndicated, i.e., published simultaneously in dozens of newspapers and magazines.
- Despite not being an excellent writer, octogenarian Khushwant Singh has been one of India's most popular columnists whose writings have appeared in Indian and foreign periodicals.
- Columnists are usually paid more highly than regular journalists and other contributors.
- New periodicals sometimes use celebrity columnists to gain new readers and increase their readership quickly.
- In most newspapers and magazines, senior journalists are allowed space to write their own columns for which no extra remuneration is paid.
- Corporate chieftains, renowned economists and veteran politicians are some of the people who are popular as columnists.

The Third Front and Other Ephemeral Alternatives: As India begins a reverse count of months towards the May 2014 General Elections, the only clear fact is that every possibility is possible were elections are to be held in today's scenario. This includes a Third Front coming to power, a fourth Federal Front making it to Parliament, a Narendra Modi-led BJP managing to cobble the highest number of seats alongside allies and independent supporters or the Congress/UPA Government sneaking back, despite strong nationwide anti-incumbency fostered by serial scams and similar shenanigans.

Under the present circumstances, both the BJP and the Congress are apparently pulling out all the stops either to win power or retain it. Unfortunately for both, they have numerous people within their party or alliance adept at shooting off their mouths, shooting themselves in the foot or scoring self-goals in some inexplicable way or the other. Consider the Congress. It is paying for Chidambaram's midnight blunder of announcing the formation of Telangana in 2009. Since then, the pressure built up steadily on the Congress/UPA till the final announcement was made about India's 29th state, Telangana, bifurcated from Andhra Pradesh.

Of course, Sonia Gandhi only acquiesced to this decades-long demand with a cynical eye on votes, since the Congress grudgingly accepts it has largely lost Andhra Pradesh, thanks to rebel Jaganmohan Reddy's YSR Congress. By birthing Telangana, the Congress hopes K C Rao's TRS Congress will finally merge with it because its raison d'être is no more. Accordingly, the Congress could win some Lok Sabha (LS) and Assembly seats in the new state. Whether the ground situation actually plays out as per such wishes cannot be considered a certainty, though.

Pandora's Box of Statehood: What's certain is that the UPA's assent to Telangana has opened a veritable Pandora's Box of statehood aspirations across India. A dozen statehood war calls are already reverberating throughout India, even triggering disruptive echoes in the Monsoon Session of Parliament. Despite fiery protests, the Congress will ignore other statehood claims and resist calls for another States Reorganisation Commission, thereby saddling whichever dispensation comes to power in 2014 with the Hobson's choice of accepting or rejecting these divisive demands.

For businesses, bifurcation into two states will yield rich dividends in the long run, after the agitations over Telangana finally die down. In the short term, pro- and anti-Telangana fires will keep simmering, causing political and business uncertainties. This could particularly affect Hyderabad, the capital city, which happens to be a pharma and IT hub too. Such uncertainties could trigger withdrawal of investments and freezing of additional investment plans. Sooner or later, though, a closure of the volatile bifurcation cauldron is bound to occur. When this happens, business in both regions will boom in right earnest again.

Meanwhile, the Congress has felt Telangana's reverse kick as some Andhra Congress MLAs and MPs have resigned in protest. With the state's Congress Chief Minister Kiran Kumar Reddy himself unhappy with the bifurcation, the party's Telangana gambit faces stormy seas ahead.

Make or Mar Monsoon Session: For now, the UPA is focussed on Parliament's Monsoon Session. The 16-working-days' session (between 5 and 30 August) presents a window of opportunity for the Government to try its best to clear at least 44 important bills from the 116 pending ones. By pushing reforms through these Bills, Prime Minister Manmohan Singh is hoping against hope to wash away the stigma of four years' non-governance and scams. Chief among these is the Food Security Bill – supposedly the game-changer to win the General Elections – earlier promulgated as an Ordinance because its passage was uncertain.

Even support from its acerbic ally the Samajwadi Party (SP) is no longer a certainty, however, after the Centre and the UP Government inadvertently entered into a spat over the contentious suspension of IAS officer Durga Shakti Nagpal, who had dared to take on the sand mining mafia. When the Centre sought details about her suspension, the UP Government hit back, citing the transfer of officers digging dirt in cases related to Sonia Gandhi's son-in-law, Robert Vadra. The conflict has escalated, with the SP's brazenness earning it public opprobrium, but the Congress is also suffering collateral damage due to its recalcitrant ally.

Interestingly, the season of discord notwithstanding, all political parties have jumped onto the same page in order to amend the RTI Act and keep political parties out of its dangerous ambit.

Mirage May Materialise: In recent weeks, the prospects of political parties in the next General Elections have repeatedly taken centre-stage. A cross-country survey by Times Now, C-Voter and India TV reveals the BJP will emerge as the single largest entity and its governing constituent the NDA will be the largest political formation. Amongst individual politicians, Narendra Modi towers as the most preferred Prime Ministerial candidate, eclipsing Rahul Gandhi and other contenders by a sizeable margin.

But these findings aren't good enough for the BJP or Modi to contemplate how they will uncork the bubbly after the General Elections. Simply stated, such survey preferences won't convert into a decisive seats advantage during the Lok Sabha polls – an unpalatable truth confirmed by The Hindu-CNN-IBN voter survey. Therefore, while the UPA may certainly suffer a significant drop in votes, the BJP/NDA won't cross the magic figure of 272 LS seats out of 543 across India.

The biggest beneficiary of an anti-incumbency wave against the UPA will be Third Front entities (SP, JD (U), Left Front, BJD, and TDP) and the fourth Federal Front (Trinamool Congress, AIADMK, BSP, etc.). In the 2009 elections, the Third Front secured 184 seats. In the present circumstances, it may win 250-plus seats – coming within striking distance of 272. This could be crossed through the support of independents and other parties, even the Congress. In such a situation, SP chief Mulayam Singh Yadav stands a strong chance of becoming Prime Minister.

Such uncertainties will spur the BJP brass and Modi to go the extra mile and deliver a stronger showing than what the opinion polls presage. In the run-up to May 2014, Modi and other top BJP leaders are slated to address more than 100 rallies across India, highlighting the economic woes, high inflation, serial scams, security threats and other problems rife under the UPA.

Despite the UPA's laundry list of problems, the BJP isn't positioned to fully capitalize on this situation. Given Modi's dictatorial, brook-no-rivals mien, he has strong detractors within and outside his party. Besides, not everybody is convinced about Gujarat's growth model, which critics lambast as non-inclusive. Pointing out that the state has one of the slowest poverty-reduction rates in India, Rural Affairs Editor of The Hindu, P Sainath, has termed the Gujarat model and Modi's reputation "the biggest public relations con job of our time."

No one can deny Modi has droves of followers on social media and across India, including ardent admirers such as economist Jagdish Bhagwati. Yet there are trenchant critics such as economist Amartya Sen, who voice serious reservations about Modi becoming the PM, given his authoritarian, non-inclusive, non-minority agenda. Significantly, Gujarat has no Lokayukta since 2003 because Modi opposes the office. Justice R A Mehta (appointed Lokayukta by the Gujarat governor on the Gujarat High Court's recommendation) has declined to take up the post because the State Government has repeatedly questioned his integrity.

The list of people covertly or overtly opposed to Modi is as long as the charge-sheet of criticism hurled at the UPA. As Arnab Goswami pointed out in Times Now vis-à-vis the channel's voter survey, there's no Modi wave across India (which the BJP fondly proclaims). The only Modi wave that exists is in Gujarat. All of which makes it increasingly likely that the mirage of a Third Front may actually materialise as the largest political dispensation in May 2014.

Print Media

• Advertisements • Notices • Posters and Pamphlets • Citation • Invitations

Advertisements

TIPS

- An advertisement is a kind of public notice asking for or offering services or buying and selling property, goods, etc. or giving information about missing persons, pets, articles, etc.
- There are two types of advertisements: Classified and Commercial.
- Classified Advertisements are categorized into columns; these are more economical; take less space; give definite information; are written in simple, common words and phrases.
- Commercial Advertisements are specially designed for these purposes; are visually attractive; carry pictures and catchy slogans with alluring expressions. They are colourful and composed in fonts of different shapes and sizes; blank space is given to add to the overall appeal of the ad.

Different Types of Classified Advertisements with Examples

Category	Details	Example
Situation Vacant	Begin with 'Wanted' or 'Required'. The Company; The Post; No. of vacancies; Age and sex of the candidate; Qualification and experience; Pay scale and perks; Contact address; Phone number; E-mail address;	Wanted smart, young, lady receptionist, between 22 and 30, for a reputed publication. Qualification: Graduate. Knowledge of and fluency in both Hindi and English essential. Salary negotiable. Apply within a week with complete bio-data to MD, Sahitya Bhawan, Agra; Ph: 05623257009; e-mail: sbpd.pubhouse@gmail.com

Property on Sale	(Begin with 'For Sale; Purchase; Wanted', as required) Details of Property: size, floor, rooms, amenities, fittings and fixtures, location/surroundings, price	For Sale: School Block Society Flat; Gr. Floor; Two Rooms Set; Full interiors; Main Street; Facing Park; Central location. Reasonable Price. Contact: Major Tiwari: 9877643556.

Vehicle	Model/year of manufacture; colour; accessories; condition, mileage, etc.	Available for Sale: Maruti 800; 2000; Self-driven; Original Scratch-less paint; AC/Stereo fitted; Price negotiable; Contact: M Dhingra 9808252544.

Household Article	Model/year of manufacture; colour; material; condition, price, address, etc.	LG Washing Machine and Fridge for sale due to transfer; both white; 3 yrs; excellent condition; negotiable price. Contact: CR Verma 9456562827

To Let	Begin with 'Wanted' or 'Required'. Size, floor, rooms, amenities, fittings and fixtures, location, rent, address, etc.	Available on rent in Preet Vihar, near Metro; close to market; fully furnished; company lease preferred; Expected rent 6k. Contact: SK Raj; D/21, Preet Vihar. Mob: 9821216744

Educational	Name of Institution; Courses offered; Duration; Eligibility; Date, Fee for Reg. Contact Add. Phone	Applications are invited from eligible candidates for admission to BBA; BCA; B.Sc. IT; B.Sc. Food Sc. by Falcon Institute of Management & Technology; Near Oberoi Farm, Delhi 37; Ph: 011-25563238/9/10/11. e-mail: office.falcon@gmali.com

Missing Persons/ Pets	Begin with 'Missing'; physical description; identifying features; reward, if any, address, phone, etc.	Missing since 08.08.17 an old man, Shankar Saran, 71; tall, weak, with specs, in nightdress. Informer will be duly rewarded. Pl. contact: Mukesh Saran, D18, Preet Vihar. Mob: 9844875080

Lost and Found	Begin with 'Lost and Found'; description of thing/s; special features; reward, if any, address; phone, etc.	Lost Blue-Coloured VIP Briefcase in Paharganj on the evening of 12th August last. The cheque book inside bears my name. Please inform Prem Thakur, Mob: 4665324654. Reward will be given.

Tours and Travels	Begin with 'Package available'	Available attractive package for Agra; 3 nights, 4 days stay; breakfast, dinner ₹ 4,000/- for two persons. Contact: Tanish Tours and Travels: 011-44335656

Matrimonial	Give caste, sub-caste, age, complexion, job, education and special condition, if any.	Wanted a suitable employed groom for a Khatri girl, sub-caste no bar, aged 24, MA, wheatish complexion, height 5 feet 5 inches, working as an editor. Contact: 9477632210

EXAMPLE **CBSE Question: 2008**

Q. You want to sell your car as you are going abroad. Draft a suitable advertisement in not more than 50 words to be published in The Hindu. Give necessary details of the car. You are Sushil from 21 Ram Nagar, Delhi.

Ans.:

THE HINDU CLASSIFIEDS

Chennai 10th August 2017

VEHICLES

Bolero	TATA SAFARI	QUALIS
	The New 2.2 VTT Safari EX 4x2 Dec '07; 11,500 kms. Extended Warranty 4yrs/150,000 kms. Beige interiors. Art leather seats, rear camera, Sony audio system worth ₹ 50,000, teflon, anti-rust coating. Mint condition, owner going abroad. ₹ 8.10 Lakhs Fixed Price. Brokers Excuse. Contact: Sushil, 21 Ram Nagar, Delhi or call: 9868082133	

 **Exercise**

1. Draft an ad to sell your house.
2. You have arranged a Tour to Amarnath. Draft an ad for the package.
3. You lost your bag with driving licence. Draw an ad announcing a reward for the finder.
4. You deal in household articles. Draw an ad for local papers to promote sales.
5. Draw a matrimonial ad for a girl working as a receptionist.

Notices

TIPS

- A Notice is used by individuals and organizations to announce events, celebrations, inaugural ceremonies, birth and deaths, issue public instructions; and to invite or make an appeal.
- An effective Notice contains: (a) Name of the organization, institution or the office that issues the notice: both at the top and the bottom. (b) Date of issuing the Notice and other relevant dates; at least the last date of implementation, etc.
- The purpose of the Notice is usually given at the top as a caption.
- Purpose of the Notice and conditions that apply.
- Details of everything that have to be notified including Date, Time, Venue, Programme, etc.
- Name, Designation and signature of the person or officer issuing the Notice.
- A Notice must be simple, straightforward, confined to essentials and within 100 words.
- Different parts of a Notice carry different marks: Format 1 mark; Name, Designation, Signature of the issuing authority 1 mark; and Content.
- The Content includes message; schedule; correct language; punctuation and arrangement.
- The Notice can be given in a box.

Format of a Notice

Name of the Organization

Date

Notice

Title

Content

Signature

Name

Designation

Mayur Vihar Phase II Welfare Association **8th September 2017**

NOTICE

Save Water Drive

Due to an acute water shortage in Delhi, and in our colony in particular, it was decided in the general body meeting that all colony residents will save as much water as possible. Please don't waste potable water to clean cars, verandahs, etc., or in watering plants. Errant families will be fined ₹ 500/- per violation. Please use water judiciously for every task.

S/d
K K Sharma
President
Mayur Vihar Phase II Welfare Association

Qs. *As Sunita Sinha, Cultural Secretary, Queen's Senior Secondary School, Patna, write a notice within 50 words for the school notice board, giving details of the cultural programme and inviting participants.*

Queen's Senior Secondry School **30th September, 2017**

NOTICE

Cultural Function on 2nd October

The College will hold a Cultural Function remembering Mahatma Gandhi on 2nd October with Songs, Recitation and Short Act Plays.

Those willing to participate should give their names, roll number, class and field of interest to the undersigned by Saturday next.

Sunita Sinha
(Secretary)
Cultural Society

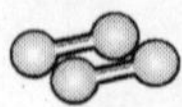 **Exercise: Write Notices to draw attention to the following –**

- Parking of Vehicles
- Change in Train Timing
- Competition for Amateur Artists
- World Elder's Day
- Scholarship
- Call for Contributions to School Magazine

Preet Vihar Police Station 03rd February, 2017

NOTICE

Parking of Vehicles

All vehicle owners and drivers are notified to park vehicles only at designated places. If a vehicle at a wrong place is creating inconvenience to others, it will be towed and a fine of ₹ 500/- imposed.

A.K. Yadav
(Station Home Officer)

Traffic Controller Northern Railway 30th September, 2017

NOTICE

Change in Train Timing

It is hereby notified that from 2nd October 2017 onwards 2057 UP Saptkranti Express will start from Muzaffarpur at 9:15 hours and reach Old Delhi next day at 7:10 hours; and 2058 DOWN Saptkranti Express will leave Old Delhi at 15:00 hours and reach Muzaffarpur the next morning at 8:30 hours.

S.P. Singh
(Station Master)

Kalkaji Temple Committee **05th June, 2017**

NOTICE

Attention Music Lovers!

All Amateur Artists of Kalkaji are requested to appear with Musical Instruments on the Night of Janmashtami in the Temple Complex for a Grand Competition of Amateur Artists where each artist or group of artists will be given half an hour to perform. The Temple Committee will distribute suitable awards to the best performing artists.

Amit Kumar
(Chairman)

Angel's Academy **30th September, 2017**

NOTICE

World Elder's Day!

All students are hereby notified to bring their grandparents on the next World Elder's Day. The School will felicitate them on the day.

S B Mishra
(Principal)

Solomon Public School **10th September, 2017**

NOTICE

Scholarship

Our ex-student Abhishek has instituted five Scholarships of ₹ 5,000/- p.m. each for students excelling in Sports, Extracurricular Activities and Academics. Deserving students wishing to avail of the Scholarship should apply to the Vice Principal by 15 September 2017 giving all relevant information.

M Manu
(Director)

Sarvodaya Public School, Jamshedpur **29th July, 2017**

NOTICE

Call for Articles in School Magazine

Our School Magazine is presently being compiled. All students who are interested in contributing Articles, Stories, Essays, Jokes and Poems to the School Magazine are requested to make their submissions by the end of August at the latest.

The School Magazine will be published in October 2017.

Prajjawal
(Student Editor)

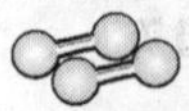
Exercise

- As a Librarian, write a notice about the change in Library timings.
- As Secretary of the Student Welfare Committee write a notice for a camp to clean the area.
- As Tarang, write a notice about a government scholarship for poor but meritorious students. Invite applications also.
- As Preeti, the Cultural Secretary of Janaki Inter College, write a notice inviting participants for a cultural function being organized to celebrate Independence Day.
- As Nikita, Secretary, Zila School Sports Club, write a notice for a meeting to be held to felicitate the players of the football team that won a shield.

Posters and Pamphlets

TIPS

- A poster or pamphlet is used to make appeals or announcements or to create awareness among people in the public interest. A poster is pasted in public places and pamphlets are distributed among the people by political parties, NGOs, government departments, institutions and even individuals.
- They are also used to promote sales of products.
- Usually posters are large in size and pamphlets are small printed sheets containing information.
- Both contain eye-catching slogans and phrases dealing with the theme, purpose or product.
- Both are also used to create awareness.
- The theme is clearly written in bold print, sometimes in capital letters.
- Different shapes and letter sizes can be used, leaving proportionate space between lines.
- Date, time, place and other useful information should be mentioned.
- Name of the promoting organization should be mentioned clearly.

- The Marks Scheme is usually 3 Marks for the Content and 2 Marks for Expression.
- Therefore, use appropriate and correct language.
- Show creativity in terms of content as well as design.

Many Can't See the Beautiful World.

Some are Born Blind.

Some Become Blind.

Some Lose Eyesight in Accidents.

Help them to See Loving Persons, Lovely Scenes.

Eyes are Useless after Death.

Donate your Eyes Today to be Removed for the Blind Only after Death.

You may See Even when No More.

It's Simple: Visit a RED CROSS Centre and Fill a Form.

President

RED CROSS SOCIETY

STOP CUTTING TREES:

TREES ARE OUR SAVIOURS

LIFE depends on **Trees.**

AIR depends on **Trees.**

FERTILITY depends on **Trees.**

OXYGEN depends on **Trees.**

ECOLOGY depends on **Trees.**

BUILDINGS depend on **Trees.**

PAPER depends on **Trees.**

INSECTS depend on **Trees.**

ANIMALS depend on **Trees.**

HUMANS depend on **Trees.**

TREES GIVE THEIR ALL; EVERYTHING, EVERY PART.

We Use	ROOTS,	STEMS,	BRANCHES
We Utilize	LEAVES,	FLOWERS,	FRUITS
We Eat	BARK,	SKIN,	PULP
We enjoy	RIND,	JUICE,	STONE

We Live and Grow and Breathe; and Life Continues.

PLANT TREES: SAVE TREES: SAVE LIFE

Scriptures Prohibited Cutting of Green Trees.

Green Trees are Like Young Progeny.

Protect Progeny to Protect Coming Generations.

PLANT TREES: SAVE TREES: SAVE LIFE

SAVE LIFE SOCIETY

Exercise

Design posters or write pamphlets to promote awareness in the following fields:

- Plastic Menace
- Control Diseases
- Stop Cruelty to Animals
- Blood Donation
- Education for All (Sarva Shiksha Abhiyan)
- Polio Eradication

BAN PLASTIC

Our Forefathers Used Leaves, Straw, Bark, Cotton and Hemp.

We have Replaced them with PLASTIC and Ruined ourselves.

PLASTIC Obstructs, Hampers, Remains as it is.

PLASTIC Ruins Fertility of Land, Man, Woman, Animals, Birds.

PLASTIC Emits Toxic Chemicals that Cause Lung Cancer.

Replace PLASTIC with Perishable things.

BE WISE, ENSURE CONTINUITY OF LIFE.

Carry a Hemp Carry-bag for purchases.

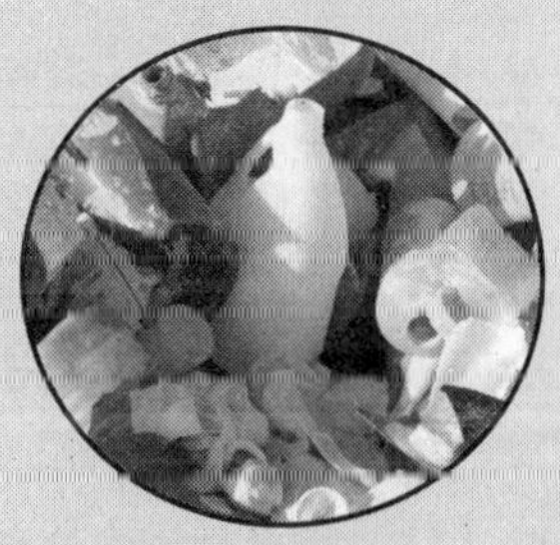

DO AWAY WITH PLASTIC BEFORE YOU ARE DONE AWAY BY IT.

Logo **SAVE ECOLOGY SOCIETY**

Curb Disease

You Spread Diseases

YOU CAN PREVENT DISEASES

Diseases are caused by Insects, Bacteria
that breed in Dirt, Filth, Clotted Water.

Diseases are caused by
Dirty, Junk and Stale Food
Avoid them for maintaining good health.

GROW, COOK AND EAT
FRESH, HEALTHY, DIGESTIBLE FOOD;

BE HEALTHY AND KEEP OTHERS HEALTHY.

ONLY HEALTH CAN ENSURE
PROSPERITY, HAPPINESS AND PEACE.

Save Ecology Society

STOP ANIMAL CRUELTY

God created animals first, then man.
Animals ensure life on Earth.
Animals are so we are.
Animals maintain ecological balance.
After plants, animals have first right on Mother Nature.
By killing them, we are killing ourselves.
We know it is suicide, yet we are committing it.
Animals have helped us.
Animals have taught us.
Animals live by themselves.
We depend on animals.
Keep Animals.

Save Animals.

Shelter Animals.

Feed Animals.

Stop Cruelty To Animals.

Save Animals To Save Life.

SAVE ECOLOGY AND SOCIETY

BLOOD DONATION:
A PIOUS DUTY

WAR
TERRORISM
MODERN DISEASES

HAVE MADE BLOOD DONATION ESSENTIAL.

S/he Needs it Today; You may Need Tomorrow.

The More We Create Heavy Machinery
and Rely on Vehicles

The More Accidents We would Face;

And
Blood Donation will be Needed
More and More.

Donate Blood **Save Others**

You Are in the Queue.

FREEDOM FROM POLIO

is POSSIBLE

ONLY WITH YOUR COOPERATION

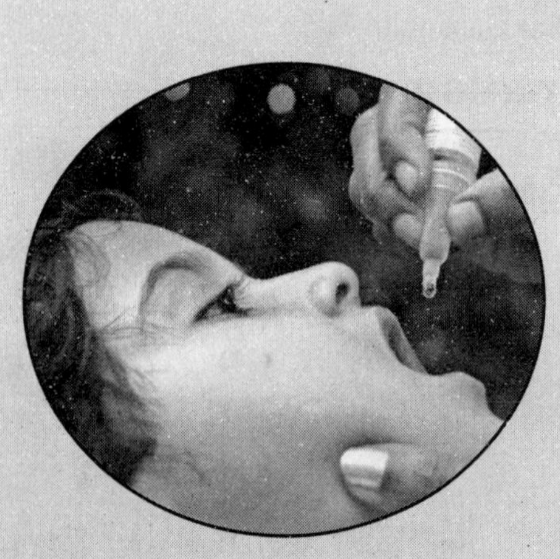

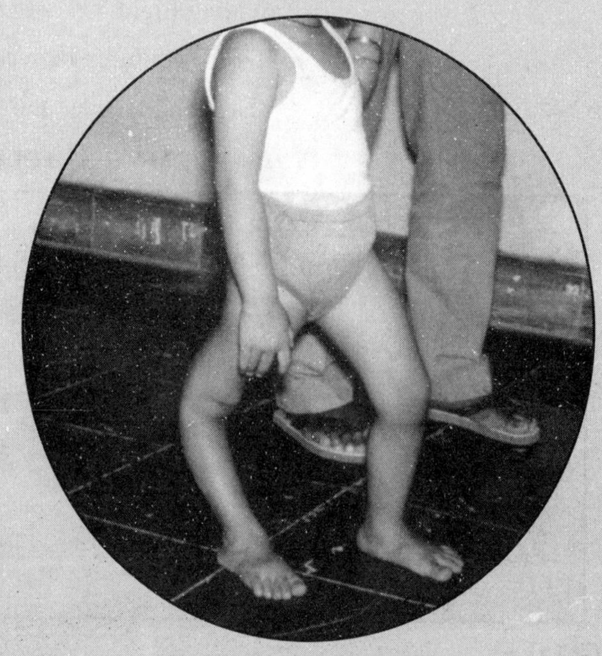

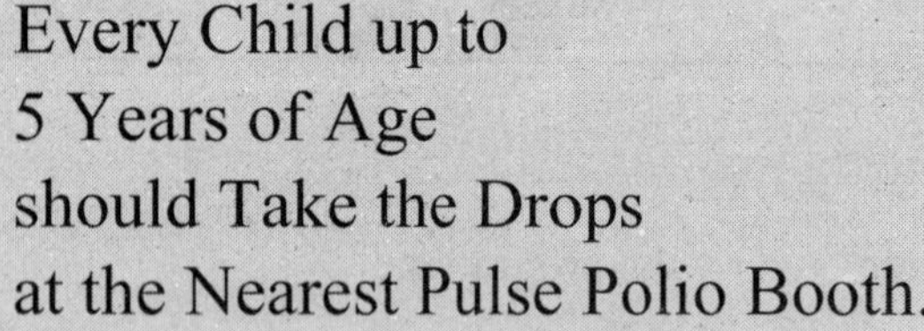

Every Child up to
5 Years of Age
should Take the Drops
at the Nearest Pulse Polio Booth.

Ensure that Your Child too
Takes the Drops
in all the Rounds

SAFETY FIRST, FOR YOUR CHILD, FOREVER

Issued by Ministry of Health & Family Welfare, Government of India

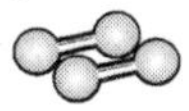 **Exercise:** Write a Pamphlet on Drug Abuse:

DARE TO SAY NO

- Is someone asking you to try drugs?
- Is someone providing them to you free?

Don't allow drugs to become a compulsion for you.

Say No,

An emphatic No!

The First Time and Always

NO DRUGS

NO DRUGS

Remember, drugs are a dead end.

They lead to destruction and death.

Life is a precious gift of God.

It's beautiful.

It's worth living; even with all its frustrations and failures.

Problems can be worked out.

Goals can be achieved.

There are people who love you.

There are people who need your love.

IF YOU ARE IN DISTRESS

Just call our toll free number: +91-222-333-4444

Your identity will be kept a secret.

Call before it is too late.

D A R E Drug Abuse Resistance Education

We are there to help you.

Exercise

1. Prepare a poster on the dangers of smoking.
2. Prepare a poster on pollution.
3. Prepare a poster on Saving Birds.
4. Prepare a poster asking people to help flood victims.

Citations

- Writing a citation means outlining reasons for awards. Many awards for different types of achievements to various persons or entities are given by governments; institutions; organizations; the corporate world and NGOs.
- While giving the awards, written, printed, embossed or engraved 'Citations' are given containing the name and address of the person and the reason for selection for the Award is stated.
- This becomes the prized possession of the person and his/her heirs.
- The older it grows the greater importance it gathers.
- That is why it is well written, though in brief.

EXAMPLE

The Akhil Bhārtiya Bāla Sāhitykār Sangh

Endows the title of **"Bāla Rachanākār Shree"**

And presents a cash award of

One Lakh One Thousand to

Āchārya Vishnukant Pandey

For his distinguished services

And distinctive contribution

In the field of Children's Literature,

On this day, Monday, 14th November 1988

President

Secretary

Akhil Bhārtiya Bāla Sāhitykār Sangh

New Delhi.

Invitations

TIPS

- Invitations on different occasions (births, birthday, marriage, engagement, other occasions, public functions, death, etc.) are part of our life. In ancient times, handwritten invitations were sent via messengers. Now almost all invitations are printed since this takes less time.
- Writing an invitation is an art.
- Invitations are complex because they are both like Letters and Posters; and they are directly sent to relatives and friends; neighbours and other known persons. Invitations or Replies to Invitations should therefore be written with due thought.
- Invitations can be formal or informal, depending upon the purpose.
- They must be deftly drafted and artistically printed on cards or written proportionately on smooth paper of good quality.
- Coloured cards or papers should be used for happy occasions, while white paper with a black border should be used for sad occasions.
- Formal or informal, invitations should preferably be completed in a single sentence.
- Third Person should be used in formal invitations.
- First Person should be used in informal invitations.
- An invitation is drafted in a way that answers all questions: who, whom, when, where, why, what for, what time, what place, and also whom to contact in the form of RSVP.
- Invitation should contain: name/names of the host; (organizers/sponsors) name/names of the invitee; occasion; place of celebrations; time of celebrations; date; (chief guest in official invitations); details of the events, if it is an event invitation.
- Use warm and simple language both in the invitation and replies.

In Replies:

- Acknowledge receipt of invitation;
- Express thanks;
- Mention acceptance;
- If regretted, specify reason;
- Be warm and polite.

Mrs & Mr Arya Priyamber

Request the pleasure of your

graceful company

on the occasion of

their son

Anag's

Birthday

on the 26th of January

7 p.m.

at their residence.

RSVP: _____________
423, Hospital Road,
Motihari, East Champaran

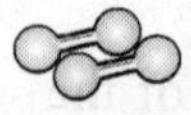

Exercise: Draft the following types of Invitations and their Replies–

1. You are Mohan. You have been invited by the Lions Club as one of the judges for a children's Fancy Dress Competition. But due to a prior engagement, you cannot accept the invitation. Write a formal reply to the president of the Club regretting your inability to accept the invitation.
2. Write an Invitation for the Fancy Dress Competition organised by the Lions Club.
3. You are Varsha. You have been invited to attend the wedding of your friend's sister during the summer vacation. Respond regretting your inability to attend the wedding.
4. Prepare an invitation card for the above marriage.
5. Prepare an Invitation for the Silver Jubilee Celebration of your school. Include necessary instructions against mobile phones and cameras.
6. Your school is organizing the Annual Day next month in one of the prestigious city auditoriums. Draft an invitation in not more than 50 words giving all essential details. Do not forget to include necessary instructions about mobile phones and cameras.
7. Prepare an Invitation for the Green Week Celebration of your school.

1.

From

Mohan Paranjape

4th October 2017

To,
Shri N K Agrawal,
President,
Lions Club, ----------

Dear Mr Agrawal,

Thank you for inviting me to judge your Fancy Dress Competition. But much as I would love to do so, I regret I will be unable due to prior commitments of delivering a few lectures in the University.

I'm sure you will understand my point and excuse me on this occasion.

Should such an opportunity arise again in the future, I will be most delighted to take it up.

Regards,

~ ~

Mohan Paranjpe

2.

INVITATION

FANCY DRESS COMPETITION

Organized by LIONS CLUB

Dear Sir/Madam,

You are cordially invited to attend a colourful Fancy Dress Competition to be held on Sunday, 7th October 2017 at 2 p.m. sharp in the Town Hall.

The District Magistrate, Shri Jivan Kumar, IAS, has kindly consented to inaugurate the function.

Alok Suman	**Chandrakishore Madan**	**N.K. Agrawal**
Competition in-Charge	Secretary	President
LIONS CLUB		

3.

S-67, Indirapuram, New Delhi

18th July 2017

Dear Kishore,

It's a pleasure to hear that your sister Nivedita is getting married. I would have loved to attend the Marriage Ceremony but at that time I will be in Mauritius on some important official assignments for which tickets have already been confirmed. There is no scope for cancellation because the contracts are crucial for the firm I'm working with.

Please inform Nivedita accordingly, since I would hate to do this myself. My absence notwithstanding, I'm sending her a wedding gift.

Yours truly,

~ ~

Varsha

4.

Mrs & Mr Kamleshwar Tripathi

Request the pleasure of your company

on the occasion of

the marriage of their daughter

NIVEDITA

to

NIRMAL

(S/o Mr & Mrs Suresh Sharma)

On Thursday, 24th July 2017

At 10 am,

Hotel Sonalika,

Azad Nagar, New Delhi.

RSVP:

302, Azad Nagar,

New Delhi. Ph: 9432788654

5.

SILVER JUBILEE CELEBRATION

M J K Inter College
Ramana Road, Bettiah

Dear Sir/Ma'am

You are cordially invited to attend the Silver Jubilee Celebrations of the school to share the joy of glorious 25 years of teaching and to encourage the students and staff to achieve much more.

Shri Krishna Kant Pandey, Hon'ble Minister for Higher Education and the school Founder has kindly consented to inaugurate the function.

Dr Purnendu Bharadwaj
Principal
M J K Inter College
Ramana Road, Bettiah

Note: For security reasons, Mobile Phones and Cameras will not be allowed within the premises.

6.

ANNUAL DAY

Siddhu-Kanhu Public School
Main Road Rourkela

Dear Sir/Madam

You are cordially invited to attend the Annual Day of the school on 25th December 2017 from 2:00 p.m. in the National Auditorium. This will include enchanting programmes, some of which will be performed by our students.

Hon'ble Minister for Higher Education, Shri Ravindra Rawat has kindly consented to inaugurate the function.

Dr Jeetendra Pandya
Principal,
Siddhu-Kanhu Public School,
Rourkela,

Note: Please do not bring Mobile Phones or Cameras.

7.

GREEN WEEK! GREEN EARTH! GREEN LIFE!

M.S.S.G. College
Areraj, Champakaranya

Dear Sir/ Madam

Plants give us everything. Let us give them our love; foster them with tender care; use them with wisdom and protect them with all our might to ensure that our great-grandchildren will be safe in the lap of the Green Earth – a fertile, generous and kind mother.

Be with us throughout the week to plant, irrigate and protect saplings for all the oxygen, shade, shelter, flowers, fruits, fragrance and pure atmosphere that they give us.

Come and celebrate GREEN WEEK with us.

Dr Vijay Shankar Pandey
Principal
M.S.S.G. College
Areraj: Champakaranya

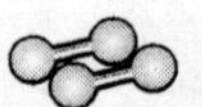

Exercise

1. Your school is organizing an Annual Sports Day. Prepare a suitable invitation.
2. The Rotary Club is organizing a Holi get-together prior to Holi. As the Secretary, prepare an invitation for the purpose.
3. You have opened a bookshop. Prepare an invitation for the inaugural ceremony.
4. Your parents are celebrating the Silver Jubilee of their marriage. Prepare a suitable invitation on their behalf.
5. You have been invited to preside over a meeting on Global Warming. Write an acceptance to the invitation.
6. You have been invited as the Chief Guest at a Public Function. Write a letter declining the offer.

Publishing Skills

• Editing • Proofreading • Scriptural Transliteration

Editing

This section is important for those who write for or wish to write for publications. All poets and writers seek to get published but most don't know how to prepare the manuscript and what is required in terms of editing; particularly the following three points:

a. Editing

b. Proofreading

c. Scriptural Transliteration

By not knowing the above, authors are bewildered and seek the help of experienced people who know something but not all the things that are required.

By knowing the process and developing the relevant skills one can prepare the manuscript in the proper manner to send it along with the proposal. Or one can even work as an editor in a publishing house. Some of the above have never been included in a book and are therefore dependent on word of mouth.

That is why this section has been included to ensure it is a comprehensive book for writers. Each topic has been dealt with sufficient detail in separate chapters.

TIPS

- Editing is a job of concentration, dedication, devotion and knowledge. It involves the finding of mistakes and correcting them; the search for loopholes and plugging them.
- It also involves arranging the text in an attractive manner and giving it a logical sequence.
- Some shortcomings are drawn to the author's attention so that additional details are given or the text is revised by the author as required.
- In fact, the job of an editor is to make a book worth reading and publishing; and to improve the quality of writing and information that would benefit the readers.
- To present the text in an attractive sequence, the matter is arranged in Sections. Chapters are also arranged accordingly. If text in one chapter has been duplicated in others, it must be deleted.

- The additional efforts to improve the quality of the book include: selection of fonts for the book title; chapter titles; other headings; sub-headings as well as an attractive font for the body copy.
- In doing this, personal preferences need to be set aside and reader preference takes precedence.
- In short, what attracts readers is of prime importance in the material presentation of the book.

Font Size:

- In the Book Title, an eye-catching, decorative or totally plain font can be used – depending upon what the publisher perceives would appeal to readers. The font size varies from 24/36/45 for the title.
- In Chapter Titles, one of the easily readable decorative fonts of size 14/16/18/20 could be used in the chapters. The same type and size is then used in all the chapters throughout the book.
- Chapter numbers are given in decorative fonts of big or bigger size, often shaded or with a double strike, usually bold or normal.
- A reasonable space of around three inches is left over the title of the chapter.
- Usually the first letter of each chapter is given in big size i.e. 36; 45; 72; invariably bold. This is called Drop cap style.
- Other Headings: In the middle of a chapter other headings are given. They should be smaller, preferably 12, 14 or 16 points and bold.
- Sub-headings: In a chapter, often there are many sub-headings. All such headings are given in bold or 2 points bigger than the size of the body text.
- Text/body: Nowadays books are printed in 8 and 9 points also but the most preferred font size is 10, 11 or 12 points. Children's books may be in 14, 16 or 18 points. Some books are in 20 and 24 points too.

TIPS

1. Capital letters or caps are termed Uppercase or u/c and small letters are called Lowercase or l/c.
2. Some prefer to print headings of chapters in all caps. But others prefer to have only the first letter of a word in caps, others in small.
3. Only nouns, verbs, adverbs and adjectives begin with caps.
4. Articles, prepositions and conjunctions are given in small letters.
5. Header is the name of the book and page number at the top of each page. Footer is the material that appears below the reading matter.
6. In most cases, the name of the book and page numbers are printed on every page either as a header or footer, particularly in books whose chapters are small or which contain many chapters.
7. In many books, mixed headers or footers are also used. The odd numbers contain the name of the book and the page number, while even numbers have the title of the chapter and page numbers. In this case, when a new chapter begins the odd page header or footer is changed accordingly.
8. Although neglected in many cases, selection of an end mark is also important. End marks should be given at the end of each chapter and, if needed, after sub-headings too. The end mark marks the beginning of a new chapter or the switchover to something different.

9. In order to indicate the end of something, small and different end marks can be given in the middle of chapters also. But in all such places in every chapter of the book the same end mark of the same size should be used.
10. The next chapter must begin from a new page. It makes no difference if a lot of space is blank at the end of the last chapter or not.
11. The book must be reader-friendly. In a cursory glance, the reader should know what is what.
12. One should not break the system used in a book. The quality of the book should not be sacrificed to save a few pages.
13. Conversely, pages should not be wasted by leaving greater space between the lines or between paragraphs.
14. Pages can be wisely saved by placing one-, two-, three-word lines side by side or in two, three or four columns or by inserting a table and adjusting that part of the matter in the table.
15. The Content page must be reader-friendly. In a chapter, major headings could be given in the Content page but not the sub-headings.
16. The chapters of sections must be given in the Section page also.
17. A Section should begin from an odd page and the back must remain blank.
18. Words or phrases taken from other languages must be given in italics but not the names of people.
19. In the text too, important statements, phrases or words should be in bold letters.
20. In dramas, single- or double-inverted commas are not given but in other books the statements or dialogues and even quotations should generally be in single-inverted comma and double-inverted commas on important occasions.
21. The pages up to the Content and the last pages as ads are not counted. Such pages are therefore not numbered.
22. The cover must be designed well and include the name of the book, author, publisher and a few catchy words or phrases that highlight the theme and content of the book; it is the cover that conveys the first impression and makes or mars the sales of a book.
23. It is best to have a short, catchy headline that attracts immediate attention and conveys the book's theme.
24. The cover photograph or illustration can also play a major role in selling or unselling a book.
25. Within 150 words, the back cover should contain something about the book that will lure readers to buy it.
26. The back cover must also contain relevant details about the author and his recent photograph.
27. An attractive book that provides ample knowledge and excellent reading is the reader's requirement and fulfilling this need is the editor's responsibility as well as the writer's duty.
28. Whether writer or editor, one should be sincere and devoted to the task.
29. Now go ahead, edit your own book and witness the difference between a writer and an editor.

Snapshot of sample editing in Track Changes

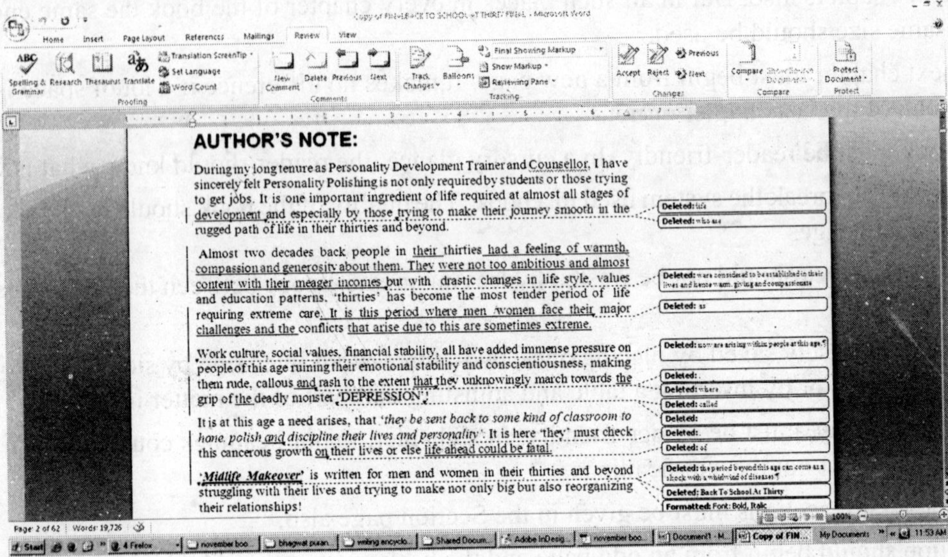

Proofreading

TIPS

- Like editing, proofreading requires concentration, dedication, devotion and knowledge. Perhaps more so because correction of mistakes is the sole responsibility of a proofreader and it is his or her responsibility to ensure an error-free book.
- This may require more than one reading to weed out all the mistakes, minor and major, besides correcting them.
- Proofreading is not an easy job and requires years of hard practice to master. There may be many mistakes in a word, line, sentence or paragraph, including the syntax.
- Even if a word is correct, it could still be substituted with a more appropriate one.
- One can't consult a dictionary at every step, which is why practice makes one perfect.
- Moreover, another difficulty is that literary words may differ from spiritual, scientific or financial words. It is, therefore, essential for a proofreader to possess a comprehensive vocabulary, even better than that of authors.
- All the same, proofreaders need to keep both light and heavy dictionaries by their side.
- Despite years of practice, some proofreaders can still end up missing mistakes, while others can speed read and detect them.
- Hard copy proofreaders don't correct the mistakes they detect. Corrections are done by DTP operators.
- To indicate the mistakes to DTP operators, the proofreader uses proofreading signs.

- In a manuscript riddled with errors, this has to be done in a neat manner so that the operator can easily understand what the proofreader wants to be corrected and how.
- For this, appropriate symbols and signs are used. Every proofreader and DTP operator need to know these signs.
- The following chart contains proofreading signs and their meanings. The signs are given after marking something or by indicating the place with a line or arrow:

Typography of Proofreading

Proofreading Abbreviations and Signs

Signs	**Meaning**	**Signs**	**Meaning**
alt.	Alter. Shift place	_	Circumflex
b.	Bold	X	Change type/font
c/ cap	Use capital letters	≈	Close; reduce space
d	Delete	:	Use colon
Pr	Darker print	:-	Use colon and dash
I/ Ital	Italicize; use italic letters	,	Use comma
L.	Less spacing; reduce space	÷	Use division mark
l.c.	Lower case/use small letter	=	Use equal to mark
lead in	Increase space	†	Use dagger mark
l. pr.	Use lighter print	_	Use dash
N P	Begin New Paragraph	‡	Use double dagger mark
Rom	Use Roman	⌐	Elevate/grow the word
run on	Arrange in one line	∟	Depress/shrink a word
>	Take from here	&c.	Et cetera
s. cap	Use small capital	!	Use sign of exclamation
Stet.	Use the line as it is	?	Use sign of interrogation
tr.	Transpose; shift it.	©	Use sign of copyright
w.f.	Wrong font	®	Use registered mark
..	Acute accent	@	Use the sign of at the rate of
=	Align	⊙	Use full stop
&	Use ampersand	˘ / -	Use macron; high sound sign
‘	Use apostrophe	¶ (N.P)	Begin New Paragraph
A v	Replace with unmarked letter	%	Use per cent sign
*	Use asterisk	ÿ ÿ	Use quotation mark
* * *	Use asterism	;	Use semi-colon
{ }	Use braces	⫡	Correct space appearance
( )	Use small brackets	#	Separate words

[ ]	Use big brackets	~	Use tilde sign
[	Carry the word further to left	$	Use dollar sign
]	Carry the word further to right	₹	Use rupee sign
^	Add left out	Ā ā	Use long aa sound

Scriptural Transliteration

What is Scriptural Transliteration?

Scriptural Transliteration is the use of special Roman alphabets to write Devanāgari, Sanskrit, Hindi or other popular Indian words with the correct sound.

When they came to India, the French, Portuguese and British were enchanted by Indian Literature, Scriptures and scientific writing.

Most of them faced a problem while pronouncing Sanskrit words and shlokas. In order to make things easier, they revised Roman letters selectively in order to write different sounds correctly.

Some examples are given below:

Sound

Original Sound	Changed Letter
आ	Ā ā
ई	Ī ī
ऊ	Ū ū
भा	Ś ś
ण	Ŋ ŋ

Words

Original Sound	Changed Letter
पुराण	Purāŋ
शिव	Śiv
शीष	Śīş
ऋषि	ŗşi
श्रुति	śruti

Shlokas with Meaning

यां विदित्वा अखिलं बन्धं निर्मथ्या खिलवर्त्मना ।
योगी याति परं स्थानं सा मां पातु सरस्वती ।।

Yāma viditvā akhilam vandham nirmathyā khilavartamanā;
Yogi yāti param sthānam sā mām pātu Saraswati.
When one comes to know Bhagawati Saraswati
then that Yogi breaks all the fetters
and gets absolute command.
May that Bhagawati save me!

* * *

सर्वमंगल मांगल्येंशु शिवे सवार्थ साधिके
शरण्ये त्र्यम्बके गौरी नारायणी नमस्तुते !
Sarva mangala māngalaye Shiva sarbārtha sādhike,
Sharanye trayambake gauri nārāyani namastute.
(O Nārāyani! You are auspicious and keep everything auspicious!
You are Shivā that fulfils every wish!
You are Gauri with three eyes and
take care of those that seek shelter!
I salute Thee!

* * *

Symbols

First: Swar: Vowels

Devanāgari	अ	आ	इ	ई	ड	ऊ	ए	ऐ	ओ	औ	अं	अः	ऋ	लृ	लॄ
Roman	a,e,i,o,u	ā	i	ī	U	ū	e,	ai	o	ou	ang	ah	ṛ	í	ḷ

Second: First Set of Vyanjanas: Consonants

Devanāgari	क	ख	ग	घ	ड.	च	छ	ज	झ	ञा	ट	ठ	ड	ढ	ण,रा
Roman	ka	kha	ga	gha	ńa	ca	cha	ja	jha	ň	t.	t.h	d.h	d.h	ŋ
Devanāgari	त	थ	द	ध		प	फ	ब	भ	म					
Roman	ta	tha	da	dha	na	pa	pha	ba	bha	ma					

Third: Second Set of Vyanjanas: Yavarga: Other Consonants

Devanāgari	य	र	ल	प	ंभा	ा	स	ह	क्ष	त्र	ज्ञ
Roman	ya	ra	la	va,wa	ś	ś	s	ḥ	ksha	tra	jna, gya

Popular Writing

• Appreciation • Synopsis • Content Writing • Blogs • Book Blurbs • Script/Screenplays/Serials

Appreciation

TIPS

- Writing appreciation is an art and demands deep critical attitude and aptitude as well as an analytical mind.
- Appreciation needs both analysis and synthesis on a higher plane. If not, it will be a superficial observation.

EXAMPLE **An Appreciation of Mahatma Gandhi**

Indomitable yet Flexible: Mahatma Gandhi possessed both a deeply attached and completely detached personality. With his religion, philosophy, objectives and works, he was deeply attached; but with material gains, desires and outcome of deeds, he was completely detached.

A worker and thinker, he truthfully translated all his thoughts and ideas into action. He was also an active convener, powerful organizer, and successful mass leader with a lofty spiritual mindset. He was the voice of millions; whatever he said was echoed by the entire country.

Mahatma Gandhi was a dream, the dream of millions of Indians. He succeeded because he worked on the real, hard surface of Truth among the people and along with the people.

He was power: pure, uncontaminated, indefatigable, celestial power. He took power from others and gave power to all.

He possessed the sharpest, most effective weapon of non-violence; the weapon of the masses that worked against Falsehood, Darkness, Excesses, Immorality, Aggression and Oppression.

Mahatma Gandhi was a grand substitute for the desires of all Indians but there is no substitute for him in the whole world.

Synopsis

TIPS

- Synopsis is the summary of a book.
- It presents the complete planning of the book in the offing.
- In other words, it is a primary sketch of the book.
- The synopsis should therefore be prepared meticulously and painstakingly.
- The pain undergone in preparing the synopsis curbs the hardships and pain during writing.
- The synopsis could become the proposal for acceptance by a university or organization and even for publication.
- A synopsis of a written article is also prepared for easy preview and acceptance.
- Herein, details spanning hundreds of pages have to be compressed into a few pages.

Synopsis of the book The Art of Sensitive Parenting – ***Published by Pustak Mahal:*** This book is about the Samvedana of parenting. Samvedana is the Hindi derivative from its Sanskrit root Sam-vedana meaning feeling with deep sensitivity. This book uses the concept of Samvedana to underline the obligation of sensitive parenting and calls for creating an adult-child relationship of 'feeling together' in favour of the growing child. It is about exploring the physical and social/emotional world of the child with the child, in understanding the issues of child development. It opens up the child's world to the adult, both the parent and the teacher, a world that has been little understood and much misinterpreted. In doing so, it provides simple but valuable techniques to parents and teachers in handling children in early stages of schooling. The book is not only about the significance of sensitivity to children's growing needs but also about growing up with children. It is about understanding their conflicts and traumas at each phase of their development and facilitating them to resolve them. It invites parents to enjoy the fascinating journey of childhood and to relive it with the growing child. It thus evokes the samvedna of parenting — to understand children's perspectives in a sensitive manner; listen to their side of the story; be open to learn from them and discover the profoundness of the inner child beyond what seems like flippant, external childishness.

The book is based on the work of the author with a number of schools and non-governmental organizations involved in implementing or promoting innovative preschool and primary education. Each issue dealt with in the book has been the subject of discussion with parents and teachers in a number of interactive sessions over the years. Many of the themes were revised based on the feedback from parents and teachers. All the ideas are based on real life experiences and personal narratives of cases from urban and rural schools with which the author has been associated over a span of more than two decades as a mentor and researcher. The book contains for teachers and parents are those who have been reported to be working well for them.

Every parent would like to see her or his child grow into a balanced person realizing one's full potential. They look for scientific but simple and easy to understand advice from real life. This is precisely what the book attempts to do – to reach out to the needy parents and teachers who are engaged in bringing up children. The most important characteristic of the book is its simple style and language. It avoids unnecessary theory and technical jargons and does not demand any specialized knowledge; yet, it is based on scientific evidences and has the potential to influence teachers and parents making them more sensitive to the growing child's cognitive, social and emotional needs. Built mainly on real life cases from their own surroundings, it has ready appeal to the common parents and teachers alike.

Finally, the book is unique in that it explicitly links home and school, work of parents and teachers, treating child's life space as one continuum between the home and the school. Thus, the proposed book traverses between home and school addressing a critical group of modern parents whose children have just begun going to school. The book, therefore, in a unique way acts as a link between the parents and the teachers, contributing to development of a shared understanding of the challenges of dealing with the growing child. It attempts to bridge the traditional gaps in knowledge and expectations between the school and the home which will invariably affect the growth and development of the child. Yet, it is not unduly a problem-centred book; nor is it prescriptive presenting to parents lists of do's and don'ts. It is crafted with a positive tone and language; it is more about helping teachers and parents alike to enjoy the playfulness, spontaneity and creativity of the growing child. Through this the book tries to introduce to parents and teachers the principles and practices of "sensitive parenting" or parenting with feeling.

A Comparative Study of Milton and Sri Aurobindo with Special Reference to 'Paradise Lost' and 'Sāvitri' – ***A Proposed Project by Prof Shrikant Prasoon:*** John Milton is a renowned author of the 17th century and Sri Aurobindo a famous writer of the 20th century. John Milton composed two related religious epics Paradise Lost and Paradise Regained. Sri Aurobindo composed Sāvitri – an epic centred on spirituality and energy.

Both Sri Aurobindo and Milton are so rich in thought and have everything in such abundance that one can begin thinking and take ideas from them and keep on collecting and expressing ceaselessly but the flow of ideas will never cease. The broadness of their poetic thought, the depth of perceptions and the height of expressions are enough to keep readers engrossed throughout.

Both Sri Aurobindo and Milton have been read and analysed and yet something seems to elude both readers and critics always. But each one is rewarded and filled with immense energy, purity and spirituality.

It is always gratifying to read an epic or an epic author in broader dimensions and with reference to other epic poets. Epics have eternal qualities, universal appeal and infinite human values. They purify and make readers grow. They help in making a reader sublime.

Paradise Lost and Sāvitri: These two epics – one composed by Milton in the 17th century and the other by Sri Aurobindo in the 20th century – have many things common and uncommon. Though composed centuries apart, somehow both are aimed at 'paving the way of God to man'.

Man has severed his relations with Nature, Natural Elements and God. To denounce God has become a fashion. Europe is bent upon making the whole world purely materialistic. Indian spiritualism has been vociferously claiming that such inclinations towards matter and materialism will ruin the Earth, making it another dead planet. The ozone layer is almost gone, whereby it's said to be a 'hole'; but 73 million kilometres can't be a 'hole'. We make designer clothes for ourselves and in the process make Mother Earth naked and devoid of greenery. Are we not helping Satan and not working like his agent? Is Yama not taking away the very life, the husband, Satyavān? Are we strong, wise and illuminated enough to fight against Yama and take our beloved 'life' back along with numerous blessings?

These are the main reasons a comparative study is needed. The Theme, Philosophy and Spirituality in both epics are universal and their study can help us in regaining Paradise and in saving the Earth and life on it from extinction. Moreover, it will serve a larger intellectual and human purpose.

It is always difficult to compare two epics or two epic authors. There are so many things in common, yet so many contradictory elements that they cannot be included in one article or even a book. This is so true in the case of Paradise Lost and Sāvitri. They are similar yet opposite; they are based on the same theme but the context and treatment are altogether different.

The comparison may not be comprehensive, complete or convincing but it is interesting and pleasing to know two legendary figures, two great books, two dignified ways of living, two apparently different philosophies and two different times, simultaneously. It will serve a great purpose in showing man his true worth, worldly and spiritual duty; bring him nearer to Nature and determine his relations with human, demonic and other living and non-living beings. Infinity will be revealed and cosmic energy will be absorbed through the panoramic views of the great epic authors.

Content Writing

TIPS

- In the hurry to put everything on the Internet, content writing has become very popular and everywhere people are writing content to be put on Internet for others to get the needed information.
- Truthfully and without prejudice the content should be prepared about a person; place; country; event; company; culture; both from the Past and the Present.
- The language must be brisk and easily comprehensible.
- There should not be any distortion in facts or addition from imagination.
- Content writing is not literary but factual writing.

The Achievements of Mrs Indira Gandhi: There are many achievements of Mrs Indira Gandhi where people usually talk about personal marks and milestones. But these are physical, political and material achievements. Yet, there are many achievements that have moulded the minds and character of the people. These are her real achievements.

Mrs Indira Gandhi showed strong will to maintain discipline. She believed in control and discipline to be the strongest stairs to success. Mrs Gandhi believed success could be guaranteed if a balance is maintained in life; if there is faith in the self, God, knowledge and the people; and if there is hope. She became a symbol of faith and hope.

The second greatest achievement of Mrs Indira Gandhi was the awakening and emancipation of women. Mrs Gandhi gave women a definite aim and immense mental, moral and social power. This changed their life and attitude. She made women come out, feel equal to men and try to be even better than men in many spheres of life.

Mrs Gandhi also motivated the youth, giving them solid dreams and fruitful ideas. With the 20-point programme, she tried to achieve unmatched success. But due to various reasons, some of these plans failed to take off fully. It would have been the best thing for India had all these plan been achieved, but because of the sacrifices needed to achieve success, people were not willing to implement some programmes.

Her handling of the short war with Pakistan in 1971 and the creation of Bangladesh showed she was an assertive leader unafraid to take tough decisions when required. Her authoritarian streak that came to the fore with the Emergency lost her quite a few supporters and she was convincingly beaten in the elections immediately after it was lifted.

But the failure of the Opposition to present a credible alternative meant she was back in power in the subsequent elections, which she won handily. Her premature death meant India lost a great leader who did not live to see her dream of India becoming a great power.

Blogs

TIPS

Blogs have evolved from online diaries into a global force that influence everything from consumer habits to pop music. Bloggers can choose a blog setup that is only visible to specific people or create one that is open to the entire world. It is estimated that there are more than 100 million blogs online.

A blog can be used to make money, to publicize a business or simply to disseminate your ideas into the blogosphere. Many bloggers maintain more than one blog with each devoted to a different goal. With so many free blogging sites available, it's simple to create a host of blogs that accomplish your online goals.

Bear in mind that few bloggers actually make money from their writings. For that to happen, you need to develop a credible, businesslike writing style that is good at promoting causes, products, ideas and other issues. One also needs to be a prolific writer with the ability to write on different topics under the sun. Of course, those who specialize in select topics or themes also create their own fan following.

It is best to write on issues or topics that are relevant or trending during that time. An eye-catching title is important to attract attention instantly so that the reader who may just be browsing the site is immediately attracted and gets down to reading your piece. Once readers take to a particular blogger's style and if the text carries substance, they are bound to revisit the site for further readings.

It's important to cultivate an authoritative, no-nonsense tone, especially when ghostwriting for someone else. Blogs that use a call-for-action line can sometimes be popular with activist readers, depending on the issue in question.

Reverse Psychology Does the Trick: I once did something that is not usually done by a newcomer – rather an apprentice. I was not even close to the team leader. I was merely assisting him.

It so happened that 12 packers and movers were doing their work since 10:00 o'clock in the morning and at 5:00 p.m. more than 30% of the work had to be done within the next hour. The workers were asked to complete the work but they refused. The team leader promised them twice the sum that was usually paid to them but to no avail. I knew the importance of the work being completed.

I thought it over and took my own decision. I moved away from the workers quietly. I then ordered a fruit hawker to prepare about 30 plates of mixed fruits, neatly cut and spiced. He took half an hour in preparing them. Then he brought his handcart up to the door of the big store.

I politely requested the workers to stop work and eat some fruit salad and then go home and return early in the morning to finish the packing and loading. I had played with their hunger and the general psychology of tired, hungry men. They happily came out and enjoyed the dish presented in leaf plates. The truck-drivers and I, too, joined them.

The team leader was obviously angry and left the place fuming, perhaps hell-bent on reporting my interference. The workers took two plates each. The first plate was finished in a jiffy but the second was eaten at leisure. They had got the rest and refreshment they so badly needed.

Suddenly, one of them proposed that they should finish the work quickly and then go home, instead of leaving with the work unfinished and returning later to finish it. The others readily agreed to this. With rejuvenated energy they resumed work and by 8:00 the entire work was over.

Empathy and human values had clearly won the day. A sympathetic approach had won over a disciplinary approach. I learnt that day that a velvet-hand approach can sometimes work miracles.

In Harmony with Nature: My family originally hailed from a village and traditionally depended on agriculture. All members of my family, including ladies, girls and boys are really very assiduous. They remain busy in some sort of physical work or the other, the motto being: the greater the sweat, the healthier the body.

Obesity is a problem only for those who fail to control their calorie intake and gorge on fattening junk foods. Physical labour keeps one healthy and fit.

Moreover, my family spends most of its time in the open. We never close the windows of our parental house. In metros though, there are big windows but these always remain closed with thick, big glass sheets. In most windows, there is no provision to open them (even occasionally). The glasses too are obstructed by heavy curtains. We shun all freshness and live on stale things, including food, water and air.

I share these experiences of hard work and living in harmony with Nature in the hope that it may inspire others to do likewise and follow eternal human values. Money alone can't keep us healthy and happy. Money is man's creation while the five gross elements are Nature's gift to all living beings.

Monsoon Session Rains Bills: Although the Monsoon Session of Parliament was hit by the inevitable disruptions, the UPA Government managed to squeeze through crucial legislations such as the 'game-changer' Food Security Bill and the Land Acquisition Bill, amongst a flurry of Bills. Though the Opposition voiced reservations against the Bills, none dared stall them for fear of being labelled 'anti-poor'.

With the Congress and the UPA upbeat about their poll prospects after the passage of crucial Bills, they could clearly be miscalculating the electoral dividends. The true impact of these Bills will not be felt across India until after the May 2014 General Elections – too late for the Congress to reap the rewards of rank populism.

What the ruling dispensation may experience is the withering gaze of disapproval from India Inc. and other critics of these Bills. The general fear is that both Bills will fuel inflation, inflate the Current Account Deficit, decelerate business growth and drive down the rupee to more than 70 to the dollar. Indeed, stock-markets reacted adversely to the Bills' passage and the rupee breached 68 to the dollar.

Corporate icons have cautioned they may be compelled to ship investments abroad if the Government doesn't quickly get its act in order. Indeed, due to unreliable power and water supplies in India, Biocon's Kiran Mazumdar-Shaw has asserted her company will invest about $200 million in a manufacturing plant in Malaysia.

Alarmingly for the UPA, an opinion poll of business leaders indicates more than three-quarters support Narendra Modi to take over as the next prime minister. Fortunately for the UPA, the vast majority of Indians, particularly from rural India, do not think along the lines of the country's business barons.

In this muddy scenario, what calmed nerves and helped the mud settle to the bottom was Raghuram Rajan assuming office on 4 September as the new RBI Governor – at perhaps the worst time any governor could take charge after 1991. As the person who predicted the 2008 global financial crisis in a November 2005 paper (Has Financial Development Made the World Riskier?), there could not have been a more astute and accomplished man to handle the job, considering his credentials as chief economist with the International Monetary Fund. Rajan's ascension has helped soothe the markets, rein in the rupee and offer Indian industry a sliver of hope where none existed.

Despite Rajan's obvious talent and business-like approach, turning things around before May 2014 seems an unlikely possibility. Clearly, the Congress needs to pull another rabbit out of its hat if it wishes to win an additional term in office.

Book Blurbs

A blurb is the book description, a summary, that you find on the back of a book or online to describe a book's contents. We do not have a fixed set pattern on writing book blurbs. When writing a back cover book blurb, feature the most intriguing parts of the content and give the reader a little taste of what's inside the book.

Use catchy words that bring up images and resonate with readers of the genre. Examples: "packed with information", "providing strategies" or a "treasure chest of..." for non-fiction and how-to-books. For fiction books "Masonic secrets, hidden esoteric wisdom" (from: The Lost Symbol by Dan Brown).

Do add a couple of endorsements from reviewers or other authors in your genre to your blurb before publishing the book.

Fifty Shades of Grey: E L James: When literature student Anastasia Steele goes to interview young entrepreneur Christian Grey, she encounters a man who is beautiful, brilliant, and intimidating. The unworldly, innocent Ana is startled to realize she wants this man and, despite his enigmatic reserve, finds she is desperate to get close to him. Unable to resist Ana's quiet beauty, wit, and independent spirit, Grey admits he wants her, too—but on his own terms.

Shocked yet thrilled by Grey's singular erotic tastes, Ana hesitates. For all the trappings of success—his multinational businesses, his vast wealth, his loving family—Grey is a man tormented by demons and consumed by the need to control. When the couple embarks on a daring, passionately physical affair, Ana discovers Christian Grey's secrets and explores her own dark desires.

Erotic, amusing, and deeply moving, the Fifty Shades Trilogy is a tale that will obsess you, possess you, and stay with you forever.

This book is intended for mature audiences.

Megaliving by Robin Sharma: Robin's first book, Megaliving is one of the most high-content and idea-rich personal development books in the market today.

For over 10 years, author Robin Sharma studied the strategies of people who have achieved lasting personal, professional and spiritual success. From leading CEOs, elite athletes and wildly successful entrepreneurs in the West to learned philosophers and wise sages living high in the Himalayan Mountains of the East. He searched for peak performers who had created lives filled with prosperity, passion and peace. This extraordinary book reveals their secrets.

Not only does it contain the 200 Lessons of Success and chapters on mental, physical and character mastery, it also has a specific 30-day coaching program to help you integrate its lessons into your daily life.

Script/ Screenplay/ Serials

TIPS

- Script or screenplay is written text that provides the basis for a film or serial that runs in cinema halls or on TV screens.
- Screenplays or scripts usually include dialogues spoken by the characters.
- Sometimes, a shot-by-shot outline of the film's or serial's actions is also written.
- Screenplays may be adapted from novels or stage plays or developed from original ideas suggested by screen writers or their collaborators.
- Each screenplay passes through multiple revisions. Screen writers incorporate suggestions and changes given by producers, directors and others involved in the film or serial production.
- Early drafts include the project or proposal and may contain brief suggestions for planned shots. This is improved and rewritten many times.
- By the date of production, a screenplay evolves into a detailed shooting script, which includes actions and gestures.
- A script or screenplay is not a literary work that cannot be changed by others. Persons involved with the film or serial can also change the dialogues and actions, if required.
- Script writers therefore need to be flexible and receptive to suggestions and changes.

My Fair Lady

— Bernard Shaw

Act – 1

Scene – I

Act – 1

Outside the Royal Opera House, Covent Garden.

Time: After theatre, a cold March night.

At rise

The opera is just over. Richly gowned, beautifully tailored Londoners are pouring from the Opera House and making their way across Covent Garden in search of taxis. Some huddle together under the columns of St. Paul's Church which are partially in view on one side of the stage. On the opposite side, there is a smudge-pot fire around which a quartet of costermongers are warming themselves. Calls of "Taxi" punctuate the icy air. Three Street Entertainers, Buskers, rush on to perform a few acrobatic tricks, stunts, and dance steps. They detain the crowd for a moment. The female member of the trio passes the hat as her two associates continue and reach the "climax" of their act.

Mrs. Eynsford-Hill— *a middle-aged lady in evening dress and her son freddy, a youngman of twenty, also in evening dress, come through the crowd in search of a taxi. One of the buskers collides into him. He is thrown backwards and strikes a figure hidden behind a group of people who now come flying forward and lands in a heap. She is a flower girl.*

***Eliza Doolittle*—** *Her basket of flowers has been knocked from her hands and her violets scat about. She is not at all an attractive person. She is perhaps eighteen, perhaps twenty, hardly older. She wears a little sailor hat of black straw that has long been exposed to the dust and soot of London and has seldom if ever been brushed. Her hair needs washing rather badly,' its mousy colour can hardly be natural. She wears a shoddy shawl, a dirty blouse with a coarse apron. Her boots are much the worse for wear. She is no doubt as clean as she can afford to be; but compared to the ladies she is very dirty. Her features are no worse than theirs; but their condition leaves something to be desired, and she needs the services of a dentist.*

***Eliza*—** *Aaaooowwwl*

***Freddy*—** *(Clumsily trying to help her) I'm frightfully sorry.*

***Eliza*—** *(Wailing) Two bunches of violets trod in the mud! A full day's wages. Why don't you look where you're going?*

***Mrs. Eynsford-Hill*—** *Get a taxi, Freddy. Do you v :t me to catch pneumonia?*

***Freddy*—** *I'm sorry, mother. I'll get a taxi right away.*

***(To Eliza)*—** *Sorry.*

(He goes)

***Eliza*—** *(Colonel pickering emerges dressed in evening clothes and looking for a taxi. He is a middle-aged gentleman of the amiable military type).*

***(To Mrs. Eynsford-Hill)*—** *Oh, he's your son, is he? Well, if you'd done your duty by him as a mother should, you wouldn't let him spoil a poor girl's flowers and then run away without paying.*

***Mrs. Eynsford-Hill*—** *Go on about your business, my girl.*

(She follows her son)

***Eliza*—** *(Muttering to herself, as she collects her flowers) Two bunches of violets trod in the mud.*

Professional Writing & Scientific Writing

• Professional Writing • Scientific Writing

Solutions to Problems of Writing and Writers

Beginning, Middle and End

Many writers argue that the hardest part of writing is the beginning. An equal number think the end is the most difficult as everything depends upon it. Others claim that to sustain in the long, middle is the toughest task. All of them are partly correct and partly incorrect. The entire writing process is fraught with perils. Insight into life, control on positive and balanced thinking, rich and lucid language helps one give a solid beginning, to maintain well during the long middle and to reach a satisfactory, acceptable and captivating end.

Some people with a mature aesthetic sense might not like this revelation that the most beautiful are usually a load of trouble. The beautiful horns of an antelope doom him; roses are plucked prematurely and wars for beautiful damsels have been common in every country and across ages. Conversely, the most useful things are usually ugly and almost hidden inside the plinth, while the top shines, is looked at, praised and talked about. The bricks that bear the load are forgotten. Therefore, the aphorism became popular that "handsome is as handsome does." Similarly, the beauty of language is easily discarded if it is meaningless or lifeless. Life in writing is more important among other important aspects. Writing must be lively.

To fill hundreds of sheets of blank pages and carve out a subject with various dimensions and bring them alive is never easy. What is the toughest thing then for a writer is to remain fully conscious from beginning to end and keep everything fresh right from a superfluous idea to the main theme.

Pain is natural, while pleasure has to be squeezed out. Dust flies in throughout the day. The homemaker has to keep the house clean by repeatedly dusting and cleaning each day. Likewise, writing should be well thought over; read and reread; corrected and re-corrected. Bizarre thoughts are common like dust; useful thoughts are hidden among the common and bizarre.

A writer has to do three things:

1. Writing must please all instantaneously: *sadyah parnorvirtaye*.
2. There must be novelty in the writing. An accomplished writer will not repeat what has already been written.

3. The writer must remain thoroughly alert and conscious. One should write only when one is refreshed, conscious and able to concentrate. This is one reason why most writers have peculiar ways and timings for writing. This is the best way for them to remain fully alert, conscious and retain full concentration.

To be thoroughly conscious is true not only for a book. It is equally true about a small letter, a minor report or writing a comment, preparing a note or concluding an article. To remain fully focused on the subject matter is the core problem of a writer. Only they can succeed who master all these aspects.

In the process of writing as a responsible writer, nothing is easy: neither the ideas nor the words; neither the presentation of ideas nor its explanations; neither the shape and form of words and ideas nor of the phrases and clauses; neither the statements nor the conclusions; neither the descriptions nor the dialogues; neither the quotes nor their relation to the context. Everything is difficult and every writer has to handle them consciously, with an alert, thinking mind, and adroitly, of course.

Selection of Topic: When one receives an assignment to write a book, it is easier because the subject has been identified. But when one has to select a subject, the writer faces many problems. The greatest problem is whether the readers and publishers will like the subject matter or not. If the subject is rejected then the writing, its standard and qualities become redundant and meaningless.

In selecting a subject one must consider whether:

- It will be liked or not;
- It will be useful or not;
- There is enough material or not;
- Justice can be done to the topic or not;
- The idea will appeal or repel society;
- It will add something to existing human knowledge;
- It will present a guideline for the future or lead to a blind alley.

If the answers to the above (and other relevant points) are positive, the writer may venture to write. If not, the writing is not essential, since the market is already flooded with books on almost every topic under the sun. Adding another book that would be lost amidst the crowd will make no sense.

Known Solution: Self-study and Entertainment

Kāvya-shāstra vinodena kālo gachchhati dheemtām;
Vyasanena cha murkhānām nidrayā kalhena wā.

(Fools spend their time in relaxing and sleeping and fighting; the wise spend their time in studying poetry and Scriptures and in entertainment.)

The books should therefore be like classics and classified as the best. To achieve this, it takes consistent, conscious and persistent effort towards the goal of becoming a poet, writer, dramatist or whatever else one wishes to be.

Study of Books and Life: The only simple solution to all problems of writers is incessant practice: reading a lot and writing a lot. Continuous, conscious practice can turn a person into an expert, popular writer. If one does not read extensively, one can't become a good writer. Thinking, pondering and comprehending what one has read is a simple solution to tough problems of writers. Combined with writing practice, it will help one develop a novel and original style of one's own.

The other determining factor is that the writer is a creator. Like the original Creator, the writer should also create something that will last for a lifetime.

Writers on Writing: For dozens of years, writers have been teaching aspiring writers how to write well. But in some cases, the teachings are ambiguous and could be interpreted in many ways. With the Internet, such lessons have become easier and more accessible.

TIPS

- Change the overwhelming task of writing into small manageable tasks. Then simply get going with the first task and so on.
- The first draft is the child's draft, where you let it all pour out and romp all over the place, knowing that no one is going to see it and you can fine-tune it later. You just let this childlike part of you channel whatever voices and visions come through onto the page.
- If one of the characters wants to say something weird, let her. No one is going to see it. If the kid wants to get really sentimental or weepy, you let him. Just get it all down on paper because there may be something great in those six crazy pages that you would never have gotten to via more rational means.
- Don't bother about your first draft not being the best. Just get going.
- Once you begin, the subsequent drafts will always get better through rereading and rewriting.

From Annie Dillard: Annie Dillard has written 11 books, including *An American Childhood* and *Pilgrim at Tinker Creek*. In *The Writing Life* she explores her life as a writer and explains what a writer needs to do for a successful book.

Here are some gems from *The Writing Life*:

1. "One of the few things I know about writing is this: spend it all, shoot it, play it, lose it, all, right away, every time. Do not hoard what seems good for a later place… Something more will arise for later, something better."
2. "Write as if you were dying. At the same time, assume you write for an audience consisting solely of terminal patients. That is, after all, the case."
3. "It is no less difficult to write sentences in a recipe than sentences in Moby Dick. So you might as well write Moby Dick."
4. "When you write, you lay out a line of words. The line of words is a miner's pick, a wood carver's gouge, a surgeon's probe. You wield it, and it digs a path you follow. Soon you find yourself deep in new territory. Is it a dead end, or have you located the real subject? You will know tomorrow, or this time next year."
5. "A work in progress quickly becomes feral. It reverts to a wild state overnight... it is a lion growing in strength. You must visit it every day and reassert your mastery over it. If you skip a day, you are, quite rightly, afraid to open the door to its room. You enter its room with bravura, holding a chair at the thing and shouting, 'Simba!'"

Seth Godin: Marketing guru and best-selling author Seth Godin, who has been called "the ultimate entrepreneur for the Information Age", generously offers 19 pieces of advice for aspiring writers. Here are three useful tips:

1. Lower your expectations. The happiest authors are the ones that don't expect much.
2. The best time to start promoting your book is three years before it comes out. Three years to build a reputation, build a permission asset, build a blog, build a following, build credibility and build the connections you'll need later.
3. Pay for an editor. Not just to fix the typos, but to actually make your ramblings into something that people will choose to read.

Explaining how he managed to be so prolific, William Stafford said: "Every day I get up and look out of the window, something occurs to me. Something always occurs to me. And if it doesn't, I just lower my standards."

Neal Bowers was told by his first creative writing teacher, Malcolm Glass, to "Trust the process and the reader." His teacher also had a colourful metaphor of grabbing the tail of a wild hog as it runs by and letting it drag you through the thicket. When he first heard it, the metaphor didn't help Neal much. He however adds the following: "These days, though, I often look back at those unplanned and unpredictable trails my writing makes through the brush, with me hanging on, and I think of Malcolm's wild hog."

James Patterson's method is simple: "I'm always pretending that I'm sitting across from somebody. I'm telling them a story, and I don't want them to get up until it's finished."

Margaret Atwood: "If I waited for perfection, I would never write a word."

Octavia Butler said: "You don't start out writing good stuff. You start out writing crap and thinking it's good stuff, and then gradually you get better at it. That's why I say one of the most valuable traits is persistence."

In Joan Didion's words: "I constantly retype my own sentences; every day I go back to page one and just retype what I have. It gets me into a rhythm."

Another common piece of advice from successful writers is to write about what you know. Hemingway was an avid hunter and fisherman – two activities that feature prominently in much of his writing – and he lived within walking distance of the fishing village in Cuba from which Santiago from The Old Man and the Sea hailed.

More from Authors for Authors: Most academics, including administrators, spend much of their time writing. But we aren't as good at it as we should be. I have never understood why our trade values, but rarely teaches, nonfiction writing.

In nearly 30 years at universities, I have seen a lot of really talented people fail because they couldn't, or didn't, write. And some much less talented people (I see one in the mirror every morning) have done reasonably well because they learned how to write.

It begins at the graduation level. There is a real transformation as people switch from taking courses to writing. Many graduate students who were stars in the classroom during the first two years – whom the people everyone admired and looked up to – suddenly weren't so stellar anymore. And some of the marginal students – who didn't care much about pleasing professors by reading every page of every assignment – were suddenly sending their own papers to journals, getting published, and transforming themselves into professional scholars.

The difference is not difficult to find. It's writing.

Many writers have talked about how hard it is to write well. Fortunately, the standards of writing in most disciplines are so low you don't need to write exceptionally well.

Below are select tips from writers on scholarly nonfiction writing that might help people write better.

1. **Writing is an exercise.** You get better and faster with practice. If you were going to run a marathon a year from now, would you wait for months and then run 26 miles? No, you would build up slowly, running most days. You might start on the flats and work up to more demanding and difficult terrain. To become a writer, write. Don't wait for that book or that external-review report to work on your writing.
2. **Set goals based on output – not input.** "I will work for three hours" is a delusion; "I will type three double-spaced pages" is a goal. After you write three pages, do something else. Prepare for class, teach and attend meetings or do whatever. If later in the day you feel like writing some more, great! But if you don't, then at least you wrote something.
3. **Find a voice; don't just "get published."** James Buchanan won a Nobel in Economics in 1986. One of the questions he asked job candidates: "What are you writing that will be read 10 years from now? What about 100 years from now?" Someone once asked me that question and it is pretty embarrassing because most of us don't think that way. We focus on "getting published" as if it had nothing to do with writing about ideas. Paradoxically, if all you are trying to do is "get published", you may not publish much. It's easier to write when you're interested in what you're writing about.
4. **Give yourself time.** Writers sit at their desks for hours, wrestling with ideas. They ask questions, talk with other smart people over drinks or dinner, then go on long walks. And later write more. Don't worry that what you write is not too good or immediately usable. You get ideas when you write; you don't just write down ideas.
5. **Everyone's unwritten work is brilliant.** And the more unwritten it is, the more brilliant it is. You will always meet those glib, intimidating graduate students or faculty members. They have all the answers. They can tell you just what they will write about, and how great it will be. Years pass and they still have the same 200-word answer to "What are you working on?" It never changes because they are not actually working on anything, except that one little act. On the other hand, you are actually working on something, and it keeps evolving. So don't be fooled by the poseur who never actually writes anything. You are the winner here.
6. **Write first – then squeeze the other things in.** Put your writing ahead of your other work. If you happen to be a "morning person", write early in the day. Or you may be a "night person" or something in between. Ensure you get into the habit of reserving your most productive time for writing. Squeeze the other things in; the writing comes first.
7. **Not all thoughts are profound.** Many people get frustrated because they can't get analytical on the big questions. Then they don't write at all. So begin small. The profound thoughts will come along the way.

8. **Your most profound thoughts are often wrong.** Or, at least, they are not completely correct. Precision in asking your question, or posing your puzzle, will not come easily if the question is hard. I always laugh to myself when new graduate students think they know what they want to work on and what they will write about for their dissertations. Nearly all of the best scholars are profoundly changed by their experiences in doing research and writing about it. They learn by doing, and sometimes what they learn is that they were wrong.
9. **Edit your work, again and again.** Exchange papers with peers or a mentor, and when you are sick of your own writing, reciprocate by reading their work. You need to get over a fear of criticism or rejection. Nobody's first drafts are good. The difference between a successful scholar and a failure need not be better writing. It is often better editing.
10. **If you have trouble writing, you have not written enough.** Writing lots of pages has always been easy for me. I could never get a job being only a writer, though, because I still don't write well. But by thinking about these tips and following them myself, I have reached the point where I can make writing work for me and my career.

Scientific Writing

While writing a scientific book, an author has no option but to write as per a scientific format. Most scientific writings are in the form of papers and projects for approval or for publication in peer-reviewed research journals.

The following format indicates the way to prepare a synopsis, proposal, project or research paper.

Abstract: State the problem, your approach and solution, and the main contributions of the paper. Include little, if any, background and motivation. Be factual but comprehensive. The material in the abstract should not be repeated word for word in the paper later.

Introduction: The Introduction is crucial. By the time a referee has read the Introduction, s/he has probably decided whether to accept or reject the paper – and will then read the rest of the paper seeking evidence to support the decision. A casual reader will continue if the Introduction is captivating or will set the paper aside otherwise. Again, the Introduction is crucial in such decisions.

Five-point Structure for Introduction: The Introduction comprises five paragraphs in straightforward language, covering five points:

1. The research topic; the problem to be solved;
2. Its need and importance;
3. Difficulties; the causes of previous failures;
4. The reason for not being solved before; the reasons for the success of the new venture;
5. Key components of approach and results, including specific limitations.

One can add a subsection: Summary of Contributions. It should present the list of major contributions in bullet form, mentioning the sections where they can be found. This material doubles as an outline of the rest of the paper, saving space and eliminating redundancy.

Related Work: The related work should be short yet detailed enough to cover most of the important points.

The Body: Any new important technical contribution must be articulated in the body, which should cover half the paper. Each section of the body should disclose something important.

Avoid detailing the history of how you got interested in the subject, what you did and how you arrived at the conclusion. Just narrate important aspects and leave out all boring details. The body should be linear, sustaining reader interest at every step, without any interruptions. Any unrelated but important material should be retained for the Appendix.

The structure of the body varies, depending upon the content. Some important components:

- Running Example: Use a running example throughout the paper introduced as a Sub-Section.
- Preliminaries: The preliminaries set up notation and terminology that is not part of the technical contribution. An important function of this section is to delineate material needed for the paper. Be succinct and straightforward.
- Content: This includes algorithms, system descriptions, new constructions, analyses, etc., with clear ideas at every step.

Experiments: The entire treatise is based on experiments. It must show:

- What is expected from it and who expects such experiments.
- Don't include meaningless experiments.
- Craft experiments to show the work in its best light.
- Discuss the possibilities of the experiment.
- Disclose the time required for experiments.
- Sensitivity to important parameters needs to be mentioned.
- Scalability in various aspects (data size, problem complexity, etc.) should be outlined.
- Mention briefly what the experiments should finally show.
- Add relative performance to naive approaches.
- Add relative performance to previous approaches.
- If possible, add relative performance among different proposed approaches.

Conclusions: Generally, a short summarizing paragraph will serve as a conclusion. But it should not repeat material from the Abstract or Introduction. In some cases, it's possible to make the original claims more concrete by referring to quantitative performance results.

Future Work: This material is important. One can enhance the paper's value by showing how the work sets new research directions. If some work is in progress in this direction or some articles have been published in Journals or Souvenirs, these should be mentioned. Future Work in a research topic adds value to it. But it must be in the same or a similar field whose outcome is valuable.

Acknowledgements: Mention all persons who have guided or helped you; otherwise, there will be hurt feelings. Acknowledge anyone who has contributed in any way: through discussions, feedback on drafts, implementation, etc. When in doubt about including some persons, include them.

Citations: Make all citations complete and consistent. Check over your final bibliography carefully and ensure each entry is right.

Appendices: Appendices should only contain detailed proofs and algorithms. These can be crucial for lengthy papers, but are still useful otherwise.

Preparing the Final Copy

- Since scientific words are tough to spell, be sure to check and recheck spellings.
- For drafts and technical reports use 12-point fonts, generous spacing, 1" margins, and single-column format.
- Don't torture others with tiny fonts and tight spacing.
- Tables, figures, graphs, and algorithms should always be placed on the top of a page or column, not in the body of the text, unless it is really small and fits into the flow of the paper.
- Every table, figure, graph, or algorithm should appear on the same page as its first reference, or on the following page.
- Before final submission or publication of a paper, procure a hard copy and read it carefully. A printout can always look different and reveal the matter in its true light.
- Preferably have this examined by a senior before dispatching it.

Noting

• Noting • Guidelines • Noting under SFS

Noting

Introduction: In many organisations, particularly the Government, noting is an important component of processing cases. Senior officers generally depend on the views of their team members, expressed through noting, before making decisions. Hence, noting assumes a significant place in the working of offices.

Besides, these organizations are accountable to their stakeholders for making their decisions. Therefore, they have to maintain records about the considerations that weighed with them in making decisions. Noting on files serves this need well.

What is Noting?: "Noting" is the act of recording remarks on a case to facilitate its disposal. The recorded remarks are called "Note."

The Note may be in any of the following forms:

1. Brief remarks on a simple or routine case.
2. A precis of previous papers, in a case in which exchange of views, through notes and / or correspondence, have been for a long period of time, and it is necessary to give an overview of the whole case so that a decision may be made.
3. A statement of the case in which views of the parties consulted have been obtained and a decision is now required.
4. An analysis of questions requiring decision in a complicated case which has been examined in detail.
5. Views, comments, and suggestions made by the persons who have considered the case at different levels. These may include suggestions about alternative courses of actions, the implications of each such course, and recommendation about the most appropriate course of action.
6. Final orders passed in the case.

Cases Where Noting is not Required: Noting is not required when, in a case, the line of action is obvious, or is based on a clear precedent or practice, or has been indicated by a higher officer, and a communication is to be sent. In such matters, a fair copy of the communication or a draft, or a draft with fair copy of the communication, as case may be, can be put up.

Noting may not be necessary when dealing with cases of repetitive nature, such as sanctioning of leave, GPF advances, forwarding of applications, and the like. In such cases, Standard Process Sheets should be devised with the approval of the Branch Officer. A Standard Process Sheet is a skeleton note developed for repetitive items of work. It shows pre-determined points of check or aspects to be noted upon, and also has space for the sanctioning or approving authority to pass his orders. By filling blanks in these sheets, answers of check points are given and the competent authority can give his orders on the basis of these answers.

Cases Where Noting is Required: Noting is necessary in cases which require examination or in which an officer has given directions for their examination.

Noting will also be necessary when the office initiates a proposal on its own for consideration and approval.

Action before Noting in a Case: Before writing a note, the dealing hand should check that all statements made in the receipt, insofar as they are open to check, are correct, and that there are no mistakes or misstatement of facts. If there are any such discrepancy, this should first be reconciled. In such a case, a brief note pointing out the discrepancy may be put up for approval of higher officers. Further action on the receipt may be taken after the discrepancy has been reconciled.

What to Write in a Note?: When writing a note, the following points should be covered, wherever applicable:

1. Draw attention, where necessary, to legal position or precedents or conventions and point out the relevant law and rules. Copies of such law, rules, and precedents should also be put up.
2. Furnish any other relevant data or information available in the office for fuller understanding of the case.
3. State the questions for consideration and bring out clearly the points requiring decision.
4. Suggest, where possible, alternative courses of action, and indicate the implications of each one of them.
5. Suggest the most appropriate course of action and give its justification.
6. If acceptance of the suggestion will involve expenditure of money, the position about the availability of funds, and, where necessary, views of the finance department or finance branch, if consulted, should also be stated.
7. Indicate the authority whose approval or sanction is required in the case.

Guidelines for Writing Notes: A note is a piece of writing intended for internal use within the organization. Therefore, the principles of effective writing should be followed in writing notes. Thus, a note should be.

1. Complete – it should answer all questions that have been raised and all other possible questions that may arise while considering the case. Answers to questions such as What, Why, How, When, Where, and Who will help in making the note complete.

2. Clear – it should be written, as far as possible, choosing short, familiar words, using short sentences, in active voice, and preferring concrete expressions in place of abstract ones.
3. Concise and to the point – it should not contain wordy expressions, or trite or unnecessary expressions, and should include only relevant statements. It should also avoid repetitions either of words or ideas.
4. Coherent – it should be logically arranged, sticking to one idea for each paragraph, and linking together sentences and paragraphs.
5. Correct – it should be factually correct, figures should be free from mistakes, and the writing should be grammatically correct.
6. Courteous – it should express ideas tactfully, without hurting anybody's feelings, and emphasise positive facts. If apparent errors or incorrect statements in a case have to be pointed out or if an opinion expressed therein has to be criticized, care should be taken to couch the observations in courteous and temperate language free from personal remarks.
7. Organised properly – it should put ideas in the best order for impact, reflecting clear thinking. The first paragraph should state the main point followed by paragraphs giving evidence and discussing it, and the final paragraph should contain recommendations.
8. Visually attractive – it should be made attractive by dividing the note in serially numbered paragraphs, using headings and limiting the paragraphs within six to ten lines. Wherever possible use bullets and other lists, and leave a small margin of about one inch on all sides (left, right, top and bottom).
    1. Notes and orders should normally be recorded on note sheets in the note portion of the file.
    2. Notes should be typed or written on both sides of the note sheet.
    3. Black or blue ink should be used by all category of staff and officers. Only an officer of the level of Joint Secretary of Government of India and above may use green or red ink.
    4. The verbatim reproduction of extracts from or paraphrasing of the paper under consideration, fresh receipt, or any other part of correspondence or notes on the same file, should not be attempted.
    5. While passing orders or making suggestions, an officer should confine his note to the actual points he proposes to make without reiterating the ground already covered in the previous notes. If he agrees to the line of action suggested in the preceding note, he should merely append his signature.
    6. Any officer, who has to put note on a file, on which a running summary of facts is available should, in drawing attention to the facts of the case, refer to the appropriate part of the summary without repeating it in his own note.
    7. Relevant extracts or a rule or instruction should be placed on the file and attention to it should be drawn in the note, rather than reproducing the relevant provisions in the note.
    8. Unless a running summary of facts is already available on the file or the last note on the file itself serves that purpose, a self-contained note should be put up with every case submitted to the highest authority of the organization. Such a note should bring out

briefly but clearly relevant facts, including the views expressed on the subject by other departments, if any, consulted in the matter and the point or points on which the orders of the highest authority are sought.

9. When a paper under consideration raises several major points which require detailed examination and respective orders, each point (or group of related points) should be noted upon separately in section notes; such notes should each begin with a list of the major point(s) dealt with therein.
10. The dealing hand should append his full signature with date on the left below his note. An officer should append his full signature on the right hand side of the note with name, designation, and date.
11. If the note has been written till the end of the page, and there is no blank sheet thereafter, a blank note sheet should be added to the file, so that the officer is not inconvenienced in writing his note or giving his orders.

Modification of Notes or Orders: Senior Officers should not require any modification in, or replacement of, the notes recorded by their juniors once they have been submitted to them. Instead, the higher officers should record their own notes giving their views on the subject, where necessary correcting or modifying the facts given in earlier notes. In any case, the replacement or modification of the notes which have already been recorded on a file, when the file has been further noted upon by others, should not be permitted.

Pasting over a note or a portion of it to conceal what has been recorded should not be done. Wherever a note recorded in the first instance requires any modification on account of additional facts or any error having come to notice, a subsequent note may be recorded, keeping the earlier note intact.

Where a final decision already communicated to a party is found later on to have been given on a mistaken ground or wrong facts or wrong interpretation of rules due to misunderstanding, such withdrawal may also have legal implications. In all such cases, in addition to consulting the Ministry of Law, wherever necessary, such a withdrawal should be permitted only after the approval of an officer higher than the one who took the original decision, has been obtained and reasons for the reversal or modification of the earlier decision have been duly recorded on the file.

Noting on Files Received from other Departments: If a reference seeks the opinion, ruling, or concurrence of the receiving department and requires detailed examination, such examination should normally be done separately through routine notes and only the final result should be recorded on the file by the officer responsible for commenting upon the reference. The officer to whom such a note is submitted will either accept that note or record a note of his own. In the former case, he may direct that the note in question or a specified portion thereof may be reproduced on the main file for communication to the department concerned. In the latter case, he should record a suitable note on the main file itself. In either case, a copy of the note recorded on the main file should be kept on the routine notes for retention in the receiving department before the file is returned to the originating department.

The department should open subject-wise files each year in which such routine notes should be kept. The inter-departmental note recorded on the file of the originating department should bear the subject file number to facilitate filing of papers and their retrieval for future reference.

Where the reference requires information of a factual nature or other action based on a clear precedent or practice, the dealing hand in the receiving department may note on the file straightaway.

Where a note on a file is recorded by an officer after obtaining the orders of a higher officer, the fact that the views expressed therein have the approval of the latter should be specifically mentioned.

In making written inter-departmental references, the following points should be observed:

1. Inter-departmental references, should normally be made under the directions of an officer not below the rank of Under Secretary or as may be provided by the departmental instructions.
2. The points on which the opinion of other departments is sought or which it is desired to bring to their notice should be clearly stated.
3. Where possible, the drafts of the orders proposed to be issued may also be shown to the departments sought to be consulted.
4. When it is necessary to consult more than one department on a case, such consultation may be effected simultaneously by self-contained inter-departmental note, unless:
   (i) it involves copying of a large number of documents available on the file; or
   (ii) the need for consulting the second department would arise only after the views of the first have become available.

When such a reference requires concurrence of one or more department the following further points should be observed:

(i) The originating department should invariably prescribe a time-limit when calling for comments or concurrence from other departments.

(ii) In case any of the departments so consulted is not in a position to send its comments/ concurrence within the prescribed time-limit, it should write back promptly, in any case before the prescribed time-limit, and indicate the additional time they would require for furnishing their final reply.

When such a reference does not require such concurrence, the originating department need not wait for the comments of other department beyond the prescribed time-limit, and it should feel free to go ahead with its scheme/ proposal without waiting any longer.

The initiating department should always feel free to recall its file from another department to which such a reference has been made on a file, if such a course is required to be adopted for expediting the process of decision making in the case. Such a decision to recall a file should be taken at a level not lower than that of a branch officer in the originating department.

Noting under Single File System (SFS): In the case of their own attached offices and subordinate offices placed directly under them, i.e. without the intervention of an attached office, as are located in Delhi/New Delhi – referred to herein as 'Non-Secretariat Organization' (NSO) - the departments should introduce the Single File System (SFS), the details of which are described in the following paragraphs.

This system will apply to matters which have to be referred by the NSO to the department for seeking a sanction / order, i.e. a decision not within its own delegated powers.

The file cover of an SFS case should prominently show the name of the (originating) NSO and likewise indicate that it follows the SFS system.

The SFS file need not bear an I.D. (Inter-Departmental) No. or other formal method of sending, but will be sent as though it is from one officer to another in the same organisation.

The SFS file should be complete in all respects, so as to enable the department to take a decision expeditiously. Hence the NSO should ensure that:

1. every point for decision / order is clearly brought out;
2. all relevant connected papers are placed on the file, properly arranged and referred to;
3. draft orders / sanctions are put up, where they are required to be approved by the department for issue; and
4. the availability of funds, etc., is certified where additional expenditure is involved in the proposal.

The officer last dealing with the SFS case in the NSO should mark it to the appropriate officer in the department, by name. Policy files should, however, be referred to the department at appropriate levels to be determined by the department and the NSO concerned, through a general order.

All SFS file, should be invariably routed through the central registry of the department concerned. Their receipt should be entered in a separate register which should also record, against the relevant receipt entry, the dispatch of the file on its return to the NSO.

As a rule, all notings in the department should be on the NSO file. However, where sensitive or delicate matters in the sphere of personnel, policy issues, and finance are involved, the recording of notes in 'duplicate' file may be permitted by issuing general or special orders by the department. This should be done at a particular stage of the SFS case or at or above a particular level, with the final decision thereafter being suitably recorded on the SFS file.

As a convention, the secretariat noting on an SFS file should start on a new page and the noting done sequentially—except in matters of the nature referred to in the para above.

Action to implement the Government decision in SFS case, should be initiated in and by the NSO on the return of the file. Orders so issued should specifically state that they have received the concurrence of Government in the department concerned. Coples of every sanction/ order so issued by The Single File System does not apply in dealings between a department and any statutory, corporate, or other autonomous body which might be owned or controlled by it.

Conclusion: Organizations today are like vast machines which work under great pressure. The work they perform has grown enormously in volume, complexity, and variety. In these circumstances, the need is for speedy disposal of work. Therefore, there is no scope today to indulge in unnecessary and repetitive notings on files. But the accountability and the answerability towards stakeholders require that there should be some record of the contributions made by functionaries at the different levels in the organization, and the circumstances and the considerations which led to the decisions that have been made. Notings in offices serve this vital need well.

Exercise

1. Shri Jamna Das, Assistant in the Budget Section of the Central Roads & Infrastructure Development Corporation (Ministry of Transport, Government of India), has applied for grant of permission to join a one-year part-time course in Journalism being conducted by the Indira

Gandhi National Open University (IGNOU), New Delhi. The application has been forwarded by the Superintendent in charge of the Budget Section.

2. You, as the dealing Assistant in Admn. I Section of the Corporation, have been allotted this receipt for necessary action. On enquiry, you have been informed that the Journalism Course will be conducted from July 2017 to June 2018. There will be two examinations-one half-yearly examination in December 2017, and a final examination in June 2018. The University will conduct contact classes for the benefit of the enrolled students on Tuesdays, Thursdays, and Saturdays from 5.00 p.m. to 7.30 p.m. each day, and attendance of students in these classes is compulsory.

3. The Corporation follows five-day week from Monday to Friday. Office timings are from 10.00 a.m. to 6.00 p.m.

Please open a new file (No. 32/8/2005-Admn. I), and put up a note giving your recommendation.

CENTRAL ROADS & INFRASTRUCTURE DEVELOPMENT CORPORATION
(Ministry of Transport)
Admn. I Section
F. No. 32/8/2005 – Admn. I

SUBJECT: Application for Grant of Permission to Attend Part-time Courses.

S. No. 1 (Receipt) – Application dated 3.5.2017 from Shri Jamna Das, Asstt, Budget Section.

1. Proposal – Shri Jamna Das, Assistant, Budget Section, has applied for permission to attend one-year part time course in Journalism being conducted by IGNOU from July 2016 to June 2017. His application has been forwarded by the Superintendent of Budget Section.

2. Details of the course – IGNOU will conduct contact classes for the benefit of enrolled students on Tuesdays, Thursdays and Saturdays from 5.00 p.m. to 7.00 p.m. each day. Attendance of students enrolled for this course is compulsory. There will be a half-yearly examination in December 2016, and a final examination in June 2017.

3. Recommendation of Budget Section – Shri Jamna Das's application has been forwarded by Superintendent of the Budget Section. The Superintendent has, however, not given his recommendation. When contacted on this point, the Superintendent clarified that it is for the Administration Section to allow Shri Jamna Das to attend the part time course or not. On his part, however, he said that he would be able to manage the work somehow in case Shri Jamna Das is granted permission on the week days when Shri Jamna Das may not be available when he may be attending contact classes, or when he takes leave for preparing for examinations during December 2016 and June 2017. Similar views were expressed by the Manager, Budget Division, when he was asked to give his recommendation.

4. Implications of the request – In case Shri Jamna Das is allowed to join the part time course and attend contact classes, he may have to leave early, say by 4.00 p.m., so that he can reach the venue of the classes. While we may have no objection to his attending contact classes on Saturdays on which days the office is closed, attending classes on Tuesdays and Thursdays

would mean that he should be allowed to leave by 4.00 p.m. on these days, i.e., at least 2 hours earlier than the closing time. This would be against office discipline.

5. Similarly, Shri Jamna Das may ask for leave for preparing for the examinations in December 2016, and June 2017. Depending upon the need of services during these times, it would be difficult to commit the grant of leave for preparing and appearing at the examinations during these months.

6. Alternatives and their implications – The following alternatives may be considered when making a decision on Shri Jamna Das's request:

    1. Shri Jamna Das may be allowed to attend the part time course in Journalism.

       It means we agree to his leaving office early on Tuesdays and Thursdays, and grant him leave, when requested, for preparing and appearing at the examinations. His leaving office early will undermine office discipline, and granting him leave may adversely affect office work. Besides, it will be difficult to resist similar demands from other employees. Also, no commitment can be given about grant of leave in connection with the examinations.

    2. Shri Jamna Das may not be allowed to join the part time course in Journalism.

       It will give a wrong message to other employees that we do not care for their welfare. We would be projected as a heartless organization in not giving chances to our employees to improve their qualifications and better their prospects. Besides, we would also lose an opportunity to have a qualified person among our staff, who can help in presenting a better image of our Corporation. Employees may also decide to agitate to set the "wrong" "right."

    3. Shri Jamna Das may be posted in the morning shift from 8.00 a.m. to 4.00 p.m. in the Receipt and Issue Section.

       This Section works in two shifts-one from 8.00 a.m. to 4.00 p.m. and the other from 12.00 noon to 8.00 p.m. An Assistant from Receipt & Issue Section may be transferred to Budget Section as substitute for Shri Jamna Dass. In this way, the question of his leaving office early will not arise because he will be able to leave by 4.00 p.m. every day. No disruption of work is likely to be caused if he is granted leave during the examination periods. The work in Budget Section is likely to remain unaffected, because that Section is prepared to manage work with whoever substitute is provided in place of Shri Jamna Das.

7. Recommendations – It is suggested that Shri. Jamna Das may be transferred to Receipt & Issue Section to work in the morning shift from 8.00 a.m. to 4.00 p.m., and an Assistant from Receipt & issue section may be transferred to Budget Section.

   It is also suggested that Shri Jamna Das may be granted permission to join the part time course in Journalism being conducted by IGNOU from July 2016 to June 2017.

8. Approval – Approval of Chairman may be obtained to the recommendations made in para 7 above.

Sd/- Chiranji Lal
6.5.2017
Supdt. (Admn. I)

 **Exercise**

1. With a view to developing cooperation and creating a spirit of healthy competition among the employees at the headquarters and in the field offices, the Rural Handicrafts Development Corporation proposes to organize a 15-day sports meet in the first half of October every year. An estimated expenditure of Rs. 10 lakhs will be incurred on this account every year and it will be met from the Employees Welfare Fund. An organizing committee of 20 members will be nominated by the Chairman to make all arrangements and incur expenditure upto the sanctioned limit.

Please prepare a note (on a new file No. 41/1/2006-Wel) for obtaining the approval of the Chairman to this proposal. (You may make reasonable assumptions about any additional information that you may need for preparing the note).

RURAL HANDICRAFTS DEVELOPMENT CORPORATION
(Ministry of Rural Development)
Welfare Section
F. No. 41/1/2006 – WEL

Subject: Annual All-India Sports Meet – Proposal regarding—

1. The background – The Rural Handicrafts Development Corporation was set up ten years ago to promote and market rural handicrafts so that the rich culture of the country comes to the notice of the people, and rural artisans get full returns for their efforts. The Corporation's headquarters are at New Delhi, and a Branch Office of the Corporation is located in the capital of each State and Union Territory.
2. It is being felt for the past some time that although the employees at the headquarters and in the field are doing good job, there is little interaction among them. They do not fully understand the achievements and the difficulties, which their colleagues in other parts of the country are experiencing, and, therefore, do not adequately appreciate the value of their contributions. It is, therefore, considered that something should be done to generate a spirit of cooperation and healthy competition among the employees.
3. The Proposal – After discussions in several meetings with the representatives of employees at the headquarters and the field, it is considered that the best way to promote cooperation and create healthy competition will be to hold an All India Sports Meet once a year. The Meet will be open for all employees at the headquarters and the field, as well as such of the rural artisans who are interested in any sports event. The Meet will be for 15 days in the first fortnight in October every year.
4. The Sports Meet will include games like hockey, football, volleyball, swimming, tennis, table tennis etc.

5. An Organising Committee of 20 members, including Executive Director (Personnel) as Chairman and Financial Adviser, 8 representatives of the employees at the headquarters and 10 representatives of the field offices will make all arrangements for the Sports Meet. The Committee will be empowered to take decisions relating to arrangements, expenditure and all other connected matters. The Chairman of the Corporation will, however, exercise general supervision and control and will be empowered to give appropriate advice, as may be necessary. The Committee will be nominated by the Chairman of the Corporation.
6. The budget for the Sports Meet is estimated at Rs. 10 lakhs. This expenditure will be met from the employees welfare fund.
7. Approval – Approval of the Chairman is requested to the proposal made in paras 3 to 6 above.

Sd/- Nishikant Roy
21.4.2017

Supdt. (Wel.)

• Drafting • Procedure • Communication and Correspondence

Drafting

Introduction: After a decision has been made in a case, action is taken to convey it to the party concerned through an appropriate form of communication. In some case in which the branch officer or a higher officer has formulated his ideas, he may prepare a communication and authorise it for issue. In other cases, a draft is prepared and put up for approval of the competent authority.

In this chapter, we shall discuss how drafting is done and what points should be taken care of while drafting communications.

What Is Drafting?: A draft is a rough copy of the communication which is intended to be issued to convey decision or decisions or views of the competent authority. Drafting is the process of preparing this rough copy.

A draft is prepared on behalf of the competent authority. It is intended to convey the decision or views of the competent authority in such a way as if such authority has written the communication himself. Thus, the time and effort of the competent authority are saved, and he could give more attention to other important and urgent matters.

Cases Where Drafting is not Required: In routine cases, such as acknowledgements, reminders, enquiries, or replies to enquiries, and when non-confidential nature of information is to be obtained or conveyed, drafting is not required. In such cases pre-printed form letters are used.

No drafting is required in cases of simple and straightforward nature or those of repetitive nature for which standard forms of communication exist. In such cases, fair copies of the communication may be submitted to the appropriate officer for signature.

Procedure for Drafting: t is not always necessary to await the approval of the proposed line of action and the draft should be put up simultaneously along with the notes by the initiating level officer. The higher officer may revise the draft if it does not conform to the approved course of action.

After a final decision is taken by the competent authority, he may have the fair communication made for his signature and authorise its issue; otherwise, he should prepare a draft and submit it to the appropriate higher officer for approval.

The officer approving the issue of a draft should append his initials with the date on the draft. It is also expected of him that he passes order on the file simultaneously whether the draft so approved should be kept on the file (along with the office copy of the communication issued in fair) or not.

Initial drafting should be done in black or blue ink. Modification in the draft at the subsequent levels may be made in green or red ink by the officers so as to distinguish the corrections made.

General Instructions for Drafting

1. A draft should carry the message sought to be conveyed in a language that is clear, concise, and incapable of misconstruction.
2. Lengthy sentences, abruptness, redundancy, circumlocution, superlatives and repetition, whether of words, observations or ideas, should be avoided.
3. Official communications emanating from a department and purporting to convey the laws or orders of the Government must specifically be expressed to have been written under the directions of Government. This requirement does not, however, imply that each communication should start with the phrase 'I am directed to say' or 'The undersigned is directed to convey', which has the effect of distancing the communicator from the reader at the very outset. A more direct and to-the-point format is to be preferred if some degree of rapport is to be established with the receiver of the communication. The obligatory requirement can be met in a variety of imaginative ways. For instance, variations of the phrase can be added to the operative part of the letter towards the end as under:

   "............. I have the pleasure to inform you that the government, on reconsideration of the matter, has decided to sanction an additional grant of ...."

   or

   "............... In the light of the above developments, government conveys its inability to accede to ...."
4. Communications of some length or complexity should generally conclude with a summary.
5. Depending upon the form of communication, the subject should be mentioned in it (including reminders).
6. The number and date of the last communication in the series, and if this is not from the addressee, his last communication on the subject, should always be referred to. Where it is necessary to refer to more than one communication or a series of communications, this should be done in the margin of the draft.
7. All drafts put up on a file should bear the file number. When two or more communications are to issue from the same file to the same addressee on the same date, a separate serial number may be inserted before the numeral identifying the year to avoid confusion in reference, e.g., A-1101/5/(I)/2005-Est., A-1101/5(II)/2005-Est.
8. A draft should clearly specify the enclosures which are to accompany the fair copy. In addition, short oblique lines should be drawn at appropriate places in the margin for ready reference by the typist, the comparers and the despatcher. The number of enclosures should also be indicated at the end of the draft on the bottom left of the page thus-'Encl.3'.

9. If copies of an enclosure referred to in the draft are available and are, therefore, not to be typed, an indication to that effect should be given in the margin of the draft below the relevant oblique line.
10. If the communication to be despatched by post is important (e.g., a notice cancelling a licence or withdrawing an existing facility) or encloses a valuable document (such as an agreement, service book or a cheque) instructions as to whether it should be sent through registered post or speed post or in an insured cover, should be given on the draft by the Superintendent/Section Officer concerned with its issue.
11. Urgent communication with bulky enclosures to far-flung areas like Andaman & Nicobar Islands should be arranged to be despatched by Air Parcel through Indian Airlines. The addressee should also be advised through wireless to take delivery of the consignment. Instructions to this effect should be given by the Divisional Head / Branch Officer/Section Officer at the time of approval of draft.
12. The name, designation, telephone number, fax number, and e-mail address of the officer, over whose signature the communication is to issue, should invariably be indicated on the draft.
13. In writing, or typing a draft, sufficient space should be left on the margin and between successive lines so that additions or interpolation of words may be made, if necessary.
14. A slip bearing the words 'Draft for approval' should be attached to the draft. If two or more drafts are put up on a file, the drafts as well as the slips attached thereto should be marked 'DFAI', DFA II', 'DFA III' and so on.
15. Drafts which are to be issued as 'Immediate' or 'Priority' should be so marked under the orders of an officer not lower in rank than a Superintendent/Section Officer.

Authentication of Government Orders: All orders and other instruments made and executed in the name of the President should be expressed to be made in his name and signed by an officer having regular or ex-officio secretariat status of and above the rank of Under Secretary, or other officer specifically authorized to authenticate such orders.

Where the power to make orders, notifications, etc., is conferred by a statute on the Government of India, such orders and notifications should be expressed to be made in the name of the Government of India.

Addressing Communications to Officers by Name: Normally, no communication, other than that of a classified nature or a demi-official letter, should be addressed or marked to an officer by name, unless it is intended that the matter raised therein should receive his personal attention either because of its special nature, urgency or importance, or because some ground has already been covered by personal discussion with him and he would be in a better position to deal with it.

Drafting of Demi-official Letters: As the objective of writing a demi-official (d.o.) letter is to call the personal attention of the addressee, the style of writing should be direct, personal and friendly. More usage of active voice is to be preferred. (e.g. 'I notice' rather than 'It is noticed'). It is expedient to come to the issue at the beginning itself e.g. 'I seek your cooperation in the matter of ....'

A demi-official (d.o.) letter should preferably not exceed one page. If the message to be conveyed is lengthy, it is better to condense it into one page in a few small and meaningful paragraphs in a manner that holds the interest of the addressee; the detailed arguments can be set out in appendices.

The colour code in demi-official (d.o.) letter will be as follows: a demi-official (d.o.) letter from a Minister will exhibit the National Emblem in blue colour and that from an officer will exhibit the National Emblem in red colour.

Communications to the Attorney – General of India: References to the Attorney–General should be made only by the Ministry of Law and Justice.

Communication to Constitutional / Statutory Authorities: References to constitutional and statutory authorities such as Election Commission of India should normally be made in the letter form addressed to Principal Secretary / Secretary. In no case office memorandum should be sent to such authorities by the Ministries / Departments.

Comunications to the Comptroller and Auditor General of India: References to the Comptroller and Auditor General of India for his views or advice can be made only by or through the Ministry of Finance. In matters of day-to-day administration, Ministries / Departments may, however, correspond direct with the Comptroller and Auditor General of India at their discretion.

Communications to the Union Public Service Commission: References to the Union Public Service Commission should normally be made in the form of letters addressed to the Secretary. In certain matters, e.g., requisitions for recruitment, formal references should ordinarily be preceded by personal discussion at appropriate level.

Correspondence with Union Territory Administrations: All communications of a routine nature which clearly relate to the business of a particular department, should ordinarily be addressed to the Secretary in the appropriate department. Other important communications may be addressed to the Chief Secretary or the Administrator.

Correspondence with State Government: Communications on the subjects which clearly relate to the business of a particular department should normally be addressed to the Secretary of that department. Other communications including those of special nature or importance warranting attention at higher levels, may be addressed to the Chief Secretary. Demi-official letters can also be sent to officers of State Governments. In case of demi-official communications to the Chief Secretary of a State, this level should not be below the level of Joint Secretary.

Communications other than those of a purely routine nature, e.g., acknowledgements, should not ordinarily be addressed to State Governments, except with the prior approval and over the signature of the branch officer. Purely routine communications can, however, be signed by a section officer.

Correspondence with the Lok Sabha and the Rajya Sabha Secretariats: Communications meant for the Lok Sabha Secretariat or the Rajya Sabha Secretariat and requiring urgent or high level attention may be addressed to the Secretaries concerned and not to the Speaker or the Chairman direct.

Correspondence with Members of Parliament: Communications received from Members of Parliament should be attended to promptly.

Where a communication is addressed to a Minister, it should, as far as practicable, be replied to by the Minister himself. In other cases, a reply should normally be issued over the signature of an officer of the rank of Secretary only.

However, where, a communication is addressed to the head of an attached or subordinate office, Public Sector Undertakings, Financial Institutions (including nationalized banks), Division/ Branch Incharge in a Ministry / Department / Organisation, it should be replied to by the addressee himself. In routine matters, he may send an appropriate reply on his own. In policy matters, however, the officer should have prior consultation with higher authorities before sending a reply. It should, however, be ensured that minimum level at which such replies are sent to Members of Parliament is that of Under Secretary and that also in letter form only.

Normally, information sought by a Member should be supplied unless it is of such a nature that it would have been denied to him even if asked for on the floor of the Houses of Parliament.

As far as possible, in corresponding with Members of Parliament, preprinted or cyclostyled replies should be avoided.

In case a reference from an ex-Member of Parliament is addressed to a Minister or Secretary, reply to such reference may be sent by the concerned Divisional Head after obtaining approval of the Secretary of the Ministry/ Department. In case the reference is addressed to a lower level officer, reply to such reference could be sent by the officer on his own in non-policy cases and after obtaining approval of the higher authorities in policy cases. However, the minimum level at which reply could be sent should be that of an Under Secretary and that too in letter form only.

Correspondence with Ministers of State Governments: The procedure laid down in the above paragraph may also be followed in dealing with communications received from the Ministers of State Governments.

Correspondence with Foreign Governments and International Organisations: Correspondence with Foreign Governments and their Missions in India, Heads of Indian Diplomatic Missions and posts abroad and, United Nations and its specialized agencies should normally be channelised through the Ministry of External Affairs. The exceptions under which direct correspondence may be resorted to are indicated in the instructions issued by the Ministry of External Affairs.

Prompt Response to Letters Received: Each communication received from the Members of Parliament, a member of the public, a recognized association or a public body should be acknowledged within 15 days, followed by a reply within the next 15 days of acknowledgement sent.

Where

(i) delay is anticipated in sending a final reply, or

(ii) information has to be obtained from another Ministry or another office,

an interim reply should be sent within a month (from the date of receipt) indicating the possible date by which a final reply can be given.

If any such communication is wrongly addressed to a department, it should be transferred promptly (within a week) to the appropriate department under intimation to the party concerned.

Where the request of a member of the public cannot be acceded to for any reason, reasons for not acceding to such a request should be given.

As far as possible, requests from members of public should be looked at from the user's point of view and not solely from the point of view of what may be administratively convenient.

Target Date for Replies: In all important matters in which State Governments, departments of the Central Government, or other offices, public bodies or individuals are consulted, time limit for replies may ordinarily be specified. On the expiry of the specified date, orders of the appropriate authority may be obtained on whether the offices whose replies have not been received, may be allowed an extension of time or whether the matter may be processed, without waiting for their replies.

Conclusion: Drafting is a crucial activity in office. A good draft will result in a good communication being sent out of the office, and thus project a good image. A poor draft may not convey intentions correctly and there is always a chance to mess things up. It is therefore necessary that drafting is done skillfully and decisions are conveyed through good communications drafted in an appropriate form.

Exercise

1. Chief Engineer, Systems, Power Development Corporation, Ministry of Power Development, had deputed several officers during the last few years on U.N. assignments. On return, these officers were required to deposit the pension and other pensionary benefits received from the U.N. in the Government account and draw them when they retired from Government service.
2. With the replacement of the Foreign Exchange Regulation Act, 1973, with the Foreign Exchange Management Act, 1999, the position has changed and now a person resident in India may open, hold, and maintain with an authorized dealer in India resident foreign currency (RFC) account out of the foreign exchange received as pensionary benefits from his employer outside. The Chief Engineer, Systems, has, therefore, proposed that there should now be no objection to his officers to open such an account and deposit pensionary benefits from the U.N. in this account. He has also proposed that the Corporation take up the matter with the Government.

Please prepare a draft letter from the Corporation to the Government in this matter.

No. 11/31/2006-Admn. - I

Government of India
POWER DEVELOPMENT CORPORATION
(Ministry of Power Development)
New Delhi, the 17th April 2017
Secretary to the Government of India,
Ministry of Power Development, New Delhi.

Subject: Deputation of Central Government Employees to U.N. Organizations – Participation in U.N. Pension Fund Scheme.

Sir,

According to existing instructions, when a Central Government servant, on the expiry of foreign service with U.N. Organizations, rejoins his parent office under the Government, the retirement benefits sanctioned by the U.N. are credited to the revenues of the Government, and paid to the Government servant when he finally retires from the service of the Government.

2. It has been pointed out that with the replacement of the Foreign Exchange Regulation Act, 1973, by the Foreign Exchange Management Act, 1999, a person resident in India may open, hold, and maintain with an authorized dealer in India a Resident Foreign Currency (RFC) Account out of the foreign exchange received as pensionary benefits from his employer outside. Accordingly, there should now be no objection to allow a Government servant, on return from his service with U.N. Organizations, to open a RFC account with an authorized dealer in India, and deposit the pensionary benefits received from the U.N. in this account.

3. It is requested that the Government may kindly consider this matter, and convey their decision to this Corporation at an early date.

Yours faithfully,

(Rajiv Mohan)
Secretary,
Tel. No. 23384185

No. 11/31/2006-Admn. I Dated: the 17th April, 2017

Copy forwarded to the Chief Engineer, Systems, Power Development Corporation,

New Delhi, for information with reference to their letter No. 12/3/2006-Estt. dated the 27th March 2017.

(Rajiv Mohan)

Secretary,
Tel. No. 23384185

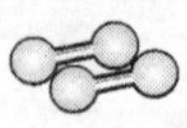

Exercise

1. It has been suggested to the Government that with a view to ensuring that Government servants free themselves from routine stresses of life and avoid falling prey to the various stress related diseases, every Government servant should compulsorily avail of at least 15 days leave every year.
2. According to rules, leave cannot be claimed as a right. It may also not be practicable to allow all Government servants to proceed on leave at the same time. Therefore, it is advisable that leave sanctioning authorities draw up a phased programme and allow leave to their employees without dislocating Government work. It should especially be ensured that leave is not denied to Government servants during the last 10 years of their service.

Please prepare a draft office memorandum from the Department of Personnel & Training to all Ministries and Departments informing them about this decision.

No. 14/28/2005-Estt. (L)

Government of India
DEPARTMENT OF PERSONNEL & TRAINING
New Delhi, the 22nd March 2017
OFFICE MEMORANDUM

Subject: Grant of Earned Leave to Central Government Employees

A suggestion has been made to the Government that the Government servants should be allowed to avail of leave periodically so that they may free themselves from the routine stresses of life and thus avoid falling prey to the various stress related diseases. It has also been suggested that every Government servant should compulsory avail of at least 15 days leave every year.

2. Under the Central Civil Services (Leave) Rules, 1972, leave cannot be claimed as a matter of right, and where exigencies of public service so require, the competent authority may refuse the grant of leave or recall a Government servant from leave. Also, it is not possible to let all those who want leave at a particular time to have it at that time. Otherwise, the staff may be depleted beyond limit and the work of an establishment may also be dislocated. But, at the same time, it is not intended that the leave entitlement of the staff is abridged and they are denied leave whenever they want it. Some mechanism has, therefore, to be evolved to balance the requirements of the public service and of Government servants.

3. The Government considers it in the public interest that Government servants take leave at periodical intervals, preferably every year, and return to work relaxed and refreshed. The leave sanctioning authorities are, therefore, advised to devise suitable procedures and chalk out an annual leave programme keeping in view the Parliament serrious and other functional requirements. The applicants for leave may be allowed to avail of the leave according to this programme. Leave is, accordingly, not to be ordinarily denied to any employee, especially in the last 10 years of his service.

4. In so far as persons serving in the Indian Audit and Accounts Department are concerned, this issues with the concurrence of the Comptroller and Auditor General of India.

(S.K. Shroff)
Deputy Secretary to the Government of India
Tel. No. 23014538

• GRE • GMAT • TOEFL • Competitive Exams

This section on Analytical writing will benefit those appearing for GRE, GMAT, TOEFL and other competitive exams. This can also prove beneficial for students in school and colleges required to write essays on burning topics.

While writing an analytical essay, ensure that you have read through the topic critically and carefully. It is important to know exactly what the examiner wants and why. One should also be careful of the allotted time frame so that one can divide his/her time accordingly.

It should be noted that no topic requires the candidate to have a specific knowledge of the subject. It is important to remember that only the students' ability to think critically on a given issue/topic is being assessed through the given topics.

TIPS

1. Read the assignment very carefully. Be aware of the differences between "consider," "explain," and "evaluate."
2. Select a topic and brainstorm around it. Try to come up with as many ideas as possible that relate to the assignment.
3. Highlight the best ideas from opposing perspectives.
4. Decide which perspective you want to defend.
5. Identify the areas you will discuss in order to defend or explain your essay, and what your point will be with regard to each area.
6. Focus on the quality, not the quantity. There may be dozens of reasons that support your view. Pick only the best.
7. Consider opposing viewpoints and possible reasons for defending them. Are any of these reasons compelling? If so, why? If not, why not?
8. Revise and rethink your essay as various arguments or interpretations emerge. You may have to try different—even opposite—conclusions before you can be sure that your position is the best one.
9. Develop a clear, focused thesis statement and keep this focus in each paragraph.

10. Each paragraph should contribute to the development of your argument. Avoid tangents!
11. Present your ideas in a natural order. The ideas should be clear, coherent and flow in a logical order.
12. Use evidence or examples wherever required to support your argument.

1. *The media today place too much emphasis on provocative images, and not enough emphasis on the ideas and events behind those images.*

   Write a response in which you discuss the extent to which you agree or disagree with the statement and explain your reasoning for your position. In developing and supporting your position, be sure to consider ways in which the statement may or may not be true and explain how these considerations shape your position.

Upon first glance at today's media, it would appear that the statement is correct. However, in my view the media's emphasis on image is largely justifiable. Moreover, the statement understates the extent to which the media also covers the substance behind those images, as discussed below.

I concede that the media today do place considerable emphasis on image. Advertisements are increasingly resorting to fast-moving, sexy, images. In fact, advertisements which provide no product information whatsoever — not even about what the product looks like or how it is to be used — are becoming increasingly common. Also, while tabloid magazines and television programs abound, intelligent discourse can be found sparingly only on public television and a few other arts and education channels, and among the stacks of scholarly journals at our libraries and at obscure websites and blogs. And, despite television's tremendous potential for airing the vital political issues of the day, the brief sound bites from our self-conscious politicians today hardly meet that potential.

Whether this emphasis on image is justifiable, it is certainly understandable — at least with respect to advertising, for two reasons. First, products are becoming more and more fungible these days; consider automobiles, for instance. Since they vary little from one make to another today, marketers are forced to resort to image for product differentiation. The second reason has to do with the fact that we are becoming an increasingly busy society. In the U.S., for instance, the average work week is now over 65 hours, compared to 40 a generation ago. Meanwhile, the number of goods and services competing for our attention seems to grow exponentially. Thus, how can the growing number of businesses compete for our limited time except by resorting to attention-grabbing images?

However understandable this focus on image, is it nevertheless unjustifiable, as the statement implies? Media critics point out that undue focus on appearances and images amounts to an appeal to our emotions and our baser, prurient instincts rather than to our intellect and reason. Taken to an extreme, argue the critics, such focus facilitates irrationality, and even sanctions demagoguery. The result is that we dissuade ourselves as a society from engaging in the sort of informed debate needed for any democracy to survive, let alone thrive. I might be convinced by the critics were the media to withhold the substance underlying the images; but they do not. Behind most newspaper headlines, magazine cover stories, and reputable Internet home pages is a wealth of substantive content; we simply need to look for it.

In sum, while I wholeheartedly agree that the media should not sacrifice substance merely to get our attention, what the statement gets wrong is that it is not the media's job to wave information and ideas in front of us; rather, it is up to us to look for them behind the hoopla and the headlines.

2. *When someone achieves greatness in any field such as the arts, science, politics, or business that person's achievements are more important than any of his or her personal faults. Comment on the above statement with reasonable arguments.*

When individuals attain greatness, their achievements are more important than their personal faults. While historians should not whitewash the personal foibles of great individuals, the impact that these mortals have had in their fields should tower over any personality defects. To focus on the personal weaknesses of great individuals is to miss the importance of their achievements.

The course of human history is decorated with individuals able to rise above their peers and reach the zenith in their fields. These individuals are often the subject of intense scrutiny from contemporaneous skeptics and later historians. But no one can lead an exemplary private life all the time; no human being is able to withstand such surveillance and historical scrutiny without personal faults coming to light. Great individuals are no exception. However, it is misguided to focus on their personal faults rather than their achievements. To do so is to miss the importance of their work, without which our culture would be worse off.

For example, Abraham Lincoln was arguably one of the greatest Presidents the United States has ever had. He managed to bring the country through a substantial revolution and to end slavery despite powerful economic and social forces working against him day and night. However, Lincoln was not a saint. He was moody and prone to depressive funks that disrupted his family life and slowly eroded his marriage. These personal faults did not reduce his success as a President. While we do not have to ignore questions about whether he was a depressive, we also should not consider them an important part of his political heritage. In contrast, many people criticize Lincoln's decision to suspend the right of habeas corpus. This (presumed) failing is not personal in nature, but relates directly to Lincoln's work in his field. Criticisms of this sort are entirely relevant, whereas personal criticisms are not.

Another example of a great individual dogged by criticism of his personal conduct is Albert Einstein. Einstein developed a number of the most important theories in modern physics, including an explanation of the photoelectric effect, an explanation of Brownian motion, special and general relativity, and Bose-Einstein quantum statistics. Each one of these theories would have been considered a great life's work for a scientist; for one man to contribute this much is remarkable. However, Einstein also had life-long problems with infidelity. The fact that he cheated on his wife is in no way relevant to his accomplishments in the field of physics, and indeed most references to Einstein properly ignore it. To focus attention on the faults of his personal life is to obscure the impact he made on history.

Great individuals have personal faults, as all human beings do. Yet it is incorrect to assert that these faults detract from those individuals' accomplishments. We are better able to appreciate the gravity of great accomplishments when we are not burying our heads in the sand, in search of personal failings.

3. Is education in management necessary to succeed in business? Provide relevant argument to the statement.

In the present day world of business, where management rules each aspect of our life, it is very essential for an individual to understand the essence of management at least to the relative terms. This is because; the world has become so complex with the times that it would not function at all when "management" is not there.

When we take up the topic of business, we can look into the past where business was carried out since primitive ages. Only the size, nature, and complexity have changed. Doing business, possessing the qualities of a businessman is an inborn or inner trait of an individual. It was present even in our ancestors who had laid down the bases of business earlier, though at a small scale.

But the scenario has changed with the fast paced world. With industrialization bringing the entire world under one network, the need for "managing" such a huge complex and multidimensional world is felt which can't be done without proper guidance and training. Having understood the need of the upcoming markets and its trend, "management education" has spread all over the world and is helping the aspirant entrepreneurs or the professionals to get the latest knowledge and skills as per the need and expectations of the developments in business. The Education system in India is limited to theoretical knowledge that is confined to just some degrees. But "management education" gives practical knowledge importance over theoretical approach. This gives a complete understanding of the activities of business and the role required to be played by the individuals at a later stage. It's not that businesses cannot run without management education. But now, with the increasing competitiveness all over the world, to become a cut over the edge, the upcoming generations of professionals need to possess the required qualities of making their place in the tough competition by constant innovation and logical and analytical thinking. And "management education" adds these to an individual's personality.

Business is required to be managed, and Management is the backbone of business. Hence, both "management" and "business" go hand in hand and that contributes to the growth of the business at a worldwide scale.

The founder of Dell, Michael Dell did not have any management education. In fact, Michael Dell did not excel academically but had great business instincts. Mukesh Ambani did not have any management education either. He went to college and graduated with a Bachelor's degree in chemical engineering. He did later pursue his MBA from Stanford but did not complete the course.

Education is also not the key to success, great ideas are. Anyone can have education and a degree, but having great ideas is what separates people from the rest of the pack. A person's education does not translate into whether they have good or bad ideas either.

Bill Gates dropped out of college, technology was being released and Bill saw it as a great business opportunity. Luckily he had great support in his parents and a great idea. So Bill Gates, the richest man in the world is another person without any sort of management education.

On the other hand, we've had thousands if not millions of people who have had management education over the years yet most of those businesses have failed. It's all about having a great idea and the intelligence to know what the next big great idea is and plan for it.

4. *Some people believe that university students should be required to attend classes. Others believe that going for classes should be optional. Which point of view do you agree with? Use specific reasons and details to explain your answer.*

Going to university is a coveted goal for most students around the world. Many parents dream of their children having the opportunity to receive a university education, as a gateway to a successful future. Although it is possible to receive a degree without attending classes, in my view, attendance plays a critical part in the university experience. The bases for my views are educational, social and intellectual.

From an academic standpoint, attending classes simply enables students to learn more. After all, professors do not simply parrot what is written in university textbooks; they add to this knowledge from their own professional experience, reading and research. This provides an opportunity for students to receive key perspectives, as well as relevant and up to date information in their specialized fields. Since acquiring knowledge and developing critical thinking skills are important goals of higher education, attendance at classes should be considered a mandatory requirement for graduation.

Socially, university life offers young people the opportunity to form meaningful friendships, relationships and connections, some of which last for life. One can make good friends or even meet a future life partner while in college or university. In addition, one's classmates may become the "movers and shakers" of tomorrow's corporations and industries. These important contacts are also made while attending university classes, studying and partying together.

Lastly, from an intellectual perspective, a student can gain tremendously by matching wits with other bright students from around the world. In the context of classes, students can discuss issues, exchange views, explore ideas, solve problems and develop cross-cultural skills through interaction with international students. This can be a critical experience that helps students define themselves and their political and ideological place in the world.

In summary, attending university classes benefits students in myriad ways. Broadly speaking, it enables students to make the best of their years in university. Therefore, it should be regarded as a desirable and meaningful means to achieving various important life goals.

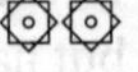

Legal & Official Templates

• Affidavit • Agreement • Sale Deed • Rent Agreement •
Partnership Deed • MOU • Relinquishment Deed • Disclaimer Deed

Any legal document must be concise, clear, and conform to the objective standards that have evolved in the legal profession.

TIPS Preparing various legal documents:

1. Know Your Reader: Every word you write should be tailored according to the needs of the reader – judge, advocate, attorney, notary, client etc. Documents that embody the same research and message may vary greatly in content and tone based on the document's intended audience. For example, a brief submitted to the court must advocate and persuade. A memorandum to a client must analyze the issues, report the state of the law and recommend an appropriate course of action. Always keep your target audience in mind when crafting any piece of writing.

2. Structure Your Writing: Organization/ structuring is the key to successful legal writing. Create a structure for your writing by using visual clues to guide the reader. Introduce your subject in an introductory paragraph. Introduce each paragraph with a topic sentence and use headings and subheadings to break up blocks of text. Limit each paragraph to one topic and sum up your message with a concluding sentence or paragraph. Organizational structure guides the reader through your text and promotes readability.

3. Avoid too much Legal Jargon: Legalese — specialized legal phrases and jargon — can make your writing abstract, stilted and archaic. Avoid unnecessary legalese and other jargon in favor of the clear and simple. To avoid legalese and promote clarity, try reading your sentence to a colleague or substituting abstract words with simple, concrete terms. For example, instead of "I am in receipt of your correspondence," "I received your letter" is clearer and more succinct.

4. Be Concise: Every word you write should contribute to your message. Omit extraneous words, shorten complex sentences, eliminate redundancies and keep it simple.

Consider the following sentence:

"Due to the fact that the defendant has not attempted to pay back the money owed to our client in the amount of 30,000 it has become absolutely essential that we take appropriate legal action in order to obtain payment of the aforesaid amount."

A more concise version reads: "Since the defendant has not paid the Rs 30,000 owed our client, we will file a lawsuit seeking reimbursement." The latter sentence conveys the same information in 18 words versus 44. Omitting unnecessary words helps clarify the meaning of the sentence and adds impact.

5. Use Action Words: Action words make your legal prose more powerful, dynamic and vivid. Add punch to your writing with verbs that bring your prose to life. Here are a few examples:

Avoid: The defendant was not truthful. Write: The defendant lied.

Avoid: The witness quickly came into the courtroom. Write: The witness bolted into the courtroom.

Avoid: The judge was very angry. Write: The judge was enraged.

6. Use Active Voice: Passive voice disguises responsibility for an act by eliminating the subject of the verb. Active voice, on the other hand, tells the reader who is doing the acting and clarifies your message. For example, instead of "the filing deadline was missed," say "plaintiff's counsel missed the filing deadline." Instead of "a crime was committed," say "the defendant committed the crime."

7. Edit like a Pro: Edit your writing ruthlessly, omitting unnecessary words and rewriting for clarity. Careful proofreading is particularly important in legal writing. Spelling, punctuation or grammatical errors in a document submitted to the court, opposing counsel or a client can undermine your credibility as a legal professional.

Legal Documents/ Templates

Affidavit

An affidavit is a written declaration made under oath before a notary public or other authorized officer. There is no standard form or language to be used in an affidavit as long as the facts contained within it are stated clearly and definitely. Unnecessary language or legal arguments should not appear. Clerical and grammatical errors, while to be avoided, are inconsequential.

The affidavit usually must contain the address of the affiant and the date that the statement was made, in addition to the affiant's signature or mark. Where the affidavit has been made is also noted. When an affidavit is based on the affiant's information and belief, it must state the source of the affiant's information and the grounds for the affiant's belief in the accuracy of such information. This permits the court to draw its own conclusions about the information in the affidavit.

An affiant is strictly responsible for the truth and accuracy of the contents of the affidavit. If false statements are made, the affiant can be prosecuted for perjury.

Agreement

Agreements are the formal accords signed before entering into an obligation between two or more parties. The terms and conditions are mentioned in detail for the sake of action in case of violation of the rules.

They may be classified into many types based on their purpose such as:

- Lease agreement (rental agreements);
- Service level agreements;
- Corporate business agreement;
- Employment agreement;
- Personal agreement;
- Wedding agreement.

The agreements are of many types based on the necessity of the contract and certain attributes are to be considered exclusively for any agreement based on the requirement.

There are certain factors that are to be followed while writing an agreement such as:

- The terms and conditions are to be discussed and clarified by all the parties who are involved in the agreement.
- The persons or the organizations involved must be identified with their legal names so as to ensure that in case of any violations the courts accept the case from any party.
- The mode of financial transactions between all the parties must be specified very lucidly so as to establish foolproof agreements which are clear in every aspect.
- As the agreements are subject to the legal enforcement, all the laws which come into play in case of breach of the terms and conditions are to be discussed in the document and the actions to be taken in such a case is to be recited.
- All the points must be in a language understandable by all the parties so that they memorize them well.
- All the parties involved must sign the agreement along with the date as an act of consent for the sake of reference in case of any discrepancy.

Sale Deed

A sale deed acts as the main legal document for evidencing sale and transfer of ownership of property in favour of the buyer, from the seller. Further, it also acts as the main document for further sale by the buyer as it establishes his proof of ownership of the property.

The sale deed is executed subsequent to the execution of the sale agreement, and after compliance of various terms and conditions detailed in the sale agreement as agreed upon between the buyer and the seller.

Rent Agreement

A rent agreement is a judicial contract which calls for owner to be paid by the user for temporary usage of a house or room. On rent agreement stamp paper, asset is termed as tangible property. It is mentioned on rent agreement form that tenant and user pays rental flat amount against usage of room/flat/house and landlord pays all taxes and duties imposed on property

Property can be used for housing, storage, parking, business, institutional etc as mentioned on rent agreement stamp paper (₹ 100 stamp paper).

Partnership Deed

A deed of partnership is a form of deed that is used to transfer real property that will be owned by a partnership. The grantees must be identified as partners in a business partnership on the face of the deed. That type of conveyance creates a tenancy in partnership, which is a survivorship arrangement. Generally, if a member of a partnership that owns real property dies their interest in the real property passes to the other partners.

(₹ 200 stamp paper).

MoU

A Memorandum of Understanding or MoU is a written agreement put in place to establish a clear understanding of how an arrangement will practically function and each party's role and responsibilities.

The MoU allows all involved to concretely see that they are agreeing to the same thing and to be a tangible reference to review should, heaven forbid, any troubles arise during the arrangement.

Primarily the format or a template of a MoU includes —

a. The date of the MoU;

b. Description of situation of parties and their relationship with each other;

c. Communication details of the parties involved;

d. Compensation details, like who handles the money and how people are going to be paid and the like;

e. Terms of agreement;

f. Any other issue.

Relinquishment Deed

Relinquishment deed is a legal document / instrument where a person legally or formally gives up or releases his legal rights of the said property being relinquished in the name of some other person i.e to give up or release ones share of an immovable property in the name of some other person. This is one of the modes of transferring of immoveable property.

As a relinquishment deed is a legal instrument / document by which a person formally gives up his claim to another person, the said deed must be systematically executed and registered as per law depending upon the needed compliances as per the statutory governance. One needs a good property lawyer for systematic legal compliances and needed documentations for drafting / making relinquishment.

Disclaimer Deed

A disclaimer deed is a deed in which a spouse disclaims any interest in the real property acquired by the other spouse. A mortgage company often asks a borrower to sign a disclaimer deed so that his spouse not having her name on the loan, cannot claim any interest in the property.

To be submitted on a ₹ 10 non-Judicial Stamp paper and duly attested by a 1st class Magistrate, Oath Commissioner or by a Notary Public with Notarial Stamp of ₹ 5.

Affidavit

I, son/daughter of .... resident of............... do solemnly declare and affirm as follows.

1. That I am the Owner/Partner of the firm operating in the name and style as having its Headquarters at...........................
2. That I am competent to sign this affidavit on behalf of the company mentioned at serial one above.
3. That we are trading in manufactured by under proper authority and we have complete in house test and repair facility.

or

That we are manufacturing the product with our own technology/Transfer of Technology (ToT) from with valid authority.

4. That our company is/is not the sole representative of this product in India on behalf of the original manufacturer of this product.
5. That we affirm and declare that the import of equipment described at serial 3 above has been within the framework or rules of Government of India as prescribed in its Export and Import policy or any other law, rule or notification in force by any competent authority of Govt. of India.
6. That we affirm and declare that we shall be responsible for any dispute arising out of ToT/ Technology mentioned above and shall bear the cost of any litigation and loss/damage caused to DOT.
7. That we hereby indemnify the Department of Telecommunication and the Telecommunication Engineering Centre against all third party claims of infringement of patent, trade mark, Industrial design rights or intellectual property rights arising from giving approval to or using the product or any part thereof.

(DEPONENT)

Witness

1.

2.

Verification

Verified this day of year 2017... that the contents of my above affidavit are true to the best of my knowledge and belief and nothing untrue has been stated nor any facts has been concealed.

Business Agreement

This business agreement is made and entered on January 28th, 2017, between

Details of the Entrepreneur:

Name: Mr. Anand Seth

Address: Plot No: 67, Industrial Area, Sector-8, Mohan Estate. Delhi-92

Contact number: =+919822456438

HEREINAFTER REFERRED AS ENTREPRENEUR PARTY

AND

Details of the Organization:

Name: Parrot Sales Pvt. Ltd

Address: 45/ L, Office No; 6, Nehru Place Towers, Delhi 93

Phone Number: =919761838244

HEREINAFTER REFERRED AS ORGANIZATION PARTY

Whereas, entrepreneur is willing to purchase the products from the Organization & the organization is interested in working with the entrepreneur by understanding the risks and benefits mentioned in this business agreement.

This business agreement is effective from January 29th, 2013 and is valid till January 29th, 2014.

Following mentioned clauses & covenants must be accepted by both the parties:

- The Entrepreneur can buy the products by making 50% of the amount in advance, whereas the remaining payment is to be made after receiving the goods.
- The organization party will dispatch the demanded goods on time, as promised, and will issue a legitimate slip for the received payment.
- In case of any violation to the above mentioned terms & conditions, this business agreement is considered as dissolved.

Agreement validation by the entrepreneur party and the organization party:

Signature of the Entrepreneur — Approval of the Organization

Anand Seth — Parrot Sales Pvt. Ltd.

Sale Deed

This DEED OF ABSOLUTE SALE executed at on this the day of.........................., 2017 by S/o...........................residing at...............................

HEREINAFTER called the VENDOR of the one part shall include his executors, administrators, legal representatives, successors etc.

To and in favour of..

W/o......................................residing at...

HEREINAFTER called the PURCHASER of the Other Part wherever the context so requires shall mean and include his heirs, executors, administrators, legal representatives, successors etc.

WHEREAS the VENDOR herein has purchased the said property more fully described in the Schedule hereunder from........................... in and by sale deed dated and registered on as Document No. of (year) of Book 1 volume No. filed at pages to on the file of the Sub Registrar of.

WHEREAS the VENDOR herein has been in exclusive possession and enjoyment of the property more fully described in the Schedule hereunder with a constructed house thereon, which was constructed by him with his self-earned funds, till date.

WHEREAS the VENDOR is the exclusive owner of the property more fully described in the schedule hereunder and he has absolute right to dispose of the same as in the manner he wishes;

AND WHEREAS the VENDOR is in need of funds in order to meet his personal commitments and family expenses and has decided to sell the property more fully described in the Schedule hereunder for a sum of ₹ /- (Rupees only) and the PURCHASER herein has also agreed to purchase the same for the said price and to the effect they entered into an agreement to sell dated

NOW THIS DEED OF SALE WITNESSETH

THAT in pursuance of the aforesaid agreement and in consideration of a sum of Rs. (Rupees only) received by the VENDOR in cash and the receipt of the said entire consideration of Rs. (Rupees only), the VENDOR doth hereby admit, acknowledge, acquit, release and discharge the VENDOR from making further payment thereof and the VENDOR doth hereby sell, convey, transfer, and assigns unto and to the use of the PURCHASER, the property more fully described in the Schedule hereunder together with the water ways, easements, advantages and appurtenances, and all estate, rights, title and interest of the VENDOR to and upon the said property TO HAVE AND TO HOLD the said property hereby conveyed unto the PURCHASER absolutely and forever.

The vendor doth hereby covenant with the purchaser as follows:

1. That the property more fully described in the Schedule hereunder shall be quietly and peacefully entered into and held and enjoyed by the PURCHASER without any interference, interruption, or disturbance from the VENDOR or any person claiming through or under him.

2. That the VENDOR has absolute right, title and full power to sell, convey and transfer unto the PURCHASER by way of absolute sale and that the VENDOR has not done anything or knowingly suffered anything whereby his right and power to sell and convey to the PURCHASER the property hereby conveyed.

3. That the property is not subjected to any encumbrances, mortgages, charges, lien, attachments, claim, demand, acquisition proceedings by Government or any kind whatsoever and should thereby and the VENDOR shall discharge the same from and out of his own funds and keep the PURCHASER indemnified.

4. That the VENDOR hereby declares with the PURCHASER that the VENDOR has paid all the taxes, rates and other outgoings due to Local bodies, revenue, urban and other authorities in respect of the property more fully described in the Schedule hereunder up to the date of execution of this sale deed and the PURCHASER shall bear and pay the same hereafter. If any arrears are found due to the earlier period, the same shall be discharged by the VENDOR.

5. That the VENDOR has handed over the vacant possession of the property more fully described in the Schedule hereunder to the PURCHASER on and delivered the connected original title document in respect of the schedule mentioned property hereby conveyed on the date of execution of these presents.

6. That the VENDOR will at all times and at the cost of the PURCHASER execute, register or cause to be done, all such acts and deeds for perfecting the title to the PURCHASER in the property hereby sold and conveyed herein.

7. That the VENDOR do hereby covenants and assures that the PURCHASER is entitled to have mutation of his name in all public records, local body and also obtain patta in the name of the PURCHASER and undertakes to execute any deed in this respect.

Schedule of Property

The Market Value of the Property is ₹..................................

In witness where of the VENDOR and the PURCHASER have set their signatures on the day month and year first above written.

Witnesses:

VENDOR

1)

2)

THE PURCHASER

Drafted by:

Rent Deed

THIS RENT DEED is made at Delhi , on this ..th day of Feb 2017..,

BETWEEN

Sh. X S/o Sh. D R/o XYZ, Delhi hereinafter called the 'LANDLORD' THE PARTY OF THE FIRST PART.

AND

Sh. A S/o C R/o XYZ, Delhi hereinafter called the 'TENANT' THE PARTY OF THE SECOND PART.

The expression both the parties shall mean and include unless repugnant to the context, their respective legal heirs, executors. Representatives, nominee and assigns respectively.

WHEREAS the first party is the owner of property No.XYZ, Delhi

WHEREAS the second party has approached the first party to take on rent, First Floor portion, consisting of two Bed Room, one Drawing-cum-dining room set, in the above said property (hereinafter called the said premises) and the first party has agreed to let out the first party has agreed to let out the said premises to the second party, on a monthly rent of ₹ 5,100/- (Rupees five thousand one hundred only) for a period of 11 months starting with effect from 00.00.200.. and ending on 00.00.200.. and the second party has also deposited ₹ 15,000 (Rupees Fifteen thousand only) by Cheque No.0……. dated 00.00.200.. drawn on HDFC BANK, Daryaganj , DELHI-110092, in advance with the first party, towards the security amount shall be refund without any interest at the time of vacation of the above said premises.

The following terms and conditions have been settled between the above said parties, WITNESSED AS UNDER:

1. That the settled rent neither shall be reduced nor shall be enhanced by either party during the settled period.
2. That the said monthly rent shall be payable on or before 7th day of each English calendar month in advance.
3. That the Bills of the electric and water shall be payable by the second party, but the House tax of the said premises shall be payable by the first party.
4. That the above said premises shall be used by the second party only for the residential/ commercial purposes and shall not be used for any other purposes and if he/she shall do so then he/she shall be liable for immediate ejectment from the said premises without any prior notice in this regard.
5. That either party can terminate this RENT DEED either with one month's notice in advance or with one month's rent in lieu thereof.
6. That the first party and/or his/her representatives, surveyors and workmen shall have right to enter into the premises at all reasonable times for the purpose either for inspection of the said premises or for repairs.

7. That the second party shall abide by the Bye-laws, rules and regulations of D.D.A., M.C.D., D.V.B., and other local authorities concerned.
8. That the second party shall not sub-let the said premises under his/her tenancy and if he/she shall do so then he/she shall be liable for ejectment from the said premises, immediately, and without any prior notice in this regard.
9. That the said security amount which is deposited by the second party with the first party, shall be returned back by the first party to the second party, (without any interest thereon) after adjustment of outstanding dues, if any, towards the second party at the time of vacating the said premises.
10. That the second party shall not make any additions or alterations in the said premises under his/her tenancy without the written permission from the first party, and if the second party shall do so then this rent deed shall stand cancelled automatically and the second party shall be bound to vacate the said premises immediately.
11. That after the expiry of the settled period, if both the parties mutually agreed to extend this rent deed for any further period, then a fresh rent deed shall be executed between the above said parties, on the fresh terms and conditions and if the first party will not agree to give the said premises on rent for any further period then the second party shall be bound to vacate the said premises and deliver the actual, physical and vacant possession of the said premises to the first party immediately, without any prior notice in this regard and if the second party does not vacate the said premises then the first party shall be entitled to get the said premises vacated from the second party through the court of law, and in the event of court proceedings, all the expenses of the first party, shall be payable by the second party.

IN WITNESSES WHEREOF the above said parties have put their respective signature on this RENT DEED on the date mentioned above.

Witnesses.

1.

FIRST PARTY

(LANDLORD)

2.

SECOND PARTY

(TENANT)

Partnership Deed

THIS DEED OF PARTNERSHIP IS MADE on this 12th day of January, 2017 by and

BETWEEN

Mr. A S/o C R/o XYZ hereinafter referred to as Party of the FIRST PART (which expression shall deem and include his heirs, executors, administrators, representatives, assigns and agents),

AND

Ms. B D/o D R/o XYZ, Party of the SECOND PART (which expression shall deem and include his heirs, executors, administrators, representatives, assigns),

AND

WHEREAS the above named partners have decided to start the partnership business of Recruitment Services in the name and style of M/s SSS with effect from …th day of January, 20.. on the terms and conditions hereinafter mentioned and have desired to reduce the terms and conditions into writing.

Now this Indenture is Witnesseth as Follows:

1. THAT the PARTIES referred above shall carry on the business of Recruitment Services in the PARTNERSHIP FIRM under the name and style of M/s SSS hereinafter referred to as the FIRM) XYZ, But by their mutual consent may start and carry on any other business or businesses under any other name or names at any other place or places.
2. THAT the business of the PARTNERSHIP pursuant to this DEED of PARTNERSHIP shall be deemed to have commenced with effect from …th day of January, 2017.
3. That the capital required for the business of Partnership shall be contributed time to time by the PARTIES in such manner in all respect as may be agreed to between them and such capital may be paid interest as may be mutually agreed from time to time at the rate of rates not exceeding 12% (Twelve Percent) per annum.
4. That all the PARTIES referred above shall be Working Partners and shall attend diligently to the business of the Partnership and carry on the same for the greatest advantage of the Firm.
5. That all the WORKING PARTNERS may be paid Salary w.e.f. … day of Feb., 2017, for the work of the FIRM as may be agreed mutually from time to time between the PARTIES in accordance with the provisions of the Income Tax Laws as well as business necessities and other factors, subject however, that the monthly Salary to each such Partner shall not exceed as under:

Name of Working Partner Maximum Basic Salary not to Exceed

a. Mr. A ₹ 12,000/- per month

b. Ms. B ₹ 12,000/- per month

6. That all business expenses shall be borne by the FIRM.

7. That the Profits or Losses, as the case may be, of the Partnership business shall be divided among the Partners as under:

Name of Working Partner	Share of Profit	Share of Loss
a. Mr. A	50%	50%
b. Ms. B	50%	50%

8. That the duration of the PARTNERSHIP shall be at WILL subject to Clause '9'.

9. That any Partner may retire from Partnership after giving a notice to the other Partner (s) of not less than one month in writing and at the expiry of such notice period he shall be deemed to have retired.

10. Upon mutual understanding, each Partner or his duly authorised agent shall have free access to the account books of the Partnership and shall be entitled to take copies or extracts from any or all such books and records of the Partnership Business.

11. That no Partner shall have the right to sell, mortgage or transfer his share of interest in the FIRM to any one else except to his heir or heirs or any one of the existing Partners or to their heir (s). In the event of heir (s) selling his/her share to any one else, the existing Partners shall have a right or pre-emotion in respect of such share (s) sold.

12. That the Partners shall keep or cause to be kept the books of account of the FIRM at the principal places of its business and make all entries therein, and that all such books of account kept shall be closed on 31st March every year or in the case of any necessity on any other date as the Partners may mutually decide.

13. That no Partner shall do any act or thing whereby FIRM or the FIRM property may be prejudicially effected.

14. That the terms of the Partnership Deed may be altered, added to or cancelled by the written consent of the Parties to this DEED.

15. That the partners can open the bank account of the firm, in any bank and bank account shall be operated by the partners jointly or individually, as the case may be.

16. That the partners shall not take any loan from any person/Financing Company, bank or any other Govt./Pvt. Department in any case, without the written consent of each other.

17. That in the case of any dispute arising out of this DEED between the Parties of this DEED, it shall be decided by Arbitration as provided for under the Indian Arbitration Act.

IN WITNESS WHEREOF the Parties hereto have set and subscribed their respective hands to these presents the day, month and year first written above.

Witnesses:

1.

Mr. A
(Party of the First Part)

2.

Ms. B
(Party of the Second Part)

Relinquishment Deed

This Deed of relinquishment is made and executed on this...day of 2017 by...................., By...................Shri...................S/o Shri..............and Miss.................Daughter of Shri.................residents of...........................hereinafter called "the EXECUTANTS/RELEASORS:.

IN FAVOUR OF

Mrs.............................W/o Shri ....residents of.................................hereinafter called the "RELEASEE".

WHEREAS the Shri.......................son of Shri...............................resident of.........................,was the absolute owner of Entire Second Floor of Freehold Property bearing No....................built on Plot No................................, in Block No............................ Built on a plot of land measuring situated at......................., by virtue of........................ Gift Deed registered as document no.........in Add............Book No........................Volume No. on.................pages.......to.........dated...............in the office of Sub-Registrar, New Delhi (hereinafter called the said portion of the said property) AND WHEREAS the said Shri...intestate died on (Death Certificate enclosed) leaving behind the following legal heirs:-

SL No.	Name	Age	Relationship	Address
1) ll) lll)				

WHEREAS consequent upon the death of Shri......................1/3rd share each in the..................of Freehold property bearing No................., built on Plot No...............In Block No..................., built on a plot of land measuring....................., situated at..........................New Delhi, has devolved upon the above legal heirs.

NOW THIS DEED WITNESSES AS UNDER:

Pursuant to their wish, as mentioned above, the Executants/Releasors out of natural love and affection and without any monetary consideration, hereby wish to release and relinquish their share each in the..............................of Freehold property bearing No......................built on Plot no.....................,in Block No............................., built on a plot of land measuring........................, situated at........................, in favour of Smt......................wife of Shri..........................as mentioned above, and hereby affirm and declare that thcy and their legal heirs shall have no claim, right, lien or interest in the entire...........................of the aforesaid property and the same shall vest absolutely in the said Smt.................wife of Shri....................., the Releases.

IN WITNESS WHEREOF, the Executants/Releasors and the Releasee have signed this Deed of Relinquishment on the day, month and year first mentioned above in the presence of the following witnesses:-

(.............)
RELEASEE

(..........................)
EXECUTANTS/RELEASORS

WITNESSES:-

1.

2.

Disclaimer Deed

This Disclaimer Deed is executed at New Delhi, on this day of........................by:.......................... .... hereinafter called "THE FIRST PARTY" ;

IN FAVOUR OF:

....

....hereinafter called "THE SECOND PARTY".

The expression of the First and Second Party shall mean and include them, their legal heirs, legal representatives, administrators, successors, executors, nominees and assignees.

Whereas the first party is the owner and lessee in respect of share of property bearing No.. situated at..New Delhi, vide Sale Deed dated.................................regd. as document No...........................in Addl. Book No.1, Volume No................................., on pages.................................to......................on........................., in the Office of the Sub-Registrar, New Delhi.

And whereas the first and second party had entered into a Memorandum of Family Arrangement (Agreement) dated.......................and as per the Memorandum of Family Arrangement (Agreement) the said Shri..............................the second party herein, has become the owner of the said share in the said property.

And whereas the first party has agreed to disclaim his right, title and interest in the said share in the said property in favour of the second party absolutely and forever in view of the said Memorandum of Family Arrangement (Agreement) the said Shri...........................the second party herein, has become the owner of said in the said property.

NOW THIS DISCLAIMER DEED WITNESSETH AS UNDER:

1. That in pursuance of the said Memorandum of Family Arrangement (Agreement) the first party doth hereby release, relinquish, disclaim and give up all his right, title interest in the said share in the said property in favour of the second party absolutely and forever.
2. That the first party now admits that he or his legal heirs and successors have been left with no right, title interest in said share in the said property and the second party has become the owner of the same with the right to transfer the same by way of sale, gift, mortgage, lease or otherwise to use and enjoy the income and sale consideration and the first party shall not claim same as legal under circumstances and shall keep the second party or nominee/s indemnify for the same.
3. That this Disclaimer Deed shall be binding upon legal heirs and successors of the first party.
4. That the first party has executed this Deed of disclaimer voluntarily, without any outside pressure and in his full sense. In witness whereof the first party have executed disclaimer Deed at the place, day, month and year as first above written in the presence of the following witnesses.

WITNESSES:

1.

2.

FIRST PARTY

SECOND PARTY

Appendices

Grammar

Parts of Speech

Nouns	Pronouns	Verbs			Adjectives		
		First	***Second***	***Third***	***Positive Degree***	***Comparative Degree***	***Superlative Degree***
Proper Nouns Mr. Sharma, Ms Rastogi, Sanjeev, Ritu, India, Germany, Chennai, Bangalore, White House, Link Road **Common Nouns** Typist, Receptionist, Secretary, Book, File, Letter, Chair, Table, Client, Manager, Supervisor **Abstract Nouns** Diligence, Punctuality, Honesty, Loyalty, Privacy, Clarity, Accuracy, Urgency, Importance **Collective Nouns** Staff, Management, Clientele, Army, Board, Government, Class	**First Person** I, Me, My/Mine, Myself, We, Us, Our/Ours, Ourselves **Second Person** You, Your/ Yours, Yourself, Yourselves **Third Person** He/She/It, Him/ Her/It, His/Her, Hers/Its, Himself/ Herself/Itself, They, Them, Their/ Theirs, Themselves **Other Pronouns** Who, Whom, Whose	Begin Bite Break Bring Catch Do Draw Drive Eat Fall Get Give Grow Know Leave Lend Pay Run See Sit Throw Write	Began Bit Broke Brought Caught Did Drew Drove Ate Fell Got Gave Grew Knew Left Lent Paid Ran Saw Sat Threw Wrote	Begun Bitten Broken Brought Caught Done Drawn Driven Eaten Fallen Got/Gotten Given Grown Known Left Lent Paid Run Seen Sat Thrown Written	Cool Tall Warm Clever Pretty Simple Large Big Small Good Bad Little Intelligent Difficult Important	Cooler Taller Warmer Cleverer Prettier Simpler Larger Bigger Smaller Better Worse Less More Intelligent More Difficult More Important	Coolest Tallest Warmest Cleverest Prettiest Simplest Largest Biggest Smallest Best Worst Least Most Intelligent Most Difficult Most Important

Adverbs	Prepositions	Conjunctions	Interjections
Adverbs of Time or Frequency (When?) Now, Before, Forever, Seldom, Occasionally, Somewhat, Once, Never, Frequently, Often **Adverbs of Place or Direction (Where?)** In, Upstairs, Under, Through, Here, There, Over, By, Down, Out, Sideways, Across **Adverbs of Manner (How?)** Carefully, Nicely, Arrogantly, Quickly, Tirelessly, Equally, Resentfully, Earnestly	About, Above, Across, After, Against, Along, Among, Around, At, Before, Behind, Below, Beneath, Between, Beside, By, Down, During, Except, For, From, In, Into, Near, Past, Towards, Under, Until, Up, Upon, With, Within, Without, Through, Throughout, To	After, Although, As much as, Because, Before, How, If, In order to, In as much as, Provided, Since, Though, Unless, Until, What, When, Where, Which, While, Who/Whom, Whoever/ Whomever	Ah, Alas, Congratulations, Great, Help, Hurry, Hey, Hooray, Never, No, Oh, Outstanding, Wow

The parts of speech include nouns, pronouns, verbs, adverbs, adjectives, prepositions, conjunctions and interjections. Each of these has its own forms, characteristics, and uses. Knowing how to use these parts will enable you to write with greater clarity, accuracy, and with better style.

Good writing requires you to master the guidelines and learn how to apply them in your writing. This section will help you understand and use parts of speech correctly. We begin with nouns.

Nouns

Nouns are words that name persons, places, or things. Things may include events, ideas, and even feelings.

For Example—

Persons	**Places**	**Things**	**Events, Ideas and Concepts**
Sunita	Office	Desk	Picnic, Freedom,
Worker	City	Window	Meeting, Equality

Types of Nouns

- *Proper nouns* name a particular person, place, or thing and are capitalised.

For Example— **Mr Sharma** will fly for **Bangalore** on **Monday**.
Ms Jyoti is our new client from **Chennai**.

- *Common nouns*, on the other hand, refer to a general category or class of persons, places, or things.

For Example— Give this letter to the **typist**.
All the **executives** have to report at 10 a.m.

- *Abstract nouns* name anything which cannot be perceived through our five sense organs.

For Example— **Diligence** at work is always appreciated.
Anita is known for her **punctuality**.

- *Collective nouns* name a group or unit and can be singular or plural.

For Example— The whole **staff** was called for the meeting.
The **management** is planning to shift the head office to Mumbai.

(Number): Singular and Plural

Nouns can be made plural in various ways. Most nouns form the plural by adding an 's' to the singular form. For other plural forms, sometimes 'es' is added to the singular form and sometimes 'y' changes to 'ies'.

Singular	Hotel, Chief, Loss, Secretary, Club, Manager
Plural	Hotels, Chiefs, Losses, Secretaries, Clubs, Managers

Possessive Nouns

A possessive noun shows ownership or possession. The possessive is formed by adding an apostrophe followed by 's' ('s) or sometimes an apostrophe (') to the end of the noun.

- *To form the singular possessive, add ('s) to all nouns.*

Singular	Singular Possessive
The profits of the company The rules of the club	The company's profits The club's rules

- *To form the plural possessive of nouns that end in 's' or 'es', add an apostrophe (') to the end of the word.*

Plural	Plural Possessive
Papers of the lawyer The wages of the secretaries	The lawyers' papers The secretaries' wages

- *For nouns that form the plural in any other way, add 's to the end of the word, except when the final 's' is a 'z' sound (houses). Then add only the apostrophe (houses').*

Plural	Plural Possessive
Men Children Notaries	The men's jobs The children's department The notaries' seal

- *When you are uncertain whether to place the apostrophe before or after the s, follow this simple rule. Rephrase the sentence by substituting an 'of' phrase for the possessive noun to help you decide if the noun is meant to be singular or plural. For instance, to decide between The employee's decision was made on the spot or, The employees' decision was made on the spot, rephrase the sentence and check whether the singular or plural as follows:*

Of Phrase	Possessive Form
The decision of the employee (singular) The decision of the employees (plural)	The employee's decision The employees' decision

Pronouns

Pronouns are used to take the place of one or more nouns. Like nouns, they refer to persons, places, events, objects, or concepts.

For Example—

- Ruth asked Sameer to come on Wednesday.
  She asked him to come on Wednesday.
  (The pronoun 'she' has replaced the noun 'Ruth', while 'him' replaces 'Sameer'.)
- The supervisor will preside over the meeting.
  He will preside over the meeting.
  (The pronoun 'he' has replaced 'the supervisor'.)
- The director and the supervisor argued about equal employment.
  They argued about equal employment.
  (The pronoun 'they' has replaced the nouns 'the director and the supervisor'.)
- Seema's application was accepted.
  Her application was accepted.
  (The pronoun 'her' has replaced the possessive noun 'Seema's'.)

- The managers' talk was enlightening.
  Their talk was enlightening.
  (The pronoun 'their' has replaced the noun 'the managers'.)
- Meena taught Meena to type.
  She taught herself to type.
  (The pronoun 'she' and 'herself' have replaced the noun 'Meena'.)

The following table shows the pronouns for the first person (I, we), second person (you), and third person (he/she/it):

Person	Singular	Plural
First	I Me My/Mine Myself	We Us Our Ours
Second	You Your/Yours Yourself	You Your/Yours Yourselves
Third	He/She/It Him/Her/It His/Her, Hers/Its Himself/Herself/Itself	They Them Their/Theirs Themselves

Who or Whom?

Even experienced writers sometimes find it difficult to decide whether to use 'who' or 'whom'. In modern usage, the tendency is to drop the more formal whom and use who in all cases. Yet the rules for using these two pronouns can be mastered easily. Once you have learned them, you would have no trouble choosing the correct pronoun.

'Who' is used as the subject of a sentence, a phrase or clause within the sentence. 'Who' is never used as an object.

For Example—

- Who talked to the director? (Here, 'Who' is the subject of the sentence.)
- I can tell who is coming. ('Who' is the subject of 'is coming'.)
- Give the package to whoever can pick it up. ('Whoever' is the subject of 'can pick' and not the object of the preposition 'to'.)

'Whom' is used as the object of a verb or preposition. It is never used as the subject of sentence, or a phrase or clause within a sentence.

For Example—

- To whom did you give your time sheets? ('Whom' is the 'object' of the preposition 'to'.)
- Whom did you see yesterday? ('Whom' is the 'object' of the verb 'see'.)

- Is that the manager whom you met last week? ('You' is the 'subject' of the verb 'met'. While 'whom' is the 'object' of that verb.)
- Give the package to whomever you call to pick it up. ('Whomever' is the 'object' of the verb 'call'. Compare this sentence with the one using 'whoever' above.)

Verbs

Verbs are words that express actions or states of being. Verbs provide the power or drive for your sentences.

For Example—

- He changed the title of the report. (action)
- The company merged with Shalimar Industries. (action)
- She appears calm in front of a group. (state of being)
- The office looks more attractive. (state of being)

Verb Tenses

Verb tenses enable you to place an action or state of being in the past, present, or future. They give you a way of talking about time. The various tenses in English are formed using the basic elements of the verb. Here is a table of these tenses for the basic verb 'go':

	Indefinite Forms	**Continuous Forms**	**Perfect Forms**	**Perfect Continuous Forms**
Present	go/goes	is/am/are going	has/have gone	has been/have been going
Past	went	was/were going	had gone	had been going
Future	shall/will go	will be going	will have gone	will have been going

Indefinite Forms

- *Present Indefinite:* It expresses a repeated or recurring action or situation that exists only now. Follow this rule for forming a sentence in present indefinite form: Subject + Verb (only first form if the subject is plural, and first form with 's' or 'es' if the subject is singular) + Object.

For Example— The secretary files the letters.

- *Past Indefinite:* It expresses an action or situation that was started and finished in the past. Follow this rule for forming a sentence in past indefinite form: Subject + Verb (second form) + Object.

For Example— The secretary filed the letters.

- *Future Indefinite:* It expresses an action or situation that will occur in the future. Follow this rule for forming a sentence in future indefinite form: Subject + shall/will + Verb (first form) + Object.

For Example— The secretary will file the letters.

Continuous Forms

- *Present Continuous:* It describes an ongoing action that is happening now.

  Follow this rule for forming a sentence in present continuous form: Subject + is + Verb (first form + ing) + Object. **For Example—**

  The secretary is filing the letters.

- *Past Continuous:* It describes a past action which was happening in the past.

  Follow this rule for forming a sentence in past continuous form: Subject + was + Verb (first form + ing) + Object. **For Example—**

  The secretary was filing the letters.

- *Future Continuous:* It describes an ongoing or continuous action that will take place in the future.

  Follow this rule for forming a sentence in future continuous form: Subject + shall be/will be + Verb (first form + ing) + Object. **For Example—**

  The secretary will be filing the letters.

Perfect Forms

- *Present Perfect:* It describes an action that happened at an indefinite time in the past or that began in the past and continues in the present.

  Follow this rule for forming a sentence in present perfect form: Subject + has (for singular subject)/have (for plural subject) + Verb (third form) + Object. **For Example—**

  The secretary has filed the letters.

- *Past Perfect:* It describes an action that took place in the past before another past action.

  Follow this rule for forming a sentence in past perfect form: Subject + had + Verb (third form) + Object. **For Example—**

  The secretary had filed the letters.

- *Future Perfect:* It describes an action that will occur in the future before some other action.

  Follow this rule for forming a sentence in future perfect form: Subject + will have + Verb (third form) + Object. **For Example—**

  The secretary will have filed the letters.

Perfect Continuous Forms

- *Present Perfect Continuous:* It describes an action that began in the past, continues in the present, and may continue into the future.

  Follow this rule for forming a sentence in present perfect continuous form: Subject + has been (for singular subject)/have been (for plural subject) + Verb (first form + ing) + Object. **For Example—**

  The secretary has been filing the letters for over an hour.

- *Past Perfect Continuous:* It describes a past, ongoing action that was completed before some other past action.

  Follow this rule for forming a sentence in past perfect continuous form:
  Subject + had been + Verb (first form + ing) + Object. **For Example—**

  The secretary had been filing the letters for over an hour when the director came.

- *Future Perfect Continuous:* It describes a future, ongoing action that will occur before some specified future time.

  Follow this rule for forming a sentence in future perfect continuous form: Subject + will have been + Verb (first form + ing) + Object. **For Example—**

  The secretary will have been filing the letters for over an hour by the time the director arrives.

The verbs must agree with their subjects in person and number. **For Example—**

Agreement in Person

Person	**Singular**	**Plural**
First Second Third	I am You receive The chair falls, she returns	We are You receive They come

Agreement in Number

Singular	**Plural**
The calculator is expensive. The assistant writes quickly. I am not ready to leave. Vishal, you get two boxes of chalk.	The calculators are expensive. The assistants write quickly. We are not ready to leave. All of you get two boxes of chalk.

Adjectives

Adjectives modify nouns, pronouns, and other adjectives by describing some quality or characteristic about them. They can be used to give your writing finer and more varied shades of meaning. They add pertinent information about the main topic.

The adjectives answer the questions: Which one? What kind? How many? **For Example—**

- We need four graphs tomorrow. (How many?)
- The director wants a small leather-bound folder. (What kind?)
- Let me have the blue file. (Which one?)

Adjectives Used in Comparisons

Adjectives are also used in making comparisons. There are three degrees of comparison: Positive (in which you tell the quality of someone/something), Comparative (where you compare two persons or things), and Superlative (where three or more items are compared).

The comparative is formed by adding 'er' or the word 'more' and the superlative is formed by adding 'est' or the word 'most'. **For Example—**

- Meena is tall. (positive)
- Reena is taller than Meena. (comparative)
- Sheena is the tallest of all. (superlative)
- Meena is hard-working. (positive)
- Reena is more hard-working than Meena. (comparative)

- Sheena is the most hard-working of all. (superlative)
- Radha is beautiful and smart. (positive)

Adverbs

Adverbs modify verbs, adjectives, and other adverbs. They answer such questions as: When? Where? How? How much? How many times?

Adverbs give additional information and describe an action or state of being, in greater detail.

For Example—

- My secretary never leaves the office before I do. (when?)
- The client will come tomorrow. (when?)
- I think they went upstairs. (where?)
- The meeting is going to take place there. (where?)
- Please type this quickly. (how?)
- The secretary jotted down the points carefully. (how?)
- I agree somewhat with your decision. (how much?)
- He understood the plan completely. (how much?)
- The secretary seldom reaches late. (how many times?)
- The director often travels to various places. (how many times?)

Adverbs Used in Comparisons

Many adverbs are used in comparisons, like adjectives. You may express them in comparative or superlative forms. **For Example—**

- They work fast. (positive)
- They work faster than the night crew. (comparative)
- They work the fastest of any group. (superlative)
- She types as well as Pankaj. (equal comparison)
- She types better than the younger workers. (comparison)
- She types best when working alone. (superlative)

Prepositions

A preposition links nouns, pronouns and phrases to other words in a sentence. **For Example—**

- The file is **on** the table.
- The file is **under** the table.
- The file is leaning **against** the table.
- The file is **beside** the table.
- She held the file **over** the table.
- She entered the cabin **without** the file.
- She searched **for** the file.
- She found the file **in** the drawer.

- She was silent **throughout** the meeting.
- She hurried **towards** the client.

Using Prepositions

Do not put unnecessary prepositions at the end of the sentence.

•	**Incorrect**: Where are the envelopes at? **Correct**: Where are the envelopes?
•	**Incorrect**: Can we go with? **Correct**: Can we go? Or, Can we go with you?
•	**Incorrect**: Where did the medical document get to? **Correct**: Where is the medical document?

In formal writing as well as in business communications, avoid placing the preposition at the end of the sentence.

•	**Avoid**: I'm not sure what data they're referring to. **Better**: I'm not sure to what data they're referring.
•	**Avoid**: Whom did they ask for? **Better**: For whom did they ask?

Conjunctions

Conjunctions are words used to join words or groups of words. Therefore, conjunctions act as connectors.

Consider the sentences given below:

- She is intelligent. She is sensitive.

With the help of the conjunction '**and**', you can combine these two sentences together.

- She is intelligent **and** sensitive. **For Example—**
- The contract was not signed. The lawyer did not approve it.
  The contract was not signed **as** the lawyer did not approve it.
- You are not taking a vacation this year. We are not taking a vacation this year.
  Neither you **nor** we are taking a vacation this year.
- The janitor is on duty. The security guard is on duty.
  Either the janitor **or** the security guard is on duty.
- You should check with the manager. You should call the supervisor.
  You should **not only** check with the manager, **but** also call the supervisor.
- I was in the bank. I filled out an application for a loan.
  While I was in the bank, I filled out an application for a loan.
- The position opened up. Three employees applied.
  As soon as the position opened up, three employees applied.

Interjections

Interjections are words or phrases used to express an emotion or to capture the reader's attention.

Strong interjections such as 'Wow', 'Call today', 'Act now', etc are punctuated with an exclamation mark.

Milder interjections, such as 'indeed', 'yes', 'well', etc are punctuated with a comma.

Interjections are rarely used in formal business writing. They appear mainly in advertising and promotional material.

Mild interjections

- Yes, we can complete your order today.
- Indeed, we appreciate our customers' concerns.

Strong interjections

- Outstanding! That's the verdict from first-time users of Formica Vinyl.
- Your suppliers may be saying, "Hey! What's happened to the old-fashioned cardboard box?"

Punctuations

In written communication, punctuation serves two main purposes. Firstly, it helps present ideas clearly and accurately and indicates where one thought ends and another begins, how ideas are related to one another, how to separate items in a series, and suchlike.

Wrong punctuation can alter the meaning of a sentence drastically. **For Example—**

- The politician said the reporter was an idiot.
- The politician, said the reporter, was an idiot.

As is clear from the above, the second sentence states exactly the opposite of the first because two commas have been used strategically.

Secondly, punctuation is used in abbreviations and in figures expressing time, quantities, measures, and suchlike.

This section explains the proper use of the period, question mark, exclamation mark, comma, semicolon, quotation marks, apostrophe, hyphens, dashes, and parentheses.

Period/ Full stop (.)

The period represents a full stop at the end of a complete sentence. It signifies that one idea has ended and another will follow. The period is followed by one full space before another sentence begins. The period is used at the end of a statement, command, or request. **For Example—**

- We will ship your order on the third of each month. (Statement)
- Order your copy today. (Command)
- Please return the enclosed card. (Polite request)

Periods are used in many abbreviations. **For Example—**

- Pvt. (Private)
- U.S.A. (United States of America)
- Dec. (December)
- M.B.A. (Master of Business Administration)

Do bear in mind, however, that using periods is no longer mandatory nowadays, and in many geographies the style is considered passé. USA and MBA could be written without periods. A period is however mandatory for words such as Pvt. and Dec., since both these words do not end with the alphabet 't' and 'c', respectively. A period would not be required, though, in the case of 'Ltd', which ends with the alphabet 'd'.

Some common words that no longer need a period include: Mr, Mrs, Dr, Ms, Mrs, etc.

Question Mark (?)

This is used at the end of a statement that asks a question. **For Example—**

- Have you met the new consultant?
- Will you please indicate your preference by 30 June?
- What price did you quote for machine parts? For replacement? For maintenance and repair? For field testing?
- The supervisor asked, "How many parts can be welded in an hour?" (The quoted words are a question.)
- Did you say "return the package today"? (The quoted words are not a question, but the entire sentence is the question.)

Exclamation Mark (!)

This adds emphasis to sentences, phrases, or clauses. In business writing, exclamation marks are used to call attention to a particular message or urge the reader to take some action. They are seldom used in formal writing. **For Example—**

- You cannot allow the competition to get ahead!
- This offer represents an unusual opportunity for us!
- Great! The sales are doubled.
- Oh! You are here! I was looking for you upstairs.

Comma (,)

This is the most frequently used punctuation mark, meant basically to group words that belong together and to separate those that do not. Some uses of the comma, however, are not for any grammatical purpose, but to follow a traditional pattern of punctuation. **For Example—**

- We learned how to use the keyboard, daisy wheel printer, and modem.
- Do you want this on the table, on your desk, or near the door?
- Please have Mr Chowdhuri reply by Thursday, and I will have his cheque ready.
- The meeting was cancelled, since no one reached the office.
- The arrangements depend, of course, on the number of people coming.

- "Sharma, I think you need to cut down your expense account."
- "Please call the field representative, Saroja, and tell him to come this afternoon."
- By the way, can you work on this weekend?
- When the final results were compiled, the interviewer was surprised.

Traditional Comma Uses

These are used in certain conventional situations including dates, addresses, the salutations and closings of a friendly letter. Commas are also used in certain forms of proper names or names followed by a title. **For Example—**

- We would like to set 5 March 2007 as our target date.

  When only the day and month are used, however, no commas are necessary:
- The stock offering on 10 May was for 5,000 shares.

  Here are more examples of the traditional use of commas:

  Dear Farouk, Sincerely yours, Truly yours,

  Dr Indu Pathak, Sudhir Karmakar, Ph.D. Jayant Pande, Director

Do not use commas to separate subject from verb. **For Example—**

•	**Incorrect:**	The sales force from Delhi, arrived two hours late. (The subject sales force should not be separated from the verb arrived.)
•	**Correct:**	The sales force from Delhi arrived two hours late.

Do not separate two subordinate clauses joined by a conjunction. **For Example—**

•	**Incorrect:**	The supervisor recommended that we work longer hours, and that we divide the work among more typists.
•	**Correct:**	The supervisor recommended that we work longer hours and that we divide the work among more typists.

Semicolon (;)

These represent a stronger break between independent clauses or in a series than a comma but not as complete a break as a period or colon. A semicolon, like a comma, is followed by one space when used in typed or printed communications. **For Example—**

- We have repaired your Desktop computer; it should run perfectly now.
- Our hiring practices should be improved; for example, we are not approaching the non-metro colleges.
- He received a copy of the complaint; he has suggested, accordingly, that his assistant should look into the matter.
- Navneet, who talked to the people in the mail room, suggested we mail the letters today; the mail delivery will be slow tomorrow.

Colon (:)

These represent a more complete stop than a semicolon but not as full a stop as a period. When a colon is used in a sentence, it could be followed by one or two-digit space.

Before a Series or List

Use a colon to indicate "Note what follows". Colons are used correctly after complete thoughts, particularly after such expressions as the following and as follows. **For Example—**

- The manufacturer gave us five colour choices: blue, orange, yellow, green, and red.
- The application form covers the following: schooling, work experience, references, outside interests, and medical history.

Time

Colons are used in numerical expressions of time. For instance:

- 5:00 p.m. 4:15 a.m. 12:00 noon 10:00 in the morning

Do note that when writing the time in figures, the words 'o'clock' are not used.

Business Letters

Use a colon after the salutation in a business letter or a memo.

•	Dear President Mukherjee:	To the Staff:
•	Dear Customer:	To All Line Managers:
•	Dear Ms Saraf:	To All Secretaries and Data Processors:

Quotation Marks (" ")

These are used to enclose a direct quotation – that is, someone's exact words. **For Example—**

- The shop supervisor said, "We must deliver the product today."
- "We were told," he said, "to deliver this product today."

Note in the examples above that when quoted material is interrupted by 'he said', 'she asked', and suchlike, the second part of the quote begins with a small letter as in the second example.

Punctuation with Quotation Marks

Commas and periods are always placed inside the closing quotation mark. On the other hand, semicolons and colons are always placed outside the quotation marks. **For Example—**

- She didn't say she was "disappointed in the group's performance".
- "The group has failed," she said.
- Look in the manual under "double-sided copying"; the instructions are clear.
- He listed the following as "unnecessary frills": glass mugs and gold-stamped pens.
- The manager said, "Please type these letters today."

Question marks and exclamation points, if they are part of the quoted material, are placed inside the quotation marks. Otherwise, they are placed outside the quotation marks. Only one end mark or comma is used at the end of the quotation. **For Example—**

- Did the article say "all employees share in the plan"? (The question mark refers to the entire sentence.)
- "Why hasn't this letter been typed?" she asked.
- "We set a new record!" Manmohan exclaimed.
- We are being asked to increase sales by "fifty-five percent".

- The news release stated, "We are pleased to announce the appointment of Rahul Mehra as the vice-president of marketing. He will provide strong leadership for our consumer products division."

Single Quotation Marks (' ')

These marks are used to enclose a quote within a quote. **For Example—**

- He said, "The letter stated that 'every effort should be made'."
- "We are instituting 'quality management' here at the plant."

Apostrophe (')

This is used to indicate possession and to form the plural of numbers, symbols, letters, and signs.

Possessive of Nouns

To form the possessive of a singular noun, add an apostrophe and an 's'. To form the possessive of a plural noun ending in 's', add only the apostrophe. For all other types of plural nouns add apostrophe and 's'. **For Example—**

- The president's opinions
- The secretary's desk
- The managers' staff
- Women's ready to wear
- Children's sports clothes

Indefinite Pronouns

Indefinite pronouns such as everyone, no one, someone, etc. require both apostrophe and 's' to form the possessive. Personal possessive pronouns do not use an apostrophe, though. **For Example—**

- Someone's ID card is here.
- That memo was hers.
- It was no one's fault.
- Is this his book?

Hyphens (-)

Use a hyphen with compound numbers from twenty-one to ninety-nine and with fractions used as adjectives. There are no spaces before or after the hyphen. **For Example—**

- Forty-five slides
- A two-thirds majority (But write Three fifths of the stockholders since three fifths is a noun)
- Sixty-two tallies

Prefixes and Suffixes

Always use hyphens with prefixes ex-, self-, all-, and with the suffix -elect. Hyphens are also used with all prefixes before proper nouns and adjectives. **For Example—**

- Self-image
- President-elect

- All-India games ex-manager
- All-important
- Pro-American

Dashes (– and —)

Use a small dash (–) to indicate an abrupt break in thought within a sentence. **For Example—**

- Call Jyoti – she will be back on Thursday – and have her look at this.
- Communication – two-way communication – is vital to business.

Use a big dash (—) to mean namely, that is, in other words, and so on before an explanation. **For Example—**

- They explained the method to us — we had to record each number.
- Many employees share this value — they desire meaningful work.

Brackets/Parentheses ( )

Use parentheses ( ) to enclose material that is not essential to the meaning of the sentence but adds additional information. **For Example—**

- Many people feel that etiquette (good manners) is important.
- Our survey indicates a declining loss rate (see Figure 3).

If material enclosed in parentheses falis at the end of a sentence, the end mark falls outside the closing parenthesis. If the material enclosed is a complete sentence in itself, the end mark falls within the parentheses. **For Example—**

- We make three forecasts (See Appendix A).
- We make three forecasts. (For complete data, see Appendix A.)

Superfluous and Simplified Words

In all forms of written communications, especially business writing, it is best to be brief and precise. While writing, however, writers inadvertently use superfluous words, some of which mean the same as the preceding word. If redundant words are deleted, the text will be easier to read and comprehend. **For Example—**

Superfluous	Simplified	Superfluous	Simplified
Consensus of opinion	consensus	Maximum possible	maximum
Exact replica	replica	Eight in number	eight
New innovations	innovations	Important essential	essential
Most unique	unique	Red in colour	red
True facts	facts	The state of Bihar	Bihar
Surrounded on all sides	surrounded	My personal opinion	my opinion
The month of May	May	Entirely complete	complete
Visible to the eye	visible	Just recently	recently

Refer back	refer
Whether or not	whether
Continue on	continue
Past experience	experience
Long period of time	long period
At a distance of 100 feet	at 100 feet
At a price of ₹20	at ₹20
Remember the fact that	remember that
I would like to recommend	I recommend
In the near future	shortly
In the event that	in case
In order that	so that
For the purpose of	for
With regard to	regarding
I am of the opinion that	I think
Please do not hesitate to let me know	please let me know
I wish to take this occasion to express my thanks	I thank
In the early part of next week	early next week
Your cheque for the amount ot	your cheque for Rs
It is quite probable that	probably
It may be that	possibly
At an early date	early
In very few cases	rarely
With reference to	as per
A large number	many
At the present time	presently
There is no doubt that	undoubtedly
Most of the time	frequently

In the same way	similarly
Terminate	end
Anticipate	expect
Assistance	help
Endeavour	effort
Ascertain	confirm
Procure	get
Consummate	complete
Advise	suggest
Alteration	change
Fabricate	make
Nevertheless	even then
Fundamental	basic
Approximately	nearly
Accomplished	completed
Accumulate	amass
Additionally	further
Commence	begin
Demonstrate	shows
Encounter	meeting
Expedite	speed up
Facilitate	make easy
Initiate	begin
Indicate	point out
Maintain	sustain
Objectives	aims
Subsequent	following
Transmit	send
Unavailability	absence
Utilise	use
Voluminous	bulky

Frequently Misspelt Words

Many common and not-so-common words are frequently misspelt by writers. The following list can serve as a handy reference guide for such words. But remember, this list is not comprehensive and it makes sense to always keep a good dictionary handy while writing to check for words not listed below.

Abbreviate
Absence
Accelerate
Accidentally
Accommodate
Accompanies
Accompaniment
Accordion
Accumulate
Accuracy
Acquaintance
Acquire
Acquit
Advantageous
Amateur
Analysis
Analyse
Anoint
Apology
Apparatus
Appreciate
Appropriate
Argument
Arrangement
Arrears
Ascertain
Association
Atheist
Authorise
Auxiliary
Axle

Bankruptcy
Believable
Believe
Beneficial
Bibliography
Bookkeeper
Brochure
Bulletin

Calendar
Camouflage
Cancelled
Cancellation
Caribbean
Category
Changeable
Choose
Chose
Collectible
Colonel
Column
Commemorate
Commission
Commitment
Committed
Committee
Competent
Comptroller
Concise
Congratulations
Conscience
Conscientious
Conscious
Consensus
Coolly
Contingency
Correspondence
Correspondents
Criticise

Debtor
Deceive
Deferred
Defendant
Definite
Depreciation
Description
Desiccate
Desirable
Desperate
Deterrence
Development
Dilemma
Disappear
Disappoint
Disseminate
Dissipate

Economical
Effect
Efficiency
Embarrass
Embarrassment
Emphasise
Enforceable
Exaggerate
Excel
Exceptionally
Excruciating
Exercise
Exhibitor
Exhilarate
Existence
Exorbitant
Extension

Facilitate
Familiar
Feasible
Fiery
Flabbergast
Flotation
Forfeit
Forewarn
Franchise
Fraud
Fraudulent

Gauge
Genius
Grammar
Grateful
Grievance
Gross

Guarantee
Guaranty

Harass
Harassment
Hindrance
Horrific
Hypocrisy
Hypothesis

Illegible
Imitate
Immediately
Imperative
Implement
Inadvertent
Incidentally
Incredible
Inconvenience
Independent
Indispensable
Inflationary
Initial
Installation
Initiative
Interruption
Interrupt
Invoice
Irascible
Irresistible
Itemise
Itinerary

Javelin
Jeopardise
Jeopardy
Juggernaut
Juvenile

Kowtow
Knowledge
Knowledgeable

Labelled
Legitimate
Liable
Liaison
Lieutenant
Likelihood
Livelihood
Liveable
Lose
Lucrative
Luscious

Maintenance
Manageable
Mandatory
Marketable
Measurable
Mediator
Medieval
Memento
Millennium
Minuscule
Miscellaneous
Mischief
Mischievous
Misspell
Misstatement
Municipal
Munificence

Necessary
Necessity
Negligible
Negotiate
Neutral
Ninety
Ninth
No one
Notarise
Noticeable

Objectionable
Observant
Occasion
Occupant
Occurrence
Omission
Omitted
Opinionated
Option
Overrated

Pamphlet
Parallel
Paralysis
Parity
Parliament
Particularly
Pastime
Peninsula
Permitted
Personnel
Phenomenon
Plagiarise
Plausible
Plenitude
Possession
Practically
Precede
Precise
Preference
Preferred
Prejudice
Presumptuous
Proceed
Pronunciation
Propagate
Privilege
Pursue

Qualify
Quantity
Qualitative
Quantitative
Questionnaire

Receipt
Receive
Recommend
Recommendation
Reconciliation
Recurrence
Reducible
Reference
Referred
Reimburse
Remittance
Remitted
Repetition
Renowned
Repetition
Respectfully

Responsibility
Returnable
Revenue
Rhapsody
Rhythm
Ridiculous
Routine

Saleable
Savvy
Schedule
Scientific
Scrutinise
Seize
Sensible
Separate
Serviceable
Similar
Sincerely
Specifically
Substantial
Supervisor
Supersede
Superficial
Superfluous
Susceptible
Synonymous

Tariff
Technician
Tendency
Their
There
Totalling
Tragedy
Transmit
Transmittal

Unanimous
Undoubtedly
Unmistakable
Unnecessarily
Until
Up to

Vacuum
Vendor
Ventilation
Versatile
Vicious
Volume

Waive
Warranty
Weird
Wholly
Withhold

Yield

Zealous

US/ UK Spelling Variations

While the Queen's English is generally followed in India, with the advent of personal computers, users tend to get confused between UK English and American English. The problem primarily arises because all spell-check software on PCs happen to be programmed according to US English.

Below are some words with UK spellings, followed by the US variations in brackets.

U.K	U.S.
Acknowledgement	Acknowledgment
Aesthetic	Esthetic
Aesthetician	Esthetician
Ageing	Aging
All right	Alright
Aluminium	Aluminum
Analyse	Analyze
Appendices	Appendixes/ Appendices
Authorise	Authorize
Behaviour	Behavior
Bejewelled	Bejeweled
Calliper	Caliper
Cancelled/Cancelling	Canceled/Canceling
Cancellation	Cancelation
Candour	Candor
Catalogue	Catalog
Centralise	Centralize
Centimetre	Centimeter
Centre	Center
Characterise	Characterize
Cheque	Check
Civilisation	Civilization
Civilise	Civilize
Colour	Color
Conceptualise	Conceptualize
Cooperate	Co-operate

U.K	U.S.
Coordinate	Co-ordinate
Cosy	Cozy
Counselling	Counseling
Customise	Customize
Datable	Dateable
Dialled/Dialling	Dialed/Dialing
Dialogue	Dialog
Dicey	Dicy
Discolour	Discolor
Dishonour	Dishonor
Disorganised	Disorganized
Dispatch	Despatch
Disrupter	Disruptor
Economise	Economize
Emphasise	Emphasize
Enamour	Enamor
Endeavour	Endeavor
Equalled/Equalling	Equaled/Equaling
Familiarise	Familiarize
Fantasise	Fantasize
Favour	Favor
Favourite	Favorite
Fertilise	Fertilize
Fibre	Fiber
Flavour	Flavor

UK	US
Fuelled/Fuelling	Fueled/Fueling
Fulfil	Fulfill
Glamour	Glamor
Globalise	Globalize
Grey	Gray
Harbour	Harbor
Harmonise	Hamonize
Honour	Honor
Honourable	Honorable
Hospitalise (Hospitalize)	
Hosteller	Hosteler
Humour	Humor
Hypnotise	Hynotize
Idealise	Idealize
Idolise	Idolize
Immovable	Immoveable
Immunise	Immunize
Individualise	Individualize
Industrialisation	Industrialization
Instalment	Installment
Interrupter	Interruptor
Italicise	Italicize
Itemise	Itemize
Jeopardise	Jeopardize
Jewelled	Jeweled
Jewellery	Jewelry
Judgement	Judgment
Labelled/Labelling	Labeled/Labeling
Labour	Labor
Labourer	Laborer
Legalise	Legalize
Legitimise	Legitimize
Licence	License
Likable	Likeable
Liquefy	Liquify
Liveability	Livability
Localise	Localize
Loveable	Lovable
Magnetise	Magnetize
Marginalize	Marginalize
Meagre	Meager
Mechanise	Mechanize
Mediaeval	Medieval
Memorise	Memorize
Mesmerise	Mesmerize
Metre	Meter
Millimetre	Millimeter
Minimise	Minimize
Misbehaviour	Misbehavior
Mobilise	Mobilize
Modelled/Modelling	Modeled/Modeling
Modernise	Modernize
Moisturise	Moisturize
Monopolise	Monopolize
Mould	Mold
Nationalise	Nationalize
Neighbour	Neighbor
Normalise	Normalize
Ochre	Ocher
Offence	Offense
Organisation	Organization
Organise	Organize
Panelled/Panelling	Paneled/Paneling
Parlour	Parlor

Penalise	Penalize
Personalise	Personalize
Philosophise	Philosophize
Phoney	Phony
Pressurise	Pressurize
Prioritise	Prioritize
Programme	Program
Prologue	Prolog
Protester	Protestor
Publicise	Publicize
Quarrelled/ Quarrelling	Quareled/Quareling
Rationalise	Rationalize
Realise	Realize
Recognise	Recognize
Rumour	Rumor
Saleable	Salable
Sanitise	Sanitize
Savour	Savor
Scandalise	Scandalize
Sensationalise	Sensationalize
Sensitise	Sensitize
Serialise	Serialize
Socialise	Socialize
Sombre	Somber
Spiritualise	Spiritualize
Stabilise	Stabilize
Standardise	Standardize
Sterilise	Sterilize
Summarise	Summarize
Synchronise	Synchronize
Synthesise	Synthesize
Systematise	Systematize
Tantalise	Tantalize
Theatre	Theater
Timbre	Timber
Tranquillity	Tranquility
Travelled/Travelling/	Traveled/Traveling/
Traveller	Traveler
Travelogue	Travelog
Trivialise	Trivialize
Tyre	Tire
Uncivilised	Uncivilized
Unfavourable	Unfavorable
Unpractised	Unpracticed
Unrecognised	Unrecognized
Urbanise	Urbanize
Utilise	Utilize
Valorise	Valorize
Valour	Valor
Vaporise	Vaporize
Vapour	Vapor
Vendor	Vender
Veranda	Verandah
Verbalise	Verbalize
Victimise	Victimize
Visualise	Visualize
Warrantor	Warranter
Westernise	Westernize
Wilful	Willful

Please note that for spelling some words (such as civilisation, customise, regularise, etc.), both 's' and 'z' are appropriate in Indian/UK English.

Politically Correct Words

Politically incorrect words are actually those words which indicate some specific gender— male or female. Instead, it is better to use common gender words so that superouracy of man or woman may not become evident. Therefore, nowadays their equivalant words are preferred to avoid being gender-specific.

Below are multiple gender-specific terms alongside common-gender equivalents.

Politically incorrect	**Correct**
Mankind	Humankind, humanity, human beings, human race
Man-made	Synthetic, artificial, manufactured, of human origin
Manpower	Workers, work force, staff, personnel
Manhole	Sewer-hole
Man-hours	Work hours
Man-sized	Husky, sizable, large, requiring exceptional ability
Founding fathers	The founders, founder members, pioneers
Gentleman's agreement	Informational agreement or contract
Housewife	Homemaker
Actress	Actor
Anchorman	Anchor
Advertising man	Advertising professional or practitioner
Airhostess	Flight attendant
Barman/barmaid	Bartender
Chairman	Chairperson
Cleaning woman	Housekeeper
Clergyman	Clergyperson
Englishmen	The English
Fireman	Fire-fighter
Fisherman	Fisher folk
Foreman	Supervisor
Headmaster	Dean; principal
Man the exhibit	Run the exhibit, staff the exhibit
Man of letters	Writer
Miss/Mrs	Ms (pronounced Miz)
Newsman	Reporter
Policeman	Police personnel
Salesman	Salesperson
Stewardess	Flight attendant
Self-made man	Self-made person
Sportsman	Sportsperson/Athlete
Statesmen	Political leaders

Swine flu	Influenza A (H1N1)
Weatherman	Meteorologist
Workman	Worker
The girls (for females above 18)	The women
The little lady, the better half	Wife
Girl Friday	Secretary, assistant, right hand
Libber or women's lib	Feminist, liberationist, women's movement
Man and wife	Husband and wife
Ladylike	Well-mannered
Layman	Layperson
Career girl/woman	Specify the person's profession
For the man on the way up	For the person or executive on his/her way up
For the lady of the house	For the homemaker or head of the household

Genderless politically incorrect terms to politically correct equivalents:

Politically incorrect	**Correct**
Crippled	Physically challenged
Mad	Mentally challenged
Government servants	Government employees
Handicapped	Physically challenged
Khalasi/jhaduwala	Safai karmachari
Peon/chaprasi	Office assistant

Exceptions to the rule: Midwives: There is no accepted male version for this job description!

Waiter/Waitress: Again, no appropriate replacement!

Most Common Confusing Words

A

accept *(v.)* : *to agree; to receive.* You must *accept* that he lied. I did not *accept* your money order.
except *(prep.)* : *with the exception that, but.* He likes everyone *except* you. Our dresses are the same *except* mine is green.

ad *(n.)* : *advertisement* .This *ad* was aired just once in the morning.
add *(v.)* : *to perform addition.* A new wing was *added* to the building.

adverse *(adj.)* : *unfortunate; strongly opposed (refers to things, not people).* I am comfortable even in *adverse* situations.
averse *(adj.)* : *having repugnance (refers to people).* He is *averse* to a military draft.

advice *(n.)* : *recommendation.* Take my *advice*. I am sure it will help you.
advise *(v.)* : *the act of giving a recommendation.* He *advised* her to leave for the day.

effect *(n.)* : *change; result.* What *effect* did that speech have on you?
affect *(v.)* : *to influence.* How do the budget cuts *affect* your staffing?

ail *(v.)* : *to be ill; to cause pain or distress.* Exercise is good for whatever *ails* one. They discussed the problems *ailing* the publications.
ale *(n.)* : *malt beverage more bitter than beer.* A drought of *ale* will cure your illness.

air *(n.)* : *what we breathe.* The doctor told me to get some fresh *air*.
err *(v.)* : to *make mistakes.* The judge had *erred* in ruling that the evidence was inadmissible.
heir *(n.)* : *one who inherits something.* He is the rightful *heir* to the throne.

aisle *(n.)* : *passageway.* I spend much of my time at the shops, wandering through the *aisles*.
isle *(n.)* : *a small island.* The visit to the British *isles* was worth-remembering.

all *(pron.)* : *entire, everything.* She left *all* her money to him.
awl *(n.)* : *a tool.* He pulled the *awl* to start his work.

allot *(v.)* : *to parcel out.* Equal time was *allotted* to each.
a lot *(pron.)* : *too much.* Please don't offer me anymore, I already had *a lot*.

allowed *(adj.)* : *gave permission to.* The dissident was *allowed* to leave the country.
aloud *(adv.)* : *said out loud; spoken.* He read the letter *aloud.*

all ready *(adv.)* : *means all are ready.* We are *all ready* to go.
already *(adv.)* : *by this or that time.* Is it summer *already*?

all together *(adv.)* : *refers to a group; all of us or all of them together.* Let's sing 'happy birthday', *all together*. It is wonderful to be *all together* now.
altogether *(adv.)* : *entirely.* It is not *altogether* his fault.

altar *(n.)* : *pedestal, usually religious.* They exchanged wedding vows at the *altar* of the church.
alter *(v.)* : *to modify.* Please don't *alter* your plans until we have the final schedule approved.

allude *(v.)* : *to refer indirectly.* He *alluded* to his past as a spy.
elude *(v.)* : *avoid capture.* The fugitive *eluded* the police for a month.
illude *(v.)* : *to mislead.* He *illuded* his real age to her.

allusion *(n.)* : *an indirect mention of something.* An *allusion* to Shakespeare's play was apparent in the movie.
illusion *(n.)* : *false perception.* You are under an *illusion*.

ambiguous *(adj.)* : *having more than one meaning.* The law was *ambiguous*.
ambivalent *(adj.)* : *to have mixed feelings.* She is *ambivalent* about her plans to attend the wedding.

amicable *(adj.)* : *friendly (refers to things, not people).* The meeting was relatively *amicable*.
amiable *(adj.)* : *easy to like (refers to people).* The *amiable* couple had a huge fight.

among *(prep.)* : *in the group, number or class of.* Who *among* us has not lied?
between *(prep.)* : *involving just two.* She couldn't decide *between* Chinese and Thai food.

amount *(n.)* : *used for things not countable.* We couldn't handle that *amount* of ill will.
number *(n.)* : *used for things that can be counted.* The *number* of accidents increased by ten percent.

ant *(n.)* : *a bug.* There were so many *ants* in the pot.
aunt *(n.)* : *the sister of a parent.* When did you last meet your *aunt*?

ante *(n.)* : *a bet placed before playing.* The antes were at the $10,000-$20,000 level.
auntie *(n.)* : *affectionate term for a parent's sister.* Hello *auntie*! How are you?

anxious *(adj.)* : *uneasy or apprehensive about something.* She is *anxious* about taking the test.
eager *(adj.)* : excited. She is *eager* to travel abroad.

any more *(adv.)* : *something additional or further.* It didn't rain *any more* this year than last year.
anymore *(adv.)* : *any longer.* Harry doesn't travel *anymore*.

appraise *(v.)* : *to put a value on something.* There is a need to *appraise* existing techniques.
apprise *(v.)* : *to notify.* I thought it right to *apprise* him of what had happened.

arc *(n.)* : *arch; crescent, half moon.* It was an *arc* shaped structure.
ark *(n.)* : *a vessel or a refuge.* Noah built the *ark* to save his family and two of every type of animal from the flood.

ascent *(n.)* : *movement upward.* The *ascent* was so troublesome that it took us a long time to reach the summit.
assent *(v.)* : *to agree.* They would *assent* to the terms you proposed.
consent *(n.)* : *agreement.* No change may be made without the *consent* of all the partners.

assistance *(n.)* : *help; aid.* The work was completed with the *assistance* of carpenters.
assistant *(n.)* : *one that assists; a helper; subordinate.* The managing director and his *assistant* had a meeting.

assumption *(n.)* : *an idea not based on evidence.* They made certain *assumptions* about the market.
presumption *(n.)* : *an idea based on evidence.* The planning shows a *presumption* in favour of development.

assure *(v.)* : *to promise or say with confidence.* Tony *assured* me that there was a supermarket in the village.
ensure *(v.)* : *to make sure something will/won't happen.* The client must *ensure* that accurate records are kept.
insure *(v.)* : *to issue an insurance policy.* Do get your car *insured*.

ate *(v.)* : *past tense of eat.* I *ate* 10 bananas yesterday.
eight *(n.)* : *the number after seven.* There were *eight* balloons in the party hall.

aural *(adj.)* : *having to do with hearing.* Information held in written, *aural*, or visual form will be accepted.
oral *(adj.)* : *having to do with the mouth.* They had reached an *oral* agreement.

awed *(adj.)* : *in a state of amazement.* He spoke in a hushed, *awed* whisper.
odd *(adj.)* : *unusual; opposite of even, when referring to numbers.* It's *odd* that she didn't recognize me. 3&7 are *odd* numbers.

aye *(exclam.)* : *yes. Aye*, you're right there.
eye *(n.)* : *organ one sees with.* Closing her *eyes*, she tried to relax.
I *(pron.)* : *pron. I* am not well.

B

bald *(adj.)* : *having no hair.* He was starting to go *bald.*
bawled *(v.)* : *cried.* All the babies *bawled* together.

ball *(n.)* : *a sphere.* He crushed the card into a *ball.*
bawl *(v.)* : *to cry or wail loudly.* All the babies *bawled* together.

band *(n.)* : *a group, sometimes a group of musicians.* I saw a musical *band* yesterday.
banned *(adj.)* : *forbidden.* Parking is *banned* around the harbour in summer.

bare *(adj.)* : *naked*. He was bare from the waist up.
bear *(n.)* : *the animal.* There wasn't any *bear* in the jungle.
bear *(v.)* : *to deal with something unpleasant.* I cannot *bear* his nasty remarks.

base *(n.)* : *the bottom; headquarters (singular).* She sat down at the *base* of a tree. There is a military *base* at Agra.
bass *(n.)* : *low vocal or instrumental range (pronounced like lace); a type of fish (pronounced like lass).* She is a singer with a *bass* voice. *Bass* is a sea-fish.

based *(adj.)* : *be dependent or supported.* Entitlement will be *based* on income.
baste *(v.)* : *to pour liquid fat or juices.* My mother *bastes* butter in chapati.

bases *(n.)* : *headquarters (plural of base).* There are many military *bases* in the country.
basis *(n.)* : *foundation; belief.* Trust is the only *basis* for a good working relationship.

be *(v.)* : *to exist or live.* She will *be* waiting.
bee *(n.)* : *insect.* I can't tolerate any *bee* hovering over my head.

beach *(n.)* : *sandy area with water.* Hey, what a fabulous sandy *beach*!
beech *(n.)* : *type of tree with smooth, gray bark.* There is a *beech* tree near my house.

beat *(v.)* : *to strike violently; to pound as with a drum; to defeat; to stir vigorously.* Aristocratic women were often *beaten* by their husbands; To *beat* it hard you need to have strength. Indians will *beat* the Australians in the cricket tournament. *Beat* the eggs into a fine paste.
beet *(n.)* : *a plant with a fleshy red or white root. Beet* root is good for health.

beau *(n.)* : *boyfriend (pronounced like owe).* Her *beau* is not coming to the party.
bough *(n.)* : *branch of a tree (pronounced like cow).* Apple *boughs* laden with blossom look lovely.

bow *(n.)* : *part of a set with arrows (pronounced like owe).* She was armed with a *bow* and arrow.
bow *(n.)* : *front part of a boat or ship* . From the distance, I could only see the *bow* of the ship.

because vs. since *(conj. & prep.)* : *because and since can be used almost interchangeably although because always indicates cause and effect and since is used for a relationship or time. Since* I have some extra money, I will buy shoes. (not cause and effect) ; I will go for the game *because* my daughter is in the team. (cause and effect) ; I wanted to talk to you *since* yesterday. (time)

been *(v.)* : *form of be used with has or have.* Have you *been* to his place earlier also?
bin *(n.)* : *container.* Throw the garbage in that *bin* only.

bell *(n.)* : *chime or alarm.* You should ring the *bell* before you come in.
belle *(n.)* : *beautiful or charming woman.* She is a *belle*.

berth *(n.)* : *a boat dock; bedroom or bed.* Ships stop in a *berth*. I'll sleep in the upper *berth.*
birth *(n.)* : *being born; beginning.* He was blind from *birth*. It was the *birth* of a new religion.

better *(adj.)* : *of higher quality.* The new facilities were far *better*.
bettor *(n.)* : *someone who places bets.* She described herself as a moderate *bettor*.

biannual *(adj.)* : *twice a year.* The *biannual* meeting of the planning committee ended with a lot of fanfare.
biennial *(adj.)* : *every two years.* The first of a series of *biennial* exhibitions looked interesting.
semi-annual *(adj.)* : *twice a year (same as biannual).* Their *semi-annual* meetings seem like a forced affair.

bite *(v.)* : *to use one's teeth to tear food.* The woman's arm was *bitten* off by an alligator.
byte *(n.)* : *computer term for eight bits of information.* A *byte* is considered as a unit of memory size.

billed *(adj.)* : *charged a fee.* He had been *billed* ₹3,000 for his licence.
build *(v.)* : *construct.* To *build* it in 2 days, you need a lot of manpower.

blew *(v.)* : *past tense of blow.* A gust of wind *blew* a cloud of smoke into his face.
blue *(Adj.)* : *the colour*. The clear *blue* sky looked amazing.

bloc *(n.)* : *a group united for a particular purpose.* The parliamentary *bloc* should be enough to solve the issue.
block *(n.)* : *city street; a cube-shaped object.* She went for a run round the *block*. Arange the *blocks* alphabetically.

boar *(n.)* : *male pig.* They eat the flesh of the wild *boar* as food.
bore *(v.)* : *someone or something not interesting.* He can be a crashing *bore*.

board *(n.)* : *piece of wood; a group of people.* Loose *boards* creaked as I walked on them. I have a seat on the *board* of directors.
bored *(adj.)* : *uninterested.* She got *bored* with staring out of the window.

boarder *(n.)* : *someone who pays for room and food.* Ramu is a *boarder* in my uncle's house.
border *(n.)* : *perimeter; boundary.* There is a refugee camp on the *border*.

bode *(v.)* : *predict.* Their argument did not *bode* well for the future.
bowed *(adj.)* : *bent (pronounced like owed).* The technique by which the pieces were *bowed* seemed like a brilliant idea.

bold *(adj.)* : *daring.* It was a *bold* attempt to solve the crisis.
bowled *(adj.)* : *to have gone bowling.* Stewart was *bowled* for 33.

boos *(eclam.)* : *sounds made by disapproving audience. Boo*! she cried, jumping up to frighten him.
booze *(v.)* : *alcohol.* I wonder where he's hidden his *booze.*

boy *(n.)* : *male child.* That *boy* is so careless.
buoy *(n.)* : *a naval beacon or marker. Buoy* floats on the sea or river to mark the places where it is dangerous.

brake *(n.)* : *stop.* He slammed on his *brakes.*
break *(v.)* : *separate into pieces.* Don't *break* the window pane.

bread *(n.)* : *a food; slang for money.* I gave some *bread* to the beggar. Nowadays he did not earn *bread.*
bred *(v.)* : *past tense of breed; raised.* The hens are *bred* for their eggs.

brewed *(v.)* : *past tense of brew; to make by soaking, boiling or fermenting.* I've just *brewed* some coffee.
brood *(v.) (n.)* : *a cluster or family.* A *brood* of chicks.

brews *(n.)* : *a kind of beer.* I have fresh *brews.*
bruise *(n.)* : *a black-and-blue mark, contusion.* His body was a mass of *bruises* after he had been attacked.

bridal *(adj.)* : *relating to brides.* Her white *bridal* gown was so pretty.
bridle *(n.)* : *a harness, usually for a horse.* Five horses, saddled and *bridled*, were tied by the reins to branches of trees.

bring *(v.)* : *you bring something towards.* What *brings* you here?
take *(v.)* : *you take something away.* He leaned forward to *take* her hand.

broach *(v.)* : *to raise a topic.* He *broached* the subject he had been avoiding all evening.
brooch *(n.)* : *a piece of jewellery with a pin on the back of it.* Where did you buy this *brooch* from?

brows *(n.)* : *the hairs in the arch above the eyes.* He wiped his *brows.*
browse *(v.)* : *search for, peruse. Browse* any new mobile on internet and let me know the feedback.

but : *(conj. & prep.)* I will come *but* I will reach a little late.
butt *(n.)* : *a push or blow given with the head.* He *butted* inside the room.

buy *(v.)* : *purchase.* I will *buy* this T-shirt tomorrow.
by *(prep.)* : *near, next to.* I think she stays very close *by.*
bye *(exclam.)* : *short for goodbye.* See you tomorrow. Take care. Bye-*bye.*

C

cache *(n.)* : *hidden stash.* There was a good supply of meat in e *caches.*
cash *(n.)* : *money.* Do you have some *cash* with you today?

calendar *(n.)* : *chart of days and months.* Check the dates in the *calendar* and let me know the date of coming Sunday.
colander *(n.)* : *sieve to drain off liquids.* Purchase a *colander* to sift rice.

can *(v.)* : *showing determination.* I *can* do it.
may *(v.)* : *permission to.* He *may* go to the park tomorrow.

cannon *(n.)* : *large, heavy gun.* They would win the fight, under cover of the defending *cannon.*
canon *(n.)* : *rule.* The appointment violated the *canons* of fair play.

canvas *(n.)* : *awning cloth, tarp.* He is used to painting large *canvases.*
canvass *(v.)* : *to poll.* They promised to *canvass* all member clubs for their views.

capital *(n.)* : *main city; assets.* Delhi is the *capital* of India. We set up a business with a *capital* of 50 lakh.
capitol *(n.)* : *statehouse.* The work is on display at the Utah state *capitol.*

carat *(n.)* : *unit of weight in gemstones.* I need a half-*carat* diamond ring.
caret *(n.)* : *a proofreading mark to show insertion (^).* Mark a *caret* wherever required.
carrot *(n.)* : *edible root.* Rabbits like to eat *carrots.*

cast *(n. & v.)* : *group of actors; to throw.* He draws sensitive performances from his inexperienced *cast.* The priceless things had been *cast* into the river.
caste *(n.)* : *a social class. Caste* issues can never be done with in India.

cay *(n.)* : *a small, low island*. He lives on a *cay.*
key *(n.)* : *instrument for opening locks.* There were two *keys* to the cupboard.
quay *(n.)* : *wharf, dock, pier*. Ships are loaded in *quays.*

cede *(v.)* : *to surrender.* In 1874, the islands were *ceded* to Britain.
seed *(n.)* : *reproductive germ.* You can grow artichokes from *seeds.*

cell *(n.)* : *prison room.* The authorities locked all remaining inmates in their *cells.*
sell *(v.)* : *to exchange for money.* This magazine of yours won't *sell.*

censor *(n.) (v.)*: *disallow; person who disallows.* The soldier's letters were *censored* before mailing.
censure *(v.)* : *to criticize strongly.* The children were *censured* by the principal.
sensor *(n.)* : *a device that measures heat, light, etc. and transmits a signal to a control or measuring instrument.* The engineers used electronic *sensors* to monitor each wheel.

cent *(n.)* : *a penny.* He was paid 40 *cents* an hour.
scent *(n.)* : *a smell, aroma* She sprayed *scent* over her body.
sent *(v.)* : *transmitted.* We *sent* a reminder letter but received no reply.

ocreal *(n.)* : *breakfast food.* A bowl of *cereal* is must every day.
serial *(adj.)* : *a series or array.* He was a *serial* adulterer.

chance *(n.)* : *accident(al).* There is little *chance* of his finding a job.
chants *(n.)* : *chorus, melody.* He was whispering something, repeating it like a *chant* or a mantra.

chased *(v.)* : *past tense of chase; to go after*. Police *chased* the stolen car through the city.
chaste *(adj.)* : *pure, virginal.* What is required of celibate Catholic clergy is to remain *chaste.*

chews *(n.)* : *wad of something chewable.* The leftover *chews* were eaten by the dog.
choose *(v.)* : *to pick; select.* It is difficult to *choose* over right from wrong.

childish *(adj.)* : *immature.* He is still so *childish.*
childlike *(adj.)* : *innocent*. She speaks with a *childlike* directness.

Chile *(n.)* : *a country in South America*. Did you go to *Chile* also?
chili *(n.)* : *a type of pepper.* Please add some more *chili* in it.
chilly *(adj.)* : *cold, brisk.* The weather is so *chilly*. Isn't it?

choral *(adj.)* : *having to do with a chorus or a choir.* My *choral* group meets on Wednesday evenings.
chorale *(n.)* : *a hymn; a group of singers specializing in church music.* A worshipper sings a *chorale*.
coral *(n.)* : *material that makes up reefs.* She was wearing a twisted rope of *coral*, pearls, and crystal.
corral *(n.)* : *a horse pen.* I drove the horses into a *corral.*

chord *(n.)* : *three or more musical tones sounded simultaneously*. Join the two *chords* to start this instrument.
cord *(n.)* : *a rope or strand of flexible material.* Her feet were tied with *cord.*
cored *(adj.)* : *removed the centre of something.* The *core* muscles of the abdomen should be strong.

chute *(n.)* : *an inclined shaft*. Cement was loaded on to barges via *chutes.*
shoot *(v.)* : *to discharge from a weapon; a stem.* The troops were ordered to *shoot* the enemy.

cite *(v.)* : *to quote from.* Authors who are highly regarded by their peers tend to be *cited.*
sight *(n.)* : *vision, the power to see.* I've always been scared of the *sight* of blood.
site *(n.)* : *a location or position.* A *site* has been chosen for the house.

classic *(adj.)* : *important; true.* Hamlet is the *classic* example of a tragedy.
classical *(adj.)* : *having to do with Greek or Roman antiquity.* Have you seen the *classical* Trojan horse?

clause *(n.)* : *part of a contract.* According to this *clause*, police cannot arrest him.
claws *(n.)* : *an animal's nails.* The kitten was *clawing* at Lovesh's trouser leg.

click *(v.)* : *a sound.* The key *clicked* in the lock and the door opened.
clique *(n.)* : *a group.* His flat became an asylum for a *clique* of young men of similar tastes.

climactic *(adj.)* : *having to do with the climax*.The film's *climactic* scenes were deleted.
climatic *(adj.)* : *having to do with the climate.* The *climatic* conditions these days are bad.

close *(v.)* : *to shut (pronounced like rose).* Please *close* the door.
clothes *(n.)* : *apparel.* Youngsters like fashionable *clothes.*

coarse *(adj.)* : *rough, lacking in fineness of texture; crude.* The poor woman wore a sari of *coarse* cloth.
course *(n.)* : *a class; a path.* A ship cannot be kept on its *course* without a compass.

colonel *(n.)* : *an officer in the military.* Some *colonel* in the paratroops came up to take care of the situation.
kernel *(n.)* : *a seed.* The *kernel* of a walnut is rich in vitamines.

complement *(n.)* : *completing part of an order.* This scarf is a perfect *complement* to that dress.
compliment *(n.)* : *praise.* I paid her a *compliment* for organising the party so well.

confidant *(n.)* : *someone confided in.* She was a close *confidante* of the princess.
confident *(adj.)* : *certain, sure.* She was a *confident*, outgoing girl.

connote *(v.)* : *to suggest, imply.* A growling dog *connotes* danger.
denote *(v.)* : *to be a sign of.* Certain clouds *denote* rain on the way.

continual *(adj.)* : *repeated but with breaks in between; chronic.* The *continual* problem with our car forced us to sell it.
continuous *(adj.)* : *without interruption in an unbroken stream of time or space.* The *continuous* dripping of the faucet drove me crazy.

corps *(n.)* : *trained group* . The Royal Army Medical *Corps* were also present there.
corpse *(n.)* : *dead body.* The *corpse* of a man lay there.

cosign *(v.)* : *to sign along with.* They *cosign* to the treaty.
cosine *(n.)* : *a trigonometry term.* Rajeev cannot solve this *cosine.*

council *(n.)* : *a group of people meeting for a purpose.* That evening, she held a family *council.*
counsel *(n, v.)* : *advise; advice.* With wise *counsel* a couple can buy a home.

creak *(v.)* : *a sound.* The stairs *creaked* as she went up them.
creek *(n.)* : *a stream.* It was a sandy beach in a sheltered *creek.*

crews *(n.)* : *many groups.* The ship's captain and *crew* may be brought to trial.
cruise *(n.)* : *a trip or vacation by sea.* They were *cruising* off the California coast.

criteria *(n.)* : *plural of criterion.* These products meet certain environmental *criteria.*
criterion *(n.)* : *a standard for evaluating or testing something.* What are the *criterion* for clearing this exam?

cue *(n.)* : *a hint; a stimulus.* She had not yet been given her *cue* to come out on to the stage. He stood and waited for a *cue* to go on.
queue *(n.)* : *a line of people.* Please stand in a *queue.*

currant *(n.)* : *small dried grape.* You need to add a *currant* bun in the dish.
current *(adj.)* : *up to date; body of air or water moving in a definite direction.* Youngsters are quick to follow the *current* trends in dressing; I saw the rising ocean *currents.*

curser *(n.)* : *someone who swears or wishes misfortune on another.* The *curser* did not think before cursing her.
cursor *(n.)* : *a blinking symbol indicating position on a computer screen.* Don't start typing until you see the *cursor.*

D

dam *(n.)* : *a barrier obstructing the flow of liquid.* The *dam* burst after torrential rain.
damn *(adj.)* : *a swear word or curse.* I treated her badly and I'll be *damned* to hell for it.

dammed *(adj.)* : *blocked from flowing.* The closed lock gates *dammed* up the canal.
damned *(adj.)* : *doomed.* She's too *damned* for commiting this act.

days *(n.)* : *twenty-four-hour periods of time.* They only met a few *days* ago.
daze *(v.)* : *to stun or overwhelm.* She was *dazed* by his revelations.

dear *(adj.)* : *affectionate.* He is very *dear* to me.
deer *(n.)* : *the animal.* I could not see any *deer* in the zoo.

desert *(n.)* : *a desolate area; to abandon.* I have seen the Sahara *desert.* He *deserted* his wife and daughter and went back to England.
dessert *(n.)* : *sweet food eaten at the end of a meal.* A *dessert* of chocolate mousse was added to the menu.

desperate *(adj.)* : *lost all hope, in despair.* I heard sounds of a *desperate* fight going on in the next room.
disparate *(adj.)* : *entirely dissimilar.* They inhabit *disparate* worlds of thought.

device *(n.)* : *a machine or tool used for a specific task.* There is a separate *device* available for this machine.
devise *(v.)* : *to invent.* A new system should be *devised* to control traffic in Delhi.

dew *(n.)* : *condensation in the morning.* The morning *dew* drops are so soothing.
do *(v.)* : *to take action.* What *do* you want to do?
due *(adj.)* : *owed by a certain date.* When is your *due* date?

die *(v. & n.)* : *to cease to live.* He *died* of AIDS.
dye *(v.)* : *to stain or colour using an agent.* I *dyed* my hair blonde.

different from vs. different than *(adj.)* : *use different from not different than.* The weather was *different from* what we expected; You may use *differently than* when a clause precedes and follows the expression. He works *differently than* she does.

discreet *(adj.)* : *careful, confidential.* We made some *discreet* inquiries.
discrete *(adj.)* : *individual, distinct*. I want a *discrete* report on this.

discussed *(adj.)* : *talked over.* The first three volumes have been *discussed.*
disgust *(n.)* : *repulsion.* I can't live with this *disgust*.

does *(n.)* : *female deer (plural)* They saw some *does* in a zoo.
does *(v.)* : *a form of to do.* She *does* this stupid thing always.

doughs *(n.)* : *unbaked loaves of bread.* Add water to the flour and mix it to a manageable *dough*.
doze *(v.)* : *to sleep.* He found his mother *dozing* by the fire.

dual *(adj.)* : *two-fold.* He played a *dual* role in the movie.
duel *(n.)* : *combat between two individuals.* He had seriously wounded men in *duels*.

E

e.g. *(abbr.)* : *for example.* My living expenses have increased, *e.g.*, rent, food and utilities.
i.e. *(abbr.)* : *that is, in other words.* My living expenses have drained my finances, *i.e.*, I have less money in the bank at the end of every month.

elicit *(v.)* : *evoke, extract, draw out.* I tried to *elicit* a smile from Riya.
illicit *(adj.)* : *illegal.* He was sharing an *illicit* relationship with him.

elusive *(adj.)* : *difficult to describe, evasive.* He remains an *elusive* personality to me, always.
illusive *(adj.)* : *not real although seeming to be.* She had the *illusive* dream of finding happiness by travelling. (plausible, possible). She had an *illusive* idea that she was qualified for the job. (deceptive, delusional)

emigrate *(v.)* : *to exit your country in order to live in another country.* Rose's parents *emigrated* from Australia.
immigrate *(v.)* : *to enter a new country to live.* They *immigrated* to Britain in 1982.

empathy *(n.)* : *to understand another's feelings.* He seemed to have some *empathy* for the guys who got dumped this week.
sympathy *(n.)* : *to feel compassion or sadness for another.* They had great *sympathy* for the flood victims.

epic *(n.)* : *saga.* The romances display gentler emotions not found in Greek *epics*.
epoch *(n.)* : *a period of time, an age.* These events marked an *epoch* in the history.

every day *(every, adj.; day, n.)* : *each day.* I learn something new *every day*.
everyday *(adj.)* : *ordinary.* These are my *everyday* clothes.

F

facts *(n.)* : *objective data.* What is the most commonly known *fact* about this book?
fax *(n.)* : *short for facsimile; technology that sends images by phone.* We got a three-page *fax* from her assistant.

faint *(adj.)* : *to go unconscious.* She *fainted* after spending an hour in the sun.
feint *(n.)* : *a deceptive blow; esp. in boxing.* It was a planned *feint* at the opponent's face.

fair *(adj.)* : *impartial.* The group has achieved *fair* and equal result.
fare *(n.)* : *payment or expense for travel.* The taxi *fare* seemed to go high.

fairy *(n.)* : *imaginary being, possessing magical powers.* She believed she had had *fairies* at the bottom of her garden.
ferry *(n.)* : *type of boat* . I caught the *ferry* at Kerala.

farther *(adv.)* : *refers to physical distance only.* We had to walk *farther* than the map indicated.
further *(adj.)* : *to help forward, advance, or promote a work, undertaking, cause, etc.* Elisa had more desire to *further* her own interests than to further the mission of the organization.

faux *(adv.)* : *fake, imitation.* Their *faux* concern for the well-being of the voters didn't fool many.
foe *(n.)* : *enemy, opponent.* His work was praised by friends and *foes* alike.

faze *(v.)* : *to perturb or fluster.* She was not *fazed* by his show of anger.
phase *(n.)* : *a period or situation.* This *phase* will also end, sooner of later.

feat *(n.)* : *an extraordinary act or accomplishment.* The new printing presses were considerable *feats* of engineering.
feet *(n.)* : *plural of foot.* My *feet* are paining a lot today.

feted *(v.)* : *celebrated, honoured.* She was an instant celebrity, *feted* by the media.
fetid *(adj.)* : *stinking. Fetid* water is injurious to health.

fewer *(adj.)* : *refers to a number that can be counted.* You people are still *fewer* in number. Look at us!
less *(pron., adv.)* : *refers to an uncountable amount. Less* rain, *less* fear.
under *(prep.)* . *in a lower position of place.* A cat is sitting *under* the chair.

find *(v.)* : *discover.* I can't *find* my keys.
fined *(adj.)* : *penalized.* She was *fined* because she disobeyed the traffic rules.

fir *(n.)* : *type of tree.* Do you know where *fir* trees are found?
fur *(n.)* : *hairy coat of an animal.* I bought a new *fur* coat.

flair *(n.)* : *style.* She had a *flair* for different languages.
flare *(n.)* : *erupt.* The *flare* of the matchstick lit up his face.

flea *(n.)* : *insect.* I can't tolerate this *flea* any more.
flee *(v.)* : *to run away.* He was forced to *flee* the country.

flew *(v.)* : *(past tense of fly) to have moved through the air with wings.* Helicopters *flew* the injured to the hospital.
flu *(n.)* : *a virus.* She was down with *flu.*
flue *(n.)* : *part of a chimney.* I think the *flue* is not working properly.

floe *(n.)* : *sheet of floating ice* . They camped on a drifting ice *floe* for five months.
flow *(n.)* : *pour, proceed, spew.* The crowd *flowed* into the building.

flour *(n.)* : *a fine white powder made from grain.* Add some *flour* to make the dish healthy.
flower *(n.)* : *the bloom of a plant.* Thank you for the lovely *flowers* dear.

for *(prep.)* : *concerning sb/sth.* Will you be going *for* an interview tomorrow?
fore *(adv.)* : *towards the front.* The *fore* legs of a kangaroo are smaller than its hind legs.
four *(n.)* : *the number after three.* There were *four* kids playing in the ground.

foreword *(n.)* : *introduction to a book written by someone other than the author.* Who has written the *foreword* of the book?
forward *(adv.)* : *moving towards a position in front.* He started up the engine and the car moved *forward.*

fort *(n.)* : *a military fortification.* The city was guarded by a ring of *forts.*
forte *(n.)* : *someone's talent.* Small talk was not his *forte.*

forth *(adv.)* : *forward.* We rose at dawn and sallied *forth.*
fourth *(det.)* : *number after third.* Who came *fourth* in the race?

foul *(adj.)* : *offensive, disgusting.* The news had put Riya in a *foul* mood.
fowl *(n.)* : *a bird that is used as food or hunted as game.* Where are the domestic *fowl* found?

freeze *(v.)* : *the state of being forzen.* This soup *freezes* well.
frieze *(n.)* : *a decorative band on the wall.* The horsemen had a *frieze* round their forehead.

G

gait *(n.)* : *a manner of walking or stepping, stride.* She had the *gait* of a peacock.
gate *(n.)* : *an opening in a wall of fence for entrance or exit.* She closed the front *gate.*

gilt *(n.)* : *gold-covered.* The sun's morning rays reflected off the *gilt* dome of the state capitol.
guilt *(n.)* : *culpability for a crime.* It is the duty of the prosecution to prove the prisoner's *guilt.*

gone *(prep.)* : *absent or having departed; used with has or have.* Riya has *gone* to the store.
went *(prep.)* : *past tense of go.* Riya and Rahul *went* to the beach.

gored *(v.)* : *stabbed with a horn or tusk.* He was *gored* to death by a charging bull.
gourd *(n.)* : *hard-shelled fruit.* Get 2 kgs of bottle *gourd* from the market.

gorilla *(n.)* : *largest of the apes.* A *gorilla* is so huge that it can scare a child.
guerilla *(n.)* : *soldier using surprise raid; irregular tactics.* This town fell to the *guerrillas.*

graft *(n.)* : *acquisition of money dishonestly.* Murder and explosions interweave with car races and *graft.*
graphed *(adj.)* : *diagrammed.* Have you *graphed* the questionnaire?

grate *(v.)* : *reduce (food) to small shreds by rubbing it on a grater. Grate* the cheese and give it to me.
great *(adj.)* : *excellent.* You did a *great* job!

grill *(n.)* : *a flat metal frame that one puts food on to cook over a fire.* Place the paneer cubes under a hot *grill.*
grille *(n.)* : *an openwork barrier for a gate.* I looked through the *grille* into the church.

groan *(n.)* : *a low, mournful sound of pain or grief.* Riya *groaned* and pulled the blanket over her head.
grown *(adj.)* : *to have increased in size.* These plants have *grown* so early. Isn't it?

guessed *(adj.)* : *conjectured, offered an opinion.* He *guessed* the child's age right.
guest *(n.)* : *company, honoree.* I have two *guests* coming to dinner tonight.

guise *(n.)* : *assumed appearance.* He visited us in the *guise* of an inspector.
guys *(n.)* : *men.* He's a nice *guy.*

H

hair *(n.)* : *what grows on one's head and body.* You have got lovely long *hair.*
hare *(n.)* : *rabbit.* Did you see any *hare* in your whole jungle trip?

hall *(n.)* : *large room.* The meeting took place in a large *hall.*
haul *(v.)* : *to pull, drag.* He *hauled* his bike out of the shed.

halve *(v.)* : *divide into two.* Please *halve* the sandwich into two.
have *(v.)* : *to possess.* I don't *have* that much money on me.

hangar *(n.)* : *shed or shelter for housing airplanes.* The size of an aircraft *hangar* is so large.
hanger *(n.)* : *something to hang a garment on in the closet.* Put the coat in the *hanger* to keep it safe.

haut/haute *(n.)* : *high-class, fancy as in haute couture (pronounced oht).* The kitty party was a *haute* affair.
hoe *(n.)* : *flat-bladed gardening tool.* It's a tough row to *hoe.*

hay *(n.)* : *dried grass.* Make *hay,* while the sun shines.
hey *(exclam.)* : *interjection used to call attention. Hey,* what's going on here?

heal *(v.)* : *to cure.* His concern is to *heal* sick people.
heel *(n.)* : *back part of the foot.* I need a shoe with low *heels.*

healthful *(adj.)* : *something that promotes health.* Organic food is thought to be *healthful.*
healthy *(adj.)* : *possessing good health.* I feel fit and *healthy.*

hear *(v.)* : *to listen; to give an official hearing.* She could *hear* men shouting. Today the jury began to *hear* the evidence.
here *(adv.)* : *in this spot.* They have lived *here* most of their lives.

heard *(adj.)* : *listened.* She had never been *heard* complaining.
herd *(n.)* : *a flock of animals.* It is a farm with big dairy *herds.*

heroin *(n.)* : *a narcotic derived from morphine.* Don't go to that market. *Heroin* is being sold over there.
heroine *(n.)* : *female admired for courage or ability.* She was a true feminist *heroine.*

hi *(eclam.)* : *a greeting, informal for hello.* '*Hi* there. How was the flight?'
high *(adj.)* : *having a relatively great elevation.* I was standing on the top of a *high* mountain.

higher *(n.)* : *more elevated.* She scored *higher* than her brother.
hire *(n.)* : *to pay for services.* We *hired* a car and headed towards our home.

him *(pron.)* : *pronoun referring to male person or animal.* He took the children with *him.*
hymn *(n.)* : *song sung in praise of a religious deity.* The film is a *hymn* to god.

hoard *(n.)* : *stockpile, amass.* He came back to rescue his little *hoard* of gold.
horde *(n.)* : *a large group, crowd.* It was a *horde* of music band which blocked the road.

hoarse *(adj.)* : *cracked voice.* A *hoarse* voice will be suitable for this character.
horse *(n.)* : *animal.* I like *horse* riding.

hoes *(n.)* : *bladed gardening tool.* Where are the *hoes*? Let's start the work.
hose *(n.)* : *a flexible tube for conveying liquid.* Use *hose* to sprinkle water to these plants.

hole *(n.)* : *an opening.* The dog had dug a *hole* in the ground.
whole *(adv.)* : *entire, complete.* He spent the *whole* day walking.

holy *(adj.)* : *religious.* I do not lead a *holy* life.
wholly *(adj.)* : *entirely, completely.* She was *wholly* given over to religion.

hostel *(n.)* : *boarding house or inexpensive lodging.* My brother is staying in a *hostel* since last 3 years.
hostile *(adj.)* : *antagonistic.* People are very *hostile* to the idea that you proposed.

hour *(n.)* : *sixty minutes.* How many *hours* are left for the exam to start?
our *(det.)* : *Our* house is just next to yours.

I

idle *(adj.)* : *not active; unemployed.* 10% per cent of the workforce is now *idle.*
idol *(n.)* : *someone admired.* Narendra Modi is my *idol.*
idyll or **idyl** *(n.)* : *a happy and peaceful place.* The rural *idyll* remains strongly evocative in most industrialized societies.

imply *(v.)* : *to indicate without being explicit.* The report *implies* that two million jobs might be lost.
infer *(v.)* : *to conclude from evidence.* From these facts we can *infer* that crime has been increasing.

in *(prep.)* : *preposition; inside.* I'm living *in* London.
inn *(n.)* : *small hotel.* Have you heard about the hotel country *inn*?

inc. *(abbr.)* : *abbreviation for incorporated.* I work with Mexaco *inc.*
ink *(n.)* : *fluid in pens.* There isn't any *ink* in this pen.

incite *(v.)* : *to prompt to action.* They conspired to *incite* riots.
insight *(n.)* : *understanding, comprehension.* His work provides important *insights.*

incredible *(adj.)* : *astonishing.* Her gymnastic moves were *incredible.*
incredulous *(adj.)* : *skeptical.* Citizens are *incredulous* about the reason for the increase in the price of gas.

ingenious *(adj.)* : *clever.* He was *ingenious* enough to overcome the limited budget.
ingenuous *(adj.)* : *naive or simple.* He eyed her with wide, *ingenuous* eyes.

innocence *(n.)* : *to be without guilt.* They must prove their *innocence*.
innocent *(adj.)* : *people who are without guilt.* The prisoners were later found *innocent.*

irregardless *(adv.)* : *paying attention.* The weather was terrible but we did not carry on *irregardless.*
regardless *(adv.)* : *in spite of, without regard.* The allowance is paid *regardless* of age or income.

it's : *contraction for it is or it has. It's* for a good cause.
its : *belonging to an animal or a thing.* The cat hurt *its* paw.

J

jewel *(n.)* : *gem.* She loved dressing up in her *jewels.*
joule *(n.)* : *(in physics) a unit of work or energy.* It consumes how many *joules*?

K

knead *(v.)* : *work with the dough.* You know how to *knead* the dough?
kneed *(v.)* : *hit with one's knee.* She *kneed* him in the groin.
need *(n.)* : *requirement.* I *need* help now.

knew *(v.)* : *past tense of know, to have understood.* I *knew* this already.
new *(adj.)* : *opposite of old.* I bought a *new* byke yesterday.

knight (n.) : *a soldier in the Middle Ages. Knights* are often shown in pictures riding horses.
night *(n.)* : *period between sunset and sunrise.* The door is always locked at *night.*

knot *(n.)* : *interlacing of cord or rope.* Tie a *knot* at the end of the cord.
not *(adv.)* : *used to express negation.* He did *not* say anything.

know *(v.)* : *understand, comprehend.* I *know* what I'm doing.
no *(det.)* : *a negative to express dissent.* There is *no* excuse.

knows *(v.)* : *understands.* God *knows* what else they might find.
nose *(n.)* : *part of the body one smells with.* He slowly breathed out the air through his *nose.*

L

lacks *(n.)* : *not having sth.* The case was dismissed for *lack* of evidence.
lax *(adj.)* : *slack, easy going.* He'd been a bit *lax* about discipline in school lately.

ladder *(n.)* : *a structure usually of wood used to climb up and down.* Climb the *ladder* fast to win the race.
latter *(adj.)* : *the second of two.* If given a choice between vanilla and chocolate ice cream, I'll take the *latter.*

lain *(v.)* : (*past participle of lie) as in lie down.* I have *lain* on the sofa.
lane *(n.)* : *narrow road or passage.* She drove along the winding *lane.*

lead *(n. & v.)* : *a metal element; to guide* . Attach a metallic *lead* to it so that it gains some power. If you *lead,* I will follow.
led *(v.)* : *guided (past tense of to lead).* A farm track *led* off to the left.

leak *(n.)* : *unintended discharge of liquid or gas.* The *leak* of fluid may occur in this container.
leek *(n.)* : *type of onion.* Do you know where the *leeks* are found?

lean *(adj. v.)* : *slim, not fat; to incline.* She was tall and *lean.* He *leaned* back in his chair.
lien *(n.)* : *a claim on property to secure debt payment.* They shall be entitled to a *lien* on any lot sold.

leased *(adj.)* : *rented.* She *leased* the site to a local company.
least *(adj.)* : *smallest in size or amount.* Who has the *least* number of troubles?

lessen *(v.)* : *to make less.* The years have *lessened* the gap in age between us.
lesson *(n.)* : *a unit to be learned or studied.* It was an advanced *lesson* in maths.

lie *(n.)* : *a falsehood; present tense of lie down.* This story is nothing but a pack of *lies;* I like to *lie* down for a nap at 2pm.
lye *(n.)* : *a caustic substance.* Does this washing powder contain *lye*?

loan *(n.)* : *something lent for temporary use.* Borrowers can take out a *loan* for remaining amount.
lone *(adj.)* : *only, solitary.* I approached a *lone* drinker across the bar.

loose *(adj.)* : *opposite of tight.* Wear *loose* clothes in summers.
lose *(v.)* : *opposite of win.* Riya was very upset about *losing* her job.

M

mach *(n.)* : *ratio with the speed of sound:* Mach 1 = the speed of sound, Mach 2 = twice the speed of sound. His fighter plane has a top speed of *Mach3.*
mock *(v. & adj.)* : *ridicule; artificial.* He *mocked* his voice, and aped a few of his guitar lines. It was a *mock* election.

made *(v.)* : *created.* My grandmother *made* a dress for me.
maid *(n.)* : *cleaning lady.* My *maid* is on leave today.

mail *(n.)* : *correspondence.* I did not receive any *mail.*
male *(n.)* : *masculine (opposite of female).* All the *males* are supposed to form a separate line.

main *(adj.)* : *primary, chief, leading.* Who is the *main* actor in this movie?
mane *(n.)* : *long hair on the neck of a horse or lion.* He had a *mane* of white hair.

maize *(n.)* : *corn.* Use *maize* flour to knead the dough.
maze *(n.)* : *labyrinth.* The house has a *maze* and a walled Italian garden.

mall *(n.)* : *shopping mall.* There is a new *mall* in our area. Have you seen that?
maul *(n.)* : *abuse, claw.* The body was badly *mauled* in the battle.

manner *(n.)* : *behaviour.* Didn't your mother teach you any *manners*?
manor *(n.)* : *palatial residence.* What a beautiful *manor*!

marquee *(n.)* : *canopy, shelter; projection over a theatre entrance.* There is no *marquee* in this theatre.
marquis *(n.)* : *aristocrat, nobleman.* I was a *marquis* in London.

marry *(v.)* : *to wed.* Will you *marry* me?
merry *(adj.)* : *cheerful.* He wished me a *merry* Christmas.

marshal *(v., n.)* : *to control; a judge.* The general *marshalled* his troops. He is the *Marshal* of the Royal Air Force.
martial *(adj.)* : *militant, aggressive.* The city remains firmly under *martial* law.

meat *(n.)* : *animal flesh used for food.* Place *meat* and poultry in the refrigerator immediately.
meet *(v.)* : *to connect, touch.* A week later I *met* him in the street.
mete *(v.)* : *to give sb a punishment.* He denounced the maltreatment *meted* out to minorities.

medal *(n.)* : *badge.* He was honoured with a gold *medal*.
meddle *(v.)* : *to interfere unwantedly.* I don't want him *meddling* in our affairs.

metal *(n.)* : *earth element.* It was an adjustable pole made of *metal.*
mettle *(v.)* : *boldness.* The team showed their true *mettle* in the second half of the match.

mind *(n.) (v.)* : *intelligence; obey.* A lot of thoughts ran through my *mind*. Please, do not *mind.*
mined *(v.)* : *excavated to extract ores.* The area was *mined* to extract ores.

miner *(v.)* : *one who excavates to extract ores.* The coal *miner* was really a brave man.
minor *(adj.)* : *someone under legal age; small.* The court would take account of the *minor's* wishes.

missed *(v.)* : *failed to hit.* A laser-guided bomb had *missed* its target.
mist *(n.)* : *fog, fine spray.* The peaks were shrouded in *mist.*

mode *(n.)* : *method, manner.* His preferred *mode* of travel was car.
mowed *(v.)* : *to have cut grass.* Rahul *mowed* the lawn.

mood *(n.)* : *an emotional state.* He appeared to be in a very good *mood* about something.
mooed *(v.)* : *to make a sound of cow.* The cows *mooed* from the barn.

moose *(n.)* : *a large deer.* I couldn't see any *moose* in the jungle.
mousse *(n.)* : *type of dessert.* Sponge topped with chocolate *mousse* attracted me.

morning *(n.)* : *start of the day, between night and afternoon.* I've got a meeting this *morning.*
mourning *(n.)* : *sorrow over someone's death.* She's still *mourning* her husband's death.

mustard *(n.)* : *yellow condiment.* Massage my head with some hot *mustard* oil so that I can feel better.
mustered *(v.)* : *assembled, gathered.* 17,000 men had *mustered* around the park.

N

naval *(adj.)* : *pertaining to ships.* Where is the *naval* officer?
navel *(n.)* : *belly button, umbilicus.* Tie this thread on your *navel.*

none *(prep.)* : *not one, not any. None* could match her looks.
nun *(n.)* : *female member of a religious order.* Was there any *nun* present there?

O

oar *(n.)* : *a blade for rowing.* When I travelled by boat I pulled the *oars.*
or *(conj.)* : You want the book *or* the pen?
ore *(n.)* : *metal-bearing mineral or rock* . Iron *ore* is obtained from underneath the earth.

one *(pron., n.,det.)* : *single unit.* Give him *one* apple every day.
won *(v.)* : *past tense of win.* Do you know who *won* the match?

ordinance *(n.)* : *a law.* They issued an *ordinance* limiting the working hours.
ordnance *(n.)* : *military weapons and ammunition.* The gun was a brand new piece of *ordnance.*

overdo *(v.)* : *to do in excess.* I'd *overdone* the garlic in the curry.
overdue *(adj.)* : *past due.* The rent was nearly three months *overdue.*

P

packed *(adj.)* : *past tense of pack.* I *packed* my bag and left.
pact *(n.)* : *an agreement or treaty.* The country negotiated a trade *pact* with the US.

pail *(n.)* : *bucket.* Get me a *pail* full of water.
pale *(adj.)* : *lacking colour.* She looked *pale* and drawn.

pain *(n.)* : *physical or emotional suffering.* She's in great *pain.*
pane *(n.)* : *a plate of glass or panel.* Stand near the window *panes.*

pair *(n.)* : *two of something.* A *pair* of gloves.
pare *(v.)* : *to remove or peel. Pare* off the rind using a peeler.
pear *(n.)* : *type of fruit. Pears* are good for health.

palate *(n.)* : *roof of the mouth.* Do not drink hot tea otherwise you will *scorch* your palate?
pallet *(n.)* : *a cloth bag filled with straw.* I want to relax on a *pallet.*
palette *(n.)* : *a board to hold and mix colours.* Have you seen my colour *palette*?

passed *(adj.)* : *past tense of pass.* He *passed* through towns and villages.
past *(adj.)* : *the time before the present.* The danger is now well *past.*

patience *(n.)* : *willingness to wait.* I have run out of *patience* with her.
patients *(n.)* : *people under medical care.* Many *patients* in the hospital were discharged on the same day.

pause *(v.)* : *to stop for a short time.* She *paused*, at a loss for words.
paws *(n.)* : *animal feet* . The cat was licking its *paws.*

peace *(n.)* : *calm.* He just wanted to relax in *peace.*
piece *(n.)* : *a portion of something.* The dish lay in *pieces* on the floor.

peak *(n.)* : *top of a mountain.* He climbed his last Swiss *peak* at the age of 80.
peek *(v.)* : *glance furtively.* She sneaked a *peek* at the map.
pique *(v.)* : *annoyed or bitter feelings.* He left in a fit of *pique.*

pealed *(adj.)* : *rang bells.* All the bells of the city began to *peal.*
peeled *(v.)* : *removed a layer* . I *peeled* off the tissue paper.

pedal *(n.)* : *foot-operated lever.* Move the *pedals* fast on the plain road.
peddle *(v.)* : *to sell, hawk, or dispense.* He *peddled* printing materials around the country.

peer *(v.)* : *to look with difficulty or concentration at someone or something.* Riya *peered* at her with suspicion.
pier *(n.)* : *a structure extending out over water.* I saw a *pier* in the sea.

perpetrate *(v.)* : *to commit, as in a crime.* A crime has been *perpetrated* against a sovereign state.
perpetuate *(v.)* : *to prolong or sustain.* The myth that the sun revolved around the earth was *perpetuated* for centuries.

pi *(n.)* : *3.1416, the ratio of the circumference of a circle to its diameter.* Tell me Ashok, what is a *pi*?
pie *(n.)* : *baked food filled with fruit or meat* . A good meal of hot *pie* and peas is refreshing.

pistil *(n.)* : *female organ of a flower.* I read a lesson on *pistils* in class 8.
pistol *(n.)* : *type of gun.* Where did you get this *pistol* from?

plain *(adj. & n.)* : *not fancy; simple; treeless area of land.* Put it in a *plain* envelope. The flat coastal *plains* of Goa attract many.
plane *(n.)* : *short for aeroplane.* She will fly to Mumbai in a *plane.*

pleas *(n.)* : *cries for help; appeals.* He made a dramatic *plea* for disarmament.
please *(exclaim.)* : *a polite word. Please* get me a glass of water.

plum *(n.)* : *a type of fruit. Plum* juice is good for health.
plumb *(v.)* : *measure.* I *plumbed* the depth and found the bottom of the shelf to be seven metres down.

pole *(n.)* : *a long, cylindrical piece of wood or metal.* Meet me at the *pole* on the right hand side of the building.
poll *(n.)* : *a collection of opinions.* The country went to the *polls* to finalize the result.

pore *(n.)* : *small hole.* Wash your face daily to keep the *pores* open.
pour *(v.)* : *to send liquid flowing. Pour* me a glass of water.

praise *(v.)* : *to express approval.* We can't *praise* Rahul enough—he did a brilliant job.
preys *(v.)* : *hunts for food; victimizes.* Small birds *prey* on insect pests.

precedence *(n.)* : *priority.* His desire for power soon took *precedence* over any other consideration.
precedents *(n.)* : *examples, criteria.* There are substantial *precedents* for using interactive media in training.
presidents *(n.)* : *chief executives.* Is *president* also invited to this meeting?

presence *(n.)* : *appearance, being present.* My *presence* in the flat made her happy.
presents *(n., v.)* : *gifts; offers.* What can you get her for a birthday *present*? A local celebrity will *present* the prizes.

pries *(v.)* : *looks closely.* I'm sick of you *prying* into my personal life.
prize *(n.)* : *award or reward.* She won first *prize* in a national contest.

principal *(n.)* : *head of school, chief.* I was appointed *principal* of the new school.
principle *(n.)* : *fundamental belief.* The basic *principles* of justice must be adhered by all.

profit *(v.)* : *gain.* It would *profit* us to change our plans.
prophet *(n.)* : *predictor, seer.* He is repeatedly hailed as a *prophet* of modernism.

Q

quarts *(n.)* : *units of liquid measure (four quarts to a gallon).* Add two *quarts* of milk to the mixture.
quartz *(n.)* : *a hard mineral. Quartz* is used to make very accurate clocks and watches.

R

rain *(v.)* : *water that falls in drops from the sky. Rain* water is good for harvesting.
reign *(v.)* : *rule, administration.* Queen Elizabeth *reigns* over the UK.
rein *(n.)* : *bit, harness.* Some of the children wore leather baby *reins*.

raise *(v.)* : *lift up.* She *raised* both arms above her head.
raze *(v.)* : *flatten, tear down completely.* Villages were *razed* to the ground.

rap *(v.)* : *to strike sharply.* He stood up and *rapped* the table.
wrap *(v.)* : *to enclose in a covering.* He *wrapped* up the Christmas presents.

rapped *(v.)* : *struck sharply.* She *rapped* her stick on the floor.
rapt *(adj.)* : *fascinated.* They listened with *rapt* attention.
wrapped *(adj.)* : *overjoyed; delighted.* The new minister declared that he was *wrapped* on hearing the results of the elections.

read *(v.)* : *present and past tense of 'to comprehend writing'.* It's the best novel I've ever *read.*
red *(adj.)* : *a colour.* The sky was turning *red* outside.

real *(adj.)* : *actual, authentic.* His *real* name is James.
reel *(n.)* : *a cylinder on which film, wire, thread, or other flexible materials can be wound.* A *reel* of copper wire is required.

recede *(v.)* : *to move back, withdraw.* His footsteps *receded* down the corridor.
reseed *(v.)* : *to seed again.* Fall is a prime time to *reseed* bare patches in the lawn.

reek *(v.)* : *stench.* The yard *reeked* of wet straw and horse manure.
wreak *(v.)* : *to cause trouble.* Torrential rainstorms *wreaked* havoc yesterday.

rest *(v.)* : *relax.* He needed to *rest* after the feverish activity.
wrest *(v.)* : *take from.* Riya tried to *wrest* her arm from his hold.

retch *(n.)* : *vomit.* The sour taste in her mouth made her *retch.*
wretch *(n.)* : *lowly being, scoundrel.* Can the poor *wretch's* corpse tell us anything about her?

review *(n.)* : *survey.* All areas of the company will come under *review.*
revue *(n.)* : *a satirical show.* What a *revue* it was. Isn't it?

right *(adj.)* : *correct; opposite of left.* I hope we're doing the *right* thing. Keep on the *right* side of the road.
rite *(n.)* : *ritual, ceremony.* All the *rites* will be performed in the spiritual way.
write *(v.)* : *to compose letters or words.* He couldn't read or *write.*

ring *(n, v.)* : *sound of a bell; jewellery worn around a finger.* When the bell *rings*, move out of the class. He had a silver *ring* on one finger.
wring *(v.)* : *to twist.* She *wrung* the cloth out in the sink.

road *(n.)* : *street, path, highway.* Wait for me in the middle of the *road.* I will be there right back.
rode *(v.)* : *past tense of ride.* We *rode* on horseback for half a mile.
rowed *(v.)* : *to move a boat.* We *rowed* down the river all day.

roe *(n.)* : *fish eggs.* Lumpfish *roe* is most like caviar.
row *(n.)* : *a number of people standing in a line.* They sat in the front *row.*

role *(n.)* : *part in a play or film.* She played her *role* so well. Isn't it?
roll *(n. & v.)* : *a bun; to rotate.* Soup and *roll* are my favourite evening snacks. She *rolled* the ball across the floor.

roomer *(n.)* : *one who rents a room.* I would like to meet the *roomer* to discuss further.
rumour *(n.)* : *innuendo, gossip.* Have you heard of the latest *rumour*?

root *(n.)* : *base of a plant.* Water should reach the *roots* of the plant.
rout *(v.)* : *defeat (pronounced rowt).* In a matter of minutes the attackers were *routed.*
route *(n.)* : *path (pronounced like root or rowt).* From which *route* are you planning to go there?

rot *(v.)* : *decay, decompose.* The human corpse began to *rot.*
wrought *(v.)* : *caused sth to happen.* She didn't get too *wrought* up about things.

rote *(n.)* : *by memory, formula.* This is one poem that I learnt by *rote* in childhood.
wrote *(v.)* : *past tense of write.* He *wrote* his name on the paper.

rude *(adj.)* : *impolite, unmannerly.* She had been *rude* to her boss.
rued *(n.)* : *regretted, repented.* Riya will *rue* the day she turned down that offer.

rye *(n.)* : *a grain.* Use *rye* to get a tangy taste in your dish.
wry *(adj.)* : *mocking, ironic.* She was passing *wry* comments.

S

sacks *(n.)* : *large bags.* I will require a *sack* of flour.
sax *(n.)* : *saxophone.* He plays the *sax.*

scene *(n.)* : *a view, a setting.* There had already been some *scenes* of violence.
seen *(v.)* : *to have viewed with eyes.* I have already *seen* that.
sea *(n.)* : *a body of salt water.* He spends long hours at the *sea.*
see *(v.)* : *to view with eyes.* I can't *see* him anywhere.

seam *(n.)* : *line formed by pieces of fabric sewn together.* The task involved clamping the panels into position and arc welding a *seam* to join them.
seem *(v.)* : *appear.* There *seems* to be plenty to eat.

sees *(v.)* : *views with eyes.* Who *sees* this department?
seize *(v.)* : *to grab hold of.* He *seized* hold of the door handle.

serf *(n.)* : *slave.* He has always been treated as a *serf.*
surf *(n., v.)* : *breaking waves.* The sound of *surf* breaking on the beach is soothing to the ears.

set *(n.)* : *a group of objects.* I have a *set* of history papers.
sit *(v.)* : *to set lower body on something.* Please *sit* down on the chair.

sew *(v.)* : *to stitch.* She *sewed* the seams and hemmed the border.
so *(adv.,conj.)* : *in the manner indicated.* Don't look *so* worried.
sow *(v.)* : *to scatter or plant seed.* Fill a pot with mud and *sow a* thin layer of seeds on top.

sewer *(n.)* : *an underground pipe or passage that carries sewage.* Close the *sewer* or else it will be risky.
suer *(n.)* : *one who sues.* He is the *suer* of the baby's father.

shear *(v.)* : *to cut.* Paul has never *sheared* a sheep before.
sheer *(adj.)* : *very steep.* She cannot climb on the *sheer* cliff.

shoe *(n.)* : *external covering for the human foot.* I want to buy a black *shoe.*
shoo *(v.)* : *interjection used to scare away an animal.* '*Shoo,*' said Mrs Riya to a dog.

sic *(adv.)* : *a Latin term used to indicate that something written is intentionally left in the original form, which may be incorrect.* She wrote, "They made their [*sic*] beds."
sick *(adj.)* : *Ill.* I am afraid she is *sick.*

sign *(n, v.)* : *an indication; a posted notice bearing a designation, direction, etc.* Flowers are often given as a *sign* of affection; Please *sign* this cheque for me.
sine *(n.)* : *a trigonometry term.* I have learnt the questions of *sine.*

slay *(v.)* : *kill.* St George *slew* the dragon.
sleigh *(n.)* : *snow vehicle* . The reindeer dragged the *sleigh.*

sleight *(n.)* : *cunning, skill.* Except by *sleight* of logic, the two positions cannot be harmonized.
slight *(adj.)* : *slender, of little substance.* The chances of success are very *slight.*

slew *(v.)* : *to slide suddenly.* The car *slewed* from side to side in the snow.
slough *(n.)* : *swamp (pronounced slew or slau).* There was a heavy *slough* last year in Assam.

soar *(v.)* : *to fly at great height.* The cost of living continued to *soar* high.
sore *(adj.)* : *in pain.* She had a *sore* throat.

sole *(adj.)* : *bottom of foot; lone.* I want a shoe with rubber *sole.* He is the *sole* owner.
soul *(n.)* : *the spiritual principle embodied in humans.* In the depths of her *soul*, she knew he would betray her.

some *(pron. & adj.)* : *a certain unspecified number.* I made *some* money running errands.
sum *(n.)* : *the total from adding numbers.* Is the *sum* of two prime numbers always even?

son *(n.)* : *male offspring.* She was blessed with a *son.*
sun *(n.)* : *star that is the central body of the solar system.* Isn't the *sun* too bright today?

sonny *(n.)* : *diminutive of son.* Look, *sonny* Jim, that's all I can tell you.
sunny *(adj.)* : *lit or warmed by the sun; cheerful.* It's a *sunny* day today.

spade *(n.)* : *digging tool.* Turn the soil over with a *spade.*
spayed *(v.)* : *to have removed the ovaries of an animal.* The animals must be *spayed* or neutered before they are given up for adoption.

staid *(adj.)* : *solemn, serious.* He is a *staid* person.
stayed *(adj.)* : *remained, waited.* She *stayed* there for long.

stair *(n.)* : *step.* He came up the *stairs.*
stare *(v.)* : *to look without blinking.* He stared at her in amazement.

stake *(n.)* : *money wagered.* You are playing cards for high *stakes.*
steak *(n.)* : *a slice of meat.* He liked his *steak* serve this time.

stationary *(adj.)* : *in one place.* A car collided with a *stationary* vehicle.
stationery *(n.)* : *writing materials such as paper, pens, etc.* The new office set up demanded a range of *stationery.*

steal *(v.)* : *rob.* If you *steal*, you will suffer.
steel *(n.) (adj.)* : *iron alloy; very firm or strong.* It was a *steel* bucket. He had a *steel* grip.

step *(v.) (n.)* : *the single complete movement of raising one foot and keeping it down.* Rohan took a *step* back.
steppe *(n.)* : *vast grasslands.* These kind of *steppe* are found mostly in Europe.

stile *(n.)* : *turnstile, passageway.* Use *stile* to climb over this wall.
style *(n.)* : *fashion.* Do you know about the latest *style* in fashion?

straight *(adv.)* : *not curved or bent.* He made sure his tie was *straight.*
strait *(n.)* : *narrow passage of water connecting two bodies of water.* The *strait* of Gibralter is quite famous.

succour *(n.)* : *relief, assistance.* The wounded had little chance of *succour.*
sucker *(n.)* : *a rubber cup that adheres to a surface by suction.* A tape recorder was attached to the phone with a rubber *sucker.*

suede *(n.)* : *leather finished with a soft, napped surface.* I want a *suede* shoes for my wedding ceremony.
swayed *(v.)* : *past tense of sway; persuaded.* He *swayed* slightly on his feet.

suite *(n.)* : *a connected series of rooms.* A *suite* of reception rooms were booked for the guests.
sweet *(adj.)* : *having the taste of sugar.* A cup of hot *sweet* tea was served to the guests.

summary *(n.)* : *an abstract or brief account.* They want the *summary* of the book.
summery *(adj.)* : *of the summer.* This dress is cool and *summery.*

sundae *(n.)* : *ice cream with syrup.* I will have *sundae* after dinner.
sunday *(n.)* : *first day of the week. Sunday* is an off.

T

tacks *(n.)* : *short nails. Tacks* held the remaining rags of carpet to the floor.
tax *(n.)* : *per cent of earnings paid to the government.* Higher *taxes* will dampen consumer spending.

tail *(n.)* : *hindmost animal appendage.* The dog began to wag its *tail* frantically.
tale *(n.)* : *story.* A delightful children's *tale* can give your child a restful sleep.

taught *(v.)* : *past tense of teach.* She *taught* you a good lesson.
taut *(adj.)* : *tightly stretched.* The fabric stays *taut* without adhesive.

tea *(n.)* : *a beverage.* Katherine sipped *tea* gracefully.
tee *(n.)* : *a peg from which a golf ball is hit.* He smashes the ball off the 15th *tee.*

team *(n.)* : *group playing on the same side in a game.* His *team* played well.
teem *(v.)* : *swarm.* Every garden is *teeming* with wildlife.

tear *(n.)* : *salt water secreted from eyes when sad (pronounced like ear)* A *tear* rolled down her cheek.
tier *(n.)* : *a row or layer.* The room was full of three-*tier* metal bunks.

than *(conj.)* : *used for comparison.* He was much smaller *than* his son.
then *(adv.)* : *indicates time, answers when.* She won the first and *then* the second game.

their *(det.)* : *possessive pronoun.* Parents are keen to help *their* children.
there *(adv.)* : *location.* We went to Paris and stayed *there* for ten days.
they're *(sf.)* : *contraction for they are.* They're happy today.

threw *(v.)* : *past tense of throw.* I *threw* a brick through the window.
through *(prep.)* : *in one end and out the other.* Stepping boldly *through* the doorway, she moved in.

throes *(n.)* : *agonizing struggles.* He convulsed in his death *throes.*
throws *(v.)* : *tosses, hurls.* The man who *throws* a race is a crook for life.

throne *(n.)* : *royal seat or office.* King Solomon has a great ivory *throne.*
thrown *(adj.)* : *was tossed.* The door was *thrown* open.

thyme *(n.)* : *herb of the mint family.* Do you have any idea where *thymes* are available?
time *(n.)* : *past, present, future sequences of events.* Things were getting better as *time* passed.

tide *(n.)* : *ebb and flow of the ocean.* The changing patterns of the *tides* cause huge destruction.
tied *(n.)* : *past tense of tie.* She *tied* him to a pole with cable.

to *(prep.)* : *in the direction of, towards; used with the infinitive form of verbs (to go, to run, to hit).* My first visit *to* Africa was productive.
too *(adv.)* : *also, to an extensive degree.* It is *too* hot to jog.
two *(adj.)* : *the number after one.* Is she *two* years old?

toad *(n.)* : *similar to a frog.* You're an arrogant little *toad.*
towed *(v.)* : *pulled, hauled.* It's a pickup van *towing* a trailer.

told : *said.* I *told* her you were coming.
tolled *(v.)* : *sounded a bell.* The cathedral bells began to *toll* for evening service.

tort *(n.)* : *a breach of contract.* Public nuisance is a crime as well as a *tort.*
torte *(n.)* : *a large cake made with little or no flour.* A hazelnut *torte* will be my delight for the evening.

tracked *(v.)* : *followed.* He *tracked* Anna to her room.
tract *(n.)* : *an extended area of land.* Large *tracts* of natural forest are good for certain species of plants.

troop *(n.)* : *a body of soldiers.* A *troop* of soldiers marched through the ground.
troupe *(n.)* : *a group of actors, singers, etc.* The dance *troupe* performed well.

V

vain *(adj.)* : *useless.* Don't wait for him in vain.
vane *(n.)* : *a blade moved by wind (weather vane).* We can easily detect the direction of the wind through this *vane.*
vein *(n.)* : *blood vessel.* He felt the adrenaline course through his *veins.*

vary *(v.)* : *to change or alter.* The properties *vary* in price.
very *(adv.)* : *extremely.* This is a *very* large amount.

verses *(n.)* : *lines of poetry.* On the walls were framed *verses* from the Quran.
versus *(prep.)* : *as compared to another choice; against.* England *versus* Australia.

vial *(n.)* : *small container for holding liquids.* Put all this liquid in a *vial.*
vile *(adj.)* : *repulsive, depraved.* He has a *vile* temper.

vice *(n.)* : *bad habit; immoral practice.* You should give up on your *vices.*
vise : *device used to hold an object firmly.* Hold the rail in the *vice.*

W

wade *(v.)* : *to walk through water.* He *waded* out to the boat.
weighed *(v.)* : *to have put on a scale.* The vendor *weighed* the vegetables.

wail *(v.)* : *mournful cry.* Riya let out a *wail.*
whale *(n.)* : *marine mammal.* I saw a *whale* in the ocean.

waist *(n.)* : *narrowest part of the human torso (usually).* He put an arm around her *waist.*
waste *(v.)* : *to squander or spend uselessly.* We can't afford to *waste* electricity.

wait *(v.)* : *to be available or ready.* He did not *wait* for a reply.
weight *(n.)* : *quantity of heaviness or mass.* He was at least fifteen stone in *weight.*

waiver *(n.)* : *a relinquishment of some right.* Their acquiescence could amount to a *waiver.*
waver *(v.)* : *to feel indecisive; vary.* The flame *wavered* in the draught.

warn *(v.)* : *to notify.* His father had *warned* him of what might happen.
worn *(adj.)* : *carried on the body.* Shoes are *worn* with socks.

warrantee *(n.)* : *person who is given a written guarantee.* Have you given guarantee to the warrantee?
warranty *(n.)* : *written guarantee.* The car comes with a three-year *warranty.*

way *(n.)* : *direction.* I hated their *way* of cooking potatoes.
weigh *(v.)* : *to measure mass.* The vendor *weighed* the vegetables.

weak *(adj.)* : *lacking strength.* She was recovering from flu, and was very *weak.*
week *(n.)* : *seven days starting with Sunday.* The course lasts sixteen *weeks.*

wear *(v.)* : *to carry on the body.* What will you *wear* tonight.
where *(adv.)* : *in what place.* Where do you live?

weather *(n.)* : *state of the atmosphere in a location.* If the *weather's* good we can go for a walk.
whether *(conj.)* : *If.* He seemed undecided *whether* to go or stay.

weave *(n.)* : *to interlace thread or yarn to make a fabric.* Textiles are *woven* from linen or wool.
we've : *contraction for we have. We've* to go there as soon as possible.

were *(v.)* : *past tense of are.* His hands *were* cold.
we're : *contraction for we are. We're* almost there.

wheeled *(v.)* : *moved on wheels.* They *wheeled* me into the operating theatre.
wield *(v.)* : *to exercise power; to handle a weapon effectively.* Don't *wield* your power here. She was *wielding* a large knife.

which *(pron.)* : *what one. Which* place you like the most?
witch *(n.)* : *sorceress.* Mrs Riya is a real *witch.*

while *(n.)* : *during or in the time that.* We chatted for a *while.*
wile *(n.)* : *a trick to fool, trap, or entice.* She had been trying out her feminine *wiles* on Rahul.

whine *(n.)* : *complaining cry.* Do not *whine* over what is done.
wine *(n.)* : *fermented grape juice that becomes an alcoholic beverage.* He opened a bottle of red *wine.*

whirled *(v.)* : *spun rapidly.* I *whirled* her round the dance hall.
world *(n.)* : *planet Earth.* He was doing his bit to save the *world.*

who's : *contraction for who is. Who's* at the door?
whose *(pron.)* : *possessive case of who. Whose* coat is this?

wont *(adj., n.)* : *accustomed; habit.* He was *wont* to fall asleep after lunch. Rising early is my *wont.*
won't *(short form)* : *contraction for will not.* I *won't* go there. It's risky for me.

wood *(n.)* : *tree trunk material.* Best quality *woods* were used for joinery.
would *(v.)* : *expressing an intention.* I would want you to take care of it.

Y

yoke *(n.)* : *harness for oxen.* Hold the *yoke* tight.
yolk *(n.)* : *yellow centre of an egg.* Egg *yolk* is good for health if prepared in less oil.

yore *(n.)* : *long past.* It was a great empire in days of *yore.*
you're : *contraction for you are You're* an angel, Riya!
your : *possessive pronoun.* What is *your* name?

English Thesaurus

A

aback *(adv.)* back, behind, rearward; suddenly, unexpectedly

abandon *(v.)* forgo, forswear, quit, relinquish; forsake, leave, resign, vacate

abase *(v.)* debase, degrade, disgrace, dishonor, humiliate

abate *(v.)* decline, decrease, diminish, ease, ebb, fade, lower, moderate, slacken, relieve, slow

abbreviate *(v.)* abridge, condense, contract, cut, reduce, shorten, truncate

abdicate *(v.)* abandon, cede, disavow, disclaim, disown, relinquish, renounce, resign, secede

abdomen *(n.)* belly, breadbasket, gut, paunch, potbelly, stomach, tummy

abduct *(v.)* capture, kidnap, seize, shanghai

aberrant *(adj.)* divergent, errant, irregular, straying; abnormal, peculiar, queer, strange, unnatural, unusual, weird

abhor *(v.)* despise, detest, disgust, hate, loathe

ability *(n.)* aptitude, bent, capability, capacity, competence, dexterity, expertise, facility, faculty, knack, proficiency, qualification, skill, talent

abjure *(v.)* forswear, recall, renounce, retract, withdraw

ablaze *(adj.)* aflame, blazing, fiery, flaming; ardent, eager, excited, exhilarated, intense

able *(adj.)* competent, efficient, fit, qualified; accomplished, adroit, dexterous, expert, gifted, ingenious, proficient, talented

abnormal *(adj.)* aberrant, anomalous, deviant, irregular, odd, peculiar, unnatural

abode *(n.)* domicile, dwelling, habitat, house, residence

abolish *(v.)* abrogate, annul, cancel, eliminate, end, eradicate, erase, extinguish, nullify, obliterate

abominable *(adj.)* abhorrent, contemptible, despicable, detestable, disgusting, hateful, horrible, loathsome, offensive, repugnant

aboriginal *(adj.)* domestic, indigenous, local, native, original, primitive

abort *(v.)* annul, cancel, destroy, fail, interrupt, miscarry, nullify, scrap, stop, terminate

abound *(v.)* overflow, pour, swarm, swell, teem

about *(adv.)* referencing, regarding; almost, around, close, near, nigh

above *(adv.)* atop, beyond, over, overhead; preeminent, superior, surpassing

abreast *(adj.)*, *(adv.)* against, aligned; apprised, familiar

abrupt *(adj.)* quick, sharp, unexpected; blunt, boorish, brusque, hasty, impatient, rude

abscond *(v.)* depart, escape, flee

absence *(n.)* dearth, deficiency, need, want; nonattendance, truancy

absentee *(n.)* defector, delinquent, deserter, fugitive, escapee, runaway, truant

absolute *(adj.)* certain, definite, faultless, ideal, sure, unconditional, unquestionable, whole

absolve *(v.)* acquit, clear, discharge, excuse, exonerate, forgive, free, justify, liberate, pardon, release

absorb *(v.)* amalgamate, assimilate, consume, devour, engulf; engage, employ, occupy; grasp, learn, sense

abstain *(v.)* avoid, decline, eschew, forgo, refrain, shun

abstract *(adj.)* conceptual, ideal, hypothetical; apart, separate, special, unrelated; complicated, deep, difficult, obscure

abstruse *(adj.)* complex, difficult, intricate, involved

absurd *(adj.)* foolish, inane, irrational, ludicrous, preposterous, ridiculous, silly

abundant *(adj.)* abounding, copious, flowing, fruitful, opulent, plentiful, prodigal, profuse, prolific, teeming

abuse *(n.)* misuse, defilement, desecration, mistreatment, profanation, subversion, violation

abyss *(n.)* chasm, gorge, gulf, hole, perdition

academic *(adj.)* collegiate, erudite, learned, lettered, literary, scholastic, schooled; established, formalistic; speculative

academy *(n.)* college, conservatory, school

accede *(v.)* acquiesce, agree, allow, assent, comply, consent, grant, permit, sanction

accelerate *(v.)* hasten, expedite, quicken, throttle

accept *(v.)* embrace, take, welcome, affirm, hold, maintain, appreciate, conclude

accessible *(adj.)* approachable, attainable, available, convenient, obtainable, reachable

accessory *(n.)* abettor, accomplice, extra, add-on

accident *(n.)* casualty, misadventure, misfortune, wreck; coincidence, fortune

acclaim *(n.)* accolades, applause, approval, jubilation, plaudits, praise

acclimatize *(v.)* acclimate, adapt, adjust, conform

accolade *(n.)* acknowledgement, esteem, praise, tribute

accommodate *(v.)* fit, harmonize, reconcile, contain, have, hold

accompany *(v.)* chaperon, escort, follow, join, see, show, usher; complement, complete, enhance, supplement

accomplice *(n.)* accessory, affiliate, associate, confederate, conspirator, partner

accomplish *(v.)* achieve, attain, complete, do, effect, execute, fulfill, make, manage, perform, realize

accord *(n.)* agreement, conformity, consent, harmony, peace, unanimity

account *(n.)* anecdote, chronicle, description, explanation, journal, narration, recital, report, story, tale; consideration, grounds, motive

accumulate *(v.)* accrue, amass, collect, cumulate, gather, heap, garner, increase, stockpile, store

accusation *(n.)* allegation, charge, complaint, denunciation, indictment, insinuation, slur, smear

accustom *(v.)* familiarize, habituate, inure, season

ace *(n.)* champion, expert, master, specialist

acerbic *(adj.)* bitter, harsh, rough, sharp, sour

ache *(n.)* agony, pain, pang, spasm, twinge

achieve *(v.)* accomplish, fulfill, finish, reach, attain, gain, get, realize, secure

acid *(adj.)* biting, cutting, sarcastic, sardonic, satirical, scornful, sharp, vitriolic

acknowledge *(v.)* admit, agree, allow, appreciate, approve, avow, concede, confess, confirm, declare, endorse, grant, ratify, recognize, reply, respond

acme *(n.)* apex, peak, summit, top, zenith

acquaint *(v.)* inform, accustom, advise, familiarize, reconnoiter, introduce, present

acquiesce *(v.)* assent, accede, accept, agree, bend, comply, concur, consent, rest, submit, yield

acquire *(v.)* attain, earn, gain, get, obtain, procure, secure

acrid *(adj.)* astringent, biting, bitter, caustic, harsh

acropolis *(n.)* bastion, citadel, blockhouse, fort, fortification, redoubt, stronghold

act *(n.)* accomplishment, deed, feat, performance; law, order, resolution, statute, writ

action *(n.)* activity, maneuver, movement, performance; exercise, conduct, response

active *(adj.)* animated, busy, dynamic, energetic, functioning, industrious, lively, living, mobile, moving, operative, spirited, tireless, working

actor *(n.)* artist, entertainer, impersonator, performer, player, thespian, trouper

actual *(adj.)* certain, definite, genuine, sure, true; concrete, material, real, tangible

actuate *(v.)* drive, impel, move, propel, push

acumen *(n.)* cleverness, discernment, insight, intelligence, keenness, sagacity, shrewdness

acute *(adj.)* keen, sharp; critical, crucial, intense, serious; astute, clever, discerning, ingenious, intelligent, keen, penetrating

adage *(n.)* cliché, maxim, motto, proverb, saying, slogan

adamant *(adj.)* firm, fixed, insistent, obstinate, resolute, set, steadfast, stubborn, unbending, unyielding

adapt *(v.)* acclimatize, accustom, adjust, conform, fashion, fit, modify, reconcile, shape, tailor

add *(v.)* annex, append, attach, augment, connect, supplement, unite; compute, figure, increase, sum, tally, total

addict *(n.)* buff, devotee, fan, hound, junkie, lover

add-on *(n.)* improvement, modernization, supplement

address *(n.)* discourse, lecture, oration, sermon; dwelling, house, lodging, residence

adept *(adj.)* able, capable, competent, expert, proficient, skilled

adequate *(adj.)* ample, enough, satisfactory, suitable

adhere *(v.)* attach, cleave, cling, fasten, hold; comply, follow, heed, obey

adjacent *(adj.)* abutting, adjoining, bordering, close, contiguous, near, nearby, neighboring, touching

adjourn *(v.)* defer, discontinue, dissolve, recess, postpone, suspend

adjure *(v.)* ask, appeal, beg, beseech, entreat, implore, petition, plead, request, supplicate, urge

adjust *(v.)* adapt, alter, calibrate, correct, modify, regulate, tune

administer *(v.)* control, direct, execute, oversee, supervise; distribute, give, parcel

admire *(v.)* esteem, honour, regard, respect, revere, venerate

admit *(v.)* allow, grant, permit; concede, confess, disclose, divulge, expose, reveal

admonish *(v.)* caution, counsel, exhort, reprove, warn
adolescence *(n.)* puberty, pubescence, teens, youth
adopt *(v.)* assume, embrace, espouse, utilize; approve, confirm, endorse, sanction
adoration *(n.)* devotion, idolatry, veneration, worship
adorn *(v.)* beautify, bedeck, decorate, embellish, garnish, festoon, ornament, trim
adult *(adj.)* developed, grown, mature, ripe
adulteration *(n.)* contamination, pollution, taint
adulterer *(n.)* debaucher, lecher, libertine, philanderer, rake, reprobate
advance *(v.)* go, move, proceed, update, upgrade; introduce, propose, present, suggest; encourage, foster, propound; lend
advantage *(n.)* benefit, edge, gain, leverage, profit
adventure *(n.)* undertaking, experience, exploit
advent *(n.)* appearance, arrival, coming
adverse *(adj.)* antagonistic, conflicting, contrary, detrimental, hostile, negative, unfavorable, unfriendly
advertise *(v.)* broadcast, communicate, divulge, exhibit, expose, proclaim, promote, publicize, show
advice *(n.)* counsel, guidance, lesson, suggestion
advocacy *(n.)* adoption, belief, espousal, promotion
advocate *(v.)* advance, bolster, champion, further, promote, recommend, support
aesthetic, aesthetical *(adj.)* artistic, discriminating, elegant, pleasing, polished, refined, tasteful
affable *(adj.)* agreeable, amiable, civil, cordial, courteous, friendly, gracious, obliging, pleasant, sociable
affair (n.) business, circumstance, pursuit; liaison, relationship, rendezvous, tryst; event, function, party
affect *(v.)* alter, change, modify, sway, stir, transform; assume, dissemble, fake, feign
affection *(n.)* devotion, fondness, friendship, liking, love, regard, respect, tenderness, warmth
affidavit *(n.)* affirmation, deposition, oath, testimony
affiliate*(n.)* agent, associate, colleague, partner
affiliation *(n.)* alliance, association, coalition, confederation, connection, federation, pact, union
affinity *(n.)* affection, closeness, fondness; correspondence, likeness, resemblance
affirm *(v.)* assert, claim, maintain, state, swear, testify; approve, endorse, ratify
affix *(v.)* add, append, attach, bind, connect, fasten
afflict *(v.)* ail, beset, distress, hurt, torment
affluence*(n.)* abundance, prosperity, wealth
afford *(v.)* allow, grant, permit, provide, sustain
affront *(v.)* insult, abuse, offend, provoke, slight
afoot *(adj.)* hiking, marching; brewing, happening, hatching, progressing
aforementioned *(adj.)* earlier, former, preceding, prior
afraid *(adj.)* anxious, apprehensive, disquieted, fearful, frightened, scared, shocked, terrified
after *(adj.)*, (adv.) afterward, following, later, subsequent, consequence, outcome, result
age *(n.)* eon, epoch, era, generation, time; adolescence, adulthood, childhood, infancy
agenda *(n.)* aims, goals, program, calendar, list, plan
agent *(n.)* ambassador, attorney, broker, factor, intermediary, proxy, surrogate; agency, cause, instrument, means, method, vehicle
aggrandize *(v.)* amplify, expand, extend, increase; boast, exaggerate, extol, praise
aggravate *(v.)* deepen, exacerbate, heighten, increase, intensify
aggregate *(adj.)* combined, complete, entire, total
aggressor *(n.)* attacker, intruder, invader, trespasser
aghast *(adj.)* appalled, astonished, horrified, shocked
agile *(adj.)* brisk, deft, lithe, lively, nimble, sprightly, vigorous; clever, keen, smart
agitate *(v.)* chum, mix, toss, tumble; discomfit, disquiet, fluster, perturb, ruffle, trouble, upset; argue, dispute
agnostic *(n.)* doubter, non-believer, skeptic, cynic scoffer
agog *(adj.)* anxious, breathless, eager, enthusiastic
agony *(n.)* anguish, distress, misery, pain, suffering, torment, torture
agree *(v.)* accede, acquiesce, allow, assent, concede; correspond, equal, harmonize, match, suit; contract, resolve, settle
agreement *(n.)* bargain, compact, contract, deal, pact, settlement, understanding; compromise, harmony, peace, unity
ahead *(adj.)*, *(adv.)* before, earlier, preceding

aid *(n.)* backing, charity, help, relief, support; aide, assistant, colleague, supporter
alert *(adj.)* ready, aware, attentive, intelligent, wary
alien *(adj.)* different, foreign, strange, unfamiliar
allay *(v.)* calm, alleviate, ease, soothe, lessen
allege *(v.)* assert, attest, declare
alleviate *(v.)* abate, ease, relieve, lessen, soften
alliance *(n.)* union, treaty, marriage
allow *(v.)* approve, grant, let, permit, sanction
alms *(n.)* charity, dole, donation
aloof *(adj.)* cool, detached, distant, reserved
alter *(v.)* change, modify, adjust
altruism *(n.)* benevolence, charity, kindness
amateur *(n.)* beginner, neophyte, novice
amaze *(v.)* astonish, dumfound, stupefy, surprise
ambitious *(adj.)* determined, industrious, intent
ambivalent *(adj.)* uncertain, wavering
amend *(v.)* improve, change, correct
amiss *(adj.)* wrong, faulty, erroneous, imperfect, awry
among *(prep.)* amid, amongst, amidst
amount *(n.)* sum, product; expense, output, outlay; bulk, mass, number
ample *(adj.)* sufficient, plenty, adequate, enough
amuse *(v.)* entertain, divert, cheer, enliven
analyze *(v.)* dissect, examine, investigate
anarchy *(n.)* disorder, turmoil, chaos
ancestor *(n.)* forebear, progenitor, forefather
anchor *(n.)* tie, mooring, support, host
anger *(n.)* ire, wrath, rage, fury, exasperation, irritation
anguish *(n.)* pain, wretchedness, agony
animate *(v.)* activate, vitalize, arouse, energize
annex *(v.)* add, incorporate, append, attach, affix
annoy *(v.)* bother, irritate, pester, trouble
annul *(v.)* invalidate, repeal, revoke, cancel
answer *(v.)* respond, retort, acknowledge, refute, react, rebut; solve, elucidate, clarify
anticipate *(v.)* expect, forecast, predict, assume, await
anxiety *(n.)* concern, trouble, misgiving
apathetic *(adj.)* unemotional, unconcerned, indifferent
appall *(v.)* horrify, amaze, dismay, shock
apparel *(n.)* clothes, attire, suit, dress
apparition *(n.)* ghost, phantom, spirit
appeal *(v.)* beg, urge, petition; attract, interest, engage, tempt
appear *(v.)* emerge, rise, loom, arrive, recur, materialize, show; seem, resemble
appease *(v.)* satisfy, do, serve
appendix *(n.)* supplement, attachment, index, addition
appetite *(n.)* hunger, thirst, craving, longing, desire
applaud *(v.)* approve, cheer, clap, acclaim, praise
appoint *(v.)* name, select, designate, delegate
appreciate *(v.)* acknowledge, honor, praise, admire
apprehension *(n.)* foreboding, trepidation, dread, misgiving, fear
apprentice *(n.)* beginner, student, learner
apprise *(v.)* notify, teach, warn
approach *(n.)* avenue, path, entrance, gate, method, program, procedure
appropriate *(adj.)* suitable, proper, suited, fitting
approval *(n.)* esteem, favour, admiration; sanction, endorsement, consent, permission
approximate *(adj.)* inexact, imprecise, close
apropos *(adj.)* applicable, appropriate, befitting
aptitude *(n.)* ability, capability, competence, capacity
archaic *(adj.)* antiquated, old, obsolete
ardent *(adj.)* fervent, impassioned, zealous, passionate, enthusiastic
argue *(v.)* dispute, contend, wrangle, bicker, debate
arid *(adj.)* parched, desert, dried, dry, barren
aristocracy *(n.)* nobility, elite, gentry, patricians
aroma *(n.)* smell, fragrance, perfume, odor
arrange *(v.)* order, regulate, systematize, organize
arrival *(n.)* entrance, appearance, landing, visitor, guest, traveller
arrogance *(n.)* insolence, audacity, haughtiness, pride
article *(n.)* writing, essay, editorial, commentary, item, object, substance, commodity, thing
articulate *(v.)* speak, enunciate, pronounce, verbalize; combine, connect, link
artifact *(n.)* antique, heirloom, relic
artistic *(adj.)* imaginative, creative, accomplished, cultured, sensitive, elegant, harmonious
ascend *(v.)* soar, rise, climb, scale
aspect *(n.)* appearance, looks, countenance, face, features, view, perspective, regard, slant, viewpoint

aspiration *(n.)* desire, inclination, ambition
assailant *(n.)* antagonist, foe, enemy, opponent
assassin *(n.)* murderer, slayer, butcher, killer
assault *(n.)* attack, charge, advance, onslaught
assemble *(v.)* convoke, convene, mobilize, gather, collect, construct, erect, join, unite, mold
assent *(n.)* approval, permission, agreement
assert *(v.)* state, say, affirm, declare
asset *(n.)* property, holdings, possessions, capital
assign *(v.)* allocate, allot, earmark; appoint, commission, name, select, deputize, charge, elect
assist *(v.)* aid, support, serve, help
associate *(n.)* comrade, peer, colleague, friend, ally, henchman, confederate, collaborator, teammate
association *(n.)* relationship, friendship, camaraderie, membership, community, recollection, impression, remembrance, organization, union, club
assume *(v.)* suppose, theorize, presuppose, postulate, hypothesize, guess, conjecture, deem, imagine, surmise, opine, estimate, speculate, deduce, infer
assurance *(n.)* guaranty, support, pledge, promise; confidence, conviction, trust, certainty, faith
assure *(v.)* guarantee, aver, attest, convince, prove, persuade, induce
astonishment *(n.)* amazement, bewilderment, wonder
astute *(adj.)* perceptive, shrewd
athletic *(adj.)* hardy, robust, vigorous, powerful
atone *(v.)* compensate, pay
atrocious *(adj.)* cruel, offensive, appalling, horrible
attach *(v.)* adhere, join, connect, append, add; attribute, associate, impute, ascribe, give
attack *(n.)* assault, raid, onslaught, offensive, siege, invasion, incursion; slander, denunciation, blame, illness, seizure, breakdown, relapse
attain *(v.)* achieve, accomplish, arrive, reach, gain
attempt *(v.)* endeavour, strike, venture, try, ratify, affirm, endorse
attention *(n.)* regard, vigilance, heed, alertness, diligence, thoroughness, recognition
attitude *(n.)* air, demeanor, disposition, inclination, nature, temperament, mood, viewpoint
attract *(v.)* draw, pull, drag, bring; allure, entice, lure, charm, fascinate
audacious *(adj.)* bold, daring, shameless
audience *(n.)* interview, spectators, witness, patrons
augment *(v.)* increase, enlarge, expand, magnify
authentic *(adj.)* genuine, real, true, actual
author *(n.)* writer, journalist, columnist, playwright, poet, novelist, essayist
automatic *(adj.)* computerized, self-regulating, automated, involuntary, instinctive, spontaneous, intuitive
auxiliary *(adj.)* subsidiary, secondary, subordinate; supplementary, reserve, supplemental, spare, extra
avarice *(n.)* acquisitiveness, greed, stinginess, meanness
average *(adj.)* ordinary, medium, common
aversion *(n.)* abhorrence, disgust, dislike, loathing
awake *(adj.)* alert, attentive, vigilant; conscious
award *(n.)* citation, honour, scholarship, prize, judgment
awareness *(n.)* discernment, alertness, keenness, attentiveness, perception, apprehension, appreciation
awesome *(adj.)* striking, moving, exalted, grand

B

babble *(n.)* chatter, jabber, twaddle, nonsense
backlog *(n.)* queue, reserve, accumulation, accretion
baggage *(n.)* luggage, gear, trunk, valise, suitcase,
bait *(v.)* entice, attract, draw, fascinate; provoke, torment, anger, nag, bother
balance *(v.)* equalize, even, compensate, adjust, coordinate, equate, match, harmonize
balcony *(n.)* gallery, verandah, terrace
balm *(n.)* salve, lotion, dressing, medicine; comfort, relief, refreshment, remedy
banal *(adj.)* dull, trite, hackneyed, prosaic, trite
bandit *(n.)* highwayman, thief, brigand, robber
banish *(v.)* exile, deport, expel, expatriate, ostracize, outlaw, extradite, isolate
bankrupt *(adj.)* failed, broke, ruined, insolvent
barbarian *(n.)* savage, brute, beast
bare *(adj.)* bald, naked, unadorned, simple, modest; barren, void, unfurnished
bargain *(n.)* agreement, pact, compact, contract, deal; discount, reduction, steal, giveaway
barrier *(n.)* obstruction, hindrance, obstacle, hurdle, restriction, restraint, impediment, barricade
bashful *(adj.)* retiring, reserved, timid, modest, shy
basis *(n.)* foundation, justification, explanation, background, source, authority, principle, grounds
bask *(v.)* relax, enjoy, wallow

beam *(v.)* radiate, glitter, glare; grin, laugh, smirk
bear *(v.)* tolerate, undergo, endure, support, sustain
beastly *(adj.)* brutal, savage, coarse, depraved, loathsome, vile, foul, base, disgusting, vulgar
beat *(v.)* bash, pulsate, pound, thump, pulse, throb; overcome, conquer, defeat
bedlam *(n.)* pandemonium, clamour, confusion, noise
befall *(v.)* occur, happen, transpire
begin *(v.)* initiate, start, inaugurate, launch, mount, create, institute, introduce, originate, found, establish, commence, arise
behaviour *(n.)* conduct, performance, ways, manner
belief *(n.)* opinion, feeling, conviction
believe *(v.)* trust, accept, think
belligerent *(adj.)* warlike, pugnacious, hostile
beloved *(adj.)* cherished, loved, adored, worshipped, idolized, precious, prized, treasured, favoured
benefit *(v.)* help, aid, serve, profit
benevolence *(n.)* altruism, charity, kindness
bequeath *(v.)* grant, give, endow, bestow
beseech *(v.)* ask, implore, beg, solicit
best *(adj.), (adv.)* first, greatest, finest, incomparable, unrivaled, unequaled, inimitable, foremost
bestow *(v.)* bequeath, present, offer, give, endow
betray *(v.)* delude, trick, deceive, divulge, disclose
bewilder *(v.)* confound, disconcert, puzzle, confuse
bewitch *(v.)* charm, enchant, fascinate, captivate
bias *(n.)* prejudice, partiality, preference, inclination
bind *(v.)* attach, adhere, fasten; oblige, compel, force; shackle, fetter, leash, restrict, hitch, yoke, tether; join, unite, connect
biography *(n.)* memoir, journal, autobiography, life
bite *(n.)* taste, morsel, nibble
bitter *(adj.)* acrid, astringent, intense, harsh, severe; sarcastic, acrimonious, caustic, biting
bizarre *(adj.)* unusual, unexpected, fantastic, grotesque
blame *(v.)* charge, condemn, denounce, disparage
blatant *(adj.)* clear, obvious, plain
blemish *(n.)* flaw, defect, stain, imperfection, dent
blind *(adj.)* unseeing, unaware; closed, obstructed, blocked; accidental, unplanned, aimless
blithe *(adj.)* gay, lighthearted, vivacious
block *(n.)* chunk, slab, cake, clod, hunk; barrier, obstruction, hindrance, bar, obstacle
bloom *(n.)* blossom, floweret, glow, blush, flush
blotch *(n.)* stain, blemish, mark, patch
blow *(v.)* blast, fan; flutter, waft, whisk, flap, wave, buffet; pipe, toot, waste, squander; miss, flounder, miscarry
bluff *(n.)* hill, cliff, precipice, steep, mountain; deception, trick, ruse, delusion
blunt *(adj.)* dull, unsharpened, unpointed, round; abrupt, brusque, curt, bluff, rude
boast *(n.)* brag, pretension, self-satisfaction, bravado
body *(n.)* fuselage, hull, skeleton; society, organization; collection, reservoir, supply, variety; anatomy, physique, figure, build, corpse, cadaver, carcass, mummy, remains
bog *(n.)* marsh, swamp, wetlands
boisterous *(adj.)* rowdy, uproarious, noisy, loud, rude
bold *(adj.)* daring, courageous, intrepid, fearless, audacious, presumptuous, strong, clear, plain, definite
bombastic *(adj.)* high-sounding, pompous
bond *(n.)* attachment, connection, affiliation, friendship, debenture, security, warranty, certificate; surety, guaranty, warrant
boost *(n.)* assistance, aid, help; addition, advance, hike
border *(n.)* edge, hem, end, trim, decoration, fringe, margin, boundary, frontier, outpost, perimeter
boredom *(n.)* apathy, doldrums, listlessness, monotony, tedium, indifference
borrow *(v.)* take, sponge, bum, beg, chisel, mooch
bottom *(n.)* underside, base, foot; depths, bed, floor impertinence, audacity
boulevard *(n.)* street, avenue, highway, road
bound *(v.)* leap, spring, vault, jump; ricochet, recoil; limit, restrict, confine, circumscribe
boundary *(n.)* border, rim, bounds, extremity, periphery, extent, limit
bounteous *(adj.)* abundant, lavish, plentiful
bow *(v.)* stoop, yield, submit, surrender, acquiesce, capitulate
boycott *(v.)* ostracize, avoid, strike
brackish *(adj.)* salty, disagreeable, tainted

brain *(n.)* intellect, genius, mentality; scholar, egg-head, intellectual

brand *(n.)* mark, scar, welt, earmark, trademark

brave *(adj.)* fearless, daring, dauntless, valiant, intrepid, bold, unafraid

brawl *(v.)* fight, quarrel, squabble

breach *(n.)* break, opening, rupture, violation, infringement, transgression, crime

break *(n.)* fracture, split, rupture; pause, intermission, interim; accident, opportunity

breathe *(v.)* respire, inhale, exhale, gasp, pant

brevity *(n.)* conciseness, shortness, terseness

bribe *(v.)* corrupt, influence, entice, tempt

bridge *(n.)* structure, connection, bond, tie, joint

bright *(adj.)* quick-witted, intelligent, clever, alert; clear, sunny, fair; lively, cheerful, vivacious, luminous, lustrous, sparkling, illuminated

brilliant *(adj.)* sparkling, shining, dazzling, gleaming, bright, talented, profound, intelligent

brim *(n.)* rim, margin, border, edge

brisk *(adj.)* keen, invigorating, stimulating, active

bristle *(n.)* hair, fiber, quill, point

broad *(adj.)* cosmopolitan, cultivated, experienced, cultured; large, extensive, spacious, expansive, roomy, tolerant, progressive, unbiased, liberal

brochure *(n.)* handout, circular, pamphlet, folder

broken *(adj.)* busted, faulty, fractured, shattered, smashed, damaged, cracked; irregular, incoherent

brood *(v.)* pine, grieve, fret, sulk, mope, muse, worry

browse *(v.)* skim, peruse, scan, inspect, examine

brush *(v.)* clean, sweep, whisk, wipe; stroke, smooth, graze

brutal *(adj.)* pitiless, harsh, unmerciful, cruel

budge *(v.)* stir, shift, move

budget *(n.)* projection, estimate, allocation, plan, funds

buffoon *(n.)* clown, jester, fool, jerk

bulge *(n.)* swelling, protuberance, bump, prominence

bull *(n.)* steer, calf, ox, cow; nonsense, balder, dash, rubbish, trash

bully *(n.)* ruffian, rowdy, tough, rascal

bunch *(n.)* cluster, clump, group, sheaf, tuft, shock, bundle, knot, collection

bungalow *(n.)* cottage, house, lodge

bunk *(n.)* berth, cot, pallet; rubbish, rot, hogwash, nonsense

burden *(v.)* hinder, encumber, hamper, strain, load, tax, try, trouble, oppress

burglar *(n.)* thief, housebreaker, robber, criminal

burial *(n.)* interment, funeral, entombment

burlesque *(v.)* imitate, mock, satirize

burly *(adj.)* strong, muscular, hefty

burn *(v.)* ignite, kindle, incinerate, blaze, scorch

burst *(v.)* explode, erupt, rupture, disintegrate; break, crack, split, fracture, destroy

butcher *(v.)* slaughter, slay, kill; ruin, mutilate, spoil, botch, destroy

buzz *(v.)* hum, drone, whir

C

cabin *(n.)* house, cottage, hut, home, shelter

cacophony *(n.)* dissonance, noise, din, racket

cafe *(n.)* coffeehouse, restaurant, cafeteria, lunchroom

cajole *(v.)* appeal, wheedle, coax, beguile

calculate *(n.)* count, measure, reckon, enumerate, determine, forecast, weigh, gauge, compute, cipher

callous *(adj.)* heartless, indifferent, unfeeling, hardened, insensitive

camouflage *(v.)* conceal, cover, veil, disguise, hide

cancel *(v.)* invalidate, rescind, repeal, retract, void

candid *(adj.)* sincere, open, frank, honest

canny *(adj.)* cautious, watchful, shrewd

capable *(adj.)* proficient, competent, able, intelligent

capsize *(v.)* overturn, invert, tip over, upset

captivate *(v.)* attract, charm, fascinate, bewitch

capture *(v.)* take, hold, seize, apprehend, arrest

care *(n.)* concern, regard, precaution, wariness, vigilance, custody, keeping, watch

career *(n.)* work, occupation, vocation, job, profession

caress *(v.)* touch, love, embrace, cuddle, pat

caricature *(v.)* mimic, ridicule, satirize

carnal *(adj.)* fleshly, worldly, sensuous, lewd

carnival *(n.)* merrymaking, festival, fair, entertainment

carry *(v.)* convey, transfer, cart, take, bring, haul, transfer, relay, support, bear, sustain, shoulder

cast *(n.)* facsimile, replica, copy; actors, players, company, troupe; appearance, aspect

caste *(n.)* position, status, birth

catalog *(n.)* register, directory, index, classification
cause *(n.)* condition, circumstances; goal, motive, foundation, basis, reason
caution *(n.)* discretion, care, heed, prudence, warning
cavil *(v.)* criticize, object, complain
cede *(v.)* relinquish, surrender, yield
celebrate *(v.)* commemorate, observe, consecrate, honour, rejoice, revel
celibate *(adj.)* unmarried, abstaining, single, pure
cemetery *(n.)* churchyard, necropolis, catacomb, tomb, vault, crypt, sepulcher, graveyard, mortuary
censor *(n.)* restrict, suppress, withhold, expurgate
census *(n.)* count, enumeration, tabulation, tally
center *(n.)* middle, nucleus, core, heart; hub, metropolis, plaza, mart; essence
cerebral *(adj.)* brainy, intelligent
ceremony *(n.)* function, commemoration, celebration, rite, observance, ritual, formality, custom, tradition
certain *(adj.)* assured, positive, untroubled, confident, conclusive, incontrovertible, irrefutable, true, unmistakable; fixed, settled, concluded, definite
certificate *(n.)* document, warrant, credentials, certification, document, warranty, guarantee
cessation *(n.)* ending, stopping
challenge *(v.)* compete, defy, denounce, invite, dare, threaten, question, dispute, inquire, ask, doubt
champion *(n.)* conqueror, victor, hero
chance *(v.)* risk, venture, stake, hazard, wager, jeopardize, speculate
change *(v.)* make different, vary, alter, transform, changeable, turn; become different, evolve, transform, adapt, moderate, adjust; displace, supplant, transpose; undress, disrobe
chant *(n.)* recitation, chorus, incantation
character *(n.)* symbol, mark, sign, figure, emblem; temperament, nature, attribute, characteristic; crank, nut, oddball, weirdo
charge *(v.)* price, cost, blame, attack, assail, assault, invade
chase *(v.)* pursue, trail, track, seek, hunt
chastise *(v.)* scold, discipline, spank, punish
cheap *(adj.)* inexpensive, competitive, reasonable, economical; shoddy, poor
check *(v.)* control, bridle, repress, inhibit, neutralize, restrain; examine, review, monitor, investigate circumspect
cheer *(v.)* hearten, console, brighten, comfort, encourage, help; applaud, shout, salute, support, yell
chest *(n.)* breast, thorax, bosom, peritoneum, ribs; box, case, coffer, cabinet, strongbox, crate
chide *(v.)* scold, reprimand, lecture
chore *(n.)* task, routine, errand, job
chunk *(n.)* lump, piece, mass, part
churn *(v.)* stir, beat, mix, agitate
circular *(adj.)* spherical, cyclical, globular, round
circumvent *(v.)* avoid, bypass, dodge, elude, evade
clamor *(n.)* outcry, din, discord, noise, uproar
clandestine *(adj.)* covert, furtive, secret, sly
clasp *(n.)* fastener, buckle, pin, clamp
classify *(u.)* arrange, order, pigeonhole, organize, categorize, label, catalogue, tag, sort, index
clean *(adj.), (adv.)* pure, unadulterated, undefiled, spotless, cleansed; clear-cut, sharp, readable; complete, entire, total, absolute
clear *(adj.), (adv.)* obvious, explicit, plain, manifest; transparent, translucent; unclouded, sunny, bright, fair; exonerated, absolved
clever *(adj.)* skillful, apt, expert, adroit, able; intelligent, smart, bright, shrewd
cliche *(n.)* slogan, banality, triviality, motto
climax *(n.)* crisis, peak, culmination, zenith, summit
clog *(v.)* obstruct, impede, seal, close, hinder
close *(v.)* conclude, finish, terminate; seal, shut, clog, block, bar, dam, cork; come together, connect, meet, unite, agree, join; shut, slam, fasten, bolt, clench, bar, shutter, lock
clot *(v.)* thicken, coagulate, set, lump
clumsy *(adj.)* ungainly, gawky, inexpert, awkward
clutter *(n.)* disarray, jumble, disorder, confusion
coalition *(n.)* union, group, association, faction
coarse *(adj.)* rough, unrefined, crude; vulgar, low, common, base, obscene, rude
coax *(v.)* cajole, wheedle, inveigle, influence, urge
coerce *(v.)* force, compel, impel, constrain
cognizance *(n.)* knowledge, awareness, understanding
coincide *(v.)* correspond, match, agree
cold *(adj.)* windy, cool, freezing, frosty, frigid, nippy, brisk, numbing, raw; unfriendly, indifferent, reserved

collapse *(v.)* drop, deflate, fall, fail
collect *(v.)* consolidate, amass, accumulate, concentrate; congregate, assemble, flock, gather
collide *(v.)* hit, strike, crash, clash, disagree, oppose
colossal *(adj.)* large, huge, enormous, immense
combat *(n.)* conflict, battle, struggle, warfare, fight
comic, comical *(adj.)* funny, silly, humorous, ironic
commemorate *(v.)* honour, solemnize, memorialize
commensurate *(adj.)* equivalent, comparable
commentary *(n.)* criticism, analysis, interpretation
commission *(n.)* authority, license, permission; committee, representatives, board; payment, fee
commit *(v.)* perpetrate, complete, perform; entrust, delegate, promise, charge, employ, dispatch
commotion *(n.)* disturbance, tumult, uproar
communicate *(v.)* impart, inform, tell, confer, talk, converse, chat, write
compact *(adj.)* small, light, dense
companion *(n.)* comrade, escort, chaperon, bodyguard
compare *(v.)* relate, associate, link, correlate; examine, contrast, weigh, analyze
compassion *(n.)* concern, sympathy, pity
compel *(v.)* force, enforce, constrain, coerce
compete *(v.)* strive, struggle, oppose, clash, encounter
compile *(v.)* gather, collect, assemble, accumulate
complacent *(adj.)* self-satisfied, egotistic, happy, smug
complex *(adj.)* combined, compounded; convoluted, intricate, complicated, tortuous, knotty
complexion *(n.)* colouration, tinge, cast, pigmentation
complicate *(v.)* snarl, confound, jumble, tangle
composure *(n.)* self-control, calmness, poise, aplomb
comprehend *(v.)* understand, grasp, discern, perceive
compulsory *(adj.)* obligatory, requisite, necessary
conceal *(v.)* cover, screen, secrete, hide
concede *(v.)* acknowledge, grant, yield, admit, allow
conceit *(n.)* arrogance, narcissism, vanity
concern *(v.)* relate, influence; bother, worry
conclude *(v.)* close, terminate, finish, complete, achieve; deduce, presume, reason, gather, assume
concoct *(v.)* make, devise, plot, hatch
condemn *(v.)* doom, sentence, damn, convict, punish
condition *(n.)* stipulation, provision; tone, shape; circumstance, situation, position, status; limitation, restriction, qualification, restraint; illness, ailment, infirmity
conduct *(n.)* behaviour, deportment, demeanour, manner
conference *(n.)* meeting, discussion, gathering
confess *(v.)* acknowledge, own, concede, admit
confidant *(n.)* friend, adherent, companion
confident *(adj.)* assured, fearless, dauntless, bold
confirm *(v.)* ratify, affirm, settle, approve, endorse; prove, validate, verify, authenticate, explain
confound *(v.)* bewilder, befuddle, puzzle, perplex, fluster, embarrass, disconcert, baffle, mystify
congenial *(adj.)* friendly, compatible, harmonious
connoisseur *(n.)* critic, expert, judge
connotation *(n.)* implication, meaning, insinuation
conscience *(n.)* duty, morals, shame
consent *(v.)* accede, acquiesce, agree, allow, approve
conservative *(adj.)* cautious, reserved, conventional
considerable *(adj.)* important, noteworthy, significant; substantial, abundant, lavish, bountiful
consistent *(adj.)* constant, rational, regular
console *(v.)* comfort, cheer, gladden, encourage
conspicuous *(adj.)* obvious, striking, prominent, flagrant, noticeable
conspiracy *(n.)* plan, intrigue, collusion, connivance
constitute *(v.)* develop, create, establish; make up, frame, compound, compose
constraint *(n.)* coercion, compulsion, pressure; shyness, bashfulness, restraint, reserve
construct *(v.)* build, erect, make, fabricate, create
consumer *(n.)* user, customer, shopper, buyer
contagious *(adj.)* communicable, infectious, spreading, epidemic, deadly, endemic, catching
contemplate *(v.)* study, ponder, consider, muse, think
contempt *(n.)* disdain, disrespect, scorn, derision
contest *(n.)* competition, trial, match, challenge, game
continue *(v.)* endure, persevere, progress; renew, reinstate, reestablish
contract *(v.)* pledge, bargain, stipulate, obligate; diminish, shrink, recede, condense, compress, decrease; catch, get, incur

contrary *(adj.)* antagonistic, hostile, counter; contradictory, unpropitious; willful, headstrong, stubborn
contrive *(v.)* create, devise, scheme, improvise, invent
controversy *(n.)* contention, debate, quarrel, difference
convenient *(adj.)* accessible, available, handy, close
conventional *(adj.)* accepted, customary, typical, commonplace, traditional, formal
converse *(v.)* speak, talk, visit
convey *(v.)* transport, transfer, communicate, send
convict *(n.)* captive, felon, criminal, prisoner
convince *(v.)* persuade, establish, satisfy, teach
cooperate *(v.)* conspire, participate, agree
copy *(v.)* mimic, ape; reproduce, duplicate, counterfeit, forge, depict, portray
corporeal *(adj.)* material, tangible, physical
corpse *(n.)* body, carcass, remains, cadaver
correspond *(v.)* compare, match, resemble, conform; communicate, write, reply, answer
corrupt *(adj.)* immoral, underhanded, fraudulent, crooked, nefarious, unscrupulous, shady, dishonest
costly *(adj.)* expensive, splendid, precious
council *(n.)* group, cabinet, directorate, committee
counsel *(n.)* advice, guidance, instruction, suggestion; adviser, lawyer, attorney, barrister
countenance *(n.)* appearance, aspect, face, features
counter *(v.)* react, respond, oppose, restrict
counter *(n.)* board, shelf, ledge, bench, table
countless *(adj.)* innumerable, incalculable, infinite
coup *(n.)* feat, achievement, exploit
courage *(n.)* valour, boldness, spirit, audacity, mettle, stoutheartedness, gallantry, daring, spunk, strength
courteous *(adj.)* well-mannered, courtly, affable, polite
cover *(v.)* envelop, enshroud, encase; shield, screen, house, shelter; mask, disguise; embrace, comprise, incorporate; traverse, cross; drench, engulf; recount, narrate, relate, broadcast, record
coy *(adj.)* shy, demur, evasive, bashful, humble
craft *(n.)* occupation, career, work, job; proficiency, competence, aptitude, ability
cramp *(n.)* spasm, crick, pang, pain
crank *(n.)* bracket, bend, arm, handle; eccentric, character, complainer, grouch
crate *(n.)* box, carton, cage, container, package
craving *(n.)* need, longing, yearning, desire
create *(v.)* originate, build, fashion, shape, fabricate
creative *(adj.)* imaginative, inventive, artistic, original
credibility *(n.)* likelihood, probability, chance
creed *(n.)* belief, doctrine, dogma, faith
creep *(v.)* slither, writhe, crawl
crevice *(n.)* crack, chasm, cleft, slit, gap
crime *(n.)* transgression, wrongdoing, offense, violation
crisis *(n.)* plight, predicament, trauma, pickle
critic *(n.)* reviewer, commentator, analyst, examiner; detractor, complainer, mud-slinger
criticize *(v.)* evaluate, study, analyze, examine; chastise, reprove, reprimand, blame
crook *(n.)* criminal, swindler, thief, rogue; notch, fork, angle, bend
crop *(v.)* trim, cut, clip
cross *(v.)* intersect, divide, traverse, span; mingle, mix
crucial *(adj.)* critical, decisive, climatic, deciding; severe, trying, taxing, hard, difficult
crush *(v.)* subdue, defeat, overwhelm, annihilate; smash, pulverize, powder, grind
cry *(v.)* weep, sob, wail, sorrow, grieve
cuddle *(v.)* embrace, snuggle, huddle, nestle
cue *(n.)* signal, hint, prompt
culminate *(v.)* finish, close, end
culture *(n.)* convention, custom, mores; breeding, gentility, manners
cunning *(adj.)* sly, crafty, clever, skillful, ingenious
curious *(adj.)* inquisitive, interested, inquiring, questioning; strange, odd, rare, queer, unique
current *(adj.)* prevailing, contemporary, fashionable
current *(n.)* drift, flow, tide
custodian *(n.)* caretaker, attendant, gatekeeper
cut *(v.)* shorten, curtail, lessen, decrease; separate, cleave; cross, intersect, pass
cynic *(n.)* skeptic, mocker, scoffer, detractor, critic

D

dainty *(adj.)* delicate, fragile, petite, airy, lacy, cute
danger *(n.)* risk, peril, jeopardy, threat, menace
dangle *(v.)* hang, droop, sway, suspend
dare *(v.)* undertake, endeavour, hazard, risk, try; defy, confront, oppose, brave, challenge, face

dark *(adj.)* sinister, evil, gloomy, dismal, immoral, corrupt; unlit, dim, shadowy, somber, indistinct, dusky, murky, gloomy, obscure, shady, hazy

dart *(n.)* missile, barb, arrow, weapon

dash *(v.)* race, sprint, speed, hurry, run; smash, dampen, dismay, dispirit

date *(n.)* appointment, rendezvous, engagement, call, visit; companion, partner, friend, lover

dazzle *(v.)* blind, amaze, awe, astonish

deal *(n.)* agreement, pledge, pact, contract

debate *(v.)* discuss, contend, contest, dispute, argue

debris *(n.)* remains, rubble, rubbish, wreckage, trash

debt *(n.)* obligation, liability, mortgage, note

deceit *(n.)* misrepresentation, trickery, fraud, duplicity, deception, dishonesty

decent *(adj.)* seemly, respectable, nice, proper, ethical, virtuous, trustworthy, upright, good

decipher *(v.)* interpret, decode, translate, explain, solve

declare *(v.)* state, assert, tell, affirm, maintain, testify, certify, contend, allege, profess, swear

decorate *(v.)* adorn, beautify, renovate, brighten, enhance, embellish, elaborate

decrease *(v.)* lessen, diminish, decline, subside, shrink, reduce, check, curb, restrain, blunt, curtail

decree *(n.)* proclamation, edict, pronouncement, declaration, judgment

dedicate *(v.)* devote, apportion, assign

deed *(n.)* act, commission, accomplishment; document, release, agreement, charter, title

defeat *(v.)* conquer, overcome, vanquish, subdue, overthrow, crush, overwhelm, repulse, decimate

defend *(v.)* protect, shield, shelter, screen; justify, plead, alibi, endorse, recommend, support

defense *(n.)* resistance, protection, security, backing; denial, alibi, explanation, justification, proof

defiance *(n.)* insubordination, rebellion, insurgence, disobedience

deficit *(n.)* shortage, paucity, deficiency, lack

define *(v.)* limit, bound, confine, circumscribe, edge; describe, designate, characterize, represent, exemplify, explain, name

definite *(adj.)* exact, fixed, precise, positive, decisive, specific, categorical; clear, sharp, distinct, unmistakable, obvious, plain; sure, certain

deform *(v.)* damage, disfigure, deface, injure

degrade *(v.)* disgrace, debase, demote, discredit, diminish, humble

degree *(n.)* gradation, size, dimension, gauge; extent, quality, potency, proportion, intensity, scope; doctorate

deify *(v.)* exalt, idealize, worship

deity *(n.)* god, divinity, divine, celestial

delay *(v.)* postpone, defer, deter, impede, detain, check, curb, procrastinate, suspend, interrupt

delegate *(n.)* legate, emissary, proxy, deputy, minister, ambassador, agent, representative

deliberate *(adj.)* intentional, conscious, studied, planned, willful, considered, calculated, intended, purposeful, premeditated, designed, unhurried

delicate *(adj.)* fine, dainty, fragile, frail, subtle, tactful; susceptible, feeble, weak

delight *(n.)* enjoyment, joy, pleasure, happiness

delight *(v.)* fascinate, amuse, please, entertain

delirious *(adj.)* demented, crazy, irrational, insane

deliver *(v.)* produce, provide; liberate, save; pass, remit, give; present, address; allot, dispense

delude *(v.)* mislead, deceive, fool, trick

deluge *(v.)* flood, overwhelm, overrun

demented *(adj.)* crazy, bemused, unbalanced, insane

demonstrate *(v.)* prove, show, confirm; illustrate, exhibit, manifest, parade, display

demoralize *(v.)* dishearten, confuse, weaken, unman, enfeeble, discourage

denounce *(v.)* condemn, accuse, charge, blame, revile, reproach, rebuke, scorn, reprimand

deny *(v.)* contradict, disagree, disavow, disclaim, repudiate, controvert, renounce

depart *(v.)* leave, go, quit, withdraw

dependent *(adj.)* poor, immature, clinging, conditional

depict *(v.)* represent, picture, portray

deplorable *(adj.)* tragic, distressing, dreadful

depress *(v.)* squash, flatten; dismay, dampen, sadden, deject, oppress, discourage

deprive *(v.)* strip, despoil, divest, seize

deranged *(adj.)* disturbed, demented, crazy, insane

derelict *(adj.)* abandoned, negligent, delinquent

deride *(v.)* mock, ridicule, scorn, jeer

derivation *(n.)* root, source, beginning, origin

derive *(v.)* obtain, determine, conclude, assume

derivative *(adj.)* borrowed, learned, copied

derogatory *(adj.)* disparaging, belittling, faultfinding, detracting, critical, sarcastic

descent *(n.)* drop, sinking, reduction, tumble, decline, fall; slide, inclination; extraction, origin, lineage, family

describe *(v.)* recount, portray, depict, picture, specify, illustrate, name, define, explain

desert *(n.)* waste, wastelands, wilderness

desert *(v.)* abandon, defect, leave

deserve *(v.)* merit, earn, rate

design *(n.)* plan, schematic, rendering, pattern, layout, diagram, drawing, sketch, blueprint, plan

desire *(n.)* aspiration, longing, craving, lust, wish, mania, hunger, yearning, hankering, itch, passion

desolate *(adj.)* forsaken, dreary, deserted, uninhabited, abandoned, isolated, disconsolate, forlorn

despair *(n.)* hopelessness, depression, discouragement, desperation, gloom

despicable *(adj.)* detestable, contemptible, abject, base

destiny *(n.)* fate, future, fortune, doom

destitute *(adj.)* lacking, impoverished, poverty, penniless, poor

destroy *(v.)* ruin, demolish, raze, eradicate, annihilate, obliterate, extinguish, finish

detach *(v.)* disconnect, remove, separate, divide

detect *(v.)* distinguish, recognize, identify, discover

deter *(v.)* discourage, caution, dissuade, prevent, warn

detest *(v.)* dislike, loathe, abhor, despise, hate

devastate *(v.)* ravage, sack, pillage, destroy

develop *(v.)* enlarge, expand, extend, promote, cultivate, intensify; grow, mature, evolve; unfold, disclose, unravel, uncover, explain

deviate *(v.)* deflect, digress, wander, stray, differ

device *(n.)* apparatus, instrument, contrivance, mechanism, appliance, contraption, implement, utensil, gadget; artifice, scheme, design, dodge, trick, ruse, plan, technique

devoid *(adj.)* lacking, empty, void

devote *(v.)* assign, apply, consecrate, bless, dedicate

devour *(v.)* eat, gulp, swallow, gorge, absorb

diabolical *(adj.)* fiendish, wicked, tricky

dialect *(n.)* idiom, jargon, cant, vernacular, patois

diatribe *(n.)* tirade, denunciation

dictator *(n.)* ruler, autocrat, despot, tyrant, oppressor

die *(v.)* expire, perish, succumb, croak; fade, ebb, wither, decay, weaken, vanish

difference *(n.)* deviation, departure, exception; divergence, opposition, dissimilarity, diversity, departure, differentiation, contrast

difficult *(adj.)* strenuous, exacting, arduous, laboured, demanding, onerous, challenging, exacting, formidable; involved, perplexing, puzzling, mystifying, bewildering, profound, complicated, deep, ambiguous, obscure

diffident *(adj.)* shy, insecure, reserved

digest *(v.)* summarize, recap; absorb, consume; learn, study

dignity *(n.)* poise, bearing, air, stateliness, splendour, majesty, class, pride

digress *(v.)* stray, deviate, wander

dilemma *(n.)* predicament, quandary, difficulty

diligence *(n.)* earnestness, perseverance, industry, vigour, carefulness, intensity, attention, care

dilute *(v.)* thin, weaken, add, mix, reduce

dingy *(adj.)* drab, dirty, grimy, muddy, soiled

diplomat *(n.)* ambassador, consul, minister, legate, emissary, envoy, agent, representative, statesman

dire *(adj.)* serious, desperate, dreadful, terrible, horrible, frightful

disability *(n.)* feebleness, incapacity, injury, weakness

disadvantage *(n.)* obstacle, restraint, inconvenience, drawback, weakness

disagree *(v.)* differ, dissent, object, oppose, quarrel

disappear *(v.)* fade, die, escape, evaporate, vanish

disappoint *(v.)* dissatisfy, disillusion, frustrate, mis carry, thwart, foil, baffle

disapprove *(v.)* condemn, chastise, reprove, denounce

disaster *(n.)* calamity, mishap, debacle, misadventure, defeat, failure, tragedy, cataclysm, catastrophe

disburse *(v.)* pay, expend, use, contribute, spend

discard *(v.)* reject, expel, dispossess, relinquish

discharge *(v.)* remove, unpack, empty; release, liberate, free, fire

discipline *(v.)* train, control; punish, chastise, correct

disclose *(v.)* reveal, confess, publish

discomfort *(n.)* annoyance, uneasiness, trouble, displeasure, embarrassment

disconnect *(v.)* detach, separate, disengage, cut, divide
discontinue *(v.)* stop, end, finish, close, cease
discord *(n.)* conflict, strife, contention, disagreement
discourse *(v.)* converse, write, speak
discover *(v.)* invent, ascertain, detect, recognize, determine, observe, uncover, find, learn
discreet *(adj.)* prudent, cautious, discerning, reserved, wary, watchful, circumspect, politic, diplomatic
discrepancy *(n.)* variance, inconsistency, conflict
discrete *(adj.)* unconnected, distinctive, separate
discretion *(n.)* caution, wariness, prudence, tact
discriminate *(v.)* differentiate, separate, distinguish
discuss *(v.)* talk, argue, debate, dispute, confer, reason
disease *(n.)* sickness, malady, ailment, illness
disfigure *(v.)* deface, mar, mutilate, damage, hurt
disgraceful *(adj.)* dishonorable, disreputable, shocking, offensive, shameful
disguise *(n.)* mask, costume, masquerade, facade
disgust *(v.)* offend, repel, revolt, nauseate, sicken, shock, upset, disturb
disheveled *(adj.)* untidy, rumpled, unkempt
dishonour *(n.)* shame, ignominy, abasement, disgrace
disinclined *(adj.)* hesitant, reluctant, unwilling
dislike *(v.)* detest, deplore, abhor, hate, abominate, loathe, despise, scorn
dismal *(adj.)* dreary, bleak, gloomy, melancholy, desolate, morbid, ghastly, gruesome, cheerless, dusky, dingy, murky, bleak, somber, creepy, spooky
dismantle *(v.)* disassemble, undo, demolish, ruin, raze, destroy
dismiss *(v.)* reject, repudiate, disperse, expel, abolish, dispossess, exile, expatriate, banish, deport
disparage *(v.)* discredit, belittle, dismiss
dispatch *(v.)* transmit, express, forward; finish, conclude, kill
dispense *(v.)* distribute, apportion, assign, allocate
disperse *(v.)* scatter, separate, disband
display *(n.)* exhibition, exhibit, presentation, demonstration, performance, parade, pageant
disposed *(adj.)* prone, inclined, apt, likely
disprove *(v.)* refute, invalidate, deny
dispute *(n.)* conflict, squabble, disturbance, feud
disrespect *(n.)* discourtesy, insolence, irreverence
disrupt *(v.)* intrude, obstruct, break, interrupt
disseminate *(v.)* scatter, spread, sow, propagate, broadcast, distribute
dissent *(v.)* disagree, refuse, contradict, differ, oppose
dissident *(adj.)* hostile, opposed, disagreeing
dissolve *(v.)* liquefy, evaporate, disintegrate, disappear
distant *(adj.)* aloof, afar, abroad, removed
distinct *(adj.)* perceptible, clear, sharp, enunciated, audible, lucid, plain, obvious, clear, definite; discrete, separate, disunited
distinguish *(v.)* discern, detect, notice, discover; honour, celebrate, acknowledge, admire, praise
distort *(v.)* alter, misinterpret, misconstrue
distract *(v.)* detract, amuse, entertain, mislead
distraught *(adj.)* troubled, distressed
distress *(n.)* pain, anxiety, worry, sorrow, wretchedness, suffering, ordeal, anguish, grief, trouble
distribute *(v.)* disburse, dispense, issue, allocate
district *(n.)* area, neighborhood, community, vicinity
distrust *(v.)* mistrust, suspect, disbelieve, doubt
disturb *(v.)* trouble, worry, perplex, startle, alarm, arouse, depress, distress, provoke, irritate, harass
diverge *(v.)* radiate, veer, swerve, deviate
diverse *(adj.)* dissimilar, assorted, different, distinct
divine *(adj.)* godlike, sacred, hallowed, consecrated, anointed, sanctified, ordained, revered, venerated
divulge *(v.)* reveal, disclose, impart, confess, expose
docile *(adj.)* submissive, meek, mild, tractable, pliant, willing, obliging, manageable, tame, obedient
doctor *(n.)* physician, surgeon, intern, veterinarian, chiropractor, homeopath, osteopath, healer, quack, anesthetist, dentist, pediatrician, gynecologist, oculist, obstetrician, psychiatrist, psychologist, pathologist, dermatologist, endocrinologist, urologist, hematologist
doctrine *(n.)* policy, conviction, tradition, canon
dogmatic *(adj.)* authoritarian, dictatorial, stubborn intolerant, opinionated, domineering, tyrannical
domain *(n.)* territory, dominion, field, specialty, area
domestic *(adj.)* indigenous, native, homemade

dominant *(adj.)* commanding, authoritative, assertive, aggressive, powerful

donate *(v.)* contribute, grant, bestow, bequeath, dis tribute, give, provide

donor *(n.)* benefactor, contributor, patron, philanthropist, giver

dote *(v.)* adore, pet, admire, love

doubt *(n.)* uncertainty, skepticism, mistrust, suspicion, misgiving, apprehension

douse *(v.)* immerse, wet, submerge, drench, soak

drab *(adj.)* dismal, dingy, colourless, dreary, dull

drag *(n.)* impedance, restraint, hindrance, burden, impediment, barrier; tiresome, bother, annoyance, hang-up, nuisance

drag *(v.)* haul, move, transport, draw; dawdle, loiter, pause; crawl, delay

drama *(n.)* play, production, dramatization, show, melodrama, tragicomedy, opera, mystery

drastic *(adj.)* extreme, extravagant, exorbitant, radical

draw *(v.)* drag, attract, lug, tow, haul; sketch, outline, trace, depict

drawback *(n.)* disadvantage, shortcoming, hindrance

dread *(n.)* awe, horror, terror, fear

drift *(n.)* tendency, bent, trend, inclination, impulse, bias, leaning, disposition

drink *(v.)* swallow, gulp, sip, guzzle

drive *(n.)* trip, outing, airing, tour, excursion, jaunt, spin, journey; driveway, approach, avenue, boulevard, road; energy, effort, enthusiasm, vigour, impulse

drop *(n.)* speck, dash, dab, bit; fall, tumble, reduction, decrease, slump, lowering

drowsy *(adj.)* sleepy, sluggish, languid, indolent, lazy

dry *(adj.)* parched, desiccated, barren, dehydrated, drained; uninteresting, tedious, dull; sarcastic, cynical, biting, funny

dubious *(adj.)* indecisive, perplexed, hesitant, uncertain, questionable; ambiguous, indefinite, unclear, obscure

due *(adj.)* expected; deserved; unsatisfied, outstanding, unpaid

dumb *(adj.)* simple-minded, dull, stupid

dumfound *(v.)* astonish, shock, startle

dungeon *(n.)* cell, vault, prison

durable *(adj.)* strong, form, enduring, permanent

duress *(n.)* threat, coercion, compulsion, control, pressure, restraint

duty *(n.)* obligation, liability, burden, responsibility

dwell *(v.)* reside, live, inhabit, stay, lodge, settle, remain, continue, occupy

dynamic *(adj.)* forceful, intense, energetic, compelling, vigorous, magnetic, electric, effective, influential, charismatic, active, powerful

dynasty *(n.)* succession, sovereignty

E

eager *(adj.)* impatient, anxious, keen, fervent, zealous, intent

early *(adj.), (adv.)* primitive, premature, preceding, unexpected, punctual

earn *(v.)* deserve, win, merit; gain, obtain, attain, get, procure, realize, acquire, secure

earnest *(adj.)* serious, intense, important, ardent, zealous, warm, enthusiastic

earthly *(adj.)* human, mortal, global, mundane

earthy *(adj.)* coarse, dull, crude, unrefined, natural

eat *(v.)* devour, chew, swallow, feast, dine, gorge, feed; erode, corrode, waste, rust, spill

ebb *(v.)* decline, recede, subside, decrease

eccentric *(adj.)* unconventional, odd, queer, strange, unusual

eclipse *(v.)* darken, diminish, obscure

economic *(adj.)* business, financial, commercial

ecstasy *(n.)* joy, rapture, delight, happiness

edible *(adj.)* palatable, good, delicious, satisfying, savory, tasty, nutritious, digestible

educate *(v.)* teach, train, inform, refine, tutor, instruct

effect *(n.)* conclusion, consequence, outcome, result

effect *(v.)* produce, cause, make, begun

effervescent *(adj.)* bubbly, lively, vivacious

effort *(n.)* attempt, undertaking, struggle, try, venture

egotism *(n.)* conceit, vanity, pride, self-love, arrogance, overconfidence, haughtiness

egregious *(adj.)* bad, outrageous, shocking

eject *(v.)* discard, reject, oust, evict

elaborate *(adj.)* gaudy, decorated, showy, dressy, flowery, flashy, ornate; intricate, complicated, involved, complex

elect *(v.)* choose, name, select

elegance *(n.)* taste, cultivation, polish, splendor, beauty, gracefulness, magnificence, courtliness, charm, sophistication, style

element *(n.)* substance, component, portion, particle, detail, part

elevate *(v.)* lift, hoist, heave, tilt; advance, appoint, further

eligible *(adj.)* qualified, suitable, fit, usable

eloquence *(n.)* fluency, wit, wittiness, expressiveness, diction, articulation, delivery, poise

elude *(v.)* evade, escape, dodge, shun, avoid

elusive *(adj.)* fleeting, fugitive, temporary

embargo *(n.)* restriction, prohibition, impediment, restraint

embarrass *(v.)* distress, disconcert, chagrin, confound, trouble, disturb, fluster, shame

embezzle *(v.)* thieve, forge, pilfer, steal

embrace *(v.)* hug, enfold, squeeze, grip

emerge *(v.)* rise, arrive, appear, form, evolve

emigrant *(n.)* exile, expatriate, colonist, migrant, pilgrim, refugee

eminence *(n.)* standing, prominence, distinction, fame

emissary *(n.)* intermediary, ambassador, consul, agent

emotion *(n.)* excitement, sentiment, passion

emphatic *(adj.)* definite, assured, strong, determined, forceful, earnest, positive, dynamic

employ *(v.)* operate, manipulate, apply; contract, procure, hire

emulate *(v.)* imitate, equal, compete, follow

encompass *(v.)* include, encircle, gird, surround

encounter *(n.)* meeting, interview, rendezvous, appointment; conflict, clash, collision, fight

encourage *(v.)* support, inspire, cheer, praise, fortify, help, aid, reassure, reinforce, back, strengthen

endeavour (v.) effort, undertaking, venture

endorse *(v.)* countersign, underwrite, subscribe, notarize; approve, sanction, acknowledge

endurable *(adj.)* tolerable, supportable, bearable

engross *(v.)* absorb, busy, fill, occupy

enhance *(v.)* embellish, magnify, amplify, increase

enigma *(n.)* problem, riddle, parable, puzzle

enlighten *(v.)* inform, divulge, acquaint, teach, tell

enormous *(adj.)* monstrous, immense, huge, large

enterprise *(v.)* undertaking, endeavour, affair, business

entertain *(v.)* cheer, delight, beguile, charm, captivate, stimulate, distract, indulge; invite, welcome

enthusiasm *(v.)* excitement, interest, fervor, ardor, eagerness, zeal

entrance *(n.)* access, entry, passage, approach, admittance, introduction, debut, enrollment

envelop *(v.)* encompass, contain, hide, surround, wrap

envelope *(n.)* pouch, pocket, container, wrapper

envy *(v.)* covet, crave, yearn, hanker

equilibrium *(n.)* balance, stability, symmetry

equipment *(n.)* tools, implements, utensils, apparatus, devices, tackle, machinery, fittings

equivalent *(adj.)* equal, corresponding, commensurate, comparable, similar

eradicate *(v.)* destroy, eliminate, exterminate

erect *(v.)* construct, fabricate, build

erratic *(adj.)* wandering, rambling, roving; eccentric, queer, unusual; deviating, inconsistent, unpredictable, irregular

erroneous *(adj.)* inaccurate, incorrect, untrue, false

erudite *(adj.)* scholarly, learned, cultured

erupt *(v.)* eject, emit, explode

escape *(n.)* flight, retreat, evasion, avoidance

escape *(v.)* elude, avoid, flee, evade, disappear, vanish

escort *(n.)* guide, attendant, guard, companion

espouse *(v.)* marry, advocate, adopt, uphold, support

essence *(n.)* pith, core, kernel, gist, nature, basis, substance, nucleus, germ

establish *(v.)* institute, organize, erect, build; verify, authenticate, confirm; fix, stabilize

ethical *(adj.)* moral, humane, respectable, decent, honest, noble

etiquette *(n.)* conduct, manners, behaviour

euphoria *(n.)* relaxation, health, well-being, happiness

evade *(v.)* avoid, dodge, shun, elude, baffle, conceal, deceive, veil, hide

event *(n.)* occasion, incident, occurrence, happening, affair, function, situation

evolve *(v.)* unfold, emerge, develop, grow

exact *(adj.)* accurate, precise, correct, perfect, definite; clear, sharp, distinct

exaggerate *(v.)* overstate, misrepresent, falsify, magnify, amplify, heighten, intensify, distort, stretch, overdo, elaborate, colour, fabricate

examine *(v.)* inspect, analyze, scrutinize, explore, probe; question, interrogate

exasperate *(v.)* annoy, irritate, provoke

exceed *(v.)* excel, outdo , surpass

excel *(v.)* surpass, transcend, exceed

excess *(n.)* profusion, surplus; prodigality, dissipation, intemperance, greed, waste

excite *(v.)* provoke, stimulate, inflame, arouse, stir, provoke, incite

exclaim *(v.)* shout, call, yell

exclude *(v.)* except, reject, ban, bar

execute *(v.)* perform, act, do, effect

exempt *(adj.)* privileged, excused, unrestricted

exhaust *(v.)* debilitate, tire, weaken, weary; deplete, use

exhort *(v.)* entreat, beg, urge

exist *(v.)* live, survive, be, endure

exotic *(adj.)* foreign, imported, extrinsic; peculiar, strange, different, fascinating, unusual

expand *(v.)* extend, augment, dilate, grow

expanse *(n.)* extent, reach, area, space, span, spread, scope, range

expect *(v.)* anticipate, await, hope; require, demand, exact; assume, presume, suppose, suspect

expedient *(adj.)* convenient, profitable, practical

expedite *(v.)* speed, quicken, advance

expel *(v.)* eject, dislodge, evict; dismiss, suspend, discharge, oust

expenditure *(n.)* outgo, payment, expense

experience *(n.)* background, skill, knowledge, practice, maturity, judgment, know-how

experience *(v.)* undergo, feel, endure

expert *(adj.)* skillful, practiced, proficient, able

explain *(v.)* interpret, elucidate, illustrate, clarify, illuminate, expound, teach, demonstrate, define

explicit *(adj.)* clear, definite, understandable

exploit *(n.)* deed, venture, escapade, achievement

exploit *(v.)* utilize, employ, use

explore *(v.)* examine, search, hunt, seek

explosion *(n.)* detonation, blast, burst, discharge

expose *(v.)* uncover, disclose, reveal, unmask, unfold; endanger, imperil

express *(v.)* declare, tell, signify, utter

expulsion *(n.)* ejection, suspension, purge, removal

exquisite *(adj.)* fine, scrupulous, precise, dainty

extend *(v.)* enlarge, lengthen, increase, reach, continue, spread

extent *(n.)* span, space, area, expanse, bulk; scope, reach, range, magnitude, intensity

exterior *(adj.)* outer, outlying, outermost, outside

exterminate *(v.)* annihilate, eradicate, destroy

extinguish *(v.)* smother, choke, douse, stifle

extort *(v.)* extract, wrench, force, steal

extra *(adj.)* additional, other, spare, reserve, supple, auxiliary, added, more

extract *(v.)* derive, secure, obtain

extraneous *(adj.)* foreign; incidental, redundant

extraordinary *(adj.)* unusual, remarkable, curious, amazing

extravagance *(n.)* excess, lavishness, improvidence, waste

extravagant *(adj.)* lavish, prodigal, immoderate, wasteful

extreme *(adj.)* outermost, utmost, immoderate, exces sive, outrageous, preposterous, exaggerated

exuberance *(n.)* fervor, eagerness, exhilaration, zeal

eye *(n.)* perception, taste, discrimination; focus, core, heart, kernel, nub

F

fable *(n.)* story, allegory, tale, parable

fabric *(n.)* cloth, textile, stuff, material, goods

fabricate *(v.)* construct, erect, make, form, build, manufacture, devise; misrepresent, contrive

fabulous *(adj.)* fictitious, remarkable, amazing, immense, unusual

facade *(n.)* face, appearance, look, front

facet *(n.)* surface, aspect, face, side, plane

facetious *(adj.)* humorous, whimsical, ridiculous, funny

facile *(adj.)* easy, simple, obvious, apparent, fluent

facilitate *(v.)* promote, aid, simplify, help

facsimile *(n.)* copy, duplicate, reproduction, mirror

fact *(n.)* certainty, truth, actuality, reality, evidence, action, deed, happening, occurrence, act, episode, incident

faculty *(n.)* ability, aptitude, peculiarity, strength, forte; instructors, mentors, professors, tutors, lecturers, advisers, scholars, fellows

fad *(n.)* fancy, style, craze, fashion, eccentricity, innovation, vogue, fashion

fade *(v.)* bleach, blanch, dim, vanish; diminish, hush, quiet, sink, decrease

failure *(n.)* fiasco, miscarriage, breakdown, stoppage, collapse, downfall, flop, washout; incompetent, underachiever, dropout, dud

faint *(adj.)* faltering, shaky, dizzy, weak, vague, thin, hazy, indistinct, dull; subdued, low, soft, quiet, muffled, hushed

fair *(adj.)* just, forthright, impartial, scrupulous, honest, decent, honorable, righteous, reasonable, even-handed, principled, trustworthy; ordinary, mediocre, commonplace; pleasant, clear, sunny, bright, calm, placid, tranquil, favourable, balmy

fair *(n.)* exposition, carnival, bazaar, festival, market

faith *(n.)* trust, confidence, credence, assurance, acceptance, conviction, sureness, reliance; belief, creed, doctrine, dogma, tenet, revelation, credo, gospel, canon, theology

fake *(adj.)* pretended, fraudulent, bogus, false

fall *(v.)* drop, decline, sink, topple, settle, droop, stumble, trip, plunge, descend, totter, recede, ebb, diminish, flop; yield, surrender, succumb, resign, capitulate

fallacy *(n.)* inconsistency, mistake, ambiguity, paradox, miscalculation, quirk, flaw, heresy, error

false *(adj.)* unfaithful, treacherous, disloyal, deceitful, unscrupulous, untrustworthy; spurious, fanciful, deceptive, fallacious, misleading, erroneous, inaccurate, fraudulent, fabricated, bogus

fame *(n.)* renown, glory, distinction, eminence, esteem, name, note, greatness, rank, position, standing, preeminence, regard, popularity

familiar *(adj.)* everyday, customary, accustomed, common, ordinary, informal, commonplace

family *(n.)* household, relatives, clan, relations, tribe, dynasty, descendants, forbears, heirs, genealogy, descent, parentage, extraction, kinship, lineage

famine *(n.)* starvation, want, misery, hunger

famous *(adj.)* known, renowned, eminent, foremost, famed, celebrated, noted, prominent, reputable, renowned, notable, notorious

fan *(n.)* supporter, follower, amateur, devotee

fancy *(adj.)* elaborate, ornamental, intricate, elegant, embellished, rich, adorned, ostentatious, gaudy, showy, baroque, lavish, ornate

fantastic *(adj.)* fanciful, whimsical, capricious, strange, odd, queer, quaint, peculiar, outlandish, wonderful, exotic, ludicrous

fantasy *(n.)* illusion, flight, figment, fiction

farce *(n.)* satire, travesty, burlesque

farewell *(n.)* good-bye, valediction, parting, departure

farsighted *(adj.)* aware, perceptive, sagacious

fascinate *(v.)* charm, captivate, entrance, enchant, bewitch, enrapture, delight, please, attract, lure, seduce, entice, intoxicate, tantalize

fashion *(n.)* manner, custom, convention, vogue, mode, usage, observance, style, craze

fasten *(v.)* lock, fix, tie, lace, close, bind, tighten, attach, secure, anchor, grip, clasp, clamp, pin, nail, tack, bolt, rivet, set, weld, cement, glue

fat *(adj.)* portly, stout, obese, corpulent, fleshy, plump, bulky, heavy

fatal *(adj.)* mortal, lethal, deadly

fate *(n.)* destiny, fortune, luck, doom

father *(n.)* parent, sire, progenitor, procreator, forebear, ancestor; originator, founder, inventor, author; pastor, ecclesiastic, parson

fatigue *(n.)* weariness, exhaustion, lassitude

fault *(n.)* wrongdoing, transgression, crime, impropriety, misconduct, malpractice, failing; error, defect, blunder, mistake, accountability, blame

favour *(v.)* indulge, prefer, pick, choose, value, prize, esteem

favourite *(adj.)* beloved, favoured, preferred, adored

favoritism *(n.)* bias, partiality, inequity, inclination

fear *(n.)* dread, fright, dismay, awe, anxiety, foreboding, concern, alarm

feasible *(adj.)* expedient, worthwhile, convenient, practicable, possible, attainable

feast *(n.)* banquet, entertainment, festival, fiesta, barbeque, picnic, dinner

feat *(n.)* deed, act, effort, achievement

feeble *(adj.)* weak, faint, fragile, puny

feel *(v.)* touch, caress, fondle, paw, grasp; experience, sense, perceive; believe, consider, hold, think

feign *(v.)* pretend, dissemble, imagine, fabricate

fellow *(n.)* youth, chap, lad, boy, stripling, apprentice, adolescent, juvenile, youngster, kid; associate, member, peer, colleague, friend

felony *(n.)* crime, misconduct, offense, transgression

feminine *(adj.)* soft, delicate, gentle, ladylike, matronly, maidenly, tender, womanly

ferment *(v.)* effervesce, foam, froth, bubble, seethe, fizz, work, ripen, rise

ferocious *(adj.)* savage, fierce, wild

fertile *(adj.)* productive, inventive, fruitful, rich, productive, fat, teeming, yielding, flowering

fervent *(adj.)* zealous, eager, ardent, enthusiastic
fervor *(n.)* ardor, enthusiasm, zeal
festival *(n.)* celebration, festivity, gala, carnival
feast *(v.)* get, retrieve, carry
fetish *(n.)* fixation, craze, mania, obsession
fetus *(n.)* embryo, organism, child
feud *(n.)* quarrel, strife, bickering, fight
fickle *(adj.)* inconstant, capricious, whimsical, mercurial, changing
fiction *(n.)* novel, tale, romance, story
fidelity *(n.)* faithfulness, loyalty, devotion
fiend *(n.)* barbarian, brute, beast, devil; fan, monomaniac
fierce *(n.)* ferocious, savage, wild, untamed, brutal, monstrous, vicious, dangerous, violent, threatening
fight *(n.)* struggle, battle, strife, contention, feud, quarrel, dispute, confrontation, brawl, bickering, wrangling, argument, debate, conflict, clash, scuffle, engagement
figure *(n.)* design, statue, shape, structure; body, frame, development, build, posture, attitude, pose, carriage; total, number; value, worth
file *(v.)* abrade, rasp, scrape, finish; classify, index, categorize, catalogue, register, list
filth *(n.)* dirt, contamination, pollution, muck, slop, squalor, grime, garbage, sludge
finance *(n.)* business, commerce, economics
find *(v.)* discover, detect, notice, perceive, discern, uncover, expose
fine *(adj.)* precise, accurate, definite; thin, subtle; powdery, granular
fine *(n.)* punishment, penalty, damage, forfeit
finish *(v.)* perfect, achieve; wax, stain, cover, paint; cease, close, end, stop
fire *(n.)* burning, flame, blaze, embers, sparks, glow, warmth, combustion, conflagration
firm *(adj.)* stable, solid, rooted, immovable, fastened, motionless, secured; solid, dense, compact, impenetrable, impervious, rigid, hardened, inflexible, unyielding; determined, steadfast, resolute, constant
first *(adj.)* beginning, original, primary, prime, initial, earliest, introductory
fishy *(adj.)* improbable, dubious, implausible, unlikely
fixture *(n.)* equipment, convenience, appliance, machine, device, equipment
fizzle *(n.)* disappointment, fiasco, defeat, failure
flabby *(adj.)* soft, yielding, limp, tender, fat
flair *(n.)* talent, aptitude, gift, ability
flamboyant*(adj.)* bombastic, ostentatious, ornate
flame *(n.)* blaze, flare, flash, fire
flatter *(v.)* adulate, glorify, praise
flaunt *(v.)* display, vaunt, brandish, boast
flavour *(n.)* taste, tang, relish
flaw *(n.)* defect, imperfection, stain, blemish
fleck *(n.)* spot, mite, dot, bit
flee *(v.)* run, desert, escape, retreat
flexible *(adj.)* limber, lithe, supple, elastic, malleable, pliable, tractable
flicker *(v.)* sparkle, twinkle, glitter, flash, shine
flimsy *(adj.)* thin, weak, slight, infirm, frail, insubstantial, fragile, decrepit
flippant *(adj.)* pert, frivolous, impudent, saucy, rude
flock *(n.)* congregation, group, pack, litter, herd
flood *(v.)* inundate, swamp, overflow, deluge, submerge, immerse
floor *(n.)* tiles, planking, carpet, rug, story, landing, basement
flourish *(v.)* thrive, increase, wax, succeed, adorn; wave
fluctuate *(v.)* waver, vacillate, falter, hesitate
fluent *(adj.)* eloquent, glib, smooth, verbose, chatty, articulate, persuasive, silver-tongued
flutter *(v.)* flap, ripple, wiggle, wave
focus *(v.)* attract, converge, convene, center; clear: adjust, detail, sharpen
foe *(n.)* enemy, opponent, antagonist, adversary
foible *(n.)* failing, weakness, defect, fault
foliage *(n.)* leaves, greenery
folk *(n.)* people, race, nation, community, tribe, society, population, settlement, clan, confederation
follow *(v.)* ensue, postdate, succeed; imitate, conform, copy, mirror, reflect, mimic; observe, heed, regard, watch, comply; understand, comprehend, catch, realize; result, happen, ensue
foment *(v.)* encourage, incite, stimulate
fond *(adj.)* loving, enamoured, attached, affectionate
food *(n.)* nutriment, refreshment, edibles, comestibles, provisions, stores, sustenance, rations, board, cuisine, nourishment, fare
fool *(n.)* nitwit, simpleton, dunce, oaf, ninny, nincompoop, dolt, buffoon, blockhead, clown

foothold *(n.)* ledge, footing, niche, step
forbear *(v.)* abstain, stop, pause, cease
forbid *(v.)* prohibit, debar, restrain, inhibit, preclude, oppose, obstruct, bar, prevent, outlaw, disallow
force *(v.)* compel, coerce, press, drive, make, impel, oblige, require, demand, command, impose, exact
forceful *(adj.)* commanding, dominant, powerful
forecast *(n.)* prognosis, divination, foresight, prophecy
forefather *(n.)* ancestor, progenitor, forebear, father, parent, sire, forerunner, predecessor, originator, precursor, procreator, patriarch, founder, kinsman
foreign *(adj.)* alien, remote, exotic, strange, distant, different, alien, imported, borrowed, abroad
foreman *(n.)* overseer, manager, supervisor, superintendent, head, boss
foretell *(v.)* prophesy, predict, divine, foresee, forebode, augur, portend, foreshadow
forethought *(n.)* provision, planning, foresight
forever *(adv.)* always, everlastingly, perpetually, eternally, endlessly, forevermore
forewarn *(v.)* admonish, alarm, warm
forfeit *(v.)* lose, sacrifice, relinquish, abandon
forge *(v.)* counterfeit, falsify, fabricate, feign, imitate, copy, duplicate, reproduce
forget *(v.)* neglect, overlook, ignore, slight, disregard, skip, exclude
forgive *(v.)* pardon, overlook, excuse, exonerate
forgo *(v.)* quit, relinquish, waive, abandon
form *(n.)* figure, appearance, arrangement, configuration, formation, structure, contour, profile, silhouette; manner, mode, custom, method; model, mold; document, chart, questionnaire, application
formal *(adj.)* regular, orderly, precise, set; polite, reserved, distant, stiff, conventional
formality *(n.)* decorum, etiquette, correctness, behaviour
former *(adj.)* earlier, previous, foregoing, preceding
formula *(n.)* equation, recipe, directions, method
forsake *(v.)* desert, abandon, leave, quit
fortify *(v.)* strengthen, barricade, entrench, buttress
fortitude *(n.)* strength, firmness, valour, fearlessness, determination
fortune *(n.)* chance, luck, fate, uncertainty; wealth, riches, possessions, inheritance, estate
fossil *(n.)* remains, specimen, skeleton, relic
foul *(adj.)* filthy, impure, disgusting, nasty, vulgar, coarse, offensive; unfair, inequitable, unjust
foundation *(n.)* basis, reason, justification, authority; footing, pier, groundwork, bed, substructure, underpinning; institution, organization, endowment, institute, society, charity
fraction *(n.)* fragment, section, portion, part, division
fracture *(n.)* rupture, shattering, breach, dislocation, shearing, separating
fragile *(adj.)* frail, brittle, delicate, dainty, weak
fragment *(n.)* piece, scrap, remnant, bit
fragrance *(n.)* perfume, aroma, smell
frame *(n.)* skeleton, framework, scaffolding, support; border, margin, fringe, hem, trim, outline
franchise *(n.)* right, privilege, licence
fraternity *(n.)* society, brotherhood, fellowship
fraud *(n.)* deceit, trickery, duplicity, guile, deception
freedom *(n.)* liberty, independence, sovereignty, autonomy; privilege, immunity, license, indulgence, latitude
freeze *(v.)* solidify, congeal, harden; control, seal, terminate, immobilize
freight *(n.)* cargo, load, encumbrance, consignment, goods, tonnage
frenzy *(n.)* excitement, rage, craze, furor, insanity
frequent *(adj.)* habitual, customary, intermittent, periodic, commonplace; regular, repeated, recurrent, incessant, continual
fresh *(adj.)* new, green, recent, current, late, untried; unsalted, uncured, unspoiled, uncontaminated, preserved; colorful, vivid, bright; cool, clear, pure, clean, refreshed, rested, restored, relaxed, reinvigorated, revived; untrained, untried, unskilled
fret *(v.)* worry, irritate, agitate, vex, bother
friction *(n.)* attrition, abrasion, erosion, grinding; trouble, animosity, quarrel, discontent, hatred
friend *(n.)* schoolmate, playmate, roommate, companion, intimate, confidant, comrade, fellow, pal, chum, crony, buddy
fright *(n.)* fear, panic, terror, dread, horror, shock
frivolous *(adj.)* unimportant, slight, trifling, superficial, petty, trivial
frontier *(n.)* boundary, wilderness, hinterland
froth *(n.)* foam, bubbles, fizz, effervescence, lather

frugal *(adj.)* thrifty, economical, sparing, saving, parsimonious, careful
fruitful *(adj.)* prolific, productive, fecund, fertile
fry *(v.)* saute, sear, singe, brown, pan-fry
full *(adj.)* saturated, crammed, packed, stuffed, jammed, glutted, gorged, loaded; abundant, copious, ample, plentiful, sufficient, adequate, lavish, extravagant, profuse
fumble *(v.)* mishandle, bungle, mismanage, botch
fund *(n.)* money, capital, endowment, gift
funeral *(n.)* interment, burial, entombment, requiem
funny *(adj.)* comic, laughable, comical, whimsical, amusing, entertaining, diverting, humorous, witty, jocular, droll; suspicious, curious, unusual, odd
furious *(adj.)* raging, enraged, fierce, angry
furor *(n.)* tumult, excitement, stir, disturbance
fury *(n.)* rage, anger, wrath
fuss *(n.)* quarrel, complaint, bother, disturbance, stir
futile *(adj.)* useless, vain, fruitless, hopeless, impractical, unsuccessful, purposeless, ineffective, ineffectual, unproductive, empty, hollow
future *(adj.)* impending, imminent, destined, fated, prospective, expected, approaching, ultimate
fuzz *(n.)* nap, fluff, fur, hair

G

gab *(vi.)* talk, chatter, gossip, jabber, babble
gadget *(n.)* device, contrivance, object, contraption
gaiety *(n.)* merriment, jollity, mirth, exhilaration
gain *(v.)* augment, expand, enlarge, grow; progress, overtake; attain, realize, reach, succeed
gait *(n.)* walk, step, pace, carriage, movement
gallant *(adj.)* noble, brave, courteous, bold, coura geous, intrepid
gallop *(v.)* leap, run, spring, bound, hurdle, swing, stride, lope, amble, trot
gamble *(v.)* bet, wager, plunge, speculate, risk, chance
game *(n.)* sport, play, recreation; fish, fowl, quarry, prey, wildlife
gangster *(n.)* criminal, gunman, racketeer
gap *(n.)* cleft, rift, hole; break, recess, pause; pass, chasm, hollow, ravine, gorge, canyon, gully, gulch
garish *(adj.)* showy, gaudy, ostentatious, ornate
gasp *(v.)* gulp, pant, puff, wheeze, blow, snort
gather *(v.)* collect, aggregate, amass, accumulate, assemble, conclude, deduce, assume; assemble, meet
gaudy *(adj.)* showy, flashy, tawdry, ornate
gauge *(v.)* measure, check, calibrate, calculate
gazette *(n.)* journal, newspaper, periodical
gem *(n.)* stone, jewel, bauble, ornament
general *(adj.)* broad, universal, extensive, ecumenical, ubiquitous; usual, customary, prevailing; indefinite, uncertain, imprecise, vague
generous *(adj.)* bountiful, lavish, profuse, prodigal, magnanimous
genesis *(n.)* generation, creation, beginning
genial *(adj.)* cordial, kind, warmhearted, friendly
genius *(n.)* talent, intellect, intelligence, gift, aptitude, astuteness, acumen, capability
genuine *(adj.)* authentic, actual, original, unaffected, reliable, staunch, trustworthy, certain, valid, positive, frank
germ *(n.)* microbe, bacterium, micro-organism, virus, parasite, bug
gesture *(n.)* movement, indication, intimation, sign
ghastly *(adj.)* terrifying, hideous, horrible, frightening, repulsive, disgusting, abhorrent, offensive
ghost *(n.)* spirit, apparition, vision, specter, phantom, spook, devil
gibberish *(n.)* jargon, chatter, claptrap, nonsense
gibe *(v.)* sneer, mock, taunt
giddy *(adj.)* high, towering, lofty, steep
giggle *(v.)* laugh, titter, chuckle, snicker
gimmick *(n.)* device, stratagem, catch, method, trick
girdle *(n.)* belt, cinch, sash, underwear
girl *(n.)* schoolgirl, lass, woman, lassie, damsel, maid, maiden
glance *(v.)* see, peep, glimpse
glare *(v.)* light, beam, glow, radiate; pierce, glower
glide *(v.)* float, drift, waft, skim, fly, flit, soar
glimmer *(n.)* view, flash, impression, sight
glitter *(n.)* luster, brilliancy, sparkle, shimmer, gleam
globule *(n.)* drop, particle, bubble
gloomy *(adj.)* dreary, depressing, discouraging, dismal, murky
glory *(n.)* grandeur, majesty, brilliance
gluttony *(n.)* voracity, edacity, intemperance, greed
gnaw *(v.)* tear, crunch, champ, masticate, bite, chew
good for nothing *(n.)* loafer, vagabond, vagrant
goodness *(n.)* decency, morality, honesty, virtue
gorge *(n.)* chasm, abyss, crevasse, ravine

gorgeous *(adj.)* beautiful, dazzling, superb, sumptuous, impressive, grand

gory *(adj.)* blood-soaked, bloodstained, offensive

gossip *(n.)* scandal, meddling, hearsay, slander, defamation; snoop, meddler, tattler, scandalmonger, muckraker, backbiter

gossip *(v.)* tattle, chat, report, blab, babble, repeat

govern *(v.)* rule, administer, oversee, supervise, dictate, tyrannize

grab *(v.)* seize, clutch, grasp, take

grace *(n.)* charm, nimbleness, agility, poise, dexterity, symmetry, balance, style, harmony; mercy, forgiveness, love, charity

grade *(n.)* rank; class, category, classification; incline, gradient, slant, inclination, pitch, ascen escent, ramp, climb, elevation, height, hill; fill, causeway, dike, dam

gradual *(adj.)* creeping, regular, continuous, regulated

grand *(adj.)* splendid, stately, dignified, regal, noble, illustrious, august, majestic, overwhelming

grant *(n.)* gift, boon, reward, present, allowance, stipend, donation, endowment, bequest

graph *(n.)* diagram, chart, design, plan

graphic *(adj.)* illustrated, visual, sketched, pictured; clear, picturesque, comprehensible, striking, expressive, eloquent, poetic

grasp *(n.)* grip, hold, clutch, cinch

grate *(v.)* rub, rasp, grind, abrade

grateful *(adj.)* thankful, appreciative, pleased, obliged

gratify *(v.)* please, satisfy, delight

gratuity *(n.)* present, tip, reward, bonus

grave *(adj.)* important, momentous, consequential, critical; somber, solemn, serious, sober

grave *(n.)* vault, sepulcher, tomb, crypt, mausoleum, catacomb

gravity *(n.)* importance, seriousness, significance

great *(adj.)* large, numerous, big, commanding, vast; exceptional, surpassing, transcendent; grand, majestic, exalted, famous, renowned, celebrated, distinguished, noted

greedy *(adj.)* avid, grasping, rapacious, selfish, miserly, intemperate, mercenary, covetous

greet *(v.)* hail, welcome, address, recognize, embrace, nod, acknowledge, bow

gregarious *(adj.)* companionable, friendly

grievance *(n.)* hardship, injury, complaint, objection

grieve *(v.)* lament, bewail, regret, sorrow, mourn

grim *(adj.)* gloomy, sulky, morose, glum; austere, strict, harsh, severe; implacable, inexorable

grimace *(n.)* smirk, smile, sneer

grin *(v.)* smirk, simper, beam, smile

grind *(v.)* crush, powder, mill, granulate, crumble

grit *(n.)* pluck, courage; sand, dust

groan *(n.)* moan, sob, grunt, cry

groceries *(n.)* food, edibles, comestibles, foodstuffs

groove *(n.)* furrow, rut, channel, trench, depression, gutter, ditch

gross *(adj.)* total, entire; corpulent, obese, huge; obscene, indecent, lewd, coarse, shameful

grotesque *(adj.)* ludicrous, odd, bizarre, malformed, ugly, distorted, deformed

grouch *(n.)* complainer, grumbler, growler, bear, sorehead, crab, crank, bellyacher

group *(n.)* assemblage, cluster, crowd; collection, accumulation, assortment, combination; organization, association, club, society

grow *(v.)* increase, expand, swell, wax, thrive, enlarge, multiply, flourish; become, develop, evolve, progress, age, ripen, blossom, mature; cultivate, raise, tend, foster, produce, plant, breed

growl *(v.)* snarl, grumble, bark, grunt, cry

grudge *(n.)* enmity, spite, rancor, animosity, hatred

gruesome *(adj.)* horrible, ghastly, grim, grisly, frightful

gruff *(adj.)* bluff, churlish, harsh, grating, hoarse

grumble *(v.)* complain, growl, whine, protest, fuss

grumpy *(adj.)* sullen, grouchy, cantankerous, irritable

grunt *(v.)* snort, groan, mutter, grumble

guarantee *(n.)* surety, promise, bond

guaranty *(n.)* warranty, contract, certificate

guard *(n.)* sentry, sentinel, watchman

guardian *(n.)* protector, overseer, trustee, custodian, keeper, defender, supervisor, baby-sitter

guess *(v.)* estimate, presume, infer, speculate, imagine, surmise, theorize, venture, suppose, presume

guest *(n.)* visitor, caller, patron, client

guilt *(n.)* blame, error, fault, liability, weakness, failing

guise *(n.)* appearance, disguise, mode, semblance

gulf *(n.)* chasm, abyss, abysm, depth, ravine, bay, inlet, sound, cove

gullible *(adj.)* innocent, trustful, simple, naive

gulp *(v.)* swallow, gasp, swig

guru *(n.)* teacher, instructor, mentor

gust *(n.)* blast, burst, blow, breeze, wind

gusto *(n.)* enjoyment, zest, zeal, fervor, ardor

gymnasium *(n.)* arena, coliseum, ring, rink, pit, gym

gymnast *(n.)* acrobat, tumbler, jumper, athlete

gypsy *(n.)* wanderer, tramp, vagrant, traveller

H

habit *(n.)* custom, mode, practice, fashion, manner; addiction, fixation

hackneyed *(adj.)* commonplace, trite, state

hag *(n.)* crone, shrew, ogress, hellcat, fishwife, witch

halfway *(adj.)* partial, midway, incomplete, partially, imperfectly, insufficiently, moderately, middling

halfway *(adv.)* half, partly, midway

hall *(n.)* public room, chamber, assembly, arena, ballroom, church, clubhouse, salon, lounge, gymnasium, amphitheater, gallery; foyer, corridor, hallway

hallmark *(n.)* label, endorsement, seal, emblem

hallucination *(n.)* delusion, vision, dream

halt *(n.)* stop, cessation, break, pause

hamlet *(n.)* town, village

hand *(n.)* helper, worker, labourer; calligraphy, script; applause

handicap *(n.)* disadvantage, obstacle, impediment, affliction, hindrance, disorder, injury

handle *(v.)* check, examine, feel, manage, operate, use, work, deal

handsome *(adj.)* attractive, impressive, stately, robust, well-dressed, slick, beautiful

hand-to-mouth *(adj.)* marginal, minimal, borderline

handy *(adj.)* near, nearby; dexterous, able, useful, beneficial, advantageous, gainful, helpful, profitable, usable

hang-out *(n.)* bar, joint, hole, headquarters, room

hang-up *(n.)* problem, predicament, difficulty

haphazard *(adj.)* accidental, random, offhand, casual, slipshod, reckless, irregular, unplanned, aimless

happy*(adv.)* joyously, gladly, cheerily, gaily, merrily, brightly, blissfully, cheerfully, gleefully

happy *(adj.)* joyous, merry, mirthful, gay, laughing, contented, genial, satisfied, cheery, jolly, sparkling, blissful, exhilarated, pleased, gratified, ecstatic, overjoyed, radiant, smiling, elated

happy-go-lucky *(adj.)* easygoing, unconcerned, thoughtless, irresponsible

harass *(v.)* annoy, attack, tease, vex, irritate, bother

harbor *(n.)* refuge, port, pier, inlet, wharf, dock

harbor *(v.)* shelter, secure, defend, lodge; consider, cherish, regard

hard *(adj.)* compact, unyielding, solid, impermeable, tough, dense, firm; difficult, arduous, tricky, trying, tedious, complex, abstract, puzzling, troublesome, laborious; cruel, perverse, unrelenting, vengeful; severe, harsh, exacting, grim

hardheaded *(adj.)* willful, stubborn, headstrong

hardly *(adv.)* scarcely, barely, imperceptibly, infrequently, somewhat, rarely, slightly, sparsely

hardship *(n.)* trial, sorrow, worry, difficulty, grief

hardy *(adj.)* tough, resistant, solid, staunch, seasoned, fit, acclimatized, rugged, robust, hearty, hale, vigorous, powerful, sturdy, solid, substantial, strong

hark, harden *(v.)* listen, heed, infliction, impairment, damage; evil, wickedness, outrage, abuse

harmonious *(adj.)* harmonic, tuneful, musical, melodic; congruous, agreeable, corresponding, suitable, adapted, similar, like, cooperative, friendly, conforming, balanced, symmetrical

harp *(v.)* carp, nag, repeat, pester, complain

harrow *(v.)* torment, distress, harass

harsh *(adj.)* rough, severe, discordant, jangling, cacophonous, grating, dissonant, creaking, clashing, jarring, clamorous, hoarse, rasping, screeching, ear splitting, tuneless, shrill

harvest *(n.)* crops, yield, fruit, grain, produce, vegetable

hassle *(n.)* dispute, squabble, struggle, bother

haste *(n.)* speed, dispatch, precipitation, rashness, impetuousness, foolhardiness, recklessness, hastiness, carelessness, heedlessness

hat *(n.)* headgear, headpiece, helmet, chapeau, bonnet, cap, derby, sombrero, topper, bowler, panama, beret, turban, hood, cowl, beret

hatch *(v.)* produce, originate, bear

hate *(n.)* dislike, animosity, enmity, hatred
haughty *(adj.)* disdainful, arrogant, proud, egotistic
haul *(n.)* tug, lift; distance, voyage, trip; spoils, take, find, booty
haunt *(v.)* frequent, habituate, visit; obsess, torment, possess, trouble, hound, terrify, plague, vex, harass, worry, frighten, annoy, bother, disturb
have *(v.)* keep, retain, use, maintain, control, treasure, hold, possess; beget, produce
haven *(n.)* harbour, port, refuge, shelter
havoc *(n.)* destruction, confusion, devastation, plunder
hazard *(n.)* chance, risk, peril, jeopardy, danger
haze *(n.)* fog, mist, smog, cloudiness
head *(n.)* skull, scalp, crown, bean, leader, chief, commander, officer, ruler; top, summit, peak, crest; front, start, source, origin; intelligence, brain, foresight, ingenuity, judgment
headache *(n.)* pain, migraine, neuralgia; problem, mess, difficulty, trouble
heal *(v.)* cure, restore, renew, regenerate, remedy, rejuvenate, medicate, revive, rehabilitate, resuscitate, help, ameliorate
health *(n.)* vigour, wholeness, healthfulness, fitness, bloom, hardiness, stamina, energy, strength
heap *(v.)* pile, add, lump, load, pack
hear *(v.)* listen, attend, catch, apprehend, eavesdrop, perceive, overhear; try, judge, examine, referee
hearsay *(n.)* rumour, scandal, report, gossip
heartache *(n.)* sorrow, pain, despair, anguish, grief
hearty *(adj.)* warm, zealous, sincere, cheery, cheerful, jovial, animated, ardent, genial, enthusiastic, genuine, passionate, intense, exuberant, devout, unfeigned, fervent, responsive, friendly
heat *(n.)* warmth, fever, fervor, ardor, passion, excitement, desire
heave *(v.)* throw, toss, move, rock, bob, pitch, lurch, roll, reel, sway, throb, slosh
heavy *(adj.)* weighty, ponderous, huge, stout, dense, substantial, hefty, large; burdensome, troublesome, oppressive, vexatious, difficult, disturbing, onerous; dull, listless, slow, apathetic, indifferent; gloomy, dejected, cloudy, overcast, dark, dismal
hectic *(adj.)* frantic, unsettled, boisterous, restless
hector *(v.)* bully, annoy, tease, vex
heed *(n.)* notice, care, note, regard
heinous *(adj.)* hateful, atrocious, wicked
heir *(n.)* inheritor, successor, descendent, heiress, beneficiary, inheritor, prince
heirloom *(n.)* legacy, inheritance, bequest, gift, antique
heist *(n.)* robbery, burglary
help *(n.)* assistance, advice, comfort, aid, support, gift, charity, encouragement, subsidy, service, relief, endowment, cooperation, guidance; aid, representative, assistant, faculty, staff; relief, maintenance, sustenance, nourishment, remedy
hem *(n.)* border, skirting, edging, edge, fringe, rim
henpeck *(v.)* nag, bully, suppress, intimidate, bother
herd *(n.)* flock, group, drove, pack, brood, swarm, lot, bevy, covey, gaggle, nest, brood, flight, school, clan
hereditary *(adj.)* inherited, genetic, paternal
heresy *(n.)* dissent, nonconformity, dissidence, sectarianism, schism, unorthodoxy, secularism
heritage *(n.)* legacy, birthright, ancestry, dowry, share, endowment, status, heredity; culture, custom, fashion, system
hermit *(n.)* ascetic, recluse, monk, loner
hero *(n.)* champion, model, conqueror, god, martyr, warrior, saint, star, knight-errant
hesitant *(adj.)* doubtful, skeptical, irresolute, uncer tain, slow, delaying, wavering, dawdling, lazy
hex *(n.)* spell, curse
hiatus *(n.)* break, pause, space, gap
hidden *(adj.)* secluded, private, covert, concealed, occult, masked, screened, veiled, clouded, obscured, disguised, unseen, camouflaged, shrouded, shadowy, clandestine, cloistered, surreptitious
hide *(n.)* skin, pelt, rawhide, fur, leather
hide *(v.)* conceal, shroud, curtain, veil, camouflage, cover, mask, cloak, screen, suppress, withhold, shield, secrete, hoard, closet, obscure, disguise
hideous *(adj.)* frightful, shocking, revolting, hateful, ghastly, grisly, ugly
hierarchy *(n.)* government, authority, ministry, regime
highway *(n.)* roadway, parkway, freeway, turnpike
hike *(v.)* tramp, tour, explore, travel, walk; raise, lift, advance, increase
hilarious *(adj.)* gay, merry, funny, amusing, lively, witty, entertaining
hinder *(v.)* stop, impede, obstruct, check, retard, fetter, block, thwart, bar, clog, encumber, burden, inhibit, shackle, interrupt, arrest, curb, oppose, deter, hamper, frustrate, intercept, prohibit, stall, slow, down, smother, disappoint, spoil, gag, annul

hint *(n.)* allusion, mention, inkling, implication, reference, observation, notice, tip, clue, omen, scent, notion, taste, suspicion, innuendo, sign, impression, indication, suggestion

hire *(v.)* engage, secure, enlist, appoint, delegate, authorize, retain, commission, empower, select, pick, contract, procure

history *(n.)* account, annals, records, archives, chronicle, writings, evidence, record

hit *(n.)* blow, slap, rap, punch; success, favourite, sellout, knockout

hitch *(n.)* loop, noose, tie; difficult, obstacle, hindrance, block

hoard *(v.)* amass, acquire, keep, accumulate, save

hoary *(adj.)* white, old, aged, grey-haired

hoax *(n.)* trick, fabrication, deceit, deception, lie

hobby *(n.)* pursuit, avocation, pastime, diversion, interest, activity, pursuit, sport, amusement, craft

hodgepodge *(n.)* mixture, jumble, combination, mess

hokum *(n.)* nonsense, trickery, chicanery

hold *(v.)* possess, keep, retain, have, accept; support, sustain, brace, buttress, prop; grasp, grip, clutch, embrace, squeeze, hug, seize; imprison, enclose, restrain; resist, persevere, continue, endure; adhere, cling, fasten, stick

hole *(n.)* cavity, perforation, puncture, slot, eyelet, split, tear, cleft, opening, fissure, gap, gash, rift, rupture, aperture, breach, crater, gorge, hollow, chasm, crevasse, burrow, den, lair; difficulty, impasse, tangle, mess, crisis, emergency

holiday *(n.)* festival, fiesta, carnival, jubilee, anniversary, celebration

holocaust *(n.)* loss, fire, destruction

holy *(adj.)* devout, pious, righteous, moral, just, good, angelic, godly, reverent, venerable, humble, saintly, innocent, godlike, saintlike, faultless, chaste, upright, virtuous, dedicated, devoted, spiritual, religious

homage *(n.)* loyalty, worship, respect, adoration, deference, devotion, reverence

home *(n.)* residence, habitation, abode, lodging, quarters, domicile, shelter; orphanage, sanitarium, hospital

homogenize *(v.)* blend, combine, integrate

honesty *(n.)* fidelity, scrupulousness, candor, openness, morality, goodness, virtue

honour *(n.)* distinction, recognition, attention, reputation, tribute, integrity

hood *(n.)* cowl, shawl, bonnet, veil, capuchin, mantle, cover; criminal, gangster, crook

hoodlum *(n.)* rowdy, thug, gangster, crook, criminal

hook *(v.)* curve, angle, crook, arch; catch, pin, secure, fasten

hoot *(n.)* howl, whoop, boo, cry

hope *(n.)* expectation, anticipation; purpose, wish, goal

horde *(n.)* crowd, swarm, pack, throng, gathering

horrible *(adj.)* repulsive, dreadful, disgusting, terrible, frightful, shameful, shocking, awful

horrid *(adj.)* shocking, hideous, disturbing, shameful, offensive, pitiful

horticulture *(n.)* cultivation, agriculture, farming

hospital *(n.)* clinic, infirmary, sanitarium, dispensary

hostile *(adj.)* unfriendly, antagonistic, hateful, opposed

hot *(adj.)* fiery, flaming, blazing, baking, roasting, scorching, blistering, searing, sizzling, broiling, scalding, parching; aroused, furious, ill-tempered, indignant, angry

hotel *(n.)* motel, lodging, inn, hostel, resort, tavern

hound *(v.)* bully, pester, badger, provoke, annoy

house *(n.)* home, habitation, dwelling, residence; family, line, tradition, ancestry; congress, council, parliament

housekeeper *(n.)* caretaker, servant, domestic

hover *(v.)* remain, wait, float, linger

howl *(v.)* cry, wail, bawl, lament, yell

hub *(n.)* center, core, middle, focus, heart

hubbub *(n.)* uproar, bustle, noise, racket

hue *(n.)* colour, tint, value, dye

hug *(v.)* embrace, hold, squeeze, clasp, press, cling, clutch, envelop, enfold, nestle, cuddle

huge *(adj.)* large, tremendous, enormous, immense

humane *(adj.)* merciful, kind, benevolent, sympathetic, understanding, compassionate, kindhearted, tenderhearted, forgiving, charitable, tender, generous, lenient, altruistic, philanthropic, magnanimous, unselfish, warmhearted

humble *(adj.)* submissive, gentle, diffident, retiring, bashful, shy, timid, reserved, deferential, mild, withdrawn, hesitant, fearful, tentative, obedient, passive, tame, restrained, subdued; modest, seemly, becoming, homespun, servile, insignificant, plain, common, homely, simple

humid *(adj.)* moist, damp, stuffy, sticky, muggy
humiliate *(v.)* humble, shame, debase, chasten, mortify, degrade, dishonour, demean, conquer, vanquish, disgrace, embarrass
humour *(n.)* comedy, entertainment, amusement, jesting, witticism, banter, joke, mirth; disposition, wittiness, gaiety, playfulness
hunch *(n.)* intuition, notion, feeling, premonition, instinct, anticipation, clue, foreboding, portent, apprehension, misgiving, qualm, suspicion, inkling
hunger *(n.)* longing, yearning, lust, want
hunk *(n.)* lump, chunk, mass, clod, slice, morsel
hunt *(v.)* pursue, follow, stalk, hound, trail, seek, track, chase; search, probe, seek
hurdle *(n.)* obstacle, barricade, blockade, barrier
hurrah *(v.)* applaud, cheer, approve
hurry *(v.)* scurry, scuttle, dash, sprint, rush, scoot, dart, spring, speed, fly, bustle, race;. urge, drive, push, spur, goad
hurt *(v.)* injure, cut, bruise, slap, abuse, flog, whip, torture, stab, harm, wound, lacerate, bite, burn, punch, pinch, scourge, lash, cane, switch; harm, maltreat, injure, spoil, damage, destroy; pain, ache, throb, sting
hush *(v.)* calm, soothe, quiet, silence, gag, stifle
husky *(adj.)* rough, throaty, growling, gruff; muscular, sinewy, strapping
hustle *(v.)* rush, push, hurry, race, run, speed
hygiene *(n.)* health, sanitation, cleanliness
hyperbole *(n.)* metaphor, exaggeration
hypnotize *(v.)* mesmerize, fascinate, captivate, stupefy, soothe, anesthetize
hypocrisy *(n.)* pretense, affectation, bigotry, sanctimony, dishonesty, lie
hysteria, hysterics *(n.)* neurosis, emotionalism, delirium, agitation, confusion, excitement, nervousness

I

icon *(n.)* image, picture, idol, hero
iconoclast *(n.)* dissenter, rebel, radical
idea *(n.)* belief, theory, hypothesis, assumption, conjecture, notion, thought; whimsy, whim, fantasy
ideal *(adj.)* typical, model, archetypal; perfect, best, theoretical, supreme, fitting, excellent
ideal *(n.)* concept, paragon, goal, prototype, model
identical *(adj.)* same, alike, twin, indistinguishable
identity *(n.)* characteristics, identification, individuality, uniqueness, name
idiom *(n.)* expression, usage, jargon
idiot *(n.)* simpleton, nincompoop, booby, fool
idle *(adj.)* unemployed, unoccupied, uncultivated, motionless, inert, resting
idol *(n.)* image, icon, god
ignite *(v.)* fire, light, enkindle, burn
ignoble *(adj.)* mean, dishonorable, low, base
ignorance *(n.)* incomprehension, incapacity, inexperience, illiteracy, simplicity, shallowness
ill *(adj.)* harmful, evil, noxious, unfavourable; unwell, unhealthy, ailing
illegal *(adj.)* unlawful, illicit, banned, outlawed, unauthorized, unlicensed, illegitimate, prohibited, forbidden
illegible *(adj.)* unreadable, faint, unintelligible, confused, obscure
illicit *(adj.)* unlawful, prohibited, unauthorized, illegal
illiteracy *(n.)* ignorance, stupidity, idiocy
illogical *(adj.)* irrational, unreasonable, absurd, fallacious, incorrect, inconsistent, unscientific, contradictory, unsound, implausible
illuminate *(v.)* lighten, illumine, decorate, light; illustrate, explain, interpret, elucidate
illusion *(n.)* deception, fancy, hallucination, mirage, apparition, delusion, trick, dream
illustrate *(v.)* explain, picture, portray, depict
image *(n.)* idol, representation, effigy, form, drawing, portrait, photograph, replica, picture; conception, perception, thought, idea
imagery *(n.)* metaphor, representation, comparison
imaginary *(adj.)* fancied, illusory, visionary, dreamy, hypothetical, theoretical, imagined, hallucinatory, whimsical, fabulous, nonexistent, mythological, legendary, fictitious, unreal
imbalance *(n.)* unevenness, inequality, irregularity
imbecilic *(adj.)* foolish, silly, jerk
imbibe *(v.)* ingest, gorge, guzzle, drink, swallow
imitate *(v.)* impersonate, mirror, mime, ape, simulate, parody; duplicate, counterfeit, falsify, reproduce; simulate, parallel
immaculate *(adj.)* pure, unsoiled, unsullied, spotless, stainless, bright, clean

immaterial *(adj.)* unimportant, insignificant, irrelevant
immature *(adj.)* childish, youthful, sophomoric, naive
immediate *(adj.)* now, next, prompt, following
immense *(adj.)* large, gigantic, tremendous, enormous
immerse *(v.)* plunge, involve, submerge, douse, steep, soak, drench, dunk, souse
immigrant *(n.)* outsider, newcomer, alien
imminent *(adj.)* impending, approaching, coming
immobility *(n.)* firm, fixed, motionless
immoral *(adj.)* sinful, corrupt, shameless, bad
immovable *(adj.)* solid, stable, fixed, firm
immune *(adj.)* exempt, free, insusceptible, privileged, excused, safe
impact *(n.)* shock, impression, contact, collision
impair *(v.)* diminish, spoil, injure, hurt, break, damage
impart *(v.)* bestow, grant, present, allow; announce, divulge, admit, reveal
impartial *(adj.)* unbiased, disinterested, equal, fair
impasse *(n.)* deadlock, standstill, cessation, pause
impatient *(adj.)* anxious, eager, feverish, restless
impeach *(v.)* charge, arraign, denounce, indict, discredit, reprimand, blame, incriminate, try
impeccable *(adj.)* flawless, perfect, exact, precise
impede *(v.)* hinder, obstruct, slow
impel *(v.)* drive, force, urge
imperfect *(adj.)* flawed, incomplete, deficient, faulty
imperious *(adj.)* haughty, arrogant, bossy
impersonate *(v.)* portray, mimic, represent, imitate
impervious *(adj.)* impassable, impermeable, impenetrable, watertight
impetuous *(adj.)* hasty, impulsive, rash
impinge *(v.)* encroach, infringe, strike, touch
implement *(n.)* tool, instrument, appliance, utensil
implicit *(adj.)* implied, certain, absolute, accurate, inevitable
imply *(v.)* indicate, intimate, suggest, hint, implicate, signify, mean, indicate
import *(n.)* meaning, signification, value, worth
important *(adj.)* significant, momentous, essential, critical, primary, foremost, marked, valuable, crucial, vital, serious, consequential; well-known, influential, famous
impose *(v.)* force, presume, burden, compel
impossible *(adj.)* inconceivable, vain, unattainable, unworkable, futile, hopeless
imposture *(n.)* fraud, deceiver, pretender, charlatan
impotent *(adj.)* powerless, inept, infirm, unable; barren, frigid, unproductive
impoverish *(v.)* bankrupt, exhaust, destroy
impregnate *(v.)* fill, pervade, soak, infuse; conceive, reproduce, fertilize
impress *(v.)* indent, emboss, imprint, dent, stamp; affect, dazzle, stir, fascinate
imprint *(n.)* banner, trademark, emblem, signature; dent, indentation
improbable *(adj.)* doubtful, unlikely, uncertain
improve *(v.)* update, refine, enrich, enhance, augment
impudent *(adj.)* bold, insolent, rude
impulse *(n.)* surge, pulsation, beat; urge, stimulus, whim, caprice, spontaneity, notion, inclination, disposition
impute *(v.)* ascribe, assign, charge
inaccessible *(adj.)* distant, rare, remote, separated
inaccurate *(adj.)* incorrect, inexact, fallacious, mistaken, wrong
inadequacy *(n.)* inferiority, weakness, defect, flaw, drawback, shortcoming, blemish, lack
inane *(adj.)* senseless, pointless, foolish, silly
inapt *(adj.)* unfit, unsuitable, ill-suited
inaugurate *(v.)* induct, begin, introduce, initiate
incantation *(n.)* chant, charm, recitation, supplication
incarcerate *(v.)* confine, imprison, detain
incarnate *(adj.)* bodily, manifest, personified
incense *(n.)* scent, fragrance, essence, perfume
incentive *(n.)* motive, spur, inducement, impetus, enticement, temptation, inspiration, encouragement, reason
incessant *(adj.)* continual, ceaseless, constant
incident *(n.)* occurrence, happening, episode, event
incise *(v.)* cut, engrave, dissect, chop, split, divide
incite *(v.)* rouse, stir, stimulate, provoke, spur
incline *(v.)* tilt, bow, nod; prefer, favour
include *(v.)* contain, embrace, involve, incorporate, constitute, intellect, insert
incoherent *(adj.)* disorganized, muddled, muffled
income *(n.)* revenue, earnings, salary, wages, profit, dividends, proceeds, receipts, commission

incompetent *(adj.)* incapable, unfit, unskilled
incongruous *(adj.)* inconsistent, contradictory
incorrigible *(adj.)* bad, difficult, unreformed
increase *(n.)* growth, addition, development, spread, enlargement, expansion, escalation
incredible *(adj.)* unbelievable, improbable, ridiculous
incumbent *(adj.)* binding, obligatory, required
incursion *(n.)* inroad, invasion, foray
indecision *(n.)* hesitation, doubt, uncertainty
indelible *(adj.)* ingrained, enduring, strong, permanent
index *(v.)* list, catalogue, alphabetize, arrange, tabulate
indicate *(v.)* symbolize, betoken, intimate, mean; show, name, point
indifferent *(adj.)* unconcerned, cool, unemotional, unsympathetic, heartless, unresponsive, unfeeling, nonchalant, impassive, detached, callous, stony, remote, reserved, distant, arrogant, unmoved
indirect *(adj.)* devious, roundabout, tortuous, twisting, devious, sinister, rambling, oblique
individual *(adj.)* personal, particular, solitary, distinctive, personalized, sole, private
indomitable *(adj.)* invincible, unconquerable, resolute
induce *(v.)* begin, cause, effect, persuade, produce
infidelity *(n.)* unfaithfulness, adultery
infirm *(adj.)* sickly, weak, frail
inflame *(v.)* arouse, incense, disturb, excite; hurt, redden, swell; burn, kindle, scorch, ignite
inflate *(v.)* expand, swell, bloat, widen; magnify, overestimate, raise
inflection *(n.)* tone, enunciation, intonation, accent
inflict *(v.)* impose, administer, deliver, strike, cause
influence *(n.)* power, authority, control, command esteem, prominence, prestige, reputation
inform *(v.)* tell, betray, instruct, relate, teach
informal *(adj.)* casual, intimate, relaxed
infringe *(v.)* encroach, trespass, transgress, meddle
infuse *(v.)* fill, inspire; steep
ingenious *(adj.)* able, clever, cunning, gifted, intelligent, original, resourceful, shrewd, skillful
ingrain *(v.)* imbue, fix, instill, teach
ingredient *(n.)* component, constituent, element
inhabit *(v.)* dwell, occupy, reside, stay
inherent *(adj.)* inborn, inbred, inherited, innate, intrinsic, native, natural
inherit *(v.)* acquire, receive, succeed, get
inhibit *(v.)* check, restrain, repress, frustrate, hinder
inhuman *(adj.)* mean, heartless, cruel, fierce, ruthless
iniquity *(n.)* crime, evil, injustice, sin, wickedness
initiate *(n.)* beginner, learner, novice
injure *(v.)* harm, damage, wound, hurt
inkling *(n.)* hint, indication, notion, innuendo, suspicion, suggestion
inmate *(n.)* occupant, patient, convict, prisoner
innate *(adj.)* inborn, native, inherent
innocence *(n.)* honesty, simplicity, purity, naivete, chastity, ignorance, virtue
innovation *(n.)* change, newness, addition
innuendo *(n.)* hint, insinuation, aside, intimation
inopportune *(adj.)* disadvantageous, ill-timed, inappropriate, awkward, untimely
inquire *(v.)* ask, investigate, probe, interrogate
inquisitive *(adj.)* curious, questioning, meddling, analytical, snoopy, nosy, interested
insane *(adj.)* demented, crazed, frenzied, lunatic, psychotic, raving, deluded, possessed, idiotic, stupid
insatiate *(adj.)* ravenous, voracious
inscribe *(v.)* address, carve, dedicate, engrave, write
insecure *(adj.)* anxious, vague, uncertain, troubled
insert *(v.)* introduce, place, inject, include
insidious *(adj.)* treacherous, deceitful, harmful
insincere *(adj.)* deceitful, pretentious, shifty, dishonest, false, hypocritical, sly
insipid *(adj.)* dull, flat, tasteless, uninteresting
insolent *(adj.)* disrespectful, insulting, rude
insolvent *(adj.)* bankrupt, broke, failed, ruined
inspire *(v.)* encourage, enthuse, fire, invigorate, motivate, stimulate
install *(v.)* establish, introduce, inaugurate
instant *(adj.)* momentary, quick, pressing, current
instill *(v.)* infuse, indoctrinate, implant, teach
instinct *(n.)* impulse, sense, intuition, feeling
institute *(n.)* establishment, organization, body, centre
instruct *(v.)* inform, teach, order, direct, educate
instrument *(n.)* utensil, apparatus, implement, device, tool; deed, document

insular *(adj.)* detached, isolated, narrow, provincial
insurance *(n.)* security, indemnity, assurance, warrant
insure *(v.)* secure, warrant, protect, guarantee
intact *(adj.)* entire, whole, together
intangible *(adj.)* indefinite, uncertain, vague
integral *(adj.)* whole, entire, essential
intellect *(n.)* understanding, intelligence, mentality
intend *(v.)* purpose, aspire, aim, indicate, signify, denote
intense *(adj.)* deep, profound, heightened, vivid, impassioned, exaggerated, violent, excessive, keen, piercing, cutting, severe
intensity *(n.)* concentration, strength, power, fervor, passion, ardor, severity, depth, magnitude
intent *(adj.)* fixed, absorbed, focused
intent *(n.)* design, plan, aim
intercept *(v.)* obstruct, ambush, block, hijack
interest *(n.)* attention, excitement, curiosity, enthusiasm; claim, right, stake
interior *(adj.)* within, inside, inland, inner, internal, inward, central, inside
interlope *(v.)* interfere, intrude, meddle
intermediate *(adj.)* intervening, medium, intermediary, median, central, middle
intermediate *(adj.)* interval, interim, recess
intermix *(v.)* mix, mingle
intermittent *(adj.)* cyclic, recurring, periodic, recurrent, changing, irregular
intern *(v.)* detain, imprison, hold
intern *(n.)* train, apprentice, tutor
interpret *(v.)* translate, explain, render, delineate, define, describe
interrogate *(v.)* question, ask, examine
interrupt *(v.)* intervene, interfere, infringe
intersperse *(v.)* scatter, strew, sprinkle
intervene *(v.)* intercede, mediate, negotiate, reconcile
interview *(n.)* meeting, audience, conference
intimate *(adj.)* close, trusted, secret, special
intimate *(v.)* hint, allude, suggest
intimidate *(v.)* frighten, threaten, alarm
intolerant *(adj.)* dogmatic, bigoted, prejudiced
intoxicate *(v.)* inebriate, muddle, befuddle
intricacy *(n.)* elaborateness, complexity, difficulty
intrigue *(v.)* plot, scheme, delight, please, attract, charm, entertain, fascinate
intrinsic *(adj.)* essential, inborn, inherent
introduce *(v.)* advance, offer, propose, acquaint; add, enter, include
introvert *(n.)* loner, recluse
intrude *(v.)* encroach, trespass, interfere, meddle
invade *(v.)* attack, intrude. infringe, trespass, interfere
invaluable *(adj.)* priceless, expensive, dear, valuable
invective *(n.)* railing, abusive, tirade
invent *(v.)* create, discover, originate, devise, fashion, form, design, improvise, contrive, build
investigate *(v.)* inquire, review, examine, study
invigorate *(v.)* animate, energize, enliven, excite, exhilarate, freshen, stimulate
invincible *(adj.)* impregnable, invulnerable, powerful, strong, unconquerable
inviolate *(adj.)* hallowed, holy, intact, pure, sacred
invoice *(n.)* notice, statement, bill, receipt
invoke *(v.)* implore, solicit, summon
involve *(v.)* associate, commit, connect, comprise, connect, entangle, implicate, include, link
iota *(n.)* jot, particle, trace, scrap, grain, bit, speck
irascible *(adj.)* irritable, temperamental, testy, touchy
irate *(adj.)* enraged, furious, incensed, angry
irk *(v.)* vex, annoy, harass, disturb, bother
irony *(n.)* satire, ridicule, mockery, derision, sarcasm
irrevocable *(adj.)* permanent, indelible, inevitable
irritable *(adj.)* cranky, testy, touchy, huffy, peevish, petulant, surly, moody, churlish, grouchy, grumpy
island *(n.)* isle, bar, archipelago
isolate *(v.)* detach, insulate, confine, seclude, divide
itemize *(v.)* list, catalogue, enumerate, number, detail

J

jab *(v.)* poke, punch, hit, blow
jacket *(n.)* coat, tunic, jerkin, cape
jackpot *(n.)* bonanza, winnings, luck, profit, success
jaded *(adj.)* cold, impassive, indifferent, nonchalant, world-weary
jam *(n.)* conserve, marmalade, jelly; trouble, dilemma, problem, difficulty
jargon *(n.)* idiom, vernacular, colloquialism, localism, dialect, slang
jaunt *(n.)* excursion, trip, tour, journey, walk

jealous *(adj.)* envious, possessive, resentful
jeer *(v.)* deride, insult, mock, ridicule, taunt
jeopardize *(v.)* endanger, imperil, expose, venture, risk
jerk *(n.)* twitch, tic, shake, quiver; scamp, scoundrel, fool, rascal
jest *(v.)* joke, tease, mock, sneer
jewel *(n.)* prize, bauble, gem, trinket
jiggle *(v.)* shake, twitch, wiggle, jerk
jingle *(n.)* rhyme, verse, clangour
job *(n.)* employment, situation, position, calling, vocation, career, pursuit, business, profession, trade; task, assignment, undertaking, project, chore, errand, duty
jocular *(adj.)* comic, frolicsome, funny, witty
join *(v.)* unite, blend, combine, connect, couple, attach, link, fuse, entwine, associate
joke *(v.)* jest, quip, banter, laugh, play, frolic, wisecrack
jolt *(n.)* bump, bounce, blow, jerk, surprise, shock, surprise
jostle *(v.)* push, elbow, nudge
jot *(v.)* write, note, scribble, record
journal *(n.)* diary, chronicle, record; periodical, publication, newspaper, magazine, daily
journalist *(n.)* columnist, commentator, reporter
journey *(n.)* trip, tour, excursion, jaunt, travel
jovial *(adj.)* affable, amiable, merry, happy
jubilee *(n.)* anniversary, celebration, festival
judge *(n.)* moderator, arbiter, referee, umpire; analyst, critic, expert, specialist
judge *(v.)* hear, decide, adjudicate, rule
juice *(n.)* sap, extract, fluid, liquid
jumble *(n.)* clutter, mess, hodgepodge, confusion
junction *(n.)* joining, coupling, joint, union; crossroads, crossing, intersection
jungle *(n.)* tangle, wilderness, undergrowth, forest
junk *(n.)* scrap, waste, garbage, filth, trash
jurisdiction *(n.)* authority, range, province, scope, domain, extent, empire, sovereignty
just *(adj.)* precisely, exactly, correctly, perfectly, accurate; hardly, barely, scarcely; only, merely, simply, plainly; fair, impartial, equal, righteous
jut *(adj.)* extend, bulge, project
juvenile *(adj.)* childish, youthful, adolescent, teenage
juxtapose *(v.)* compare, contrast, match

K

keepsake *(n.)* memento, token, remembrance, reminder
kernel *(n.)* seed, grain, core, nut, germ
kettle *(n.)* vessel, cauldron, saucepan, stewpot, pot
kid *(n.)* child, son, daughter, boy, girl
kid *(v.)* mock, tease, joke
kidnap *(v.)* abduct, capture, shanghai
killjoy *(n.)* grouch, sourpuss, spoilsport
kiln *(n.)* dryer, oast, oven
kind *(adj.)* accommodating, agreeable, charitable, compassionate, considerate, generous, kindhearted, loving, obliging, sensitive, tactful, tender
kind *(n.)* classification, species, genus; type, sort, variety, description, denomination, designation
kindle *(v.)* fire, excite, light, ignite
kingdom *(n.)* realm, domain, country, empire, diligence, strain, stress, effort, dominions, territory
kinship *(n.)* affiliation, relationship, connection, alliance, family
knack *(n.)* dexterity, trick, skill, faculty, ability
knead *(v.)* work, shape, twist, press
knickknack *(n.)* bric-a-brac, ornament, trifle, bauble, trinket, showpiece, gewgaw
knife *(n.)* blade, dagger, stiletto, lancet, machete, scalpel, dirk
knit *(v.)* unite, join, intermingle, affiliate
knob *(n.)* bulge, protuberance, node, bump; handle, doorknob, latch
knot *(n.)* bond, tie, cinch, hitch, splice, group
knowledge *(n.)* information, learning, wisdom, enlightenment, expertise, awareness

L

label *(v.)* identify, mark, name, specify
labour *(n.)* work, activity, toil, operation, employment, undertaking, energy, industry, diligence, strain, stress, effort
lacerate *(v.)* tear, wound, cut, rip
lack *(n.)* deficiency, scarcity, insufficiency, inadequacy; need, privation, poverty, distress
laconic *(adj.)* concise, curt, succinct, terse
ladle *(n.)* spoon, skimmer, scoop
lady *(n.)* woman, female, matron, gentlewoman
lame *(adj.)* halt, unpaired, handicapped, limping
lament *(v.)* grieve, deplore, bemoan

lampoon *(v.)* satirize, burlesque, ridicule

land *(n.)* property, estate, tract, ranch, farm, lot; country, province, region, nation

landscape *(n.)* countryside, scenery, panorama, view

language *(n.)* expression, tongue, word, sign, signal, gesture, vocabulary, diction, dialect, idiom, vernacular, speech, jargon

lanky *(adj.)* lean, rangy, thin

lantern *(n.)* light, torch, lamp

lapse *(v.)* pass, void, slip, deteriorate, decline, weaken

larceny *(n.)* theft, burglary, thievery, robbery, crime

lascivious *(adj.)* bawdy, carnal, immoral, lewd, lurid, sensual, sexual

lass *(n.)* girl, woman, lady, damsel, maiden

lassitude *(adj.)* weariness, listlessness, fatigue

lasting *(adj.)* enduring, abiding, constant, permanent

latent *(adj.)* potential, undeveloped, dormant

lather *(n.)* foam, froth, bubbles

latitude *(n.)* freedom, degree, measure

latter *(adj.)* after, following, late, last, recent

laud *(v.)* glorify, honour, praise

laugh *(v.)* chuckle, snicker, titter, chortle, cackle, guffaw, giggle

lavatory *(n.)* basin, privy, bathroom, washroom, toilet

lavish *(adj.)* profuse, extravagant, generous, unsparing, plentiful

lawful *(adj.)* legal, legitimate, decreed, permitted, constitutional; legislated, enacted, official, enforced, protected, legitimized, established

lawyer *(n.)* attorney, solicitor, jurist, defender, counsel, solicitor, barrister, advocate

laxity *(n.)* slackness, negligence

layout *(n.)* arrangement, design, organization, plan

leave *(n.)* departure, farewell, consent, vacation

lazy *(adj.)* indolent, idle, sluggish, apathetic, loafing, flagging, slothful, lethargic

leader *(n.)* guide, conductor, director, manager, officer, captain, master, ruler, boss

leaflet *(n.)* brochure, handbill, circular, pamphlet reprimand

league *(n.)* union, alliance, group, unit, organization

leap *(v.)* jump, bound, spring, vault, bounce

learn *(v.)* acquire, read, master, ascertain, determine, unearth, hear, memorize, study

lethal *(adj.)* deadly, fatal, mortal, malignant, harmful

lethargy *(n.)* stupor, dullness, drowsiness

letter *(n.)* message, memo, note, memorandum, epistle, line, mail; symbol, character, type

leverage *(n.)* power, purchase; lift, hold, support

leviathan *(n.)* monster, beast, mammoth

levity *(n.)* flippancy, frivolity, silliness

lewd *(adj.)* smutty, indecent, sensual; wanton, lascivious, licentious, lecherous, dissolute, debauched, corrupt, depraved, vulgar

lexicon *(n.)* dictionary, vocabulary, glossary

liable *(adj.)* accountable, answerable, exposed, obliged; apt, inclined, likely, tending

liaison *(n.)* agent, connection, emissary, proxy; affair, intrigue, romance, tryst

liar *(n.)* deceiver, perjurer, falsifier, fibber

liberal *(adj.)* progressive, broad-minded, nonconformist, permissive, radical, tolerant; generous: indulgent, lavish, magnanimous

libertine *(n.)* lecher, pervert, rake, rouge

liberty *(n.)* emancipation, enfranchisement, rescue, freedom; leave, relaxation, rest, leisure, recreation; privilege, permission, decision, selection; rights, freedom, independence

license *(n.)* consent, authorization, permission, sanction; permit, certificate, registration; freedom, looseness, excess, immoderation, latitude

licit *(adj.)* authorized, lawful, sanctioned

lid *(n.)* cover, cap, top, roof, hood

lie *(v.)* falsify, prevaricate, deceive, misinform, exaggerate, distort, concoct, misrepresent, dissemble, delude; prostrate, recline, retire, rest, sleep

life *(n.)* being, entity, presence, consciousness, vitality; biography, story, memoir; duration, lifetime, span, generation, season, cycle; excitement, zeal

lift *(v.)* elevate, raise, hoist; steal, filch, pilfer

light *(adj.)* illuminated, radiant, luminous, bright; vivid, colourful, rich, clear; slight, frivolous, trivial, unimportant; lively, spirited, animated, active; ethereal, airy, fluffy, downy, dainty, thin, sheer, insubstantial, graceful

light-headed *(adj.)* inane, fickle, frivolous, silly; tired, delirious, dizzy, weak

light-hearted *(adj.)* gay, joyous, cheerful, happy

like *(v.)* enjoy, relish, savour, fancy; admire, esteem, approve; prefer, choose, desire, fancy

likely *(adj.)* probable, conceivable, rational, plausible, apt, tending, prone, liable

limb *(n.)* branch, arm, bough, offshoot; appendage, arm, leg, part

limit *(n.)* boundary, frontier, border, extent, extremity

limp *(adj.)* weak, pliant, flaccid, flabby, pliable, slack, loose, flimsy

line *(n.)* border, limit, boundary, edge, row, rank, file, order, arrangement, sequence, column, groove, profession, career, vocation; cord, filament; descent, pedigree, lineage, family, heredity

linear *(adj.)* successive, direct, straight

linger *(v.)* remain, loiter, tarry, lag, delay, dawdle, wait

lingerie *(n.)* underwear, dainties, unmentionables

linguist *(n.)* lexicographer, translator, grammarian

link *(n.)* loop, ring, coupling; seam, weld, intersection, fastening, splice, articulation, joint

liquid *(adj.)* watery, molten, moist, aqueous, liquefied, dissolved, melted, thawed, wet; running, splashing, thin, moving, viscous, fluid, juicy

list *(v.)* catalogue, register, tally, inventory, index; pitch, slant, incline

listen *(v.)* hear, heed, attend, overhear

litany *(n.)* form, ritual, recital, list

literacy *(n.)* scholarship, education, knowledge

literal *(adj.)* actually, exactly, strictly, verbatim

literate *(adj.)* lettered, learned, scholarly, educated

lithograph *(n.)* print, copy

litter *(n.)* debris, mess, jumble, hodgepodge, trash, clutter; brood, piglets, puppies, kittens, offspring

little *(adj.)* small, diminutive, tiny, wee, slight, miniature, puny; inadequate, inconsiderable, insufficient; shallow, petty, superficial, frivolous, trivial; base, weak, shallow, mean, petty

live *(v.)* exist, subsist, survive, breathe, be; relish, savour, experience; dwell, inhabit, abide; continue, remain, survive, endure, last

livelihood *(n.)* job, career, means, subsistence

lively *(adj.)* active, animated, brisk, energetic, spirited, vigorous, vivacious

load *(n.)* cargo, capacity, bundle; responsibility, charge, obligation, trust, duty

loan *(v.)* lend, provide, advance

loath *(adj.)* disinclined, unwilling, opposed

loathe *(v.)* detest, dislike, hate

lobby *(n.)* entryway, antechamber, foyer, hall, vestibule

locale *(n.)* vicinity, territory, district, area, region

locate *(v.)* discover, find, establish, determine, place, settle, inhabit, dwell

lodge *(n.)* retreat, inn, hostel, hotel, motel, resort, cabin, cottage; society, club, fraternity

lodge *(v.)* shelter, board, harbor, quarter; place: fix, leave, deposit, embed

logic *(n.)* reasoning, deduction, induction, thought

logy *(adj.)* lethargic, sluggish, dull

loiter *(v.)* linger, dawdle, idle, tarry, wait

lonely *(adj.)* abandoned, homesick, forlorn, deserted, lonesome, solitary, secluded

longing *(n.)* craving, yearning, pining, desire, wish

loom *(v.)* appear, rise, emerge; threaten, hulk, hover, approach

loop *(v.)* curve, encircle, connect, bend

loose *(adj.)* slack, free, careless; wanton, unrestrained, dissolute; unattached, disconnected, baggy, free; vague, random, obscure

loot *(n.)* plunder, spoils, take, booty

lopsided *(adj.)* uneven, unbalanced, tipped, irregular

lost *(adj.)* misplaced, mislaid, obscured, strayed, vanished; perplexed, puzzled; wasted, ruined

lotion *(n.)* cream, balm, salve, unguent, cosmetic

lounge *(n.)* sofa, couch, divan; room, bar, lobby, parlour, salon

love *(n.)* attachment, infatuation, rapture, ardor; respect, regard, admiration

lover *(n.)* suitor, sweetheart, admirer, escort, paramour, fiance, boyfriend, girlfriend, steady

low *(adj.)* crouched, sunken; muffled, hushed, quiet; sad, dejected, moody, blue; vulgar, base, mean, coarse; moderate, inexpensive, cheap

loyal *(adj.)* fair, true, dependable, firm, faithful

loyalty *(n.)* fidelity, allegiance, faithfulness, constancy, attachment, support, devotion

lucid *(adj.)* clear, obvious, unmistakable; bright, luminous; rational, normal

luck *(n.)* prosperity, wealth, windfall, blessings; fate, opportunity, break, accident

lucrative *(adj.)* profitable, fruitful, productive, gainful

ludicrous *(adj.)* absurd, ridiculous, laughable, farcical, incongruous
luggage *(n.)* baggage, trunks, bags, valises
lukewarm *(adj.)* cool, tepid, chilly
lull *(n.)* pause, hiatus, stillness, hush, silence
lull *(v.)* soothe, quiet, calm
luminous *(adj.)* lighted, glowing, radiant, bright
lump *(n.)* mass, clump, block, chunk, hunk
lunacy *(n.)* madness, dementia, mania; foolishness, silliness
lunge *(v.)* thrust, surge, bound, jump
lure *(v.)* entice, enchant, bewitch, allure
lurid *(adj.)* ghastly, gruesome, sensational
luscious *(adj.)* toothsome, palatable, delicious
lush *(adj.)* verdant, dense, grassy; rich, juicy, succulent; elaborate, extravagant, luxurious, ornamental, ornate
lust *(n.)* desire, appetite, passion, sensuality
luster *(n.)* brightness, radiance, glow, brilliance, light
luxurious *(adj.)* comfortable, affluent, expensive, rich
lyrical *(adj.)* melodious, sweet, rhythmical, poetic

M

machine *(n.)* contrivance, device, implement
macrocosm *(n.)* universe, world
made *(adj.)* fashioned, built, formed, manufactured
magazine *(n.)* periodical, journal, publication
magic *(n.)* occultism, wizardry, sorcery, divination, witchcraft, voodooism, soothsaying
magnanimous *(adj.)* charitable, noble, unselfish, forgiving, generous
magnate *(n.)* tycoon, mogul
magnetic *(adj.)* alluring, appealing, attractive, irresistible, captivating, fascinating, charming
magnificent *(adj.)* splendid, grand, exalted, majestic
magnify *(v.)* amplify, expand, increase, enlarge
magnitude *(n.)* extent, quantity; importance, greatness, consequence, significance
maim *(v.)* disfigure, mutilate, disable, damage, hurt
main *(adj.)* principal, chief, leading, dominant, foremost
maintain *(v.)* uphold, support, sustain, affirm, defend; state, attest, declare, say; preserve, keep, conserve, reserve, save, manage
majesty *(n.)* grandeur, nobility, greatness
make *(v.)* manufacture, construct, fabricate, assemble, fashion, produce, build, form; create, originate, generate, devise, conceive, invent; constrain, compel, coerce; wage, conduct, engage, prepare, ready, arrange, adjust, cook; earn, gain; reach, arrive
maladroit *(adj.)* awkward, bungling, clumsy, inept
malady *(n.)* affliction, ailment, disease, sickness
malice *(n.)* hatred, spite, animosity, resentment
malign *(v.)* vilify, defame, slander
mall *(n.)* market, shop, arcade
malodorous *(adj.)* stinking, fetid
mammoth *(adj.)* huge, large, colossal
manacle *(v.)* chain, handcuff, shackle
manage *(v.)* control, lead, oversee, mastermind, engineer, handle, supervise; contrive, accomplish, effect, achieve; endure, survive
mandatory *(adj.)* imperative, compulsory, obligatory
maneuver *(v.)* plot, scheme, contrive, design, conspire
manger *(n.)* trough, tub, crib
mania *(n.)* craze, lunacy, madness, desire, obsession
manifest *(adj.)* apparent, clear, evident, obvious
manipulate *(v.)* control, shape, mold, form
mannequin *(n.)* model, dummy, display
manner *(n.)* conduct, deportment, demeanor, behavior; custom, habit, use, way, practice
mansion *(n.)* house, villa, hall, estate, home
mantle *(n.)* cloak, blanket, role, job
manual *(n.)* handbook, guidebook, reference
manufacture *(v.)* make, fabricate, produce, build
manuscript *(n.)* book, paper, document, composition
mar *(v.)* damage, spoil, disfigure, harm, scratch, deface
margin *(n.)* edge, border, lip, shore, boundary
marine *(adj.)* nautical, maritime, oceanic
mark *(v.)* brand, imprint, label, identify, earmark; signify, denote, mean, characterize, qualify
market *(v.)* sell, trade, vend, exchange, barter
marry *(v.)* wed, espouse; join, unite, combine
marsh *(n.)* swamp, morass, bog, quagmire
martyr *(n.)* saint, victim, sufferer, offering, scapegoat
marvel *(v.)* wonder, awe, stare

mash *(v.)* crush, bruise, squash, pulverize, press
mask *(v.)* disguise, cloak, conceal, veil, hide
massacre *(v.)* slaughter, kill, exterminate, annihilate
massage *(v.)* rub, knead, stimulate, caress
massive *(adj.)* weighty, bulky, huge, cumbersome, large
master *(v.)* conquer, subdue, humble, succeed, overcome; understand, comprehend
match *(n.)* equal, peer, equivalent, counterpart, approximation; race, rivalry, competition
material *(adj.)* physical, real, tangible; essential
maternal *(adj.)* motherly, protective, nurturing
matrimony *(n.)* marriage, wedlock, union
matrix *(n.)* mold, die
matter *(n.)* substance, material, constituents, object, thing, element; subject, interest, focus, theme; affair, concern
mature *(adj.)* developed, ripe, grown, cultured
maudlin *(adj.)* tearful, sentimental, over-emotional
maxim *(n.)* saying, proverb, aphorism, adage, epithet
maximum *(adj.)* greatest, supreme, highest, best
mayhem *(n.)* crime, violence, chaos
maze *(n.)* labyrinth, tangle, convolution, intricacy
meager *(adj.)* lean, scanty, spare, wanting
mean *(adj.)* humble, servile, pitiful, vicious, contemptible, despicable, degenerate, unscrupulous; base, low, vulgar, common
mean *(v.)* signify, symbolize, imply, suggest, designate, denote
meander *(v.)* wander, wind, roam, flow, ramble
meaning *(n.)* sense, import, definition, implication, intent, connotation, context, significance
means *(n.)* machinery, method, system, agency; wealth, resources, substance, property
measure *(n.)* degree, dimension, capacity, weight, volume, distance, quantity, area, mass; rule, test, example, norm, criterion
mechanical *(adj.)* automated, programmed, automatic; stereotyped, unchanging, monotonous
medal *(n.)* badge, award, commemoration, decoration
meddle *(v.)* interfere, interlope, intervene, encroach
mediate *(v.)* arbitrate, negotiate, intervene
medication *(n.)* remedy, pill, vaccination
mediocre *(adj.)* middling, average, common, ordinary
meditation *(n.)* contemplation, reflection, thought
medley *(n.)* mixture, conglomeration, variety
meek *(adj.)* humble, unassuming, passive, docile
meet *(v.)* engage, battle, match, face; touch, coincide, join, intersect; assemble, gather, converge, congregate; satisfy, fulfill, suffice
melancholy *(adj.)* gloomy, depressed, dispirited, sad
mellow *(v.)* ripen, mature, age
melodramatic *(adj.)* artificial, sensational, exaggerated
memento *(n.)* keepsake, reminder, souvenir
memoir *(n.)* biography, autobiography, account
memorable *(adj.)* unforgettable, notable, significant, monumental, eventful, exceptional, singular
memorize *(v.)* retain, learn, remember
menace *(v.)* threaten, intimidate, portend
mend *(v.)* repair, patch, fix, aid, remedy, cure, correct
medial *(n.)* servant, domestic, maid, lackey
mental *(adj.)* thoughtful, rational, intellectual, subconscious, telepathic, psychic
mention *(v.)* remark, comment, infer, intimate, suggest
merchandise *(v.)* advertise, sell, trade, market
merciful *(adj.)* lenient, softhearted, mild, tolerant
mere *(adj.)* minor, insignificant, little
merit *(n.)* worth, excellence, honour, character, virtue
merriment *(n.)* mirth, joy, gaiety, happiness, humour
mesh *(v.)* engage, coincide, suit, agree, fit
mess *(n.)* confusion, disorder, jumble, clutter
message *(n.)* communication, tidings, information
metamorphosis *(n.)* transformation, change, conversion
metaphorical *(adj.)* figurative, symbolical, allegorical
method *(n.)* procedure, process, technique, system
meticulous *(adj.)* mindful, cautious, thorough
miff *(v.)* offend, annoy, upset
might *(n.)* power, ability, strength, force, sway
migrate *(v.)* move, emigrate, leave
mild *(adj.)* moderate, gentle, meek, temperate

militant *(adj.)* aggressive, warlike, belligerent
mimic *(v.)* imitate, copy, simulate, impersonate; mock, burlesque, caricature, ridicule
mind *(n.)* mentality, perception, judgment, wisdom, intellect; intention, inclination, determination
miniature *(adj.)* small, tiny, little, minute
minister *(n.)* clergyman, ambassador, delegate
minister *(v.)* attend, tend, help
minor *(adj.)* inferior, secondary, lesser, trivial
miracle *(n.)* marvel, revelation, wonder
mirage *(n.)* illusion, phantasm, hallucination, fantasy
mirth *(n.)* gaiety, laughter, frolic, jollity, fun
miscellaneous *(adj.)* diverse, unmatched, unlike; mixed, muddled, scattered, confused, disordered
mischievous *(adj.)* playful, roguish, naughty
miser *(n.)* niggard, skinflint, money-grubber
miserable *(adj.)* wretched, distressed, troubled
mislead *(v.)* delude, trick, beguile, dupe, misrepresent
miss *(n.)* failure, slip, blunder, mishap, mistake, deviation, woman, lass, maid, female, girl
mission *(n.)* purpose, charge, commission
missionary *(n.)* apostle, evangelist, messenger
mist *(n.)* vapour, cloud, rain, haze, fog
mistake *(v.)* err, blunder, misjudge, botch, bungle
mix *(v.)* blend, combine, mingle, stir, unite; confuse, jumble, tangle; associate, fraternize
moan *(v.)* groan, wail, whine
mob *(n.)* throng, crowd, rabble, multitude, horde
mobile *(adj.)* movable, loose, free
mock *(adj.)* imitation, counterfeit, sham
mode *(n.)* manner, fashion, method
model *(n.)* example, prototype, ideal; pattern, design, standard; poser, sitter, mannequin, nude
moderate *(adj.)* inexpensive, cheap, economical; modest, temperate, calm, reserved; tolerant, restrained, cautious; temperate, mild
modem *(adj.)* stylish, chic, smart, fashionable; contemporary, new, current, renovated, improved
modest *(adj.)* humble, unassuming, meek, diffident; plain, seemly, tasteful, unadorned, unaffected; moderate, reasonable, inexpensive, economical; proper, pure, chaste, seemly, decent; lowly, simple, unaffected
modify *(v.)* change, vary, alter
moist *(adj.)* wet, humid, dank, moistened, damp
mold *(n.)* form, matrix, shape, frame, pattern, cast, growth
molest *(v.)* harm, bother, annoy, irritate, badger
molten *(adj.)* melted, liquefied, flowing
moment *(n.)* time, instant, jiffy, importance, significance, note, consequence
momentum *(n.)* impetus, impulse, drive, energy
monetary *(adj.)* pecuniary, financial, fiscal
monologue *(n.)* speech, talk, discourse, address
monopoly *(n.)* trust, syndicate, cartel
monster *(n.)* chimera, werewolf; abnormality; criminal, rascal, savage
monument *(n.)* memorial, shrine, statue, monolith
mood *(n.)* state, condition, temper, humour, disposition
moot *(adj.)* disputable, arguable, debatable
moral *(adj.)* virtuous, proper, scrupulous, honorable, aboveboard, principled, chaste, noble
morale *(n.)* assurance, resolve, spirit, confidence
morbid *(adj.)* sickly, unhealthy, ailing; gloomy, melancholic, depressed
morning *(n.)* dawn, daybreak, cockcrow, sun-up
morose *(adj.)* surly, downcast, gloomy
morsel *(n.)* piece, bite, chunk, bit, part
mortal *(adj.)* malignant, lethal, deadly; human, transient, perishable, temporary
motel *(n.)* hotel, cabin, inn, resort
motif *(n.)* theme, melody, design
motion *(n.)* change, act, action, passage; suggestion, proposition, plan
motto *(n.)* maxim, adage, saw, aphorism, sentiment, slogan, catchword, axiom, proverb, saying
mound *(n.)* pile, heap, knoll, hill
mount *(v.)* ascend, rise, scale, clamber
mourn *(v.)* grieve, sorrow, bemoan, languish, pine
move *(v.)* arouse, stir, stimulate; impel, actuate; introduce, submit; go, walk, run, travel, progress, proceed, traverse
mow *(v.)* cut, scythe, reap, harvest
muddle *(v.)* confuse, disarrange, mix, jumble, snarl
muffler *(n.)* scarf, neckpiece, choker
mumble *(v.)* mutter, utter, murmur
munch *(v.)* chew, masticate, crunch, bite, eat
mundane *(adj.)* normal, ordinary, everyday

municipality *(n.)* community, district, village, town
murder *(n.)* homicide, carnage, slaying, butchery
murky *(adj.)* gloomy, dark, dim, dusky, dingy, dirty
muscular *(adj.)* brawny, powerful, husky, strong
museum *(n.)* collection, archives, treasury, depository
music *(n.)* melody, harmony, tune, air, strain
mutation *(n.)* change, modification, deviation
mute *(adj.)* speechless, silent, bewildered, unspoken
mutiny *(n.)* insurrection, revolt, resistance, revolution
mutter *(v.)* mumble, murmur, grumble, complain
myriad *(n.)* variable, innumerable, endless, multiple
mystical *(adj.)* occult, spiritual, mysterious, secret
myth *(n.)* legend, fable, saga, parable, tale, story

N

nab *(n.)* grab, take, snatch, seize
nag *(v.)* scold, vex, annoy, pester, bother
naive *(adj.)* unaffected, artless, innocent, unsophisticated, gullible, credulous, trusting, inexperienced
naked *(adj.)* uncovered, unclad, bare, exposed
name *(n.)* reputation, renown, fame; title, designation; star, hero, lion, celebrity
narrate *(v.)* tell, recite, describe, reveal, report
nasty *(adj.)* offensive, foul, gross, vulgar; indecent, immodest, smutty, lewd, sarcastic, mean
nation *(n.)* people, populace, community, society, state, realm, country, domain
natural *(adj.)* original, fundamental, inherited, native; characteristic, usual, customary, ingenuous, artless, spontaneous, real, actual, tangible, physical
naughty *(adj.)* mischievous, wayward, roguish
neat *(adj.)* tidy, trim, prim, spruce, dapper, orderly, precise; clever, dexterous, skillful, agile
necessary *(adj.)* essential, important, requisite, required, imperative, compulsory, mandatory
nefarious *(adj.)* vile, wicked, evil, foul, sinful
negative *(n.)* refusal, contradiction, disavowal, refutation, denial; picture, film, image, plate
neglect *(v.)* disregard, disdain, affront, ignore, spurn; evade, defer, procrastinate, postpone
negotiate *(v.)* bargain, mediate, conciliate, arbitrate
niche *(n.)* recess, cranny, position, vocation
night *(n.)* evening, nightfall, twilight, bedtime
nimble *(adj.)* light, quick, spry, active, graceful; alert, bright, clever, intelligent
noble *(adj.)* exalted, courtly, lordly, dignified, distinguished; meritorious, virtuous, refined, chivalrous; aristocratic, patrician; stately, impressive, imposing
noise *(n.)* sound, clamor, racket, fracas, din, uproar
nomad *(n.)* wanderer, migrant, vagabond, traveller
nominate *(v.)* name, appoint, propose, designate
nonchalant *(adj.)* casual, unconcerned, impassive, detached, indifferent; careless, negligent, trifling
nonsense *(n.)* inanity, trash, senselessness, fun, jest, absurdity
noose *(n.)* loop, hitch, lasso, rope
nostalgia *(n.)* longing, homesickness, wistfulness
nosy *(adj.)* snoopy, curious, inquisitive, interested
notch *(n.)* nick, indent, cut, dent, groove
noted *(adj.)* well-known, celebrated, notorious, famous
notice *(n.)* warning, notification, announcement, attention, interest
notion *(n.)* whim, fancy, idea, assumption
notorious *(adj.)* infamous, known, disreputable
nourish *(v.)* feed, encourage, sustain
novel *(adj.)* new, strange, odd, unique, unusual
novel *(n.)* story, tale, fiction, romance
novice *(n.)* beginner, neophyte, amateur
noxious *(adj.)* injurious, harmful, deadly
nudge *(v.)* poke, bump, tap, push, touch
nugget *(n.)* lump, ingot, chunk, rock
nuisance *(n.)* bother, annoyance, vexation, trouble; breach, infraction, affront
null *(adj.)* void, invalid, vain, unsanctioned
numb *(v.)* deaden, stupefy, paralyze, stun, dull
numerous *(adj.)* many, copious, diverse, infinite
nuptials *(n.)* wedding, marriage, matrimony
nurse *(v.)* tend, minister, aid, treat
nurture *(v.)* nourish, feed, sustain
nutritious *(adj.)* nourishing, wholesome, healthful

O

oath *(n.)* promise, vow, pledge; profanity, curse, swearword, blasphemy
obdurate *(n.)* stubborn, hardhearted, firm
obedient *(adj.)* dutiful, loyal, devoted, deferential, faithful; docile, submissive, compliant

obese *(adj.)* fat, corpulent, plump, stout
obey *(v.)* yield, conform, submit, serve comply
object *(n.)* article, gadget; goal, aim, objective
object *(v.)* disapprove, protest, dispute, complain
obligate *(v.)* bind, restrict, constrain, force
oblige *(v.)* accommodate, assist, aid, contribute, help; constrain, bind, force, compel, coerce
oblivion *(n.)* obscurity, void, emptiness, nothing
obnoxious *(adj.)* offensive, annoying, disagreeable
obscure *(adj.)* vague, indistinct, unclear, hazy, arcane
observant *(adj.)* alert, discerning, perceptive, bright
observe *(v.)* watch, scrutinize, see, notice; remark, note, mention; commemorate, dedicate, solemnize; comply, follow, obey
obsessed *(adj.)* haunted, beset, controlled, troubled
obsession *(n.)* fixation, fascination, passion, mania
obsolete *(adj.)* antiquated, archaic, out-of-date
obstacle *(n.)* hindrance, restriction, obstruction
obstruct *(v.)* block, interfere, bar, hinder, prevent
obtain *(v.)* get, take, acquire, seize, procure
obvious *(adj.)* apparent, perceptible, open, clear, intelligible, comprehensible, understandable
occasion *(n.)* event, occurrence, incident, happening
occult *(adj.)* hidden, mysterious, supernatural, secret
occupation *(n.)* vocation, employment, job, profession
occupy *(v.)* seize, conquer, invade, pervade, engage, absorb, engross, involve, fascinate
occur *(v.)* happen, transpire, befall
odd *(adj.)* unusual, unique, strange; single, sole, unpaired, unmatched, lone
odious *(adj.)* hateful, offensive, repulsive
odour *(n.)* smell, perfume, fragrance, bouquet
offense *(n.)* misdeed, crime, wrong, insult, injury, hurt
offer *(v.)* present, tender, propose, submit
offer *(n.)* proposal, submission, attempt
offhand *(adj.)* impromptu, informal, improvised
offspring *(n.)* child, progeny, issue, descendant, heir
ointment *(n.)* salve, lubricant, lotion, cream, balm
old *(adj.)* aged, elderly, venerable, seasoned, enfeebled; archaic, prehistoric, antique
omen *(n.)* warning, portent, augury, indication, sign
omit *(v.)* exclude, drop, skip, overlook, disregard
omnipotent *(adj.)* all-powerful, almighty
omnipresent *(adj.)* universal, pervasive, ubiquitous
once *(adj.), (adv.)* formerly, previously, earlier
only *(adj.)* solely, exclusively, entirely, totally; simply, barely, hardly; sole, single, isolated, unique
onset *(n.)* beginning, opening, start, origin
ooze *(v.)* leak, seep, exude, flow
opaque *(adj.)* dim, dusky, darkened, murky, gloomy
open *(adj.)* clear, divulged, revealed, unobstructed; free, public; unguarded, accessible; frank, plain, candid, straightforward
operate *(v.)* functional, work, serve, run, percolate; manipulate, conduct, administer
opinion *(n.)* belief, view, sentiment, conception
opponent *(n.)* rival, competitor, adversary, antagonist
oppose *(v.)* contradict, dispute, defy, confront, resist; fight, compete, encounter, assail, storm, clash
oppress *(v.)* harass, maltreat, abuse, bother
optimal *(adj.)* favourable, desirable, optimum
optimism *(n.)* faith, cheerfulness, confidence, enthusiasm, expectation, certainty
option *(n.)* choice, selection, alternative
opulence *(n.)* riches, wealth, affluence
oracle *(n.)* prophet, seer, sage, fortune teller
oral *(adj.)* spoken, vocal, verbal, uttered, voiced
ordain *(v.)* establish, install, appoint; destine, fate, consecrate, invest, bless
order *(n.)* arrange, plan, system, command, stipulation, mandate, injunction; class, kind, hierarchy, classification, progression, succession, series
order *(v.)* classify, organize, direct, instruct, require; buy, secure, request
ordinance *(n.)* law, direction, mandate
ordinary *(adj.)* usual, normal, common; average, mediocre, accepted, typical, characteristic
organise *(v.)* arrange, systematize, coordinate, classify; establish, build, found, plan, formulate
orientation *(n.)* familiarization, introduction
originate *(v.)* introduce, found, start, begin
ornament *(n.)* decoration, embellishment, adornment, beautification
ornate *(adj.)* showy, gaudy, adorned, embellished
orphan *(n.)* foundling, waif, stray
oust *(v.)* eject, expel, discharge, evict, dislodge

outbreak *(n.)* explosion, outburst, commotion, tumult; violence, mutiny, revolution
outburst *(n.)* discharge, eruption, outbreak
outcast *(n.)* exile, fugitive, vagabond, undesirable, refugee
outcome *(n.)* upshot, consequence, result
outcry *(n.)* complaint, clamor, objection
outfit *(v.)* supply, equip, provide
outlandish *(adj.)* foreign, grotesque, queer, rude
outlaw *(v.)* forbid, ban, banish, condemn
outlook *(n.)* viewpoint, scope, vision, prospect, likelihood, possibility, opportunity, probability
outrage *(v.)* offend, wrong, affront, insult
outright *(adj.)* unmitigated, unconditional, obvious
outside *(adj.)* outermost, external, outer
outskirts *(n.)* suburbs, limits, boundary, edge
outwit *(v.)* trick, bewilder, confuse, deceive
over *(adj.)* above, overhead, higher; beyond, past, farther; accomplished, finished
overcast *(adj.)* cloudy, gloomy, dark
overcome *(v.)* conquer, overwhelm, vanquish
overconfident *(n.)* reckless, impudent, heedless, rash
overdo *(v.)* amplify, overreach, exaggerate, enhance; tire, fatigue, exhaust, overtax
overdue *(adj.)* late, delayed, belated, tardy
overhaul *(v.)* recondition, modernize, renew, repair
overpower *(v.)* overwhelm, master, subjugate, defeat
overrate *(v.)* overvalue, magnify, exaggerate
oversee *(v.)* superintend, superwise, manage
oversight *(n.)* failure, overlooking, mistake, error
overt *(adj.)* apparent, open, obvious, public
overture *(n.)* suggestion, advance, tender, prelude, prologue, preface, introduction
overwhelm *(v.)* defeat, overcome, overthrow, conquer; bewilder, confound, confuse, surprise
own *(v.)* acknowledge, grant, admit, declare; possess, hold, have, enjoy, retain, keep

P

pace *(n.)* step, gait, movement, speed
pacify *(v.)* calm, soothe, conciliate, appease, placate
padding *(n.)* stuffing, wadding, waste, filling
pagan *(adj.)* heathen, unchristian, idolatrous
page *(n.)* leaf, sheet, folio, side, surface, recto, verso
page *(v.)* call, summon, seek
pageant *(n.)* parade, celebration, pomp
paint *(v.)* sketch, picture, depict; brush, swab, daub, cover, spread
palace *(n.)* manor, mansion, castle
palpitate *(v.)* tremble, quiver, pulsate
paltry *(adj.)* worthless, small, insignificant, trifling
pamper *(v.)* overindulge, spoil, pet, humour, gratify, coddle, please
pandemonium *(n.)* noise, disorder, uproar, anarchy, riot, confusion
pang *(n.)* pain, throb, sting, bite
panic *(n.)* dread, alarm, fright, fear
panorama *(n.)* view, spectacle, scenery, prospect
pant *(v.)* gasp, desire, wheeze, throb, palpitate
pantomime *(n.)* sign, charade, mime
pantry *(n.)* storage, provisions, storeroom, larder, cupboard, closet, room
pants *(n.)* trousers, breeches, slacks, jeans, overalls, cords, shorts, corduroys, pantaloons, chaps, knickers, bloomers, rompers
parable *(n.)* fable, allegory, moral, story, tale
parade *(v.)* march, demonstrate, display, exhibit
paradox *(n.)* mystery, enigma, ambiguity, puzzle
paraphernalia *(n.)* trappings, equipment, gear
parasite *(n.)* dependent, sponger, hanger-on, toady
parch *(v.)* scorch, dry, shrivel, desiccate, dehydrate
pardon *(v.)* exonerate, clear, absolve, reprieve, acquit, liberate, discharge, free, release, forgive, condone, overlook, exculpate, excuse
parental *(adj.)* paternal, maternal, familial, genetic
park *(n.)* plaza, square, lawn, green, promenade, tract, grounds, woodland, meadow
parody *(v.)* mimic, copy, caricature, imitate, joke
parole *(v.)* release, discharge, pardon, liberate, free
parson *(n.)* clergyman, cleric, preacher, minister
partial *(adj.)* incomplete, unfinished; prejudiced, unfair, influenced, biased, inclined
participate *(v.)* compete, play, strive, engage
particle *(n.)* jot, scrap, atom, molecule, fragment, piece, shred, bit, part
partition *(n.)* division, distribution, barrier, separation, wall, obstruction
partner *(n.)* associate, worker, ally, comrade
party *(n.)* affair, reception, gathering, function; group, company, crowd, assembly; organization, faction

passage *(n.)* journey, voyage, crossing, trek; passageway, entrance, hall; excerpt, section, portion, paragraph, quote
passenger *(n.)* traveller, commuter
passion *(n.)* feeling, craving, desire, emotion
passive *(adj.)* complacent, inert, lifeless, idle
passport *(n.)* pass, permit, visa, identification
password *(n.)* countersign, watchword, identification
past *(adj.)* former, preceding, foregoing, earlier
pastor *(n.)* priest, rector, clergyman, minister
pasture *(n.)* grass, grazing, meadow, field
pat *(v.)* tap, touch, stroke, pet, rub
patch *(n.)* piece, bit, scrap, spot
patch *(v.)* repair, darn, mend
path *(n.)* trail, way, track, byway
pathetic *(adj.)* sad, touching, affecting, moving, pitiful
pathos *(n.)* pity, sorrow, grief
patience *(n.)* forbearance, fortitude, composure, endurance, perseverance, persistence
patient *(adj.)* submissive, forbearing, unruffled, imperturbable, passive, persevering, calm
patriarch *(n.)* ruler, master, ancestor, chief
patriot *(n.)* statesman, nationalist, loyalist, chauvinist
pattern *(n.)* model, original, guide, copy
pause *(v.)* stop, halt, cease, interrupt, suspend; reflect, deliberate
payment *(n.)* reimbursement, restitution, refund, reparation; portion, part
peace *(n.)* pacification, conciliation, agreement; tranquillity, harmony, silence, stillness; composure, contentment
peak *(n.)* summit, zenith, height, summit
peculiar *(adj.)* unusual, wonderful, singular, outlandish, strange; unique, characteristic, eccentric
pedestal *(n.)* base, stand, foundation, support
peek *(n.)* sight, glimpse, glance, look, spy
peep *(v.)* chirp, twitter, squeak, chirrup
peeve *(v.)* irritate, annoy, anger, bother
penalize *(v.)* chasten, castigate, punish
penchant *(n.)* inclination, taste, bias
pendant *(n.)* locket, lavaliere, decoration, jewellery
pending *(adj.)* continuing, awaiting, undecided
penetrate *(v.)* pierce, perforate, puncture
perceive *(v.)* observe, note, look, notice; comprehend, sense, grasp
perch *(v.)* roost, land, rest, sit
peremptory *(adj.)* decisive, final, imperious, dictatorial
perforate *(v.)* bore, pierce, drill, slit, stab, penetrate
perform *(v.)* accomplish, do, achieve, fulfill, discharge, effect, complete, finish, realize; enact, show, exhibit, display, dramatize, execute
perfume *(n.)* scent, fragrance, aroma, odor
perilous *(adj.)* precarious, unsafe, dangerous
period *(n.)* epoch, era, age, end, limit, conclusion
periphery *(n.)* circumference, perimeter, border
perjury *(v.)* false statement, falsify, lie
permanent *(adj.)* fixed, enduring, abiding, continuing, lasting, imperishable, persevering, constant
permeate *(v.)* penetrate, pervade, saturate, fill
permission *(n.)* liberty, consent, license, authorization, approval, sanction, endorsement, affirmation
perpetrate *(v.)* perform, commit, act, do
perpetual *(adj.)* continual, unceasing, constant, endless; repetitious, repeating, recurrent
perplex *(v.)* puzzle, confound, bewilder, confuse
persecute *(v.)* oppress, harass, victimize, abuse
perseverance *(n.)* grit, resolution, pluck, determination
persist *(v.)* persevere, pursue, strive, continue, endure
person *(n.)* individual, being, character, personage
personal *(adj.)* private, secret, confidential; individual, peculiar, particular, special
personify *(v.)* represent, symbolize, exemplify
personnel *(n.)* employees, workers, group, staff
perspective *(n.)* view, vista, aspect, attitude, outlook
persuade *(v.)* influence, induce, convince, cajole
pertain *(v.)* belong, relate, refer, concern
perturb *(v.)* disturb, pester, worry, irritate, bother
pervade *(v.)* penetrate, spread, suffuse, permeate
perverse *(adj.)* deviant, wayward, delinquent, bad
pervert *(u.)* corrupt, ruin, vitiate, divert
pessimism *(n.)* unhappiness, gloom, sadness
pester *(v.)* annoy, harass, provoke, bother

petition *(n.)* request, prayer, supplication, appeal
petrified *(adj.)* stone, hardened, mineralized, firm
petty *(adj.)* small, contemptible, insignificant, frivolous, trivial, unimportant
phantasm *(n.)* vision, illusion, specter
phenomenal *(adj.)* extraordinary, unique, remarkable
philanthropic *(adj.)* benevolent, humanitarian, kind
phlegmatic *(adj.)* calm, sluggish, indifferent
phobia *(n.)* avoidance, aversion, hatred, resentment
phony *(adj.)* affected, imitation, artificial, false
physical *(adj.)* material, corporeal, visible, tangible, palpable, substantial, real
physique *(n.)* structure, build, constitution, body
pick *(v.)* choose, select, separate; gather, pluck, pull
picture *(n.)* view, photograph, image, portrait; description, depiction, portrayal
picturesque *(adj.)* charming, pictorial, scenic, graphic, striking, arresting, quaint
piece *(n.)* part, portion, share, section
pierce *(v.)* penetrate, stab, probe
piety *(n.)* reverence, devotion, devoutness, veneration, grace
pile *(n.)* heap, collection, mass, quantity
pilgrim *(n.)* traveller, wayfarer, wanderer, sojourner
pill *(n.)* tablet, capsule, pellet, medicine, drug
pillage *(v.)* plunder, loot, rob, destroy, steal
pillow *(n.)* cushion, pad, support, headrest
pinnacle *(n.)* apex, zenith, crest, summit, climax
pious *(adj.)* reverent, devout, divine, holy, religious
piracy *(n.)* robbery, theft, pillage, holdup
pitch *(n.)* slant, incline, angle, grade; throw, toss, hurl, cast; frequency, tone, sound
pith *(n.)* center, essence, heart, core
pity *(n.)* compassion, charity, tenderness, kindliness, benevolence, clemency, humanity, sympathy
pivot *(v.)* turn, whirl, swivel, rotate
place *(n.)* position, point, spot; locality, locus, site, area, region; status, position
plague *(n.)* pestilence, illness, epidemic
plain *(adj.)* obvious, open, manifest, clear, understandable; simple, unadorned, unpretentious, mod est; ordinary, everyday, commonplace; blunt, out spoken, candid, impolite, rude
plan *(n.)* design, scheme, project, idea, undertaking, plot, conspiracy, strategy, arrangement, layout, disposition, order
plateau *(n.)* tableland, elevation, hill
plausible *(adj.)* convincing, probable, credible, likely
player *(n.)* athlete, contestant, actor, performer
playful *(adj.)* joking, whimsical, comical, funny
playwright *(n.)* writer, author, tragedian
plea *(n.)* appeal, request, supplication, pleading
pleasant *(adj.)* affable, agreeable, obliging, charming, gracious, amiable, polite, civii, cordial, sociable
please *(v.)* gratify, delight, satisfy
pleasure *(n.)* enjoyment, delight, happiness, amuse ment, preference; desire
pledge *(n.)* security, surety, guarantee, agreement
plentiful *(adj.)* bountiful, prolific, profuse, lavish, extravagant, copious, abundant, abounding
plenty *(n.)* abundance, lavishness, deluge, torrent, bounty, profusion, avalanche
plight *(n.)* condition, dilemma, state
plump *(adj.)* obese, stout, fleshy, fat
plunge *(v.)* cast, fall, rush, dive, jump
poach *(v.)* steal, filch, pilfer, smuggle
poetic *(adj.)* lyrical, romantic, imaginative
poetry *(n.)* verse, rhythm, rhyme, poesy
poignant *(adj.)* penetrating, moving, touching
point *(v.)* indicate, show, name, denote; direct, guide, steer, influence, lead
pointless *(adj.)* prosaic, trivial, unnecessary; ineffective, useless, impotent, incompetent, weak
poise *(n.)* carriage, bearing, grace, composure, dignity
poisonous *(adj.)* noxious, venomous, toxic, harmful
poke *(v.)* jab, punch, crowd, push,
polish *(v.)* smooth, burnish, finish, shine
polite *(adj.)* polished, mannerly, amiable, gracious, cordial, diplomatic, civil, sociable, respectful
pollute *(v.)* soil, defile, stain, dirty
pompous *(adj.)* pretentious, arrogant, haughty, proud
ponder *(v.)* meditate, think, deliberate, consider
poor *(adj.)* indigent, penniless, destitute, needy, starved, beggared, broke, weak, puny, feeble, infirm; mediocre, shoddy, deficient, cheap, flimsy
poppycock *(n.)* drivel, nonsense, gibberish
populace *(n.)* people, multitudes, masses, people
popular *(adj.)* liked, favourite, beloved, celebrated, admired, famous, widespread

porous *(adj.)* absorbent, pervious, permeable
portable *(adj.)* movable, transportable, transferable
portend *(v.)* foretell, predict, herald
portion *(n.)* part, scrap, fragment, piece; allotment, share, quota
portray *(v.)* draw, describe, depict, characterize
pose *(n.)* position, attitude, affectation, pretense
posh *(adj.)* rich, smart, comfortable
position *(n.)* location, whereabouts, bearings; view, belief; job, office, occupation; status, rank; posture, carriage, bearing
positive *(adj.)* decisive, clear, emphatic, assertive, resolute, certain, confident, sure
possess *(v.)* have, hold, own, occupy, control, maintain
possibility *(n.)* plausibility, feasibility, chance, hazard, hope, prospect
post *(n.)* column, pillar, pedestal, upright, mast
posterior *(adj.)* subsequent, after, succeeding, next, following, later; behind, back
posterity *(n.)* eternity, descendants, children, offspring
postpone *(v.)* defer, delay, suspend, retard, withhold, shelve, adjourn, pause
postscript *(n.)* appendix, addition, supplement
posture *(n.)* pose, carriage, aspect, presence; feeling, sentiment, disposition
potable *(adj.)* clean, fresh, unpolluted
potency *(n.)* power, energy, vigour; authority: influence, control, dominion, command
pouch *(n.)* bag, sack, receptacle, container
pounce *(v.)* seize, spring, attack, bound, surge, jump
poverty *(n.)* want, privation, insolvency; lack, shortage, inadequacy, scarcity
power *(n.)* vigor, stamina, authority, jurisdiction, dominion, dominance, control, supremacy; compulsion, coercion, horsepower, potential, dynamism
practical *(adj.)* useful, feasible, workable, rational, utilitarian, serviceable, efficient, effective
practice *(n.)* usage, mode, manner, fashion, exercise, rehearsal, system
pragmatic *(adj.)* logical, sensible, practical, realistic
praise *(v.)* commend, applaud, acclaim, endorse, eulogize, compliment, celebrate, honor, glorify, extol, congratulate
prank *(n.)* trick, antic, game, escapade, caper, joke
preach *(v.)* lecture, teach, sermonize, discourse, exhort, moralize, talk, harangue, inform, address
precarious *(adj.)* uncertain, unsafe, risky, doubtful, dubious, dangerous
precede *(v.)* lead, antedate, preface, introduce, herald, forerun
precious *(adj.)* valuable, costly, expensive; beloved, cherished, prized; delicate, fragile, dainty
precipice *(n.)* cliff, crag, bluff, hill, mountain
precise *(adj.)* exact, accurate, definite, careful
predecessor *(n.)* forerunner, antecedent, ancestor
predicament *(n.)* difficulty, strait, plight, scrape, circumstance, mess, pinch, crisis
predict *(v.)* foretell, prophesy, prognosticate, divine
predominant *(adj.)* supreme, almighty, powerful; first, transcendent, surpassing, superlative, principal
preeminent *(adj.)* distinguished, eminent, outstanding
preface *(v.)* introduce, commence, precede, begin
preference *(n.)* choice, election, option, selection, pick
prehistoric *(adj.)* ancient, primitive, antiquated, old
prejudice *(n.)* bias, inclination, partiality
preliminary *(adj.)* preparatory, preceding, introductory
prelude *(n.)* introduction, preamble, prologue, preface
premature *(adj.)* rash, precipitate, untimely, early
premise *(n.)* supposition, assumption, proposition
premium *(adj.)* excellent, select, prime, superior
premonition *(n.)* foreboding, portent, sign, warning
preparation *(n.)* rehearsal, anticipation, build-up; preparedness, readiness, fitness, training, mixture, compound, medicine
prerequisite *(n.)* requirement, necessity, essential
prerogative *(n.)* privilege, advantage, exemption, right
presence *(n.)* occupancy, residence, inhabitancy; nearness, closeness; appearance, behaviour
preserve *(v.)* guard, protect, shield; keep, process, cure
preside *(v.)* officiate, direct, lead, control, manage
pressure *(n.)* tension, burden, stress, squeeze
prestige *(n.)* influence, reputation, fame, esteem

presume *(v.)* believe, consider, suppose, assume
pretend *(v.)* feign, affect, imitate, simulate, represent
pretty *(adj.)* attractive, lovely, beautiful; pleasant, delightful, cheerful, pleasing
prevalent *(adj.)* prevailing, common, widespread
prevent *(v.)* preclude, block, stop, thwart, halt, impede, check, frustrate, obstruct, inhibit, restrain, hinder
previous *(adj.)* former, antecedent, prior, preceding
prick *(v.)* pierce, stick, cut, hurt, puncture
pride *(n.)* egotism, haughtiness, disdain, condescension
prim *(adj.)* exact, stiff, formal, demure, decorous, polite, proper, precise
primp *(v.)* dress, prepare, paint, powder
principal *(adj.)* chief, leading, first, main, foremost, preeminent, dominant, prevailing
prior *(adj.)* before, antecedent, foregoing, preceding
prisoner *(n.)* captive, convict, detainee, hostage
privacy *(n.)* seclusion, solitude, isolation, aloofness, separation, concealment, secrecy
privilege *(n.)* right, perquisite, prerogative, indulgence, affluence
probable *(adj.)* likely, seeming, presumable, feasible, plausible
procedure *(n.)* fashion, mode, method, system, order
proceed *(v.)* move, progress, continue, advance
process *(n.)* operations, means, manner, method
prod *(v.)* provoke, crowd, shove, push
product *(n.)* result, output, outcome
profanity *(n.)* irreverence, abuse, cursing, swearing
profession *(n.)* career, occupation, calling, avocation, vocation, position; declaration, vow, oath
professor *(n.)* teacher, educator, instructor, lecturer
proficiency *(n.)* learning, skill, knowledge, ability
profit *(n.)* gain, return, proceeds, remuneration
profound *(adj.)* scholarly, learned, sagacious, intellectual, great, intense
progress *(n.)* headway, impetus, motion, improvement, advancement, development, growth
prohibit *(v.)* forbid, interdict, obstruct, prevent, ban
project *(n.)* plan, scheme, outline, design
prominent *(adj.)* famous, notable, leading, distinguished, striking, noticeable
promiscuous *(adj.)* indiscriminate, unrestricted, lewd, wanton, loose, immoral
promote *(v.)* further, encourage, help, aid, assist, support, back, champion, advocate, bolster, nourish, nurture, subsidize, boost, advance
prompt *(adj.)* timely, precise, punctual
prone *(adj.)* disposed, inclined, predisposed, likely
pronounced *(adj.)* noticeable, clear, definite, obvious
pronouncement *(n.)* report, declaration, statement
proof *(n.)* verification, confirmation, substantiation, corroboration, testimony
propensity *(n.)* talent, capacity, ability, inclination
prophecy *(n.)* prediction, forecast, prognostication
prophet *(n.)* seer, oracle, soothsayer, astrologer
proponent *(n.)* defender, advocate, champion, protector
propose *(v.)* offer, recommend, submit, volunteer
propriety *(n.)* accordance, compatibility, congruity, modesty, dignity, pleasantness
prospect *(n.)* expectation, promise, outlook, possibility
prosper *(v.)* thrive, flourish, flower, succeed
protection *(n.)* shield, screen, shelter, defense, safeguard, security, guaranty
protest *(n.)* meeting, rally, demonstration, dissent
proud *(adj.)* stately, distinguished; vain, vainglorious, haughty, arrogant
provide *(v.)* furnish, equip, outfit, stock, supply
provision *(v.)* requirement, stipulation, prerequisite
provoke *(v.)* vex, irritate, aggravate, bother, incite, stir, rouse, arouse, cause, make, produce, begin
proxy *(n.)* agent, broker, representative, delegate
prudent *(adj.)* careful, cautious, circumspect, wary, discreet; practical, sensible, wise, discerning
pry *(v.)* snoop, spy, nose, inquire, meddle
pseudo *(adj.)* imitation, quasi, sham, false
publish *(v.)* distribute, print, issue; advertise, announce, promulgate, proclaim
pudgy *(adj.)* fat, chubby, chunky, stout
pulpy *(adj.)* soft, smooth, thick, fleshy
pun *(n.)* witticism, quip, joke
punctual *(adj.)* prompt, precise, exact, meticulous
puny *(adj.)* small, feeble, inferior, diminutive, weak
pure *(adj.)* unimixed, unadulterated, simple, clear, undiluted, clear, immaculate, germ-free, sterilized, sanitary, refined; chaste, virginal, continent, celibate; absolute, sheer, utter, complete

purge *(v.)* cleanse, evacuate, eliminate

purpose *(n.)* aim, intention, end, goal, mission, objective, expectation, intent, aspiration

putrid *(adj.)* rotten, corrupt, putrefied, decayed

puzzle *(v.)* perplex, obscure, bewilder, complicate, confuse, wonder, marvel, surprise, astonish

Q

quaint *(adj.)* odd, strange, fanciful, whimsical

quake *(v.)* tremble, shake, quiver, move, rock

quality *(n.)* attribute, trait, endowment, condition, character, nature, essence; grade, class, merit, worth, excellence, variety, rank

qualm *(n.)* scruple, suspicion, doubt, uncertainty

quarrel *(v.)* dispute, wrangle, contend, squabble, clash, bicker, contest, disagree, argue, feud

queasy *(adj.)* squeamish, sick, uneasy, uncomfortable

queer *(adj.)* odd, peculiar, strange, curious

quiet *(adj.)* silent, calm, peaceful, hushed, muffled, noiseless, still, reserved, reticent

quirk *(n.)* whim, caprice, fancy, peculiarity

quiver *(v.)* vibrate, shudder, wave, shiver, tremble

quote *(v.)* excerpt, extract, say, repeat; price, request, demand, value

R

rabble *(n.)* crowd, mob, masses, riffraff, people

rabid *(adj.)* fanatical, obsessed, zealous; insane, deranged, mad

racket *(n.)* uproar, clatter, din, disturbance, noise, conspiracy, scheme, corruption, crime, theft

radial *(adj.)* branched, outspread, spreading

radiant *(adj.)* shining, luminous, radiating, bright

radical *(adj.)* fundamental, original, primitive, native, organic; extreme, progressive, militant, seditious, riotous, rebellious, revolutionary, heretical

raft *(n.)* flatboat, barge, float, catamaran, boat

rage *(n.)* fury, frenzy, tantrum, uproar, storm, out burst; fad, fashion, style, mode, vogue, craze, mania

ragged *(adj.)* tattered, frayed, frazzled, threadbare

raid *(n.)* attack, invasion, foray, assault, roundup

rain *(v.)* pour, drizzle, shower, sprinkle, mist, storm

raise *(v.)* lift, elevate, hoist, boost; rear, breed, cultivate, produce; erect, construct, build

rake *(n.)* rascal, lecher, drunkard, scoundrel

ramble *(v.)* saunter, stroll, roam, wander; drift, stray, diverge, meander, digress

rampant *(adj.)* raging, uncontrolled, violent, turbulent, tumultuous, unruly, unrestrained

rancid *(adj.)* unpleasant, tainted, stale, bad, rotten

random *(adj.)* aimless, haphazard, casual, unpredictable, irregular

rank *(n.)* row, column, file, string, line; eminence, position, distinction, standing, status, ancestry

ransack *(v.)* search, rummage, scour, seek; loot, pillage, plunder, ravish, strip, rifle

rant *(v.)* rave, fume, rail, rage, yell

rapid *(adj.)* swift, speedy, accelerated, hurried, fast

rapt *(adj.)* awed, transported, entranced, enchanted

rapture *(n.)* delight, ecstasy, pleasure, satisfaction

rare *(adj.)* exceptional, singular, extraordinary, unusual; scarce, expensive, precious, select, superlative, excellent

rascal *(n.)* scoundrel, rogue, rake, knave, cad, scalawag, reprobate, miscreant

rash *(adj.)* hasty, impetuous, impulsive, foolish, heedless, foolhardy, brash

rational *(adj.)* logical, stable, thoughtful, sensible, impartial, objective, sober; intelligent, sensible, wise; responsible

rattle *(v.)* disconcert, bother, unnerve, confuse, disturb, embarrass

raucous *(adj.)* hoarse, harsh, loud, gruff, rough

ravage *(v.)* pillage, devastate, despoil, plunder, sack

rave *(v.)* talk, babble, gabble, jabber; rage, storm, splutter, rail, rant

ravenous *(adj.)* voracious, starved, hungry

raw *(adj.)* natural, crude, rough, immature, inexperienced; cold, biting, windy, bleak, chafed, bruised

react *(v.)* respond, reciprocate, behave, answer

ready *(adj.)* prepared, alert, handy, expectant, available; eager, willing, ardent, zealous

real *(adj.)* authentic, original; existing, actual, substantive, tangible

realism *(n.)* authenticity, naturalness, actuality, reality

realize *(v.)* fulfill, complete, accomplish; recognize, apprehend, discern; obtain, receive, get

realm *(n.)* kingdom, province, domain, sphere

rear *(n.)* back, hindmost, tail, posterior, rump, butt

reason *(n.)* intelligence, sanity; logic, speculation, rationalism, analysis; motive, end, rationale, aim, mind, brain, mentality, intellect

reassure *(v.)* console, comfort, encourage, guarantee

rebel *(n.)* revolutionary, agitator, insurgent, mutineer, nonconformist

rebound *(v.)* recoil, reflect, ricochet, bounce

rebuke *(v.)* chide, reprove, condemn, reprimand

recede *(v.)* retreat, shrink, ebb, lower, abate, decline, decrease, fall

receipt *(n.)* acquisition, receiving, acceptance, arrival; voucher, acknowledgment, notice, stub

recent *(adj.)* modern, fresh, novel, contemporary

reception *(n.)* gathering, party, soiree, entertainment

receptive *(adj.)* alert, perceptive, observant

recess *(n.)* nook, cell, cubicle; intermission, interlude

recipient *(n.)* receiver, beneficiary, heir

recite *(v.)* render, enact, dramatize, interpret, soliloquize, narrate, recount

reckless *(adj.)* heedless, thoughtless, wild, rash

reclaim *(v.)* recover, redeem, regain, mend, improve

recognize *(v.)* place, recall, remember, acknowledge, appreciate, realize

recommend *(v.)* commend, praise, endorse, suggest, prescribe, urge, advise

reconcile *(v.)* adjust, adapt, arrange, regulate

record *(n.)* document, manuscript, account, history, deed; disk, phonograph

recover *(v.)* salvage, redeem, rescue, reclaim; convalesce, heal, mend, revive, recuperate

recreation *(n.)* pastime, amusement, relaxation

recuperate *(v.)* recover, convalesce, heal

recur *(v.)* return, reappear, happen, repeat

redeem *(v.)* recover, repay, purchase, atone, compensate; save, liberate, free, deliver, rescue

redemption *(n.)* regeneration, salvation, rebirth, rescue

redress *(n.)* compensation, payment, reparation

redundant *(adj.)* superfluous, wordy, verbose, dull

referee *(n.)* arbitrator, umpire, conciliator, judge

refine *(v.)* strain, filter, clean, separate; improve, better, clarify, explain

reflect *(v.)* ponder, contemplate, concentrate, weigh, consider, think

reform *(n.)* reformation, betterment, improvement

refrain *(v.)* avoid, cease, forbear, abstain

refuge *(n.)* shelter, sanctuary, retreat, haven

refund *(n.)* return, reimbursement, repayment, remuneration, compensation, rebate, settlement

refuse *(v.)* reject, decline, rebuff, spurn, deny

refute *(v.)* disprove, answer, deny

regard *(n.)* look, gaze, glance; estimation, appreciation, affection, admiration

regard *(v.)* observe, notice, mark; consider, view, think; respect, esteem, value, admire

region *(n.)* territory, area, realm, locale, domain, sphere

regret *(n.)* remorse, compunction, repentance, qualm, grief, pain, anxiety, sorrow

regret *(v.)* mourn, lament, rue, repent, grieve, sorrow

regular *(adj.)* customary, conventional, usual; orderly, methodical, precise, systematic, organized, consistent, rhythmic, periodic, measured

regulate *(v.)* control, rule, legislate, direct, govern, manage; adjust, adapt, standardize, rectify, correct

rehabilitate *(v.)* restore, reinstate, change, reestablish

reign *(v.)* rule, govern, manage

reimburse *(v.)* repay, compensate, refund

reinforce *(v.)* encourage, strengthen, support, boost

reject *(v.)* refuse, repudiate, decline, renounce, deny; discard, expel, eliminate

rejuvenate *(v.)* reinvigorate, refresh, strengthen

relapse *(v.)* backslide, revert, regress, deteriorate, degenerate, weaken, sink

relate *(v.)* tell, recount, recite, retell, describe, report; connect, associate, correlate, compare

relax *(v.)* slacken, repose, recline, unbend, rest

release *(v.)* liberate, acquit, loose, free

relevance *(n.)* connection, pertinence, importance

reliable *(adj.)* unimpeachable, trustworthy, reputable, irrefutable, incontestable, dependable, unfailing

relic *(n.)* vestige, trace, heirloom, antique, keepsake, memento, token

relief *(n.)* softening, alleviation, comforting; aid, assistance, support, help, succor; relaxation, comfort, contentment, restfulness

religion *(n.)* faith, belief, persuasion, theology, doctrine, communion, piety

relish *(v.)* fancy, like, enjoy

reluctance *(n.)* unwillingness, disinclination, qualm, hesitation, doubt

remark *(v.)* say, state, speak, mention, observe

remarkable *(adj.)* exceptional, extraordinary, unusual

remedy *(v.)* help, aid, heal, counteract, repair, cure

remnant *(n.)* remainder, residue, leavings, dregs

remorse *(n.)* anguish, guilt, compunction, contrition, grief, regret

remote *(adj.)* distant, removed, secluded, isolated; ancient, aged, old; separated, unrelated, irrelevant

rendition *(n.)* interpretation, translation, version

renew *(v.)* refresh, regenerate, rehabilitate, invigorate, restore, freshen, stimulate

renounce *(v.)* disown, disavow, deny, discard

renovate *(v.)* remake, rehabilitate, renew

repair *(v.)* restore, fix, correct, refurbish, mend

repel *(v.)* rebuff, resist, oppose, repulse, offend

repentance *(n.)* sorrow, remorse, self-reproach, regret, guilt, penitence

replenish *(v.)* refill, restock, renew

replica *(n.)* copy, likeness, model, duplicate, imitation, reproduction

represent *(v.)* depict, render, portray, enact, symbolize, describe; imitate, substitute, impersonate

repress *(v.)* check, restrain, control, curb, hinder

reprieve *(n.)* delay, respite, suspension

reprimand *(v.)* reprove, rebuke, chide, reproach, denounce, criticize, scold

reproach *(v.)* censure, upbraid, condemn, scold, blame

repudiate *(v.)* reject, retract, repeal, revoke, abandon

repulsive *(adj.)* offensive, disgusting, odious, forbidding, horrid

reputable *(adj.)* distinguished, celebrated, honorable, trustworthy, honest, worthy, brave, noble

request *(v.)* ask, solicit, beseech, entreat, sue, beg

rescue *(v.)* save, recover, redeem, salvage, retrieve; free, deliver, liberate, release

resemblance *(n.)* likeness, correspondence, coincidence, similarity

resentment *(n.)* annoyance, irritation, anger

reservoir *(n.)* supply, store, reserve, pool, cistern

residue *(n.)* remainder, leavings, scraps, shavings

resilient *(adj.)* rebounding, elastic, springy, flexible

resist *(v.)* oppose, endure, bear, persist, suffer, abide, persevere, last, repel

resolve *(v.)* decide, determine, conclude, decree

resource *(n.)* reserve, support, means, stratagem

resourceful *(adj.)* ingenious, capable, active, intelligent

respect *(n.)* regard, relation, esteem, honour, admiration

respite *(n.)* delay, postponement, reprieve, pause

respond *(v.)* reply, rejoin, acknowledge, answer

responsible *(adj.)* accountable, liable, obligated, obliged, pledged, bound, answerable; reliable, capable, dutiful, dependable, competent

rest *(n.)* repose, quiet, slumber, peacefulness, relaxation, doze, nap, respite; residue, surplus, remnant, balance; intermission, interval, inactivity, pause, recess

restless *(adj.)* fidgety, jumpy, nervous, uneasy, agitated, unsettled, restive, impatient, jittery

restrain *(v.)* curb, bridle, rein, regulate, muzzle, inhibit, deter, hamper, restrict, gag, limit, contain, check

restrict *(v.)* limit, circumscribe, contract, shorten

result *(n.)* consequence, outcome, aftermath, upshot, settlement, determination, payoff, end

resurrection *(n.)* transformation, rebirth, renewal

retard *(v.)* hinder, postpone, delay, impede

retort *(n.)* reply, counter, repartee, response, answer

retraction *(n.)* denial, revocation, cancellation

retreat *(n.)* refuge, sanctuary, port, haven, resort

retribution *(n.)* punishment, reprisal, retaliation

retrieve *(v.)* recover, regain, reclaim

return *(v.)* reappear, recur, repeat, revive, rebound; restore, replace; reply, respond, retort; repay, reimburse, recompense, refund; interest, profit

reveal *(v.)* disclose, publish, betray, announce, declare, show

revenge *(n.)* retaliation, reprisal, retribution

revenue *(n.)* income, return, earnings, yield, receipts, proceeds, profits

reverence *(n.)* veneration, respect, admiration, regard, esteem, adoration, praise

review *(v.)* correct, criticize, revise; examine, analyze, check

revise *(v.)* improve, correct, reconsider, rewrite, edit, change, modify

revoke *(v.)* annul, reverse, recall, retract, cancel

revolve *(v.)* roll, spin, rotate, twirl, turn

rich *(adj.)* wealthy, moneyed, affluent; luxurious, magnificent, resplendent, lavish, ornate, splendid, elegant; fertile, lush, fruitful, luxuriant

riches *(n.)* wealth, fortune, possessions, money

ricochet *(v.)* carom, rebound, reflect, bounce

riddle *(n.)* enigma, puzzle, dilemma, complexity

ridicule *(v.)* mock, gibe, scoff, sneer, taunt, mimic, deride, scorn, caricature, satirize

righteous *(adj.)* virtuous, just, honorable, exemplary, noble, trustworthy, ethical, impartial; religious, devout, pious, saintly, angelic, devoted, reverent, spiritual, holy

rigid *(adj.)* stiff, unyielding, inflexible, solid, firm; strict, exact, rigorous, severe; fixed, set, unmoving, definite, determined

rim *(n.)* margin, edge, border, verge, brim, lip, brink

ring *(n.)* circle, circlet, girdle, jewellery, band, signet, bracelet; group, party, bloc, faction, group, gang, band; sound, clangor, jangle

riot *(n.)* uproar, tumult, confusion, disorder, disturbance, protest

ripen *(v.)* develop, evolve, advance, grow

risk *(n.)* hazard, peril, jeopardy; contingency, prospect, uncertainty

rival *(n.)* competitor, antagonist, opponent

rival *(v.)* approach, match, equal

rivalry *(n.)* competition, contention, opposition, dispute

rob *(v.)* burglarize, plunder, defraud, cheat, pilfer, filch, embezzle, pillage, sack, loot

robust *(adj.)* vigorous, husky, hale, hearty, sound

rogue *(n.)* knave, outlaw, miscreant, criminal

romantic *(adj.)* poetic, fanciful, chivalrous, courtly

rooted *(adj.)* grounded, based, fixed, firm

rot *(n.)* decay, decomposition, corruption, disintegration, nonsense, trash, silliness, foolishness

rotate *(v.)* turn, twist, wheel, revolve, move

rotten *(adj.)* spoiled, putrefying, decaying, rancid; unsound, defective, impaired, weak; corrupt, contaminated, polluted, tainted, defiled, dirty

rough *(adj.)* uneven, irregular, bumpy, jagged, coarse; severe, harsh, strict, stem; crude, boorish, uncivil, uncultivated, rude; turbulent, buffeting, stormy, tumultuous; unfinished, incomplete, imperfect; approximate, inexact, uncertain

rouse *(v.)* waken, arouse, raise, awaken; stimulate, urge, stir, provoke, animate, excite

routine *(adj.)* usual, customary, conventional, habitual

rove *(v.)* walk, meander, wander, roam

rowdy *(adj.)* noisy, rebellious, mischievous, unruly

royal *(adj.)* regale, imperial, sovereign, supreme, noble; stately, dignified, majestic, courtly, aristocratic, lordly, imposing, resplendent

rubbish *(n.)* waste, debris, nonsense, litter, trash

rude *(adj.)* boorish, brutish, uncouth, vulgar, harsh, gruff, abusive, brazen, audacious, hostile, insensitive, rough, violent; coarse, unrefined, unpolished, crude; primitive, ignorant, barbarous

rugged *(adj.)* rough, uneven, hilly, broken, mountainous; strong, vigorous, hale, sturdy, hardy, healthy

ruin *(v.)* destroy, demolish, wreck, ravage; impoverish, beggar

rule *(v.)* govern, control, dictate, manage, regulate

rumble *(n.)* reverberation, resounding, roll, noise

rumour *(n.)* report, gossip, tidings, hearsay, tale

rumple *(v.)* wrinkle, crumple, crush, fold

rupture *(v.)* break, burst, crack, tear

rural *(adj.)* country, rustic, agrarian, suburban

ruthless *(adj.)* cruel, savage, brutal, merciless, fiendish, unmerciful, ferocious, vengeful, barbarous

S

sabotage *(v.)* subvert, undermine, attack, destroy

sacrifice *(n.)* tribute, atonement; loss, discount, deduction, reduction

sad *(adj.)* unhappy, downcast, gloomy, sorrowful, glum, dispirited, depressed, melancholy, blue; pitiable, disheartening, discouraging, dreary, disquieting

saint *(n.)* paragon, martyr, altruist, believer

salute *(v.)* greet, recognize, praise

salvage *(v.)* save, retrieve, recover, regain

sanction *(v.)* approve, confirm, authorize, countenance

sanctuary *(n.)* church, shrine, temple; shelter, refuge, asylum, resort, haven

sane *(adj.)* rational, normal, lucid, sober, sound, balanced, sensible, reasonable, wise

sanitary *(adj.)* hygienic, wholesome, sterile, healthful

sarcastic *(adj.)* scornful, mocking, ironical, satirical, taunting, derisive, sneering, snickering, cynical

satire *(n.)* irony, sarcasm, mockery, ridicule, caricature
saturate *(v.)* soak, overfill, drench, steep, immerse
savage *(adj.)* primitive, crude, simple; cruel, barbarous, inhuman, brutal; wild, untamed, uncivilized, uncultured, uncontrolled
savor *(v.)* partake, enjoy, relish, appreciate, like
scaffold *(n.)* platform, gallows, framework, structure, block, gibbet
scald *(v.)* burn, steam, char, blanch, parboil
scamper *(v.)* hasten, speed, haste, hurry, run
scanty *(adj.)* scarce, meager, small, inadequate, thin, skimpy, sparse, diminutive
scare *(v.)* panic, terrify, alarm, frighten
scene *(n.)* occurrence, spectacle, view, display
scent *(v.)* smell, perfume, odour, fragrance, redolence
scholarly *(adj.)* erudite, cultured, studious, learned
scoff *(v.)* mock, deride, jeer, ridicule
scorching *(adj.)* fiery, searing, sweltering, burning, hot
scorn *(v.)* refuse, despise, disdain
scoundrel *(n.)* rogue, scamp, villain, rascal
scowl *(v.)* frown, glower, disapprove, grimace
scramble *(v.)* mix, combine, blend, beat; climb, clamber, push, struggle
scrap *(n.)* trash, junk, waste, cuttings, chips; bit, fragment, particle, piece, morsel; fight, quarrel, brawl, squabble
scratch *(v.)* wound, hurt, cut, mark, injure, scar
scrub *(v.)* rub, cleanse, scour, clean, wash
scrupulous *(adj.)* exact, punctilious, strict, careful
scrutinize *(v.)* examine, view, study, stare, watch
scuffle *(n.)* struggle, shuffle, strife, fight
seam *(n.)* joint, union, stitching, closure, suture
seasonal *(adj.)* periodically, biennial, annual, yearly
secede *(v.)* withdraw, retract, leave, retreat
seclusion *(n.)* solitude, aloofness, privacy, retirement, retreat, concealment
secrecy *(n.)* hiding, seclusion, privacy, mystery, dark, darkness, isolation, reticence, stealth
secrete *(v.)* hide, conceal, cover, disguise; emit, discharge, produce, exude
secure *(adj.)* safe, guarded, defended; assured, determined, confident
sediment *(n.)* dregs, silt, grounds, residue
seek *(v.)* search, delve, dig, ransack, look, sniff, prowl
seethe *(v.)* boil, simmer, stew
seize *(v.)* grasp, take, catch, grab, clutch, snatch
seldom *(adv.)* rarely, infrequently, occasionally, un commonly, scarcely, hardly
select *(v.)* pick, decide, elect, choose
sell *(v.)* market, vend, barter, exchange, trade, bargain, peddle, retail, wholesale, contract, retail
sellout *(n.)* betrayal, deception, deal, trick
semblance *(n.)* resemblance, aspect, appearance
senile *(adj.)* aged, infirm, feeble, old, sick
senior *(adj.)* older, elder, higher, superior
sensation *(n.)* consciousness, perception, feeling
sense *(n.)* sensation, feeling, touch, sight, hearing, taste, smell; intellect, perception, reason, cleverness, knowledge, thought; reasonableness, judg ment, discretion, fairness; tact, understanding
sensitive *(adj.)* tender, delicate, sore, painful; touchy, tense, nervous, irritable, unstable
sensuous *(adj.)* passionate, physical, exciting, sensual, gratifying, hedonistic
sentiment *(n.)* feeling, emotion, opinion, thought
sentry *(n.)* sentinel, watch, protector, watchmen
sequel *(n.)* continuation, progression, sequence, series
sequence *(n.)* succession, order, continuity, progression, flow; arrangement, distribution, classification; series, chain, string, array
serene *(adj.)* calm, unruffled, tranquil, composed, sedate, placid
sermon *(n.)* discourse, lesson, doctrine, lecture
service *(v.)* maintain, sustain, repair
setback *(n.)* hindrance, check, delay, difficulty
settle *(v.)* prove, establish, verify; finish, end, achieve; locate, reside, dwell, colonize
sever *(v.)* separate, part, split, cleave, cut, divide
severe *(adj.)* exacting, inflexible, harsh, cruel, oppressive, rigid, rigorous, difficult, oppressive, relentless
sew *(v.)* join, fasten, stitch, tack, bind, piece, baste
sewage *(n.)* excrement, offal, waste, residue
shabby *(adj.)* threadbare, worn, ragged, faded, dilapidated, deteriorated, seedy
shadow *(adj.)* slight, inconsiderable, superficial; silly, trifling, inane, frivolous, petty, foolish
sham *(adj.)* pretended, false, misleading, untrue
shame *(v.)* humiliate, mortify, dishonor, disgrace

shape *(n.)* form, contour, configuration; pattern, frame, mold; condition, fitness, health
shatter *(v.)* break, sliver, split, burst
sheath *(n.)* scabbard, case, covering
sheer *(adj.)* abrupt, steep, precipitous, perpendicular; transparent, delicate, fine
shine *(v.)* radiate, glitter, sparkle, twinkle, glimmer, glow, blaze; reflect, glisten, gleam, mirror; polish, scour, brush, burnish, wax
shiver *(v.)* shake, tremble, vibrate, quiver
shore *(n.)* coast, beach, seaside, bank; support, prop, buttress, strut
shortage *(n.)* lack, deficiency, failure, dearth, shortfall
shove *(v.)* push, nudge, jostle, press
showy *(adj.)* conspicuous, flamboyant, pretentious
shred *(n.)* strip, fragment, splinter, rag
shrewd *(adj.)* cunning, sharp, keen, intelligent, canny, crafty, cagey
shrine *(n.)* temple, altar, church, sanctuary
shrivel *(v.)* wither, shrink, decrease
shroud *(v.)* hide, cover, conceal, obscure, veil, screen
shudder *(v.)* tremble, shake, shiver, quiver
shun *(v.)* avoid, ignore, eschew, evade
shy *(adj.)* timid, reserved, distrustful, suspicious
siege *(n.)* attack, assault, onslaught, blockade
sieve *(v.)* strain, purify, filter
sigh *(n.)* moan, groan, gasp, cry
signify *(v.)* mean, indicate, communicate, denote, imply, intimate, portend
silence *(n.)* serenity, hush, tranquillity, quiet
silly *(adj.)* foolish, imprudent, ridiculous, absurd, inane, frivolous
simple *(adj.)* unaffected, plain, clear, unadorned, uncomplicated, bare, innocent, artless
simplify *(v.)* clarify, explain, elucidate, interpret
sincere *(adj.)* honest, genuine, earnest, faithful
sinister *(adj.)* ominous, menacing, base, bad, evil
sink *(v.)* submerge, depress, fall, lower, droop
sip *(v.)* drink, imbibe, taste, sample, savor
situation *(n.)* circumstances, predicament, state, job, trade, status, station, rank
skeleton *(n.)* bones, framework, outline, structure
skeptic *(n.)* doubter, cynic, unbeliever, agnostic
skid *(v.)* slip, slide, swerve, veer, glide
skill *(n.)* dexterity, ability, expertise, competence, talent; occupation, craft, vocation, trade, job
skin *(v.)* strip, peel, husk, scale, scalp
skinny *(adj.)* thin, lean, bony, gaunt, emaciated
skirmish *(n.)* scuffle, scrimmage, engagement, combat
slack *(adj.)* lax, loose, lazy, indolent, sluggish, slow
slander *(n.)* gossip, libel, scandal, misrepresentation
slang *(n.)* jargon, lingo, dialect, colloquialism
slap *(v.)* smack, strike, hit, spank, cuff, buffet
slaughter *(n.)* slaying, bloodshed, carnage, massacre
sleazy *(adj.)* flimsy, shoddy, cheap, trashy, rundown
slender *(adj.)* thin, slim, slight, spare, fragile, flimsy
slight *(v.)* disregard, insult, snub, neglect, overlook
slime *(n.)* mire, muck, mud, ooze
slit *(v.)* cut, gash, slash, rip, slice, split, tear, pierce
sloppy *(adj.)* careless, lax, untidy, messy, disorderly
sluggish *(adj.)* languid, lethargic, indolent, slothful
slumber *(v.)* sleep, rest, nap, doze, snooze
slur *(n.)* insult, innuendo, slight, affront, blemish
sly *(adj.)* cunning, wily, deceitful, deceptive, tricky, shifty, evasive, elusive, shrewd, clever, calculating, treacherous, shady, slick, smooth, slippery
smash *(v.)* break, shatter, crush, pound, destroy, demolish, wreck, ruin
smear *(v.)* slander, libel, sully, slur; smudge, daub, plaster, spread, apply
smell *(n.)* odour, aroma, fragrance, scent, stench, stink
smirk *(n.)* sneer, leer, grimace
smooth *(adj.)* level, flat, flush, polished, sleek, uniform; suave, glib, polite, courteous
smother *(v.)* suffocate, stifle, asphyxiate, strangle, subdue, suppress
smudge *(n.)* smear, blot, blur, stain, blemish, streak
smug *(adj.)* conceited, egotistical, satisfied
snare *(v.)* catch, entangle, trap, trick, lure
sneak *(v.)* lurk, prowl, creep, slink, steal
sneer *(v.)* criticize, deride, ridicule, scoff, gibe, taunt
snip *(v.)* clip, pare, cut, lop, nip, slice, slit
snivel *(v.)* weep, whine, bawl, bemoan, blubber
snobbery *(n.)* contempt, arrogance, insolence
soak *(v.)* steep, saturate, douse, permeate, infuse
sob *(v.)* cry, moan, weep, wail, lament, whimper, bewail

social *(adj.)* genial, pleasant, polite, civil, pleasant
society *(n.)* fellowship, association, brotherhood, fraternity, club; community, civilization, people, nation
soggy *(adj.)* saturated, damp, wet, soaked, sodden
sojourn *(n.)* stay, visit, stopover, vacation, abide
solace *(v.)* comfort, console, soothe, cheer, relieve, assuage, allay, soften, mitigate
solemn *(adj.)* sacred, grave, serious, grim, imposing
solicit *(v.)* supplicate, beg, implore, urge, request, ask, inquire, question, proposition
solid *(adj.)* whole, regular, unbroken, firm, substantial, sound, hard, stable, dense, stout
solidify *(v.)* harden, crystallize, set, coagulate, congeal
solitary *(adj.)* single, sole, individual, singular, isolated, lonely, remote, separate
solitude *(n.)* isolation, seclusion, privacy
somber *(adj.)* dull, gloomy, dark, dim, drab, dismal, depressing, dreary, melancholy
sonorous *(adj.)* resonant, reverberating, vibrant
sooty *(adj.)* blackened, dirty, grimy, dingy, filthy
soothe *(v.)* calm, comfort, ease, quiet, refresh, soften, alleviate, assuage, mitigate
soothsayer *(n.)* prognosticator, diviner, oracle, prophet, astrologer, seer, mystic
sophisticated *(adj.)* worldly, refined, cultured
sorcery *(n.)* magic, witchcraft, alchemy, enchantment
sore *(adj.)* sensitive, raw, tender, painful, inflamed
sorrow *(n.)* grief, affliction, anguish, remorse, misery, sadness, woe, trouble, affliction
sorry *(adj.)* regretful, repentant, apologetic
sort *(v.)* order, arrange, classify, distribute, assort
soul *(n.)* spirit, essence, ghost, being
source *(n.)* origin, beginning, inception, cause, root
souvenir *(n.)* keepsake, token, memento, relic, trophy
space *(n.)* room, area, gap, expanse, distance, interval
spad *(n.)* distance, measure, length, extent, stretch
spare *(adj.)* thin, gaunt, slight, emaciated; excess, additional
sparse *(adj.)* meager, inadequate, scanty, thin, spare
spasm *(n.)* convulsion, fit, contortion, seizure
spatter *(v.)* splash, slosh, spray, shower, speckle
special *(adj.)* specific, certain, particular, designated, unique, distinctive, uncommon, unusual
specify *(v.)* stipulate, designate, cite, name, define
specious *(adj.)* deceptive, misleading, false
speck *(n.)* bit, particle, trace, grain, iota
spectacle *(n.)* sight, show, demonstration, wonder
specter *(n.)* ghost, spook, phantom, spirit, apparition
speculate *(v.)* consider, theorize, contemplate, consider, infer
speech *(n.)* language, oration, communication
speedy *(adj.)* quick, fast, hasty, brisk, swift, hurried
sphere *(n.)* globe, orb, shell, planet; province, realm, environment
spirit *(n.)* ghost, apparition, phantom, specter; vivacity, vigor, zeal, ardor; significance, meaning, sense
spiteful *(adj.)* vindictive, malicious, cruel, malevolent, nasty
spleen *(n.)* anger, petulance, wrath, rancor
splendid *(adj.)* grand, magnificent, impressive, dazzling
spoil *(v.)* decay, ruin, damage, decompose, putrefy
sporadic *(adj.)* occasional, infrequent, scattered
sprawl *(v.)* recline, lounge, relax, slouch
spring *(v.)* bound, leap, issue, jump, hop, vault
sprout *(v.)* germinate, bud, burgeon, grow, develop
spurious *(adj.)* false, fake, deceptive, phony, feigned
spurn *(v.)* reject, shun, slight, snub, scorn, disdain
spurt *(v.)* burst, gush, spout, issue, spring
squabble *(v.)* wrangle, quarrel, bicker, argue, feud
squalor *(n.)* filth, poverty, misery
squeamish *(adj.)* queasy, modest, prudish, finicky
squeeze *(v.)* compress, crush, squash, press, pinch
squirm *(v.)* wriggle, writhe, fidget, twist, shift
stab *(n.)* wound, cut, puncture, thrust
staff *(n.)* personnel, employees, crew, cast
stagnant *(adj.)* inert, stale, dirty, filthy, fetid
stalwart *(adj.)* stout, sturdy, strong, rugged, robust, vigorous, bold, gallant, steadfast, formidable
stamina *(n.)* endurance, strength, vigor, vitality, power
stammer *(v.)* sputter, falter, stumble, hesitate, stutter
staple *(adj.)* basic, necessary, essential, fundamental
stark *(adj.)* simple, desolate, dreary, grim, harsh
startle *(v.)* surprise, alarm, scare, frighten, disturb
state *(n.)* country, nation, condition, situation, circumstances, status, position, standing, station

stately *(adj.)* majestic, dignified, regal, grand, elegant
stationary *(adj.)* fixed, static, permanent, rooted, stable
statue *(n.)* sculpture, image, icon, figurine
stature *(n.)* height, bulk, build, status, standing
status *(n.)* state, condition, position, rank, standing
statute *(n.)* law, decree, act, bill, rule, ordinance, edict
steadfast *(adj.)* resolute, unwavering, constant, faithful, dependable, firm
steep *(adj.)* precipitous, sheer, abrupt
steer *(v.)* guide, direct, pilot, conduct, lead, navigate
stereotype *(v.)* classify, categorize, typecast, label
stem *(adj.)* severe, rigid, hard, strict, austere, rigorous
stiff *(adj.)* rigid, formal, inflexible, firm, stubborn, obstinate, unyielding, formal, uncompromising, severe
stiffen *(v.)* harden, congeal, thicken, coagulate
stigma *(n.)* disgrace, shame, infamy, blemish, blot, stain, taint
stigmatize *(v.)* disgrace, discredit, dishonor, defame, shame, brand, humiliate
stingy *(adj.)* niggardly, miserly, tight, closefisted
stipulate *(v.)* specify, determine, designate, indicate
stir *(n.)* tumult, bustle, excitement, commotion, disorder, uproar, furor, agitation, fuss
stockpile *(n.)* reserve, supply, deposit, hoard, store
stoic *(n.)* impassive, apathetic, indifferent, nonchalant, composed, poised
stolid *(adj.)* impassive, unemotional, dispassionate, indifferent, imperturbable
stomach *(n.)* belly, paunch, abdomen
stoop *(v.)* bend, bow, crouch
story *(n.)* tale, anecdote, yam, parable, fable, legend, report, account; level, floor
stout *(adj.)* plump, portly, heavy, bulky, corpulent; resolute, brave, courageous, bold, fearless, indomitable, firm, strong, robust, hardy
straight *(adj.)* direct, honest, fair, just, virtuous, open
strain *(n.)* effort, exertion, force, pressure, anxiety, tension, stress
strange *(adj.)* unusual, abnormal, bizarre, peculiar, extraordinary, outlandish, unfamiliar, unknown
stratagem *(n.)* trick, deception, wile, scheme, plan, contrivance, device
stray *(v.)* wander, drift, roam, deviate, digress
streamer *(n.)* flag, banner, pennant, standard, ensign
strength *(n.)* power, force, might
strenuous *(adj.)* vigorous, spirited, laborious
strident *(adj.)* raucous, shrill, harsh, piercing
strife *(n.)* conflict, fight, discord, clash
stringent *(adj.)* strict, harsh, severe
stroll *(v.)* walk, saunter, meander, wander, roam
struggle *(n.)* battle, clash, conflict, exertion, endeavour
stubborn *(adj.)* obstinate, headstrong, stiff, resolute, inflexible, intractable
stupendous *(adj.)* amazing, astounding, marvelous, extraordinary, incredible, spectacular, wondrous
stupor *(n.)* daze, trance, numbness, lethargy
sturdy *(adj.)* robust, rugged, stalwart, strong, muscular, firm, indomitable, stout
stylish *(adj.)* fashionable, chic, smart, modish
suave *(adj.)* sophisticated, smooth, cultured, worldly
subjective *(adj.)* biased, prejudiced, individual
subjugate *(v.)* conquer, enslave, subdue, defeat
submerge *(v.)* immerse, engulf, plunge, sink
submit *(v.)* comply, obey; suggest, volunteer, propose, present, tender
subordinate *(adj.)* inferior, lower, junior, subservient
subsequent *(adj.)* following, ensuing, succeeding, later, after
subservient *(adj.)* subordinate, servile, deferential
subsidy *(n.)* endowment, allowance, grant, bequest
substantial *(adj.)* plentiful, abundant, ample, considerable, wealthy, affluent, influential, valuable
subterfuge *(n.)* ploy, scheme, stratagem, device, expedient, deceit
subtle *(adj.)* delicate, understated, refined, elusive, deceptive, inferred, insinuated, artful, insidious
subtract *(v.)* deduct, decrease, diminish, lessen, lower
succession *(n.)* sequence, order, continuation
succinct *(adj.)* brief, concise, terse, abbreviated
succor *(n.)* aid, help, sustenance, assistance
succumb *(v.)* submit, concede, relent, capitulate, collapse, fail
suffer *(v.)* endure, tolerate, bear, undergo, agonize
suffuse *(v.)* saturate, pervade, soak, impregnate

suitor *(n.)* wooer, admirer, gallant, beau
sulk *(v.)* pout, scowl, frown, glower
summary *(n.)* condensation, digest, abridgment, brief
summit *(n.)* peak, pinnacle, apex, crown, culmination
summon *(v.)* call, invite, invoke, request, petition
sumptuous *(adj.)* luxurious, elegant, lavish, opulent
sundry *(adj.)* various, several, divers
supersede *(v.)* replace, supplant, succeed
supplant *(v.)* replace, displace, succeed, supersede
supply *(v.)* equip, stock, replenish
support *(n.)* aid, assistance, help, relief, succor; brace, prop, column, buttress, strut
suppress *(v.)* overpower, repress, curb, quell, crush; bury, cover
surcharge *(n.)* tax, duty, surtax, tariff, levy, toll
surface *(n.)* rise, appear, emerge
surmise *(v.)* speculate, guess, infer, imagine, suppose
surmount *(v.)* conquer, transcend, hurdle, overcome
surplus *(n.)* excess, abundance, remainder, residue
surrender *(v.)* submit, abandon, capitulate, yield
surrogate *(adj.)* substitute, backup, alternative
survey *(n.)* poll, study, review, outline, critique
survival *(n.)* subsistence, continuation, durability
suspect *(v.)* mistrust, doubt; suppose, imagine, conjecture
suspend *(v.)* postpone, delay, defer, interrupt
suspense *(n.)* apprehension, indecision, anxiety
suspicion *(n.)* skepticism, misgiving, mistrust, cynicism, notion, impression
swagger *(v.)* strut, prance, boast, brag, gloat
swallow *(v.)* drink, eat, gulp, consume, devour
swamp *(n.)* marsh, mire, morass, slough
swarm *(n.)* horde, mass, flock, multitude, host
swear *(v.)* declare, testify, affirm; damn, curse
sweet *(adj.)* luscious, aromatic, fragrant, clean, fresh, melodious, harmonious, mellow
swift *(adj.)* fast, rapid, expeditious, fleet, prompt, quick
swindle *(v.)* trick, deceive, dupe, defraud, victimize
switch *(v.)* swap, trade, exchange, replace, substitute
sycophant *(n.)* flatterer, flunky, parasite, toady
sylvan *(adj.)* picturesque, pastoral, idyllic
symbolize *(v.)* signify, connote, mean, represent
sympathize *(v.)* commiserate, console, pity
synopsis *(n.)* summary, abridgment, condensation
systematic *(adj.)* methodical, orderly, precise, regular

T

tabloid *(n.)* newspaper, periodical, publication
taboo *(adj.)* forbidden, banned, prohibited
tacit *(adj.)* implied, understood, assumed, inferred
taciturn *(adj.)* reserved, quiet, reticent
tag *(v.)* label, ticket, designate, identify
tailor *(v.)* customize, adapt, adjust, conform
tale *(n.)* narrative, account; fib, lie
talisman *(n.)* amulet, charm
talk *(n.)* conversation, dialogue, discourse, speech
tame *(adj.)* docile, gentle, obedient
tame *(v.)* domesticate, train
tamper *(v.)* alter, change, meddle, damage
tangible *(adj.)* material, corporeal, tactile, discernible, evident, actual, real, genuine
tantamount *(adj.)* equivalent, parallel, identical
tarnish *(n.)* blemish, blot, stain, taint
taste *(n.)* partiality, liking, bias, preference
taunt *(v.)* insult, jeer, mock, provoke
tavern *(n.)* bar, saloon, pub, cafe, inn, lodge
tawdry *(adj.)* cheap, sleazy, flashy, ostentatious
tease *(v.)* annoy, taunt, torment, harass, irritate, vex
tedious *(adj.)* monotonous, tiresome, dull, boring
tell *(v.)* recount, describe, report, speak, mention, explain, reveal, declare, divulge
temper *(n.)* disposition, temperament, humour, composure, poise
temperament *(n.)* disposition, attitude, mood, emotion, nature, character
temperate *(adj.)* calm, composed, cool, reasonable
tenable *(adj.)* defensible, justifiable, maintainable
tenant *(n.)* renter, leaseholder, inhabitant
tender *(adj.)* fragile, frail; sympathetic, kindhearted, considerate
tenet *(n.)* belief, conviction, dogma, creed, doctrine
tenuous *(adj.)* fine, narrow, insubstantial, flimsy, feeble
tepid *(adj.)* lukewarm, indifferent, halfhearted, languid
terminate *(v.)* complete, conclude, eliminate, cancel

terminology *(n.)* vocabulary, language, jargon
terrible *(adj.)* frightful, appalling, dreadful, horrible, horrendous, disastrous, disturbing, extreme
terrific *(adj.)* splendid, marvelous, wonderful, outstanding, super
terror *(n.)* fright, horror, alarm, dismay, consternation
terse *(adj.)* brief, succinct, concise, precise, curt
test *(n.)* inspection, experiment, examination, quiz
testy *(adj.)* irritable, cranky, grouchy, edgy, short-tempered, touchy, peevish
theorem *(n.)* principle, hypothesis, postulate, premise
theory *(n.)* conjecture, speculation, rationale, explanation, view, conception, outlook
therapeutic *(adj.)* restorative, curative, recuperative, remedial, corrective
thesis *(n.)* opinion, contention, argument, assumption, assertion, hypothesis
thick *(adj.)* abundant, dense, packed, crowded
thin *(adj.)* lean, gaunt, scanty, meager, scarce
think *(v.)* contemplate, meditate, consider, remember, recall, recollect, believe, suppose
thirst *(n.)* longing, desire, yearning, eagerness
thoroughfare *(n.)* artery, highway, expressway, boulevard, concourse, freeway
thought *(v.)* concept, conviction, notion, opinion, theory, hypothesis, supposition
threadbare *(adj)* worn, shabby, tattered, frayed, seedy
threaten *(v.)* endanger, menace, terrorize, scare
thrift *(n.)* economy, husbandry, conservation
thrive *(v.)* flourish, succeed, increase, grow
throng *(n.)* mass, multitude, horde, swarm, host, assemblage, crowd
through *(adj.)* completed, done, finished
thrust *(v.)* shove, plunge, jab, push
thug *(n.)* hoodlum, goon, gangster, criminal
tiara *(n.)* crown, diadem, coronet
tie *(n.)* rope, band, strap, cord, necktie, bow, scarf, cravat, choker, connection, relation, bond, link, knot, draw, deadlock, stalemate
tiff *(n.)* quarrel, dispute, disagreement, scrap, spat
tighten *(v.)* squeeze, compress, constrict, clench
time *(n.)* age, epoch, generation, cycle; interval, duration, span, rhythm, tempo, beat, cadence
timid *(adj.)* shy, retiring, fearful, withdrawn, reticent, indecisive, vacillating
timorous *(adj.)* timid, fearful, apprehensive, anxious, scared, afraid
tinker *(v.)* dabble, putter, potter, trifle
tiny *(adj.)* small, diminutive, minute, microscopic
tirade *(n.)* harangue, denunciation, outburst
title *(n.)* designation, name, appellation, epithet; interest, holding, ownership
titter *(v.)* laugh, giggle, snicker, chuckle
token *(adj.)* nominal, superficial, minimal
token *(n.)* symbol, mark, sign, note
tolerable *(adj.)* endurable, sufferable, bearable; adequate, decent, average
tolerant *(adj.)* unprejudiced, moderate, merciful
tomb *(n.)* grave, vault, crypt, sepulcher, mausoleum
tonic *(adj.)* refresher, restorative, stimulant
topical *(adj.)* local, isolated, provincial, regional
torment *(n.)* anguish, suffering, distress, misery
torpid *(adj.)* inactive, inert, lethargic, sluggish, motionless, dormant, hibernating
torpor *(n.)* idleness, inactivity, indolence, sluggishness
torrent *(n.)* cloudburst, deluge, flood
tortuous *(adj.)* winding, serpentine, twisted, snaky, crooked, bent
toss *(v.)* throw, fling, pitch, cast, hurl, chuck
totter *(v.)* stumble, falter, weave, reel, lurch
tough *(adj.)* rugged, hardy, durable, sturdy, unyielding, incorrigible
tourist *(n.)* visitor, sightseer, wayfarer
tournament *(n.)* competition, rivalry, contest, match, event, series
toxic *(adj.)* poisonous, deadly, lethal, virulent
trace *(n.)* vestige, indication, hint, suggestion
track *(v.)* hunt, trail, pursue, trace
tragedy *(n.)* disaster, calamity, catastrophe, affliction, suffering, tribulation
trait *(n.)* characteristic, quality, property, attribute, mannerism, habit
tramp *(n.)* vagabond, vagrant, gypsy
tranquil *(adj.)* peaceful, serene, placid, still, pleasant, cool, restful
transform *(v.)* alter, transfigure, convert, change
transgress *(n.)* overstep, infringe, violate, trespass
translate *(v.)* reword, explain, interpret, decipher

translucent *(adj.)* transparent, clear, limpid

transparent *(adj.)* translucent, diaphanous, lucid, clear, thin, sheer

transpire *(v.)* happen, occur, ensue, result

transpose *(v.)* switch, swap, exchange, transfer

trap *(n.)* snare, trick, stratagem, maneuver, artifice

traumatic *(adj.)* alarming, upsetting, frightful

travesty *(n.)* parody, satire, spoof, burlesque, lampoon, farce

treacherous *(adj.)* unfaithful, deceitful, deceptive, insidious, disloyal, treasonous, unstable

treatise *(n.)* dissertation, thesis, essay, discourse

treaty *(n.)* agreement, settlement, covenant, pact

tribulation *(n.)* distress, suffering, hardship

tribute *(n.)* accolade, homage, recognition, applause

trinket *(n.)* bauble, adornment, decoration, ornament

triumph *(v.)* prevail, conquer, overwhelm, overpower, win, revel

trivial *(adj.)* insignificant, inconsequential, unimportant, irrelevant, frivolous

trophy *(n.)* award, citation, medal

trot *(v.)* canter, jog, lope, amble

trouble *(n.)* calamity, distress, misfortune, tribulation, worry, stress

trough *(n.)* channel, furrow, rut, crater, ditch

truculent *(adj.)* fierce, mean, malevolent, pugnacious, belligerent, contentious, hostile

trunk *(n.)* chest, strongbox, coffer, case

try *(v.)* endeavour, strive, test, examine

tryst *(n.)* meeting, rendezvous, assignation

tumble *(v.)* fall, slip, descend, decline, totter, drop

tumult *(n.)* disorder, commotion, turmoil, melee, agitation, ferment

turbulent *(adj.)* violent, blustery, disorderly

turmoil *(n.)* chaos, commotion, disorder, tumult,

turpitude *(n.)* depravity, baseness, perversion, vileness. evil, sinfulness, corruption

tussle *(v.)* scuffle, grapple, struggle, brawl

tweak *(v.)* nip, pinch, grasp, squeeze, pull, twist

twinge *(n.)* twitch, tingle, spasm, crick, stitch, throb

twirl *(v.)* twist, gyrate, turn, rotate, pivot

typify *(v.)* represent, personify, epitomize, exemplify, illustrate

tyrannical *(adj.)* oppressive, despotic, arbitrary, domineering, unjust, cruel

U

ubiquity *(n.)* prevalence, pervasiveness, commonness, omnipresence, universality

ulterior *(adj.)* concealed, shrouded, obscured

ultimate *(adj.)* extreme, final, decisive, concluding, eventual, maximum, utmost, preeminent

unassuming *(adj.)* modest, unpretentious, humble, simple, plain, diffident

unauthorized *(adj.)* unsanctioned, prohibited, illicit, forbidden, banned

unbalanced *(adj.)* unstable, maladjusted, biased, untrustworthy, treacherous

unbend *(v.)* relax, rest, soften, ease, relent

unbiased *(adj.)* impartial, objective, neutral, unprejudiced, tolerant, disinterested

uncanny *(adj.)* strange, odd, weird, mysterious, eerie

unceasing *(adj.)* continual, incessant, chronic, perpetual, persistent

uncivilized *(adj.)* primitive, barbarous, crude, uncouth

uncommon *(adj.)* exceptional, extraordinary, unique, remarkable, rare, scarce

unconditional *(adj.)* absolute, certain, unrestricted

unconscious *(adj.)* senseless, oblivious, benumbed

uncouth *(adj.)* rude, ill-mannered, vulgar, crass

underestimate *(v.)* misjudge, miscalculate, slight

undergo *(v.)* endure, tolerate, suffer, bear, abide

undermine *(v.)* weaken, erode, corrode, decay, threaten

underrate *(v.)* devaluate, lessen, downgrade, depreciate

understand *(v.)* comprehend, grasp, perceive, discern, interpret, hear, accept, conclude

underwrite *(v.)* guarantee, support, endorse

undo *(v.)* cancel, efface, erase, expunge, obliterate

undulate *(v.)* wave, surge, heave, flap, pulsate

uneasy *(adj.)* restless, perplexed, troubled, apprehensive, fidgety, nervous, jittery, uncomfortable

unequal *(adj.)* disparate, unlike, uneven, odd

unfathomable *(adj.)* incomprehensible, enigmatic, mysterious, inscrutable, profound, baffling, puzzling

uniform *(adj.)* regular, routine, normal, unwavering, invariable, consistent, steady

unify *(v.)* combine, integrate, consolidate, compact, concentrate, arrange, blend, integrate, synthesize

unintentional *(adj.)* involuntary, accidental, inadvertent, unplanned, unconscious

unique *(adj.)* singular, particular, peerless, unrivaled, unequaled, matchless, unusual, uncommon, odd, peculiar, rare

unison *(n.)* coincidence, agreement, concord

unity *(n.)* union, harmony, agreement, concert, unison, concord, rapport, congruity

unjust *(adj.)* unfair, partial, prejudiced, biased, inequitable, shabby, undeserved, unjustified, unmerited

unkempt *(adj.)* disorderly, disheveled, messy, tousled, untidy, crude, vulgar

unnerve *(v.)* upset, unsettle, aggravate, fluster, discourage, disconcert

unprecedented *(adj.)* unparalleled, unique, unequal, unusual, uncommon, untoward

unravel *(v.)* explain, elucidate, clarify, justify, resolve, interpret, solve, untangle, unwind, disengage

unveil *(v.)* reveal, show, expose, divulge, announce

upheaval *(n.)* eruption, earthquake, volcano, outbreak, explosion, outburst

uphold *(v.)* maintain, support, champion, sustain, endorse, sanction, bolster, help

upright *(adj.)* upstanding, honest, good, outstanding, moral, ethical, principled, just, righteous, pure, true

uproar *(n.)* clamor, commotion, disturbance, furor, hubbub, melee

uproot *(v.)* remove, transport, liquidate, excavate, extirpate, eradicate, eliminate, dislodge

upset *(adj.)* irritated, worried, uneasy, shaky, troubled, unsettled, disturbed, aggravated, concerned, perturbed, disconcerted

urban *(adj.)* city, metropolitan, civic

urbane *(adj.)* suave, poised, polished, refined, smooth, elegant, gracious, courteous

urchin *(n.)* waif, stray, foundling, orphan, ragamuffin, child, infant

urge *(n.)* drive, desire, impulse, craving, passion, push, influence, stimulus, impulse

urgent *(adj.)* pressing, compelling, demanding, driving, forcing, imperative, anxious, insistent

usable *(adj.)* useful, employable, applicable, functional, serviceable

useful *(adj.)* beneficial, helpful, effective, practical, functional, handy

usual *(adj.)* common, customary, ordinary, familiar

usurp *(v.)* capture, commandeer, appropriate, assume, seize

utensil *(n.)* instrument, device, implement, gadget

utmost *(adj.)* ultimate, maximum, maximal, entire, greatest, undiminished, unlimited

utopian *(adj.)* idealistic, ideological, visionary, perfect, ideal, fanciful, theoretical

utter *(adj.)* complete, entire, total, unconditional, unqualified, thorough

utterance *(n.)* assertion, declaration, enunciation, proclamation, pronouncement

V

vacant *(adj.)* empty, uninhabited, abandoned, deserted, expressionless, vapid

vacation *(n.)* holiday, furlough, respite, sabbatical

vaccinate *(v.)* immunize, inoculate, inject

vacillate *(v.)* waver, hesitate, fluctuate, alternate, sway, falter

vacuum *(n.)* void, emptiness, vacuity, nothingness

vagrant *(n.)* beggar, tramp, hobo, idler, loafer

vague *(adj.)* obscure, indistinct, indefinite, imprecise, unspecified, uncertain, loose, unclear

valet *(n.)* servant, attendant, butler, steward

valour *(n.)* bravery, courage, boldness, spirit

valuable *(adj.)* expensive, precious, rare, priceless, useful, beneficial, profitable, serviceable

vandalism *(n.)* defacement, damage, mutilation, dis figuration, marring, spoiling

vanish *(v.)* disappear, depart, evaporate, fade, dissolve, exit

vanity *(n.)* conceit, pretension, self-esteem, pride, folly, arrogance

vanquish *(v.)* conquer, overwhelm, overpower, defeat, quell, quash, subdue, suppress, subjugate, crush

vapour *(n.)* fog, haze, mist, gas, smog, condensation

variance *(n.)* difference, divergence, discrepancy, incongruity, disagreement, discord

variety *(n.)* category, group, classification, division

varnish *(v.)* embellish, disguise, mask, veil, falsify

vault *(n.)* crypt, tomb, mausoleum, sepulcher

vaunt *(v.)* boast, gloat, brag, strut, swagger, flaunt

vehement *(adj.)* fervent, energetic, impassioned

vehicle *(n.)* conveyance, medium, means, agency, instrumentality

velocity *(n.)* speed, swiftness, quickness

venerate *(v.)* admire, worship, revere, esteem, respect

vengeful *(adj.)* vindictive, unforgiving, unrelenting, spiteful, rancorous, intractable, malicious

venial *(adj.)* excusable, justifiable, forgivable

venom *(n.)* bitterness, virulence, malice, anger, contempt, spitefulness, malevolence, hate

vent *(v.)* express, air, assert, verbalize, articulate, expound, release, unleash, discharge

venture *(n.)* undertaking, enterprise, adventure, investment, speculation, endeavor, attempt

venture *(v.)* chance, wager, risk, gamble, hazard, dare, plunge, imperil, jeopardize, endanger

veracious *(adj.)* truthful, accurate, precise, honest, sincere, trustworthy, righteous

veracity *(n.)* truth, honesty, sincerity, accuracy, precision, exactness, correctness

verandah *(n.)* terrace, porch, deck, patio, courtyard

verbal *(adj.)* oral, spoken, stated

verdict *(n.)* decision, judgment, ruling, adjudication, decree, determination, sentence

verge *(n.)* edge, brink, border, limit, margin, rim, brim

verify *(v.)* confirm, prove, authenticate, corroborate substantiate, validate

vernacular *(adj.)* native, indigenous, regional, informal, colloquial, everyday, ordinary, familiar

versatile *(adj.)* flexible, pliable, adaptable, tractable, all-round, resourceful

versed *(adj.)* experienced, seasoned, competent, adept, capable, skilled, practiced, trained

vertical *(adj.)* erect, upright, perpendicular, plumb

vestige *(n.)* trace, indication, shred, fragment, remainder, hint, suggestion

veteran *(adj.)* experienced, seasoned, skilled, versed

vex *(v.)* annoy, harass, irk, bother, disturb, irritate, plague, torment, agitate

vibrate *(v.)* shake, flutter, tremble, quiver, undulate, fluctuate, oscillate, reverberate

vicinity *(n.)* area, locality, neighborhood, environment, proximity, nearness

vicious *(adj.)* immoral, base, degenerate, vile, depraved, reprehensible, wrong, malicious, malevolent, spiteful, malignant, unruly

victim *(n.)* casualty, dupe, gull, prey, sucker, fool

victor *(n.)* winner, champion, vanquisher, conqueror

vigilant *(adj.)* watchful, alert, observant, attentive, careful, wary

vigour *(n.)* strength, power, potency, stamina, energy, endurance, vitality, soundness

vile *(adj.)* evil, depraved, wretched, repulsive, contemptible, revolting, disgusting, offensive, vulgar

village *(n.)* town, community, hamlet, municipality

villain *(n.)* miscreant, cad, rascal, rogue, scoundrel

vindicate *(v.)* exonerate, acquit, absolve, clear, defend, justify, support, uphold, corroborate, assert

vintage *(adj.)* classic, antique, old, excellent

violation *(n.)* transgression, infringement, breach, debasement, assault, outrage

violent *(adj.)* intense, fierce, furious, rough, vicious, brutal, barbarous, savage, fierce

virgin *(n.)* pure, undefiled, unsullied, unadulterated. unmixed, fresh, unspoiled

virile *(adj.)* vibrant, strong, forceful, vigorous, robust, masculine

virtue *(n.)* integrity, justice, temperance, purity, decency, merit, distinction, excellence

virulent *(adj.)* malignant, venomous, poisonous; bitter, malicious, antagonistic

virus *(n.)* infection, disease, germ, microbe

visa *(n.)* endorsement, permit, authorization

visage *(n.)* countenance, appearance, aspect

visible *(adj.)* discernible, perceptible, perceivable, obvious, apparent, clear, evident, conspicuous

visibility *(n.)* distinctness, perceptibility, prominence, clarity

visitor *(n.)* guest, caller, company

vista *(n.)* view, perspective, prospect, outlook

vital *(adj.)* essential, necessary, important, critical, requisite; vigorous, lively, energetic, active

vivacious *(adj.)* lively, animated, brisk, spirited, sprightly, energetic, spry

vivid *(adj.)* shining, intense, lucid, lively, spirited, energetic, vivacious, realistic, picturesque, distinct, graphic, striking, clear, discernible

vocabulary *(n.)* lexicon, glossary, dictionary

vocal *(adj.)* spoken, oral, expressed, articulated, verbalized; outspoken, open, honest, assertive, candid, blunt, frank

vociferous *(adj.)* noisy, boisterous, uproarious, blatant, loud, ranting

vogue *(n.)* fashion, style, custom, trend, fad, popularity, acceptance, rage
volatile *(adj.)* explosive, unstable, fickle, erratic, frivolous, passing, transient, ephemeral
volume *(n.)* book, manuscript; size, magnitude, bulk; loudness, intensity, strength
voluntary *(adj.)* willing, disposed, inclined, prone, deliberate, intended, intentional, planned, willful
volunteer *(v.)* offer, extend, render, submit, tender, propose, suggest, recommend
voluptuous *(adj.)* sensual, indulgent, carnal, erotic, lustful, licentious
voracious *(adj.)* greedy, insatiable, ravenous, hungry, rapacious, grasping
vouch *(v.)* certify, attest, swear, state, assure
vow *(v.)* swear, promise, assure, attest, certify, affirm, pledge
voyage *(n.)* journey, excursion, trip, tour
vulgar *(adj.)* coarse, tasteless, gross, crude, unrefined
vulgarity *(n.)* obscenity, rudeness, indelicacy, coarseness, crassness, impropriety, immodesty
vulnerable *(adj.)* unprotected, unguarded, defenseless, exposed, susceptible, unsafe

W

waft *(v.)* float, hover, drift, skim, flit, flutter
wager *(v.)* bet, stake, risk, gamble, hazard
waif *(n.)* stray, foundling, orphan, urchin, ragamuffin
wad *(v.)* lament, bemoan, sob, whine, mourn
waive *(v.)* forgo, sacrifice, relinquish, renounce, resign, postpone, defer, shelve, table
wand *(n.)* baton, staff, stick, scepter
wander *(v.)* roam, drift, ramble, meander, rove, range, stroll, saunter, digress, stray, veer
wanton *(adj.)* malicious, hateful, spiteful, reckless, willful, unruly; lewd, lascivious, lustful, dissolute
ward *(n.)* child, minor, orphan; district, territory, precinct, parish
warm *(adj.)* gracious, amiable, pleasant, kind, intimate, amicable, sympathetic, close
warrant *(v.)* certify, approve, authorize, sanction
wash *(v.)* clean, cleanse, scrub, swab, bathe
watch *(v.)* observe, view, see, regard, scrutinize, inspect, guard, patrol, protect
waver *(v.)* fluctuate, vacillate, hesitate
wax *(v.)* increase, grow, enlarge, expand, flourish
waylay *(v.)* ambush, assail, lurk, trap
wealth *(n.)* riches, affluence, assets, abundance
weary *(adj.)* tired, exhausted, drained, fatigued
weary *(v.)* harass, annoy, bother, badger, pester, irk, vex, distress
weigh *(v.)* consider, contemplate, ponder, study
weird *(adj.)* mysterious, eerie, spooky, uncanny, unnatural, ghostly, puzzling, arcane
well *(adj.)* healthy, strong, hardy, robust, fit, sound
whereabouts *(n.)* location, position, situation, locale, place, spot, site
whimper *(v.)* cry, whine, sniffle, snivel, weep
whimsical *(adj.)* capricious, fanciful, playful, impulsive
whine *(v.)* cry, complain, grumble, snivel, whimper
wholesome *(adj.)* nourishing, healthy, nutritious, beneficial, advantageous, good
wicked *(adj.)* evil, corrupt, vile, immoral, nefarious
wild *(adj.)* untamed, uncivilized, unrestrained
wile *(n.)* trickery, deception, deceit, artifice, ruse
wilt *(v.)* droop, wither, shrivel, decay, slump
wince *(v.)* flinch, recoil, cringe, falter, twitch
windfall *(n.)* blessing, godsend, boon, bonanza
winnow *(v.)* sift, separate, sieve, extract, eliminate
winsome *(adj.)* winning, beautiful, charming, captivating, lovely, cute, engaging, comely, delightful
wisdom *(n.)* sagacity, understanding, discretion, insight, tact, intelligence, knowledge
wish *(v.)* crave, yearn, want, need; direct, order, bid, instruct; request, beg, entreat, solicit
wistful *(adj.)* melancholy, longing, yearning, sentimental, nostalgic, wishful, plaintive
witchcraft *(n.)* sorcery, wizardry, divination, magic
wither *(v.)* shrivel, wilt, shrink, atrophy, languish
withstand *(v.)* oppose, defy, confront, resist, endure
witness *(n.)* spectator, bystander, onlooker, eyewitness, observer
witticism *(n.)* quip, jest, pun, gag, joke, wisecrack
wizard *(n.)* magician, conjurer, soothsayer, sorcerer
woeful *(adj.)* mournful, sad, sorrowful, doleful
wonder *(v.)* question, ponder, doubt, speculate; marvel, gape, stare
wonderful *(adj.)* extraordinary, marvelous, astounding, awesome, remarkable, excellent, superb

woo *(v.)* court, charm, pursue, cultivate, entice, entreat, seek

worry *(n.)* anxiety, apprehension, fear, disquiet, uneasiness, misgiving

worship *(n.)* adoration, devotion, reverence, veneration, praise, idolize

worth *(n.)* value, importance, quality, excellence

wrangle *(v.)* dispute, bicker, quarrel, squabble

wrap *(v.)* enfold, envelop, swathe, bandage, swaddle, cover

wrath *(n.)* anger, fury, ire, irritation, resentment

wreak *(v.)* perpetrate, do, perform, commit

wreath *(n.)* garland, bouquet, decoration

wreckage *(n.)* remains, debris, wreck

wretch *(n.)* miscreant, rogue, villain, rascal, brute

wrinkle *(n.)* fold, crease, pucker, furrow, ridge

writ *(n.)* law, decree, order, edict

write *(v.)* inscribe, scrawl, sign, compose, record

wrong *(adj.)* immoral, evil, false, inaccurate, improper

wrong *(v.)* harm, abuse, oppress, maltreat, dishonor

Y

yardstick *(n.)* measure, standard, scale, guide, gauge, model, norm

yearning *(n.)* longing, craving, desire, want, wish

yell *(v.)* cheer, root, shout, call, holler, scream

yield *(v.)* surrender, abdicate, cede, concede, resign, grant, acquiesce, give

yoke *(n.)* couple, harness, join, link, attach, connect

youth *(n.)* immaturity, adolescence, minority

Z

zany *(adj.)* crazy, funny, silly, nonsensical, wacky

zeal *(n.)* enthusiasm, fervor, passion, spirit, ardor

zealot *(n.)* fanatic, devotee, partisan

zealous *(adj.)* enthusiastic, eager, fervent, passionate, spirited, ardent, earnest

zenith *(n.)* top, peak, crest, elevation

zest *(n.)* relish, enthusiasm, gusto, enjoyment, delight, keenness